The Women
Who Clothed
the Stuart Queens

The Women Who Clothed the Stuart Queens

Gender and Work in the Royal Wardrobe and the Fashion Marketplace

Sarah A. Bendall

BLOOMSBURY VISUAL ARTS
LONDON • NEW YORK • OXFORD • NEW DELHI • SYDNEY

BLOOMSBURY VISUAL ARTS
Bloomsbury Publishing Plc, 50 Bedford Square, London, WC1B 3DP, UK
Bloomsbury Publishing Inc, 1359 Broadway, New York, NY 10018, USA
Bloomsbury Publishing Ireland, 29 Earlsfort Terrace, Dublin 2, D02 AY28, Ireland

BLOOMSBURY, BLOOMSBURY VISUAL ARTS and the Diana logo are trademarks of Bloomsbury Publishing Plc

First published in Great Britain 2026

Cover design by Paul Smith
Cover images: [left] Portrait of Maria II Stuart, gift of D. Franken, Le Vésinet, Rijksmuseum; [right] Nicolas Arnoult, La Bonne Couturierre, 1692, etching with engraving, detail. Private collection of the author.

A catalogue record for this book is available from the British Library.

A catalog record for this book is available from the Library of Congress.

ISBN: HB: 978-1-3504-0734-3
         PB: 978-1-3504-0731-2
         ePDF: 978-1-3504-0735-0
         eBook: 978-1-3504-0736-7

Typeset by RefineCatch Limited, Bungay, Suffolk
Printed and bound in India

For product safety related questions contact productsafety@bloomsbury.com.

To find out more about our authors and books visit www.bloomsbury.com and sign up for our newsletters.

Contents

List of tables vii

Acknowledgements viii

Notes to the reader x

Abbreviations xi

Introduction: 'She craveth allowance' 1

    The royal court and the fashion marketplace 3

    Women and work in early modern Europe 7

    Work in the household and the shop 10

    Accounting for work and fashion: sources 15

    Chapter outlines 20

1   Wearing: The Stuart queens and elite fashions in the long seventeenth century 21

    The early Stuarts: Anna of Denmark and Henrietta Maria 22

    The Restoration: Catherine of Braganza and Mary of Modena 32

    The later Stuarts: Mary II and Queen Anne 45

    Conclusions 57

2   Managing: The Office of the Robes and the work of the Mistress of the Robes 61

    The Mistresses of the Robes and their office 62

    The management and finances of the Office of the Robes 73

    By her direction: material literacy, fashionability and shopping 82

    Elite women's careers? Work and identity 89

    Conclusions 93

3   Selling: Fashion retailers, milliners and their social networks 95

    Suppliers to the early Stuart queens and their networks 96

    Changing shopping locations, busy decoration and evolving trades 100

Female milliners, French novelties and East Indies goods in the late seventeenth century 112

Milliners, Indian women and their social networks 121

Conclusions 133

4 Making: Seamstresses, silkwomen and the rise of the mantua-maker 135

Seamstresses, silkwomen and embroiderers to the Stuart queens 136

Later women makers and their ambiguous occupational identities 143

Changing patterns of work in the Robes and in the City 152

The skills, training and working relationships of early mantua-makers 160

Conclusions 174

5 Caring: Maintaining clothing and appearances in the care economy of the royal household 177

Storing clothing: wardrobes, the Mistress of the Sweet Coffers and the dressing room 178

Getting dressed: tirewomen, dressers and the *toilette* 186

Cleaning clothing: brushers, laundresses and starchers 201

Dynasties of service and social mobility 205

Conclusions 210

Conclusion: Women's patronage and women's work 213

Appendix I: Makers and suppliers to the Stuart queens 219

Appendix II: Clothing and accessories of the Stuart queens 245

Appendix III: A list of Queen Mary II's jewels, 1695 251

Appendix IV: Debts owed to Robert and Elizabeth Graydon, 1701 253

Glossary of clothing, textile and sewing terms 257

Image credits 263

Notes 267

Bibliography 315

Index 333

Tables

Table 2.1:	Mistresses of the Robes to the Stuart queens	65
Table 5.1:	The women of Mary II's bedchamber, 1689–94	191
Appendix I, Table 1:	Tradespeople to Anna of Denmark, 1603–19	219
Appendix I, Table 2:	Tradespeople to Henrietta Maria, 1627–39	222
Appendix I, Table 3:	Tradespeople to Catherine of Braganza, 1662–92	225
Appendix I, Table 4:	Tradespeople to Mary of Modena whose bills were unpaid after 1688	230
Appendix I, Table 5:	Tradespeople to Mary II, 1689–94	232
Appendix I, Table 6:	Tradespeople to Queen Anne, 1702–14	238
Appendix II: Table 7:	Clothing and accessories of the Stuart queens	246

Acknowledgements

This book was conceptualized during a Covid-19 lockdown when closed borders and libraries prompted me to re-examine household sources that I had previously collected. I became increasingly fascinated by the women whose names and signatures were recorded in the piles of paperwork created by the bureaucracy of Stuart courts. My so-called 'small' project soon became one that extended over many continents and years, and I am grateful to many people for offering their time and expertise as this book took shape.

First and foremost, my deepest thanks go to my amazing research assistants and colleagues – Zara Kesterton, Eilish Gregory, Marlo Avidon, Sarah Randles, Megan Shaw and Celeste van Gent – who visited archives for me in the United Kingdom and helped me sort through many of these archival documents. I extend this thanks to Greg and other staff at the National Archives in Kew for helping me locate documents during the many hours I spent there. I would also like to thank Amanda, Diane and Vicky at West Sussex Record Office who assisted me with the Petworth House Archives and gave me handy tips during my visits to Chichester. I am grateful to Heather Conopo at Buckminster Archives and Louise Kennedy at Helmingham Hall for their assistance in locating and scanning documents for me. I would also like to recognize archival staff at the British Library and National Art Library for their valuable assistance.

The collection of this archival material would not have been possible without the financial help of the Institute for Humanities and Social Sciences (IHSS) at Australian Catholic University. Huge thanks to Kathryn Perez for assisting me in arranging travel and getting invoices paid. This research was also funded by a Research Project Grant from the Pasold Research Fund which allowed me to view records held at various archives in the UK.

In addition to financial aid, this project would also not have been possible without the generous knowledge offered by others studying the Stuart courts and London's fashion makers and retailers. I am indebted to Susannah Lyon-Whaley for sharing sources relating to Catherine of Braganza with me, including the papers held at the Kresen Kernow Cornish Archives and Lincolnshire Archives. I thank Amy Lim for directing me to the Petworth House Archives and for sharing her Chatsworth and NatWest archives finds with me. I would also like to the thank Kerry-Louise Apps for sharing her research on the Duchess of Lauderdale, and Marlo Avidon for directing me to sources containing some of the tradespeople featured in this book.

I am also grateful to Michelle Barker, Sarah Birt, Serena Dyer, Jemma Field, Elisabeth Gernerd, Laura Gowing, Erin Griffey, Maria Hayward, Ninya Mikhaila, Rebecca Morrison, Tessa Murdoch, John Styles and Annabel Westman for discussing their own research with me and for their guidance. Additionally, I would like to thank audiences at conferences and seminars in the UK, France, Australia, New Zealand and online, who provided valuable feedback on my research in progress.

While much of this research was facilitated by international travel and collaborative discussions around shared research interests, I would also like to acknowledge my colleagues in Australia who have supported me while writing this book. I am endlessly grateful to Joy Damousi for hiring me into my current position at IHSS, and to Susan Broomhall for fostering and encouraging my research at the Gender and Women's History Research Centre. I thank Kristie Flannery for encouraging me to pursue this monograph idea during our lockdown walks, even when I claimed it was just going to be a 'small book'.

I am extremely grateful to colleagues who have read chapter drafts from this monograph, including Clare Davidson, Sally Fisher, Ming Gao, Minerva Inwald, Jessica O'Leary, Laura Saxton and Mary Tomsic. I also must thank others who have provided valuable feedback or general support in other settings where I have presented or discussed this work, including Diana Barnes, Lorinda Cramer, Nicole Davis, Antonia Finnane, Kate Fullagar, Sally Gray, Darius von Güttner Sporzyński, Pauline Hastings, Peter Holbrook, Laura Jocic, Catherine Kovesi, Jessica Lake, Rachel Matthews, Una McIlvenna, Adelina Modesti, Ebony Nilsson, Lisa O'Connell, Jon Piccini, Jenny-Lynn Potter, Susan Scollay, Rachel Stevens, Natalie Tomas and Linda Young. A huge thank you also to Minerva Inwald, Ming Gao, Guillermo Ruiz-Stovel and Antonia Finnane for their help translating and interpreting the hanzi characters that were inked into the silk sample featured in Chapter 3.

Citations and transcriptions from the Petworth House Archives are courtesy of Lord Egremont. Some of the content in this book has previously been published in *Women's History Review* (Taylor & Francis Group). I thank the journal editors and publishers for permission to use revised material from these articles. I'm deeply grateful to the editorial and production teams at Bloomsbury, particularly Frances Arnold and Martin Thompson for their enthusiastic support of this book (and all my many proposed images), and to the anonymous readers of my manuscript materials for their feedback.

To my friends and family, thank you for your continued support with my research endeavours which can sometimes become all-consuming. I am extremely grateful to Robert for allowing me to spend time, sometimes too much time, at my desk pursuing various rabbit holes of research when I should be doing other things, and also for offering advice, and not judging (too harshly) my amateur Excel skills. Final thanks go to my furry home office manager, Raffy, who in the final push of writing this book always made sure that I made time to get up, take a break and go outside for a walk – all things I plan on doing a lot more of now that it is finished!

Notes to the reader

Original terminology has been retained to refer to objects of dress and textiles, unless otherwise specified. A glossary of dress, textile and sewing terminology is provided.

Most English spelling has been modernized but original punctuation, grammar and word order have been retained. Most abbreviations and contractions have been extended. English translations have been given in the body of the text; original quotations are given in the endnotes. All translations are my own unless otherwise noted.

The prices of English goods are written in pounds (£), shillings (s.) and pence (d.). There were 12d. in a shilling and 20s. in a pound during the early modern period. Throughout the book these currencies are abbreviated into £ s. d. Roman numerals have been written in Arabic numerals when quoting from an original manuscript or printed sources.

Dates have been converted from the Julian Old-Style calendar and given in the modern Gregorian calendar (with the new year starting on 1 January).

Abbreviations

BA	Buckminster Archives
BLO	Bodleian Libraries
BL	The British Library
CUL	Cambridge University Library
DCCH	Devonshire Collections, Chatsworth House
KKCA	Kresen Kernow Cornish Archives
LA	Lincolnshire Archives
LMA	London Metropolitan Archives
NAL	National Art Library, Victoria and Albert Museum
NWA	NatWest archives
RAO	Royal Archives Online
RBSC	Rare Books and Special Collections, University of Sydney
ROLLCO	Records of London's Livery Companies Online
TNA	The National Archives
WRO	Warwickshire Record Office
WSRO	West Sussex Record office

Introduction: 'She craveth allowance'

A portrait dated to 1702 of Queen Anne depicts the last Stuart monarch of England in a version of her coronation clothes (see Fig. 0.1). The queen stands next to a red velvet cushion bearing the orb of the crown jewels, the royal sceptre and the St Edward's crown, and around her neck hangs the royal garter of St George, all symbols of her monarchical authority. In addition to this regalia, the queen is dressed in the fashions of the time. Her gold-coloured mantua gown of brocaded silk and purple mantle were made by her mantua-makers Anne Clifton and Anne Howe, and the matching petticoat was constructed by her petticoat-maker Elizabeth Banks. Her hair has been cut and carefully styled by her tirewoman Mary Ducaila and the linen garments that peek out from under her sleeves were constructed by her seamstress Mrs Duran. Even the Order of the Garter regalia worn by Anne was supplied by tradeswomen. The blue ribbon holding her St George insignia of the Order of the Garter was provided by her famous milliner Elizabeth Graydon and the star pinned to her breast symbolizing the heraldic shield of St George was completed by the embroiderer Mrs Hunter.[1]

During Queen Anne's reign (1702–14), her royal appearance was artfully constructed and maintained by a mixture of people from various backgrounds and social positions: the queen herself; her Mistress of the Robes Sarah Churchill, Duchess of Marlborough; her Yeoman of the Robes Rachel Thomas; her fashionable mantua-makers, petticoat-makers and milliners, mercers, drapers and lacemen; as well as teams of dressers, seamstresses, starchers and laundresses. The Stuart era saw the rise of women in many of these roles: the Mistress of the Robes was a position created under the Stuarts and women came to dominate the millinery and mantua-making trades during their reigns. It is the work of these women, many unknown until now, preserved in portraits of the Stuart queens that was key to shaping the enduring image of not only elite women at the Stuart courts but seventeenth-century fashions more generally.

This book explores the work and lives of courtiers, servants, retailers and makers who 'craved allowance', a phrase frequently used in their surviving bills, for their work clothing six Stuart queens

Fig. 0.1 *Michael Dahl,* Queen Anne, c. *1702–5, oil on canvas. National Portrait Gallery, NPG 6187.*

between 1603 and 1714. The vast piles of paperwork generated by these individuals were preserved by the Office of the Robes, an administrative department of the queen's household that managed some of her most valuable assets: her clothing.[2] When examining these papers, one cannot help but be struck by the sheer number of women whose names appear within them, highlighting their increasing prominence during the Stuart period; the women employed both within and outside the royal household to clothe Queen Anne vastly outnumbered those who had been employed one hundred years earlier when the first Stuart Queen of England, Anna of Denmark, took the throne in 1603. Using this paperwork and tracing the recorded names in additional archives, this book examines the nature and growth of women's work within the royal household and London's fashion marketplace during the seventeenth century, exploring how elite desires for novel consumer goods – fuelled by global trade and the influence of French fashion – influenced the marketplace of London and propelled burgeoning female trades.

The Women Who Clothed the Stuart Queens establishes the strong connections between the worlds of the Stuart courts and London's fashion marketplace. These were not totally separate spheres. Court women had multiple interactions with common tradespeople and, increasingly by the late seventeenth century, men and women not connected to the courts could commission royal tradespeople too. In addition to changing market forces and guild structures, I argue that it was the consumption and patronage practices of influential elite women at the courts that were integral to legitimizing 'milliner', 'mantua-maker', 'petticoat-maker', 'Indian woman', 'tirewoman' and other trade identities as professions for women during what this book defines as the Stuart seventeenth century (1603 to 1714). This contributes to our understanding of the growing importance of women's work and women's cultural and economic influence in early modern England more broadly.

The royal court and the fashion marketplace

The rule of the Stuart dynasty in England oversaw a period of radical politics and rapid religious and social upheaval (see Fig. 0.2). Civil war, regicide and revolution, leading to the eventual creation of a constitutional monarchy and of 'Great Britain', all took place under the Stuarts. At this same time, England also began to build its empire, with colonies and trade networks in the Americas and Asia. The Stuart era also sits at a key nexus in the history of fashion, consumption and production during the early modern period. Since Neil McKendrick influentially proclaimed that the late eighteenth century was the moment of the consumer revolution, when modern patterns of consumption first appeared as 'a greater proportion of the population than in any previous society in human history' had the ability to 'enjoy the pleasures of buying consumer goods', several studies have shown that increased consumption during the late eighteenth century was not so much a revolution, but rather, the next phase in a long evolution of European consumption practices.[3] Indeed, established practices of consumption identified by McKendrick began in countries such as England, France and the Dutch Republic during the seventeenth century.[4] This century oversaw several shifts in patterns of production and consumption associated with broadened consumer choice: the rise of ready-made goods, the increased importance of globally imported commodities and the growth of shop-based retailing, all of which were fuelled by favourable economic conditions due to increased trade and colonization and the rise of the middling sorts.[5]

The seventeenth century was also marked by significant labour shifts in the fashion marketplace, particularly in London. During this period the capital rapidly developed and grew in size and population, and it dominated England's import and export market. Fashionable English and Scottish

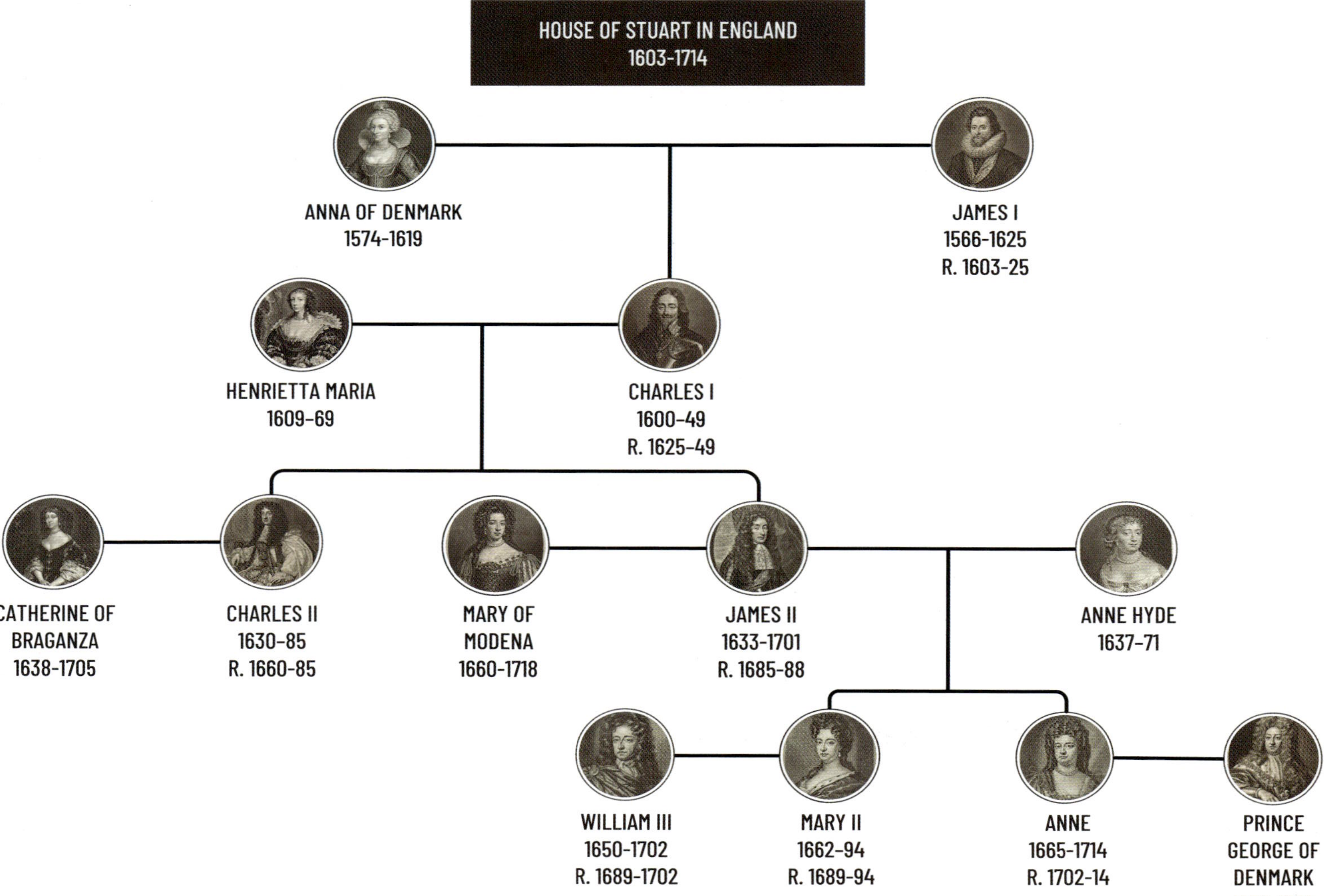

Fig. 0.2 *The House of Stuart in England, 1603–1714.*

subjects patronized London's tradespeople for the latest wardrobe goods, and over a third of Londoners worked in clothing and leather-related trades to meet this demand.[6] This made London a centre of innovation and consumption where fashion makers and suppliers, if skilled, versatile and adaptable, could thrive. New retailing trends and techniques, as well as cheaper less-durable goods, that promoted novelty began to emerge, and this stimulated demand and more frequent purchasing among consumers.[7] It was in the late seventeenth century that the fashion press also began giving more and more people access to new styles, which helped create the annual fashion cycle, further stimulating novelty and consumption.[8] Many garments exclusively made by tailors in the sixteenth century were, by the end of the seventeenth century, crafted by a variety of artisans. At this time women also became key makers and suppliers not only of women's clothing and accessories, but also, as this book will show, of imported French and East Indies goods too. The period also saw the continuation of the ubiquity of women in service roles as both managers and carers of clothing in households and wardrobes that were increasingly filled by a variety of new consumer goods.

The Stuart court was not a static institution that sat separately from the wider fashion marketplace of early modern London, or that of England and Europe more broadly. Early modern royal courts were locales centred on the sovereign and their family, consisting of networks of people such as nobility, diplomats, agents and servants, and structures like buildings, gardens and parks, usually in metropolitan areas. They were epicentres of government, finance, religion, patronage and culture. The royal court was also a much more open and accessible place than one might think. As R. O. Bucholz has argued, at this time it was 'possible for any reasonably prosperous looking individual to wander the halls of his sovereign's abode; explore the rooms within which he lived; examine his most treasured possessions; observe him at his dinner; and, if properly introduced, engage him in conversation'.[9] This was certainly the case with contemporary observers and social climbers such as Samuel Pepys, the son of a well-connected London tailor who rose through the ranks to become a naval administrator and Member of Parliament. He often visited court, noting the dress of those he saw, and he even shopped at the same places as the Stuart monarchs.

During the seventeenth century increasing numbers of English nobility and gentry also participated in trade and commerce, or married into merchant or trading families, to pursue commercial wealth.[10] Thus, many courtiers were involved in commercial enterprises like merchant trade, manufacturing and retailing, or had frequent contact with those who were. The Stuart court and London's bustling streets were thus inextricably linked, and make the daily records generated by the court fruitful places to look for all types of commercial activities, including women's work in relation to clothing.

There were no laws that restricted dress after 1603 when the first Stuart king of England, James I, repealed the country's loosely implemented sumptuary legislation.[11] By the middle of the seventeenth century, new moneyed middling sorts, including wealthy merchants, not only began to share power and status with traditional titled elites but also took advantage of England's lack of sumptuary laws.[12]

Rather than consuming or wearing different things, distinctions between different sorts or classes of people in England began to be determined by the quality and types of materials and trimmings used to make their goods, their value, as well as the quantity owned.[13] Fashion, referring to new popular or desirable styles that were novel, was therefore frequently dictated or promoted by those in London who were connected, in one way or another, to the royal courts. This is because courts were spaces where sartorial display, innovation and novelty were common, if not expected.

Unlike some European courts, such as the French court of Louis XIV or the later Georgian courts of the eighteenth century, the Stuart court in England did not set strict dress codes or have a static uniform of court dress, and very few tradespeople were exclusively patronized by the royal family. Instead, it was a dynamic environment that at times set fashion trends and at others responded to the changing fashion marketplace. This was made apparent by multiple authors throughout the century such as Richard Braithwaite, who warned women not to emulate those in fashionable London society and the court, and even Hannah Woolley who advised gentlewomen that the court was 'the source and foundation' of most fashions during this time.[14] Petitions from tradespeople in the lead up to the English Civil Wars also claimed that they would be utterly ruined by the departure of the court from London.[15] The slow movement of fashionable shopping districts to the West End of London near palaces and Parliament during the seventeenth century is also indicative of the increasing influence of the court on fashion and the reliance of London's tradespeople on the court.

This book gives particular attention to changes that took place in the fashion marketplace in the second half of the seventeenth century. The four decades after the Restoration of the Stuarts in 1660 saw many changes to women's and men's fashions and consumption habits, but also to women's role in the fashion trades. Rather than treating this period as merely the beginning of the long eighteenth century, this book shows that many of these changes were the result of very clear seventeenth-century processes, such as the changing nature of royal appointments and residences under the Stuarts, the changing influence of the guilds in London and the ongoing processes of global trade that had begun in the late sixteenth century. I also challenge the assertion that under the later Stuarts, such as Queen Anne, London's fashion industry was left without 'effective court patronage' and the court became an 'isolated and esoteric corner' of the fashion world.[16] As this book will demonstrate, Anne and others were guided by her 'favourite', Sarah Churchill, Duchess of Marlborough, who was a fashion leader of the emerging 'beau monde', and during Anne's reign the most widespread and varied consumption of goods by any Stuart queen took place.[17]

While the wardrobes of the Stuart queens are certainly not representative of the clothing worn by all women during this century, their fine dress embodied the aspirations of many who could, for the right price, access royal artisans and suppliers.[18] Anna of Denmark and Henrietta Maria's farthingale-makers Robert Hughes and John Ager both had shops in Cheapside in London where members of the public could commission garments.[19] Some of the mantua-makers and tailors discussed in this book had clients ranging from queens and duchesses to those who were simply given the title 'Mrs' or

'Widow', and retailers like milliners were located in key shopping areas such as the New Exchange and Covent Garden, where they were patronized by both royalty and London's fashionistas alike. It is through these interactions with the tradespeople of London, between client and maker, as this book demonstrates, that new garments were not only popularized and disseminated during the seventeenth century, but women's reputations and fortunes in the court and the fashion trades were made.[20] By examining these relationships, and the connections between the Stuart courts and London's marketplace, we can examine both continuities and changes to the gendered nature of work within the royal household and the fashion trades, account for the types of interactions between women in the court and those in the shops of London, and, in some cases, trace the complex lives and relationships of the women involved in these exchanges.

Women and work in early modern Europe

Women have always worked. However, in the past and even now women's labour, especially inside the home, has been shaped by gender biases that have prioritized some types of industries (usually male-dominated) over other types (usually female-dominated), meaning that activities undertaken by women have often been unrecorded in relation to official measures of economic activity. This book primarily focuses on women's paid or transactional work; that is, labour that was exchanged for payment, goods or favours. However, it also acknowledges that historically much of the work performed by women, such as childcare or household management – which contributed to local, national and global economies – was both unpaid and unrecorded.[21] Indeed, some of the types of work examined in this book, such as tasks relating to managing budgets and buying goods, doing the laundry or making and mending clothing, was usually performed by women on a much smaller scale, unpaid or low-paid, within the family home during the early modern period.

Alice Clark's influential study, *Working Women in Seventeenth-Century England* (1919), argued that during the late seventeenth century increasingly capitalist and industrial modes of production took work away from the domestic and family economy and disadvantaged women's employment opportunities.[22] Since Clark's study was published in the early twentieth century, there has been a tendency to characterize women of middling social levels as withdrawing from commerce during the seventeenth and eighteenth centuries.[23] However, unlike nineteenth-century notions of middle-class femininity and respectability, which framed women's place as in the home engaging in domestic labour rather than paid outside labour, for most of the early modern period women of various social levels were expected to work and contribute financially to the household. By the early eighteenth century, Amy Erickson and Peter Earle have found that a great majority of London wives continued to be engaged in 'gainful occupations' after their marriage, with about half of those from the middling socio-economic levels working in the same trade as their husbands, usually in textiles or retail.[24] It was not until the late eighteenth century that wealthy male professionals (such as officials, merchants and craft guild masters) began to perceive female family members 'who did not engage in productive labour' as status symbols and began to dismiss women's domestic roles as work.[25]

Recent scholarship on the working lives of early modern women has refined or debated Clark's claims, with many arguing that the relocation of work to outside the home gave both single and married women 'significant, rewarding participation' in the workforce and demonstrates that most women continued to work for a living, albeit not without discrimination.[26] As Laura Gowing has articulated, 'being trained, earning money, and doing work that could be rewarded or substituted with pay was a normal experience for seventeenth-century women', and it shaped their sense of identity.[27] As this book will show, the work of the women who clothed the Stuart queens, both elite and non-elite, married and unmarried, certainly formed a key part of their identities and social networks. The work undertaken by the Mistresses of the Robes in their court offices was a key part of their identities, and women such as the Duchess of Marlborough used her good management work in her court offices to defend her reputation. For women such as Elizabeth Graydon and Jane Potter, their identities as milliners and Indian women were a key part of their social rise. Their successful shops were patronized by a wide array of customers, which allowed Graydon to dine with Mary II and take trips to the Duke and Duchess of Marlborough at their St Albans residence, or, in Potter's case, to broker marriages between her elite patrons and engage in the politics of the period.

Moreover, the women of this study were connected to the growing global economy. As Margaret R. Hunt and Alexandra Shepard have articulated, the early modern period saw unprecedented economic growth in parts of Europe that was 'linked both to the global redistribution of resources and to new ways of organising labour'.[28] In England, Jan de Vries' analysis of the 'Industrious Revolution' generally holds true: new patterns of employment and household interaction with global markets emerged during the seventeenth century and this saw more women and children undertake waged labour. The increased purchasing power of these groups helped to fuel the demand for new fashionable consumer goods.[29] Many of the new occupations taken on by the women in this study, such as Mary Devet's retailing of East Indies goods and Madame Cheret with her French shop in Covent Garden, were directly related to the demand for foreign novelties by Londoners, many of whom were women. The earning power of the female consumer, and the jobs for women that it created, therefore played a part in enabling rising consumption and fashion innovation in Europe and drove the profitable global trade in commodities such as clothing, textiles and haberdasheries.[30]

While this book highlights the work and stories of women in the Stuart household accounts, as its subtitle indicates, this research is also interested in gender and the similarities or differences between the work of the men and women who clothed the queens. Women's patterns of work cannot be understood without comparing them to that of men. Additionally, many of the women discussed in this book worked alongside their husbands, something that Heide Wunder has called 'the working couple', or what has also been referred to as the 'two-supporter model'.[31] While many women worked in their husband's shops and carried on their businesses as widows, my research shows that some couples did not always work in the same trade and men's occupations did not always determine women's work. The case of Jeanne and François Haite (Jane and Francis Heath), discussed in Chapter 4, shows that couples also migrated due to women's skilled occupations: Jane was brought to London to teach the art and trade of mantua-making, and Francis, a periwig-maker who admitted to knowing nothing of his wife's trade, came with her.

Gender norms are not static and expectations of both men and women change over time, and are affected by class, age, marital status and race.[32] One way that this book understands women's work in early modern Europe is through the concept of 'agentic gender' norms or expectations. This term, coined by Allyson Poska, highlights the fact that in the early modern period there was an 'expectation that women had the opportunity to act independently, achieve success, and exert power and authority in many aspects of their lives'.[33] This should not be viewed as reactive or an exception to the patriarchal norm. Rather, it acknowledges that there were parallel sets of expectations for women within early modern society, expectations which they constantly had to navigate.

The realities of early modern life required most women to engage in some sort of paid labour, even if it was commonly 'low status, badly paid, and rarely full-time'.[34] Much of this labour was unrecorded; however, even when occupational titles for women did exist they were often infrequently used, vague or misleading and titles often do not account for those, including men, who had multiple occupations.[35] Thus, to track the distribution of labour amongst those servicing the queens' households, I have used verb-orientated approaches pioneered by Rosemarie Fiebranz, Erik Lindberg, Jonas Lindström and Maria Ågren.[36] Rather than relying on occupational titles, verb-orientated approaches identify and extract from sources 'verb-phrases' that describe tasks or actions which were performed to make a living.[37] By doing so, we can track women's economic activity and examine the myriad ways that both men and women described women's labour and how this work was valued. The verb-orientated titles of each chapter in this book have been informed by this approach. Each chapter broadly seeks to represent the types of activities or work performed by the women it discusses: the Stuart queens wore clothing that was managed, sold, made or cared for by others.

Looking for descriptions of work done, rather than just occupational titles, also shows the variety of work tasks completed by men and women for the Stuart courts. Many of the tradeswomen discussed in this book were not assigned specific occupations. Sometimes this was because there were not occupational titles available to accurately capture the range of activities they performed, as was the case with many early mantua-makers and milliners, or, even when they were given job descriptors, women often performed many tasks not acknowledged by them. On the other hand, elite women in the courts were given titles such as Mistress of the Robes or Mistress of the Sweet Coffers, but these have usually been viewed as sinecures, as these offices do not appear to be 'occupational' at first glance.

However, looking for descriptions of their tasks in household papers, whether in their own words or through descriptions made by others, shows us that they were indeed exchanging labour for their salaries, boardwages and other benefits. Such descriptions include checking and signing off artisan's bills, instructing others within the household or noting that they had distributed payments.

The household accounts of the Stuart queens show that women of all different social backgrounds were expected to be competent and economically productive just like their male counterparts, even if they had to battle patriarchal expectations regarding gendered abilities and spaces. In practice, patriarchy did limit the sorts of economic, social or political roles that women could take on, and not all women wanted to partake in such roles. Social, political, religious and economic factors have all played a part in restricting or enabling women's paid and unpaid work in the past, just as they still do today. However, analysing household accounts using verb-orientated approaches and the lens of agentic gender norms, as I have done in this study, offers, as Polska has argued, a new way of understanding the 'full spectrum of expectations of women, as it extends the range of acceptable behaviour'.[38]

In other words, we should not view the economic activities of the women uncovered in this book as an exception to the norm, even if they present examples of the capabilities of some of the most successful women of the time. Rather, in certain times, places and contexts women were viewed as, and expected to be, 'capable, economically productive, rational, qualified, skilled, and competent'.[39] The research presented in this book shows that by looking for evidence of women's names and work in places such as household accounts we can uncover a wider view of women's economic activities. I hope that this work will inspire others to dig into collections of household papers in Europe and beyond to write more histories of gender and work in a range of historical fields.

Work in the household and the shop

The first location of women's work examined by this book is the household, particularly the royal household of the Stuart queens. It was here that elite women worked for wages commissioning tradespeople, managing finances and storing clothing, while non-elite women laundered and cleaned wardrobe spaces, as well as taking part in dressing practices. The royal household was an administrative unit of the court responsible for balancing income and expenditure, with each key member of the royal family, including the queen, having her own household that employed treasurers, managers, clerks, attendants and servants. In addition to being centres of power and political and cultural influence, the court employed thousands of people and was, as Bucholz has argued, the 'largest single employer of the central government – indeed, possibly in British society at large – in one location' during the seventeenth and eighteenth centuries.[40] The lives of the men and women in the royal households of the Stuart queens of England, like many other European courts, remain largely unknown.

Elite women in the courts of Europe are often considered in relation to their families, their proximity to the queen and their role in court intrigues, that is if they are even considered at all. Nadine Akkerman and Birgit Houben have noted that the role of ladies-in-waiting in early modern court culture is understudied and not very well understood. This is even though women in queens' households across Europe 'became powerful political players', both individually and collectively, and were 'instrumental in creating and enhancing the image of female rulers across Europe'.[41] Many of these women were able to wield such political power through their appointment to court offices within the queen's household, where they swore allegiance to serve and attend her. The intimate nature of spaces within the household usually required that men served kings and women served queens as both high-status royal officers and as servants. Such appointments 'provided formal, official roles for women at court' which resembled those in the king's household.[42] Importantly, as this book demonstrates, court women served as conduits for fashion knowledge in ways that men, who did not consume or wear the same clothing, simply could not have. Despite this, the day-to-day role these women played in the functioning of the royal household itself is understudied. The paperwork of the royal household shows that while they may have come from powerful or influential families, on paper these women performed daily activities that ensured the household ran correctly and were often treated like any other employee when receiving their wages.

Jane Whittle and Elizabeth Griffiths have identified that work, consumption and gender interacted in three main ways in the early modern household: through management of consumption; the 'work' of consumption such as shopping and laundry; and the use of consumption to 'construct gendered identities'.[43] Although an analysis of the similar roles performed by men in the king's household is beyond the scope of this book, arguably, managing roles within the royal household complemented women's training and skillsets more than it did men's.[44] Moralizing and religious literature from the early modern period characterized women's place as primarily being within the home. The household was a woman's 'proper sphere of influence' and wives were expected to manage the day-to-day running of the household, provide for all its members and properly allocate its resources, with various degrees of freedom and permissions granted to them by their husbands.[45] This was especially true of elite households of the gentry and nobility, which 'were not small private family units' but large establishments that often had more employees than actual family members and played important roles in the local communities and economies.[46] Over the course of the seventeenth century 'quantitative culture' also increased among all social levels in England, particularly in the household where women's work coincided with the consumption of goods.[47] Women had important roles in the household as those who controlled or regulated consumption. In many instances, it was women who managed or directed the purchase and use of food, household goods and clothing.

In addition to elite women at court, there were also several non-elite women (and men) who undertook clerical, manual or otherwise drudge work of cleaning and caring for spaces and clothing. A large portion of England's workforce, both male and female, spent portions of their life in service.

Service work was ubiquitous and included both domestic servants in the home and husbandry in the fields.[48] Thus women, especially elite women, were expected to be able to manage vast sums of money, people and goods, to accurately account for expenditure and credit, and to have some sort of financial literacy. The royal household accounts make much household work performed by elite officeholders visible. However, a significant portion of this work was not unique to the royal court. It also took place in smaller country estates, in middling urban households in bustling cities, and in smaller poorer rural households, where it was usually unpaid labour. In this way, the work that went into managing and caring for the clothing of the Stuart queens is reflective of the continuous roles that women of different social ranks played in clothing and caring for their families all over England and Europe more widely.

Moving outside the household and away from consumption, this book also examines the work of production in the artisanal workshops and retail premises of London. Women's work in urban production is still regularly obscured by the sources that have survived. The rise of female milliners and the mantua-maker in England, Scotland, France and North America has been the subject of numerous studies over the last thirty years. However, most studies focus on the eighteenth and nineteenth centuries, when these trades were firmly established, rather than on the seventeenth century, when they emerged.[49] Studies of these female trades also continue to rely on guild records: sources that were created by traditionally male institutions that attempted to limit female participation. English guilds, or Companies as they were known in London, had originated from medieval fraternities that oversaw the training and practice of their craft and enforced quality control. They created a representative body for the trade that protected its interests in a certain town or region, while in the City of London they granted citizenship to its members, giving them considerable political influence. Many studies of these institutions have argued a 'decline' thesis, which proposes that there was a gradual exclusion of women in guilds across Europe during the medieval and early modern periods, which in turn limited women's economic activity in urban areas.[50]

Yet in the English context, the decline theory is problematic as guilds did begin to apprentice more women. Gowing, Erickson and Sarah Birt have shown that by the end of the seventeenth century London's guilds, known as Livery Companies, began to apprentice more girls and women.[51] As my study demonstrates, household accounts also contained an increasing number of bills from female tradespeople. While tradeswomen were certainly also present in the household papers of the Stuart kings, the Stuart queens' household accounts are much more fruitful places to look for women's work (see Appendix I). This is because many of the new, female-dominated trades of the seventeenth century, such as mantua-making, millinery and tiring, primarily catered to other women. As this book demonstrates, their success relied on their sometimes close relationships with other women, including elite courtiers, forming a symbiotic relationship that would not have been permissible with male customers, given the gender norms of the time.

Women had always dominated market spaces throughout Europe during the early modern period as both buyers and sellers.[52] Alongside the consumer revolution there was also a retail revolution that occurred between 1650 and 1800. At this time the numbers of small shops and peddlers increased in North-West Europe and the 'retail ratio' of retailers to inhabitants rose enormously in places like England and the Netherlands.[53] Through quantitative analysis of work tasks performed in England between 1500 and 1700, Whittle and Mark Hailwood have found that commerce, defined as buying and selling or running a shop or stall, was the largest category of work attributed to women in South-West England, with women making up 60% of those who sold food and drink, 68% of those who sold clothing and 72% of those who sold textiles.[54] Earle has estimated that between 1695 and 1725 nearly 30% of women in London worked making or selling clothing and other small goods.[55] While women had always had a place in the retailing of clothing and textiles, they were excluded from crafts such as tailoring around 1500 before being integrated back into them after 1650.[56]

The Stuart queens' household accounts, which are representative of elite female consumption habits in London, tell a slightly different story. In the early seventeenth century, women account for only a quarter of makers in the bills submitted to the early Stuart queens. Many were widows and none of these women made their outer garments. However, by the reign of Queen Anne in the early eighteenth century, women account for just over half of the makers in her accounts, with all her outer garments constructed by women (see Fig. 0.3).[57] The number of pure retailers also increased during this period and while women did not dominate retail, due to limitations of capital and merchant opportunities, their numbers increased in specific areas such as millinery and as suppliers of miscellaneous small wares (see Fig. 3.4).

But why such a change to patterns of women's work in London's fashion marketplace during the Stuart period? In many ways, London was unique when it came to women's working rights. Due to its

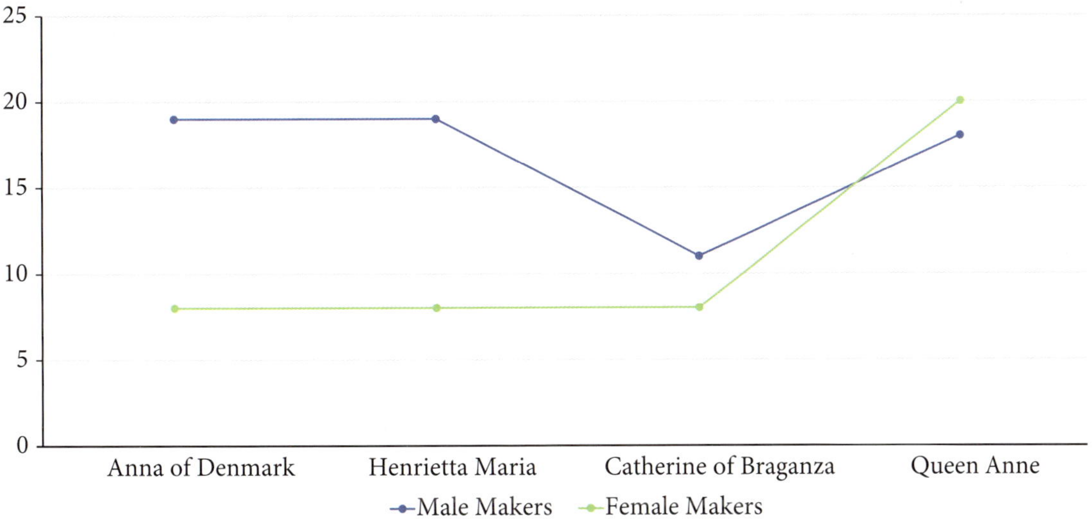

Fig. 0.3 *The gender of makers in the queens' Office of the Robes accounts, 1603–1714. Data source: Appendix I.*

size and place as an economic hub, it had allowed businesswomen to operate as 'feme sole' traders since the fourteenth century. This enabled married women to bypass couverture under English common law, which transferred her legal being, assets and property to her husband upon marriage. It also separated her assets and debts from her spouse, meaning that she could conduct business activities under her own name.[58] This had created a unique framework for women's work within the City of London, but it is still unclear how common this practice was before the seventeenth century.[59]

In addition to this pre-existing legal framework, during the seventeenth century London's livery companies struggled to control entry into craft industries as the metropolis expanded beyond the square mile of the old City of London centre. The opportunities offered by Company membership also became less desirable, particularly to those who were not motivated to participate in City politics, or to women who were excluded from positions of power within the Company and City administration.[60] It also became less necessary to undertake formal Company apprenticeships to practice a trade. As a result, less than a quarter of male Londoners belonged to a Company by 1660.[61] Of those who did start apprenticeships, many left before their indenture was complete to seize business opportunities elsewhere, while others finished and moved to the expanding suburbs to work away from Company control.[62] This process was intensified by the Great Fire of London in 1666 which destroyed much of the old city. The pragmatic need to retain paying Company members therefore appears to have paved the way for the apprenticing of girls.

Yet, even when women were permitted to be apprenticed in London, Companies still 'adopted ambivalent attitudes' towards female labour and gave them fewer rights. The 'formulaic records of apprenticeship' also continued to minimize women's place in the craft trades.[63] Not only did women begin to enter London's guilds in larger numbers, but they also began to work in large numbers outside of the guilds' control, particularly in the West End and Middlesex (see Appendix I). The experiences of these women who worked outside the guilds is much harder to trace and has not, until now, been explored in great depth. We must look for their work in tax records, non-guild apprenticeship records, court cases and in the bills they left behind in household papers. This book shows that there were several women who serviced elite clients and became wealthy and well known yet do not appear in the guild records. In particular, the archives studied in this book also capture the work of significant members of London's fashion marketplace that are often missing in guild records: French migrants. These include the aforementioned Haites and Cherets; women such as Marie Mandoue (Mary Mandove), who made Indian gowns for Catherine of Braganza; and even the tirewoman Mary Ducaila, whose brother was also Queen Anne's stay-maker. Tracing these names in the records reveals networks of French artisans living in London in the fashionable West End, plying their trades and training the next generation of English tradespeople. Their working lives as skilled migrants offer a different perspective of women in the fashion trades in London during the seventeenth and eighteenth centuries.

What studies of women's work in the craft trades that rely on guild records also struggle to reveal is the knowledge and skills involved in their work, and the social networks forged with the clients that they drew on for their success. As Deborah Simonton has noted, shifting notions of gender are demonstrated by how 'skill' is defined and used in relation to divisions of labour.[64] Indeed, there has been a tendency to characterize certain skills within the craft trades as male or female, by contemporaries and historians alike. However, tracing the working lives of the tradeswomen located in the Stuart queens' accounts nuances these divisions of labour and the changing nature of men and women's work during the late seventeenth century in London. Household bills and other documents such as court cases allow us to assess the skills and craft knowledge held by women, and the esteem that others had for them, in ways that guild records often cannot. This book demonstrates that if we look beyond institutions like guilds and their ways of classifying and recording work, a much more holistic understanding of early modern men and women's work in the craft trades emerges. Such an understanding, as this book will show, reveal not only the work tasks women performed, their skills and knowledge, but also their working arrangements, client relationships and social connections with elite patrons.

Accounting for work and fashion: sources

All early modern royal courts had dual roles as both political and household spaces. These large and complex institutions were filled with administrators and servants who recorded the political functions of government, as well as the day-to-day processes of feeding, clothing and otherwise entertaining the royal family, their relatives, other courtiers and international guests. As a result, these households produced copious amounts of paperwork, much of which has survived. These household accounts are an underexplored resource for histories of not only monarchy, court culture and fashion, but also histories of work, administration and life in Stuart England more broadly. They contain descriptions of goods bought and sold, as well as daily tasks performed, often described in their own words by the person directly involved.

The sources at the centre of this study are the thousands of loose papers and transcribed manuscripts compiled in English, Scots, French and Latin by the Stuart queens' Office of the Robes that describe clothing and furnishings.[65] The Office of the Robes was an administrative sub-department in a royal household that dealt with clothing, as well as furnishings and other goods (see Fig. 0.4). This department sat separately from the Great Wardrobe, which, during the Stuart period, primarily oversaw livery, furnishings such as beds, carpets and hangings, as well as 'Provisions for Coronations, Marriages and Funerals'.[66] Every member of the royal family had their own household which contained an Office of the Robes that accounted separately from the Great Wardrobe to the Treasury.[67] The king

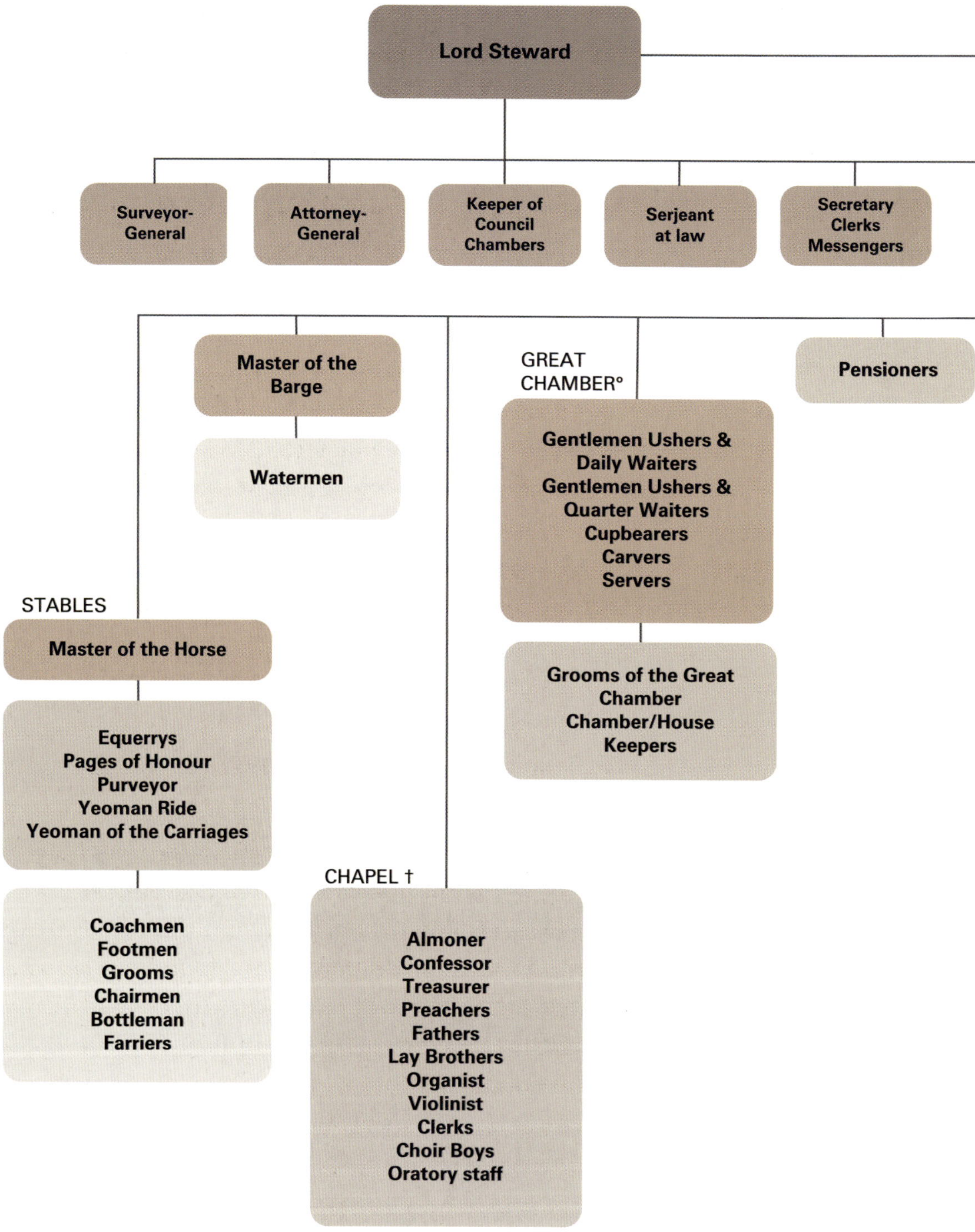

Fig. 0.4 *Organizational structure of the Stuart queens' household, including the Office of the Robes and Bedchamber.*

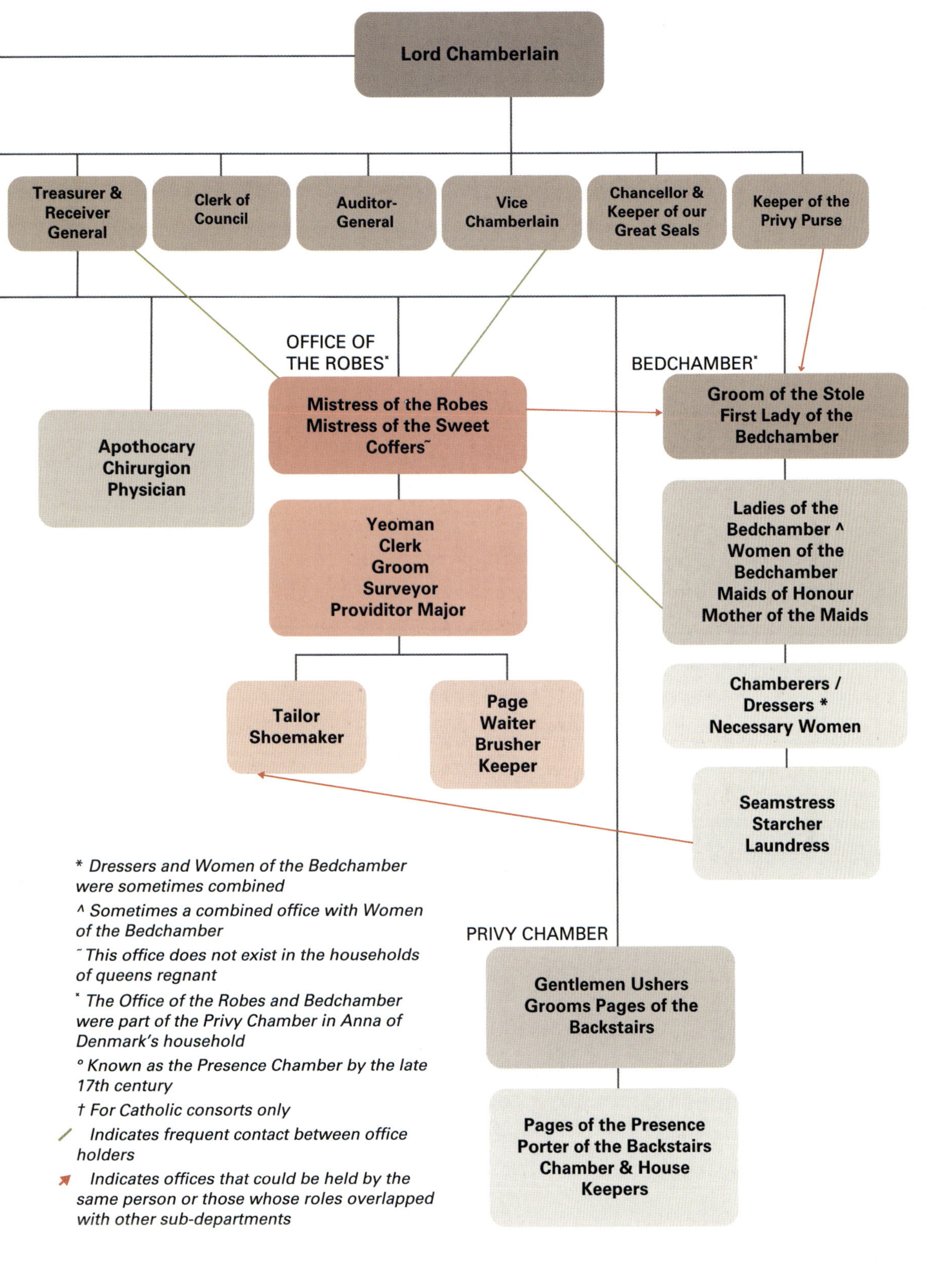
Lord Chamberlain
Treasurer & Receiver General
Clerk of Council
Auditor-General
Vice Chamberlain
Chancellor & Keeper of our Great Seals
Keeper of the Privy Purse
OFFICE OF THE ROBES*
Apothocary
Chirurgion
Physician
Mistress of the Robes
Mistress of the Sweet Coffers˜
Yeoman
Clerk
Groom
Surveyor
Providitor Major
Tailor
Shoemaker
Page
Waiter
Brusher
Keeper
BEDCHAMBER*
Groom of the Stole
First Lady of the Bedchamber
Ladies of the Bedchamber ^
Women of the Bedchamber
Maids of Honour
Mother of the Maids
Chamberers /
Dressers *
Necessary Women
Seamstress
Starcher
Laundress
PRIVY CHAMBER
Gentlemen Ushers
Grooms Pages of the Backstairs
Pages of the Presence
Porter of the Backstairs
Chamber & House
Keepers
* Dressers and Women of the Bedchamber were sometimes combined
^ Sometimes a combined office with Women of the Bedchamber
˜ This office does not exist in the households of queens regnant
* The Office of the Robes and Bedchamber were part of the Privy Chamber in Anna of Denmark's household
° Known as the Presence Chamber by the late 17th century
† For Catholic consorts only
Indicates frequent contact between office holders
Indicates offices that could be held by the same person or those whose roles overlapped with other sub-departments

and queens' privy purse, which was a private income allowance used for personal expenses, was separate to the accounts of the Office of the Robes. However, some of the queens' privy purse accounts have survived and are also utilized in this study.

Due to the varied political upheavals of the period, not all the household papers of the Stuart queens have survived in the same condition or in their entirety, nor are they housed at the same location.[68] The surviving papers of James I's consort, Anna of Denmark (1574–1619), are in the National Archives, Kew. They sporadically cover the period of her reign in England from 1603 to 1620 and consist of declared accounts from her Office of the Robes kept by her Vice Chamberlain and Receiver General, audited accounts from her Mistress of the Robes and documents relating to staff and wages kept by her Lord Steward. An inventory of wardrobe goods dating between 1608 and 1611 and one taken of Somerset House after her death in 1619 also detail the queen's clothing and furnishings.[69] While Anna's papers consist of transcriptions of bills and accounts settled, the accounts of Charles I's consort, Henrietta Maria (1609–69), consist of hundreds of loose artisans bills and vouchers, warrants for payment and declared accounts that were compiled by her Office of the Robes staff, approved by her Mistress of the Robes and then given to her Treasurer and Receiver General.[70] These household papers, which are also located in the National Archives, largely date from 1627, after the dismissal of her French household, to 1639 at the beginning of the Wars of the Three Kingdoms, although multiple payments to staff are recorded up until the execution of Charles I in 1649.[71]

Henrietta Maria's accounts are by far the largest in terms of the sheer volume of bills and paperwork that has survived. However, the queen consort of Charles II, Catherine of Braganza (1638–1705), has the longest spanning accounts. Her privy purse books record personal expenditure from the start of her reign in 1662 to 1681.[72] Her Office of the Robes accounts mostly date from her time as dowager from 1684 to 1705 and consist of boxes of loose bills, vouchers and warrants for payment for tradespeople and household staff that were deposited with the Auditor of Land Revenue, or compiled by her Lord Steward and Lord Chamberlain. For this study, I have focused on those sources covering her time in England as queen consort and dowager before she returned to Portugal in 1692.[73] Several bills, inventories and other warrants relating to Catherine's expenditure that I have also included in this study survive in the personal archive of her principal secretary, Sir Richard Bellings.[74] The most enigmatic queen of this book is Mary of Modena (1658–1718), the consort of James II. Detailed household papers have not survived, likely due to the circumstances around her sudden departure from England during the Glorious Revolution. Those papers that I have discovered are in the Bodleian Library Oxford. These consist of a mix of documents that date to the period of Mary's time as queen consort (1685–8), as well as those that were later submitted by tradespeople claiming payments long after she had fled to France.

For queens regnant such as Mary II (1662–94) and Queen Anne (1665–1714), references to clothing and furnishings are spread across their private Office of the Robes and privy purse accounts, as well as those of the Great Wardrobe. Several of Mary II's early papers from the beginning of her reign in 1689 are missing. Her Office of the Robes accounts are in the British Library and consist of bills that were submitted in 1694 or settled after her death in December of that year. Queen Anne's Office of the Robes accounts are also in the British Library and consists of a transcribed volume of bills and receipts for clothing that cover the period in her reign from 1702 to 1711, when the Duchess of Marlborough was the Mistress of the Robes.[75] Some original bills and receipts do survive in other papers from Anne's court, as well as those from Sarah Churchill's personal archive. Of those that I have been able to compare, the transcriptions are faithful copies. It is unclear where Queen Anne's accounts for the period 1711–14 (the final years of her reign) are located and indeed they may not have survived. However, civil lists detailing payments owed to household staff and tradespeople from these years do exist and have been used for this study.

Using the queens' household accounts as a starting point, I have been able to use genealogical records (birth, marriage and burial records), probate wills and inventories, the household papers of other elite women, as well as letters, and even court cases relating to financial disputes, to trace many tradeswomen through the historical record and uncover more about their lives, skills and work. To help interpret these sources, and the wider world of seventeenth-century fashion, I also utilize printed literature and a wide variety of visual and material sources. Importantly, French visual sources such as fashion plates from the Restoration onwards are, when appropriate, utilized.[76] Elite portraiture in the second half of the seventeenth century is characterized by the *en deshabille* styles of relaxed undress that are not necessarily representative of all the garments worn by their sitters in daily life, so accurate depictions of elite dress at this time are hard to come by. French fashions heavily influenced the Stuarts, and recent work has shown that French fashion prints are relatively representative of real garments that English consumers were keenly interested in.[77] My research has also revealed that many of the queens' tradespeople were French and had trained in France before relocating, either temporarily or indefinitely, to London. Thus, many of the French sources I utilize are crucial to understanding the training and skills of the people commissioned by the Office of the Robes.

I also treat the paperwork produced by the royal household as material sources. These papers were working documents that passed to many different people and contain evidence of many different hands, of how much they were handled and even whether women could sign their names, which allows us to follow the paper trail of work tasks inside and outside the household. Such papers can therefore be read for evidence of both men and women's work, their knowledge, skills and titles, and the differences between them.[78] All these records – archival, printed, visual and material – provide alternate sources to court gossip and diplomatic accounts that do not recount the work tasks performed by elite women within the royal household; to legal or tax records that focused only on male heads of households and erased the contributions of wives, children and servants under coverture; or to guild records that tended to undervalue or erase evidence of women's work in these institutions and their representative trades.[79]

Chapter outlines

By using this large body of royal records to explore the changing relationship between gender, work and fashion during the long seventeenth century, this book opens wider conversations about the nature of women and work in relation to clothing, during a time when professional identities and household positions were in flux.

Chapter 1 establishes the contexts and meanings of the dress of the Stuart queens. It demonstrates how each queen, influenced by their natal backgrounds and their different positions (as consort, dowager or regnant), interacted with wider trends in the fashion marketplace in their consumption of clothing, patronage of tradespeople and sartorial politics. Chapter 2 explores the work and networks of the Mistress of the Robes who managed the queen's Office of the Robes and commissioned tradespeople. It shows that the work undertaken by women in this position gained them power and influence and helped dictate fashion both in and outside the court. It argues that their patronage played a crucial role in supporting the rise of women's work in the fashion marketplace.

Chapter 3 examines the suppliers of the Stuart queens, particularly the rise of female milliners and fashion retailers such as Indian women. Operating outside guild control, many of these women cultivated famous public personas and influential networks, using their business success to rise through the ranks of Stuart society. Their connections with influential court women were pivotal in legitimizing their roles in the marketplace. Chapter 4 traces the emergence of female mantua-makers and the ambiguous occupational identities that they held as they competed for patronage alongside tailors. These women leveraged their training in various trades and relied on elite support in the courts to establish themselves. The chapter also examines the role of migrant French *couturières* in training the first generation of English mantua-makers and highlights their impact on English fashion.

Finally, Chapter 5 explores what happened to clothing in the Office of the Robes, encompassing storage, cleaning and dressing practices, including cosmetics, skincare and hairstyling, much of which was performed by women, including the Mistress of the Sweet Coffers and tirewomen. The chapter stresses the vast amounts of labour and materials involved in the care for elite clothing and explores how care work within the royal household provided many opportunities for paid work, social mobility and lifelong careers for tradeswomen as well as women from dynasties of service.

The conclusion focuses on what we can learn from studying women's work in the fashion marketplace alongside the work of women in the courts. The royal household accounts, as well as letters and court cases relating to the women of this study, detail a symbiotic relationship between the fashion marketplace of London and the royal court. Such a relationship challenges and revises understandings of women's work in these spheres. It reveals how women from different social backgrounds who worked with clothing, whether making, selling, managing or caring for it, participated in a complex and interconnected system that blurred the lines between court and marketplace, facilitated women's economic activities and identity formation and, finally, shaped the fashion landscape of seventeenth- and eighteenth-century England.

1

Wearing: The Stuart queens and elite fashions in the long seventeenth century

Early modern royal courts were theatrical spaces with complex rules of courtesy and precedence. Kings and queens used dress to impart a sense of wealth and magnificence associated with divine monarchy, and courtiers dressed to impress their monarch as they competed for honours and favour.[1] Royals and their courtiers were always aware of how their appearance and actions were viewed by others, and wealth and competition often gave way to innovations in fashion.[2] Structured garments, sumptuous fabrics and expensive jewels helped to shape and materialize elite bodies that were defined by power and wealth, and were themselves an expression of the power and wealth of the crown they served or wore. In this sense, intense focus on self-presentation and novel expressions of magnificence through clothing was 'both the prerogative and the duty of the elite'.[3] The profound significance of dress, both as a symbol of status and a form of moveable wealth, explains why the monarchy invested vast sums on teams of suppliers, artisans, managers and caretakers. Thus, before we can focus on the work of the women and men who worked behind the scenes to clothe the Stuart queens, we must first understand the meanings of elite dress during the Stuart period.

Elite women were diplomatic and cultural agents in early modern Europe, who used clothing for personal and political ends in what has been termed 'sartorial politics'.[4] For royal women, clothing communicated personal messages about their nationality, familial and factional connections, confessional identity and piety, and even love and marital harmony.[5] Queenly sartorial displays were therefore mediated by the nature of their rule, as queens consort or regnant. Of all the queens whose accounts are studied in this book, only Mary II and Queen Anne were English-born. Anna of Denmark, Henrietta Maria, Catherine of Braganza and Mary of Modena were all foreign-born queens consort.[6] Their continental backgrounds influenced both their reception and life in England, as well as their tastes in clothing and the household staff and tradespeople they employed. These women often brought new materials, ideas and fashions from their homelands, acting as agents of cultural transfer between their natal and marital courts. This not only helped to 'promulgate a pan-European court culture that transcended national boundaries', but it brought the English court into contact with new ideas, merchants, suppliers and artisans.[7] Once settled into their new courts, various Stuart queens also championed certain styles and partook in fashionable local consumer culture, sometimes even promoting English modes at their natal courts.

I am primarily interested in the everyday dress of the Stuart queens, rather than costumes related to court masques or their robes of state used for coronations and Parliaments. I also give more attention to the queens after the Stuart Restoration of 1660. Unlike Anna of Denmark or Henrietta Maria, whose wardrobe accounts and dress has been expertly studied by Jemma Field, Michael Pearce, Caroline Hibbard and Erin Griffey,[8] the later queens have received less attention.[9] Those Stuart queens of the post-Glorious Revolution (1688) period have been especially neglected. It is only recently that the visual representation, collecting and patronage practices in art, architecture and the decorative arts of these later Stuart queens have been investigated in any great depth.[10]

This chapter does not give an exhaustive account of each queen's wardrobe or the meanings of aristocratic dress during the entirety of the Stuart era. However, it does contextualize the dress and wardrobe of each queen and their use of clothing during three periods of the seventeenth century: the early Stuarts, the Restoration and the later Stuarts. Such periods are not only separated by time and chronology, but also by major social, cultural, political and economic changes to the monarchy and in the fashion marketplace, at the local, European and, increasingly, global levels. This chapter establishes the contexts and meanings of the dress of the Stuart queens. In doing so, I demonstrate how each queen's background (Danish, French, Portuguese, Italian and English) and their different life stages and positions, as consort, dowager or regnant, interacted with wider trends in the fashion marketplace to influence her consumption of clothing, her patronage of tradespeople and her sartorial politics. While their dress was always political, over time the wardrobes of the Stuart queens became more influenced by the fashion marketplace and commercial interests. It is only after establishing the meanings and motivations behind the consumption of dress for these well-known women that we can investigate the gendered labour and the lives of those who worked to manage, sell, make and care for their clothing.

The early Stuarts: Anna of Denmark and Henrietta Maria

The first Stuart queen of England was James I's consort, Anna of Denmark. Born on 12 December 1574, Anna was the daughter of King Frederick II of Denmark and his wife Sofie of Mecklenburg-Güstrow. During her youth she had grown up in the sophisticated Oldenburg court of Denmark, which, at that time, was one of the most affluent and politically powerful states in early modern

Europe, owing to its territories that extended from Greenland and Iceland to modern day Denmark, Sweden and northern Germany. After her father's death in 1588, Anna was betrothed to King James VI of Scotland, son of Mary Queen of Scots and cousin to Elizabeth I of England.[11] They were married by proxy on 20 August 1589 when Anna was fifteen years old. She was crowned as queen the following year. As both Scottish and Danish courts were Protestant, the match was well received, and Anna's pan-European connections were deemed to be advantageous for the Stuarts.[12]

When Anna arrived in Scotland in May 1590, she brought with her a trousseau of costly jewels and apparel made by over 300 tailors, embroiderers and jewellers, which signified the wealth of her Danish family and her status as a new queen of Scotland.[13] These themes continued to be important during her reign as queen of Scotland and then England, as her royal body remained a physical symbol of the wealth and power of both the Oldenburg and Stuart dynasties.[14] As Field and Pearce have found, Anna kept many Danish and German wardrobe staff in her Scottish household, and her Danish tailor Paul Rey helped her to fashion a Danish–German style in conjunction with local fashions in Scotland.[15] Although the Scottish crown faced financial difficulties, after James VI was named as Elizabeth I's successor the English crown subsidized much of the Stuart household's expenditure, including their clothing which was made from large amounts of imported fabrics and trimmings from Europe, particularly Spain and Italy.[16]

Elizabeth I died on 24 March 1603 and James VI of Scotland was proclaimed as James I of England. In preparation for her departure to England, Anna's Scottish household accounts show that new clothing made from expensive textiles was ordered and existing clothing was altered to suit fashions in England which tended to lean more towards French and Spanish styles.[17] James even ordered that Tudor goods from the Great Wardrobe be taken and sent to Anna in preparation for her procession into London where, as Field has argued, she 'cut a magnificent spectacle' and conformed to English dress standards.[18] The latter was especially important; Anna was not just a foreign queen consort, but the Stuarts were a foreign dynasty being placed on the English throne. Thus, it was essential they win the support of the people. Anna was crowned as queen alongside James on 25 July 1603 in Westminster Abbey. England was more financially and politically stable than Scotland and such conditions allowed Anna to 'redefine herself' through her cultural patronage of the arts – including the visual arts, architecture, masquing and material goods – to build a high court culture that she used for 'aesthetic and political' gain.[19] Such political ends are apparent in her wardrobe accounts and portraiture.

An inventory of the queen's clothing for the period 1608–11, with 479 entries, gives a detailed overview of the many types of garments owned, reflecting Anna's personal tastes as well as the dress of fashionable elites in England during this period.[20] The most numerous types of garments in this inventory are mix-and-match ensembles comprised of separate bodies (bodices), petticoat-skirts and sleeves made from satin or taffeta. Other gowns are described as 'night gowns', referring to loose garments worn as informal wear. Several types of close fitting, upper body garments such as doublets, jerkins and waistcoats (see Fig. 4.3) are also recorded.[21] Pinking, a technique whereby the fabric was cut to form little decorative shapes such as stars, zigzags and scallops, was commonly noted, as were copious amounts of buttons, lace and braid used to trim the edges of garments or to cover seams.[22] All these outer garments were worn with kirtles and petticoats, as well as a mixture of linen accessories (see Chapter 4), and were intended to be mixed and matched to create a variety of outfits that were commonly worn by elite women at this time.[23]

The inventory also records many garments used to shape the queen's silhouette into one that conveyed an imposing sense of aristocratic power.[24] Several pairs of 'whalebone bodies' and farthingales,

Fig. 1.1 *John De Critz the Elder,* Anna of Denmark, c. *1606–8, oil on canvas. National Portrait Gallery, NPG 6918.*

all made from satins, taffetas and damasks of various colours, are mentioned.[25] Some have argued that Anna strategically wore the French wheel farthingale upon her arrival to England, after it had ceased to be fashionable, in order to create a visual and sartorial connection to her predecessor, Elizabeth I (see Fig. 1.1).[26] While this may have been one motivating factor, in the early seventeenth century this style of farthingale was still common on the continent among England's close neighbours such as France. It was also part of fashionable dress at courts with whom Anna had frequent contact, such as those of Denmark-Norway, Brandenburg, Sweden and Wolfenbüttel.[27] Thus, this undergarment that shaped the skirts created not only an imposing, aristocratic silhouette, but also a visual connection for Anna and the Stuarts with both the Tudors and with her peers throughout Europe.

No Danish gowns are mentioned in the queen's English inventory. However, several garments are described as Spanish. In April and May 1611, the queen wore several 'hanging sleeves of the Spanish Fashion', which could have represented Anna's championing of an Anglo-Spanish marriage alliance.[28] Support for the French King Henri IV of France was also shown when a plain black gown was recorded as a 'morning gown per French King death' on 19 May 1610 after his assassination by a Catholic fanatic five days earlier.[29] Thus, Anna's clothing was strategically used to emphasize a variety of political and cultural ties across Europe.

The political stakes of royal dress are evident in descriptions of the decorative embroidery on Anna's garments.[30] Some of this embroidery contained ciphers or heraldry. The bodice of a gown of white satin was described as 'embroidered all over with borders of Silver owes', referring to spangles, and with the letters of 'A· & ·S.', meaning Anna Sovereign or Anna Stuart, whilst other motifs included 'esses' (letter 'S') for Stuart.[31] Red fleur-de-lys are also depicted on a gown in a portrait of Anna painted in the period 1617–18 (see Fig. 1.2). The garment in this painting closely matches a description given of another gown in 1610:

> One gown of Ash colour Damask, the upper part of the bodies wearing and watchet sleeves Embroidered in bias guards with gold Carnation and watchet Silks . . . and Flowered all over with the Same Embroidery Like Flower Deluces [fleur-de-lys].[32]

While it is unclear if this is the exact gown shown in the painting, the use of this heraldic symbol was indicative of Anna's royalty, purity and the historical claims of the English monarchy to the French throne.

Finally, jewellery, of which Anna had a large collection, was a key and very conspicuous way that she engaged in sartorial politics. She often wore jewels that contained ambiguous or cross-confessional meanings which helped her to navigate the Catholic and Protestant divisions in Europe, particularly after her suspected conversion to Catholicism during the 1590s. Additionally, she owned many cipher jewels such as crowned 'S's and 'C's that referenced her mother, Sofie of Mecklenburg-Güstrow, and brother, King Christian IV of Denmark. Many of her portraits depict her wearing these jewels (see Fig. 1.2).

Fig. 1.2 *Paul van Somer,* Anna of Denmark, c. *1617–18, oil on canvas. Royal Collection Trust, RCIN 405813.*

When championing a marriage match between her eldest son Henry (who later died aged eighteen) and the Spanish Habsburg Infanta, Anna Maria, she also wore jewellery that referenced Henry alongside miniatures depicting Habsburg family members.[33] Anna therefore used her clothing and jewellery to emphasize her natal ties to the Oldenburg court in Denmark and to support the Anglo-Spanish marriage matches of her children.[34]

Anna of Denmark died on 2 March 1619. Although she had sought a strategic Spanish marriage for her second son Charles, it was abandoned due to an impasse with Spain over the Stuarts' Protestant faith and the place of Catholics within the realm.[35] Instead, a new match was proposed with the Bourbon French princess, Henrietta Maria. Henrietta Maria was born on 25 November 1609 at the Louvre Palace in Paris. She was the youngest daughter of King Henri IV and his Italian wife Marie de' Medici. After negotiations with the French, the marriage was agreed to, and Henrietta Maria was wed to Charles by proxy in a sumptuous Catholic ceremony at the Cathedral of Notre Dame in Paris on 1 May 1625. A month later, Henrietta Maria stepped foot on English soil at Dover and met her new husband, King Charles I.

Of all the Stuart queens, Henrietta Maria is perhaps the most maligned and misunderstood. As Malcolm Smuts has summarized, poets and artists 'crafted an image of Henrietta Maria as a symbol of chaste beauty, monogamous love and harmony' in the 1630s; however, during the wars of the 1640s she became a polarizing figure, 'a cavalier heroine and malignant villain, the reputed patron of a Papist and libertine faction' who was blamed for many of the grievances that Parliament and its supporters directed at Charles I.[36] Although recent work has shown her to be a sophisticated patron of the arts who played a formidable cultural role in Caroline England, her time as queen consort is often still characterized by the Puritan and pro-Parliament sentiments that framed her as a frivolous, extravagant and naïve French Catholic who threatened the stability of the realm.[37]

The marriage between the Protestant Charles I and Catholic Henrietta Maria was 'the first transnational, cross-confessional marriage' of any king and queen in Europe since the Reformation.[38] As such, the Anglo-French match immediately caused tensions within Parliament. As well as allowing Henrietta Maria to continue to practise her Catholic faith in private chapels built in the royal palaces, the marriage negotiations also stipulated that concessions should be granted to English Catholics. There was a deep fear, and perhaps one that was well-founded, that the Pope in Rome wished to use Henrietta Maria to convert Charles to Catholicism and regain England as a Catholic nation.[39] Such fears were not abated by the fact that over time the queen's faith became more visible through new chapel building projects, the hosting of papal envoys, her patronage or commissioning of art with explicit Catholic themes and her proselytizing within the court.[40]

While the English Parliament had been deeply suspicious of any Catholic match for Charles I, the king's own actions during the 1630s also reflected negatively on his wife. In 1629, after a series of disputes about taxation and matters of foreign policy, the king dissolved Parliament and it would not meet again until 1640. This eleven-year period of personal rule with only an advisory council of royal appointees undoubtably set England on the path towards civil war. During this time there was fear that the queen was wielding an illegitimate influence over her husband that subverted existing patriarchal power structures.[41] Thus, it is within this context of deeply fraught religious and political tensions, of the queen's Catholicism and her French origins, that we must understand Henrietta Maria's household accounts and dressing practices during the 1630s, as well as the wider interpretation of her public image.

Henrietta Maria's Office of the Robes accounts show that she was a queen with discerning and expensive tastes. When she had arrived in England in 1625, she brought with her a rich trousseau filled with clothing, jewellery, ecclesiastical textiles and paraphernalia, furniture and decorative arts, as well as coaches and horses, that reflected her status as a Bourbon Princess of France.[42] Like Anna of Denmark before her, Henrietta's clothing choices during the early years of her reign were heavily influenced by her natal court, and the high standards that had been instilled in her at the French courts influenced her extravagant spending. Griffey's meticulous analysis of the queen's household

Fig. 1.3 *Hendrick Pot*, Charles I, Henrietta Maria and Charles, Prince of Wales (later Charles II), c. *1632, oil on panel. Royal Collection Trust, RCIN 405541.*

bills show that 'rich', 'best' and 'fine' were the most common adjectives used to describe the garments and furnishings ordered by the queen, and almost all of her clothes were made from high-quality European silks and richly adorned with embroidery, metallic lace and spangles.[43] The king and queen both spent staggering amounts in the early years of their reign on jewellery too, sometimes for themselves and often as gifts for their courtiers.[44] Such spending was essential to showcasing Henrietta's magnificence as queen consort and as a French princess. However, an audit conducted in 1626 showed that after only a year in England the queen owed debts to various creditors and artisans amounting to £30,000 and a council was set up and measures were taken to limit her expenditure.[45]

Portraits of the queen painted during the 1630s portray her in both French and English styles. In Hendrick Pot's 1632 portrait of Charles I and Henrietta Maria with their infant son (the future Charles II), the queen wears an outfit typical of the French court: a petticoat, a bodice and stomacher with ballooning virago paned sleeves and a standing Medici collar (see Fig. 1.3).[46] Many similar garments were listed in her trousseau and in the same year that this portrait was painted, the queen's French tailor billed for making 'a pair of paned sleeves of flowered satin'.[47] Although the queen was increasingly depicted in portraits during the 1630s wearing English styles of dress, consisting of a bodice and a petticoat (see Fig. 1.4), there was a notable disjunction between formal portraits that presented the queen in English styles and the French and continental garments that were in her wardrobe.

During the 1630s the queen's surviving accounts show that her outer clothing was primarily fashioned by two French tailors, named George Gelin and Jacques Bardou, as well as a Frenchman named Charles Genty, who was described in various bills as both an 'embroiderer' and a 'cutter', meaning he patterned and cut the fabric pieces to be sewn up by her tailors. In the early years of her reign, the queen was also served by a French farthingale-maker named John Huguitt and a French shoemaker named Jean Fausse.[48] These artisans, some of whom came from France with Henrietta Maria, helped the queen to maintain the French aspects of her appearance in England. In addition to having French artisans, the queen also bought clothing from France. In 1630, Gelin altered a 'white satin gown for her Majesty which Mistress Grynie brought from France'.[49]

A French ensemble consisting of a hungerline and petticoat was by the far the most common outfit made for Henrietta Maria during the 1630s (see Fig. 1.5).[50] Hungerlines were popular garments in France derived from the male *justacorps*. While the English waistcoat was a sleeved jacket-bodice that often contained short gored 'skirts' that flared over the hips, the hungerline was a jacket-bodice defined by its voluminous and flowing long skirts. Special farthingale rolls were even constructed to be worn under this garment; a 'Roll to wear with a Hungerline' was made by the queen's farthingale maker in 1639.[51] Petticoats at this time referred to a skirt that often, but not always, had an attached stiffened 'bodie' (petticoat-bodies, or stays). They could be worn as outer garments with a waistcoat, hungerline or bodice, or as undergarments. Petticoats made by Gelin for Henrietta Maria are often described as containing whalebone bodies with sleeves and stomachers, meaning that they likely formed a skirt-bodice combination frequently seen in England and France.[52]

Fig. 1.4 *Wenceslaus Hollar,* Ornatus Muliebris Anglicanus *[The Clothing of English Women], 1640, etching. Rijksmuseum Amsterdam, RP-P-1920-2683. This costume book presents several styles of English women's dress, including this formal style, from the late 1630s.*

What often singled out the French styling of such an ensemble was the addition of an outer, sleeveless black floor-length gown, which was common in portraits from the French court, and this was something that Henrietta Maria's accounts show that she commissioned regularly.[53] In addition, the queen also commissioned 'Italian gowns' and 'simares', perhaps the Italian *zimarra*, which was a type of loose over-gown. Griffey has suggested that perhaps the queen's use of Italian styles was a nod to her Italian Medici lineage.[54] While this is certainly possible, French writings from the 1630s also mentioned hungerlines and simares as the latest fashions in France.[55]

Fig. 1.5 *Anthony van Dyck,* Queen Henrietta Maria with Sir Jeffrey Hudson, *1633, oil on canvas. National Gallery of Art Washington DC, 1952.5.39. The long skirts of this pinked blue jacket-bodice indicate that it could have been a French garment known as a 'hungerline' in Henrietta Maria's Robes accounts.*

Part of Henrietta Maria's value as a bride to the king of England was her background as a Bourbon princess, her very presence at the English court signifying the relationship between the two countries and their ruling families.[56] Although it seems that she preferred French fashions over English ones, her choice of dress, whether it be French, English or Italian, was a strategic part of her cultural patronage and her sartorial politics. She was also clearly a trend-setter as her style was mirrored by many courtiers who also began to buy clothing and accessories direct from France, much to the dismay of critics who saw such continental, Catholic influences on fashions as symptomatic of the moral weaknesses of the court.[57]

Anti-court writings of the early seventeenth century increasingly spoke of a divide between the court and the rest of society due to the strained relationship between the king and Parliament. Conduct literature began to address men and women of the lower gentry and middling sorts, warning them against lavish spending and corruption like that of the courts. Richard Brathwaite stated in his popular conduct manual, *The English Gentlewoman* (1631), that 'she is not to be accounted a Court visitant, who restrains her self either in her choice of *delicacy* or *variety* of habit'.[58] The ideal English gentlewoman who practised restraint in dress was therefore the opposite of the queen and her courtiers. Dress, and particularly Henrietta Maria's dress, entered national discussions in the decades leading up to the English Civil Wars (1642–51) about both royal expenditure and what it was to be English.

The reliance of fashion retailers and suppliers on the queen's patronage was made explicit in a 1641 petition from 'Tradesmens wives'. On behalf of 'their husbands, their children, and their families, amounting to many thousand souls', these women claimed that their families had undertaken apprenticeships and set up 'houses and shops both in the City and Suburbs, and also in the Exchanges at very great rents', and they urged Parliament to halt the queen's possible departure from England. They pleaded for Parliament to 'give some speedy assurance to her Majesty' that the 'Authors and Instigators' of the 'seditious tumults and scandals' increasingly levelled at the queen should be punished and that she should receive 'public vindication by Parliament'. If they did not, they would be unable to pay their rents and 'live in good repute' as they relied heavily on the 'splendour and glory of the English Court and principally upon that of the Queens Majesty' for the sale of their 'commodities'.[59] Although the vast majority of Henrietta Maria's tradespeople were men (see Appendix I, Table 2), female petitioning was common during the pre-war and Civil War era, and it seems that these tradespeople hoped that this feminine form of petitioning would sway Parliament. However, it was not enough. Amid increasing tensions with Parliament and threats of violence in the capital, Charles I and Henrietta Maria left London on 10 January 1642. A month later Henrietta Maria fled for Europe; she would not return to England again until the Stuart Restoration in 1660. Although she has been maligned for her French tastes while queen consort, the growing pan-European influence of French styles under her nephew, King Louis XIV of France, and the beginnings of the consumer revolution soon saw court women chase and popularize trends generated by the market during the reign of her son, Charles II.

The Restoration: Catherine of Braganza and Mary of Modena

Catherine of Braganza was born on 25 November 1638 in Vila Viçosa, Portugal. She was the youngest daughter of King John IV of Portugal and his wife, Luisa de Guzmán.[60] When Catherine was seven years old a marriage with the Stuart Prince Charles had been proposed. However, anti-Catholic sentiment in England at the time of the Wars of the Three Kingdoms and English Civil Wars (1639–53) led King Charles I to reject the match. After the execution of his father in 1649, young Charles was crowned King of Scotland and lived in exile in France, the Dutch Republic, the German states and the Spanish Netherlands. While in exile he bided his time and sought to gain support for the return of the Stuarts to their English and Irish thrones. Following the death of Oliver Cromwell, Lord Protector of the Interregnum Commonwealth government in 1658, and a successful coup against his son Richard Cromwell in 1659, Charles was invited back to England by Parliament. He entered London in May of 1660 to much rejoicing and nearly a year later, on 23 April 1661, he was crowned King Charles II of England.

At the opening of his Parliament in May 1661, Charles II announced that he would marry the Portuguese Infanta. The marriage treaty was considered a 'great diplomatic victory of the House of Braganza' and was celebrated in Portugal.[61] In England the reception was not quite as positive. Although the Portuguese bride came with an immense dowry that helped to alleviate the Stuarts' money troubles, the match took place during the Portuguese Restoration War and pitted England against Spain. Worryingly for many, Catherine was also Catholic. Indeed, her religion would lead to tensions during Catherine's time in England, particularly during the Popish Plot and Exclusion Crisis of 1678–81, a fictitious conspiracy that claimed the queen and her household were planning to assassinate Charles II.[62]

Catherine was married to Charles on 21 May 1662 in separate Catholic and Anglican ceremonies.[63] Despite their different personalities and levels of piety, Catherine and Charles did have a fondness for each other. However, their marriage was plagued by the king's infidelities and Catherine's inability to produce a living heir. These troubles were inevitably heightened by the culture of the Restoration court, which has been described as 'rakish' and 'bawdy'.[64] Satires frequently connected the vices of courtiers with national weakness, while Restoration court culture was perceived to disrupt traditional models of marriage, family and morality.[65] Women also began to take on a much more public role in court life and that of fashionable London society more generally.[66] Charles II was the first English king of the seventeenth century to openly keep several mistresses drawn from English, French and Italian nobility, as well as non-elite sorts. These women, including Barbara Palmer, Duchess of Cleveland, and Hortense Mancini, Duchess of Mazarin (see Fig. 4.22), were celebrated for their beauty and they exploited their influence on the king for economic and political ends.[67]

In contrast, Catherine of Braganza framed herself, as Maria Hayward has argued, as a 'good wife' to assert herself as queen and 'thereby came to represent normative, virtuous, women at court and in the country at large'.[68] As such, historians have tended to treat Catherine unfavourably compared to her husband's more beautiful and outspoken mistresses.[69] Rarely is the queen identified as one of the Restoration court's beauties.[70] Although not conventionally beautiful, Catherine's wardrobe accounts

Fig. 1.6 *Dirk Stoop,* Arrival of Queen Catherine of Braganza in Portsmouth, c. *1662, etching and engraving. Rijksmuseum Amsterdam, RP-P-1879-A-3176. This print is part of a series recording the journey of Catherine of Braganza from Portugal to London in 1662. Note the difference between Catherine's Portuguese dress and the dress of English ladies on far left.*

show that she was far from unfashionable. Later in her reign, as Chapters 3 and 4 will show, Catherine's tailors, mantua-makers and milliners were patronized by other elite women, including many of the so called 'Windsor Beauties' of Charles II's court.

When Catherine of Braganza and her ladies first arrived in England in 1662, they were dressed in Portuguese styles, including the large oblong-shaped *guardainfantes*. Their appearance seemed rather peculiar to the English who had grown accustomed to fashion trends emanating from France and the Dutch Republic.[71] The engravings made of her progress from Lisbon to Hampton Court by her court painter Dirk Stoop depict the princess and her ladies departing Lisbon and arriving in Portsmouth wearing this Portuguese dress (see Fig. 1.6). However, upon her arrival at Hampton Court Palace with Charles II, after their marriage, the prints show the new queen dressed in Anglo-French styles of the English court.

Unlike Anna of Denmark and Henrietta Maria who continued to reference fashions from their home countries in their dress, Catherine very quickly abandoned Portuguese styles. In 1663, Samuel Pepys wrote in his diary that the queen looked 'mighty pretty' in an informal Anglo-French style consisting of a 'white laced waistcoat and a crimson short petticoat' and a French hairstyle he described as '*à la negligence*'.[72] For more formal occasions during this decade, Catherine would have worn the typical formal gown of the time which consisted of a long-waisted, fitted bodice with a low round neckline and elbow-length sleeves that was worn with a petticoat-skirt (see Fig. 1.7). Around the same time, portraits of the queen by court painters such as Peter Lely and Jacob Huysmans depicted Catherine with Anglo-French hairstyles and in the popular formal and *en deshabille* gowns of the Restoration court (see Fig. 1.8).[73] The Office of the Robes accounts show that Catherine's dress was distinctly Anglo-French. Privy purse accounts dating from 1668 to 1679 detail her regular purchases of fashionable garments and accessories from French artisans, merchants and retailers. In comparison, there is only one reference to 'the Italian Milliner for 2 hoods' at this time.[74] The queen also imported many fashionable goods directly from France. In November of 1675 'a box lately brought from France, containing three pair of embroidered bodies' was delivered to the 'Queen's Robes at Whitehall'.[75]

Catherine of Braganza's decision to adopt French styles so quickly likely stemmed from the familial connections that the Stuarts maintained with France and the chokehold that French fashions had on much of Europe during this period.[76] After the royal family was deposed, during the Interregnum (1649–60) Henrietta Maria and some of her children, including the future Charles II and James II, fled to France. There they lived in exile in Paris, Bruges and The Hague. Charles II's sister, Henrietta, with whom he had a close relationship, had also married Philippe I, Duke of Orleans, brother of Louis XIV in 1661. Despite the efforts of Charles to create a distinctly English style in the woollen vest, it is no surprise that the tastes of the restored Stuart monarchy tended towards the continental and French.[77]

By the mid-seventeenth century, this was generally true in most of North-West Europe. While French dominance in English court culture was not new, as the case of Henrietta Maria demonstrates, the wide embrace of French influences around Europe in the latter half of the century was the result of a combination of several things: Louis XIV's centralized court at Versailles with its strict etiquette, his economic policies that promoted French textiles and fashions implemented by the French first minister of state, Jean-Baptiste Colbert, and the influence of French salons and popular media such as fashion prints.[78]

Catherine's time as queen saw several changes to fashionable dress worn in England. This included the introduction of new mantua gowns from France, which were primarily referred to in English during this time as 'mantos'.[79] The manto initially consisted of a casual T-shaped gown that was draped and pleated to create an unstiffened bodice with attached overskirts. It was worn over a pair of bodies and a contrasting petticoat and secured using a girdle or belt (see Fig. 1.9). In 1678, the *Extraordinaire du Mercure galant* noted that almost every fashionable woman in Paris wore a mantua gown as daily attire to see friends or to promenade.[80] Members of the Francophile Restoration court were early adopters too. In 1669, the French ambassador in England, Colbert de Croissy, wrote to his French contacts informing them that if they were to continue to try to gain favour with Charles II's influential French mistress, Louise de Kérouaille, they should gift her with 'trifling tokens [such] as a pair of

Fig. 1.7 *Silver Tissue Dress, c. 1660s, English. Fashion Museum Bath. This gown is typical of elite styles of the 1660s and believed to have been worn by Lady Theophilia Harris at the court of Charles II.*

Fig. 1.8 *Peter Lely,* Catherine of Braganza, *c. 1663–5, oil on canvas. Royal Collection Trust, RCIN 401214.*

French gloves, ribbons, a Parisian undress gown, or some little object of finery'.[81] That same year, Pepys noted in his diary that his wife had begun to wear a 'French gown called a sac', perhaps another early style of manto.[82]

Charles II was unwilling to set a strict dress code like that of Versailles, where gowns with fully boned bodices were still required to be worn, and so the relaxed French elegance of the manto was a common sight on London's streets and at the English court.[83] In October 1673 Queen Catherine's privy purse records indicate that she paid thirty-five pounds for 'a French Embroidered manto', making this one of the more expensive pieces of clothing in her accounts.[84] In the years after this, the Duchess of Cleveland and the Duchess of Mazarin also imported goods from France that included mantos of

Fig. 1.9 *Jean Lepautre,* Dame en habit d'été *[Woman in Summer Fashions], c. 1676–8, hand–coloured engraving. Rijksmuseum Amsterdam, RP-P-2009-1109. The woman wears a mantua gown over a contrasting petticoat and sleeves, with a hood, gloves and a fan. The print is part of the second series of* Suite de Costumes *partly commissioned for the gazette* Le Nouveau Mercure galant.

'gold and silver stuff' and those 'flowered with gold and silver', as well as fabrics, ribbons, muffs, gloves, shoes and fashion dolls.[85] While it is impossible to read into all the subtleties of taste in these sorts of accounts, it is clear that at this time, on paper at least, Catherine was wearing the same styles as her husband's mistresses and other much-praised Restoration court beauties.

During the 1680s Catherine continued to patronize French artisans in both Paris and London.[86] There were large communities of fashionable French makers, merchants and retailers in London during the seventeenth century. Although French artisans had long been migrating to England, their numbers substantially increased during the late seventeenth century and specifically after 1685, when Louis XIV revoked the Edict of Nantes, which had given religious freedoms to French Calvinist Protestants. Suddenly facing religious persecution, approximately 25,000 French Huguenots migrated to England in the last two decades of the seventeenth century, bringing with them their expertise and skills in textile manufacturing and the fashion trades.[87] France's loss was England's gain. Yet while the queen benefitted from the arrival of many French refugees, her wardrobe was not immune from the various economic and political measures taken during the seventeenth century to protect English industry against foreign trade. Various French commodities, including French linens, silks and colbertin lace, were banned in England in the periods 1678–85 and 1688–1780, and during these years these French wares were not purchased by the queen.[88]

In addition to linens, silks, wools and other mixed-fibre fabrics of European origins, Catherine was the first queen of England to wear large amounts of 'Indian' silk and cotton fabrics that were imported from the East Indies, now India, China, Japan and the Middle East. Her accounts from the 1680s include frequent references to fabrics described as 'Indian satin', 'Indian Serge', 'Persians', 'Indian painted calico' and 'muslin' (see Appendix II), and she purchased goods such as Indian fans and an 'Indian satin screen'.[89] Mantos and garments known as Indian gowns were frequently made for the queen with these textiles. The Indian gown was a kimono-style gown worn by both men and women as informal wear at home (see Fig. 1.10). It was likely derived from Japanese styles imported by the Dutch (called *japonse zijde rok*) that were combined with traditional European nightgowns.[90] Samuel Pepys bought Indian gowns for himself and his wife, and King Charles II had more than ninety Indian gowns made between 1662 and 1685.[91] For women, these gowns were frequently referred to as morning or night gowns and they may also have been the loose garments depicted in *en deshabille* portraits of the period (see Fig. 2.13). Indian gowns probably inspired the relaxed style of the manto, as both these garments made frequent use of lightweight Asian textiles and were made by mantua-makers (see Chapter 4).[92]

When Catherine of Braganza arrived in England in 1662, she brought Indian cabinets with her, which John Evelyn noted 'had never before been seen here'.[93] Alongside spices, in the sixteenth century Portuguese traders had begun to deal in textiles and porcelain, trading within the Indian Ocean and South China Sea as well as to Africa and Europe.[94] Before the English East India Company (EIC) and the Dutch East India Company (*Vereenigde Oostindische Compagnie*, or VOC) established a control of trade during the seventeenth century, it was Portuguese ships that had delivered cargoes of spices, cloth and 'Indian wares' such as porcelain and lacquerware to England.[95] Additionally, Catherine's dowry provided England with control of Tangiers and Bombay (modern day Mumbai) and additional trading privileges to the Portuguese East Indies and Brazil. Thus, the queen's consumption of these goods demonstrated not only her fashionability, but also the wealth and power of global trade networks and colonies held by both her Portuguese homeland and increasingly by the English.

Fig. 1.10 *Nicolas Bonnart,* Homme en Robe de Chambre *[Man in a Chamber Robe], c. 1676, French. Los Angeles County Museum of Art, M.2002.57.43. The engraving is from a series depicting French Court Fashions. It calls the gown a 'Robe d'Armenien', or Armenian gown, which is largely synonymous with the term 'Indian Gown' used in English. Many fabrics came to France via French merchants living in Smyrna in Turkey and who traded in Armenian and Persian goods that were brought to the city by trade caravans.*

Major personal life events are also visible in Catherine's Robes accounts. In the early 1680s, white was the most common colour of the queen's outer garments, followed by black, gold and silver, reds (crimson and scarlet), blues, purples, greens and browns. Many garments she ordered in 1684 were flowered, striped or otherwise patterned with these multiple hues. That year she also wore a 'Birth Day Green Petticoat' to her birthday ball, with Evelyn writing of the event that the 'court had not been seen so brave and rich in apparel since his Majesty's Restoration'.[96] However, the death of Charles II on 6 February 1685 marked not only a distinct shift in Catherine's place at court, from consort to dowager, but also changed the colour of her wardrobe. The queen's apartments were 'hung with black' and all the formal clothing she commissioned was either black or dark grey, usually made of plain wool or crape, a fabric associated with mourning.[97] Blue waistcoats were the only exception, and it is likely these were worn in private. Her period of formal mourning appears to have ended in 1686, but for the remainder of her time in England her wardrobe was dominated by blacks, greys, 'dark[s]' and browns of various shades (sad coloured, cinnamon, philamot), as well as some white, blue, purple and gold in her informal waistcoats and nightgowns. Thus, in her final years Catherine continued to use this darker and duller colour palette in her dress to assert her place as widow and dowager.

Catherine of Braganza was not the unfashionable queen that scholarship has often, whether meaning to or not, implied her to be. Her Robes accounts show, as Hayward has also argued, that her position as queen was 'visible and dominant'.[98] Like others in the Restoration court, including her husband's mistresses, she was tapped into French fashion networks and helped to popularize East Indies textiles and furnishings, as well as the mantua gown. In fact, when Catherine returned to Portugal in 1692 it was reported that her brother, King Dom Pedro II, had requested that she discard her Anglo-French garments and dress again in Portuguese styles. However, the ladies of the Portuguese court soon asked for her assistance in convincing the king to allow them to dress in the French manner. Eventually, French styles succeeded at the Portuguese court too.[99] In this context, Catherine's fashion knowledge and tastes that were refined at the Stuart courts were adopted by those in her home country.

After the death of Charles II in 1685, his brother, James, Duke of York, was crowned King James II, and his young Italian wife, Mary of Modena, became queen consort.[100] The duke's first wife was the gentry-born Anne Hyde, whom he had met when she was maid of honour to his sister Mary of Orange. The couple had eight children but only two daughters, Mary (born 1662) and Anne (born 1665), survived childhood (see Fig. 1.11). When their mother died in March 1671 the sisters' education was overseen by their uncle Charles II, who provided them with Anglican chaplains ensuring that they would not be influenced by the increasing Catholic leanings of their father.[101] By this time, it became increasingly apparent that Catherine of Braganza was unable to have children and that the crown would pass to James, who was keen to secure his own male heir. Although Mary of Modena had wished to become a nun, she was married to James in 1673 at the age of fifteen.[102]

Detailed household accounts for Mary of Modena, as both Duchess of York and then as queen, have not survived and there are few portraits during her reign that depict her in clothing that was not staged *en deshabille* dress or coronation robes (see Fig. 1.12). As a result, little can be determined about how Mary actually dressed. One rare depiction of her in hunting attire from 1675 shows the duchess in a heavily embroidered *justacorps* and a cravat, mimicking men's hunting styles (see Fig. 1.13). Like

Fig. 1.11 *Peter Lely,* James II, when Duke of York with Anne Hyde, Princess Mary, later Mary II, and Princess Anne, later Queen Anne, c. *1668–85, oil on canvas. Royal Collection Trust, RCIN 405879.*

Catherine of Braganza, who was described as wearing a 'cavalier riding-habit, hat and feather, and horseman's coat' in 1666, and various other women at the French court, Mary enjoyed wearing playful masculine-inspired styles of riding habit.[103] A description by John Verney of the Duchess of York at the horse races at Newmarket in early 1683 also mentioned her fondness for mantos, as he wrote that the duchess gave 'the Country Ladies leave to come to her in mantos, her court was every night full'.[104] While it does not describe what Mary herself was wearing, it is clear that mantos were acceptable attire at her court and perhaps she wore the style too.

The few surviving bills dating from 1687–8 reveal that Mary of Modena patronized many of the same tradespeople as the queen dowager and other court women (see Appendix I, Table 4). A bill from her

Fig. 1.12 *After Godfrey Kneller,* Queen Mary of Modena, c. *1685–1742, mezzotint. Rijksmuseum Amsterdam, RP-P-OB-32.789.*

mercer lists a range of European silk fabrics in colours such as white, crimson, gold and silver, as well as different greens, yellows, dark browns and purples.[105] Trims from her laceman include silver and gold lace, fringe, tassels and buttons, much like those supplied to Catherine of Braganza in the same period (see Appendix II). There are also sporadic references to garments such as embroidered petticoats and satin shoes and slippers of various colours. However, without surviving bills from the queen's makers it is impossible to know exactly what she was wearing, but it is likely that her wardrobe consisted of many of the same sorts of fashionable garments and accessories as worn by Catherine of Braganza in the 1680s.

Fig. 1.13 *Simon Verelst,* Mary of Modena when Duchess of York, c. *1675, oil on canvas. Royal Collection Trust, RCIN 404920.*

Mary of Modena's reign as queen consort lasted a little over three years. Her husband, James II, had controversially converted to Catholicism in 1669 and concerns about the future of the monarchy reached fever pitch when Mary gave birth to a son in June 1688. Opponents, including the king's own daughter Anne, disseminated rumours alleging that the pregnancy was fake and the baby an imposter. The birth of this Catholic heir triggered the Glorious Revolution of 1688, whereby the Protestant

William of Orange, husband of James's daughter Mary (and also his nephew), was invited by politicians and religious leaders to invade England.[106] The invasion was swift, forcing Mary of Modena and her infant son to flee for France. James, fearing the same fate as his father, Charles I, did the same soon after. In France, Mary of Modena, James II and their children lived in exile for the rest of their lives.

The later Stuarts: Mary II and Queen Anne

Mary II and William III were crowned as joint monarchs on 11 April 1689. The Bill of Rights signed that same year ensured that the monarch remained Protestant and set limits on their powers.[107] In addition to these changes in how monarchical power functioned, not least being England's first and only joint sovereigns, Mary and William also popularized new cultural styles and tastes, such as those popular in the Dutch Republic. The queen's English household accounts show that the eleven years she had spent as Princess consort of the Orange-Nassau dynasty of the United Provinces of the Netherlands had shaped her tastes in decorative arts and dress.[108] Bills due at the time of her death in 1694 demonstrate that she was still in contact with many Dutch tradespeople and manufacturers in places such as The Hague and Delft, from whom she directly imported delftware, furniture and Dutch linens.[109] Mary utilized English-based Dutch merchants with connections to the VOC, which grew increasingly powerful in the late seventeenth century. Bills from the Dutch merchant and army contractor, Solomon de Medina, record that he 'sold and Delivered' Indian textiles, lacquered furniture and tea to Mary's household.[110] Another Anglo-Dutch merchant, John van Collema, also delivered goods such as a 'Japan chest', 'China ink pots', 'China jugs' and Indian 'White Cane sticks'.[111] As Amy Lim has argued, Mary's Dutch-inspired displays of Asian decorative arts were a 'visible manifestation of Dutch trade power, and the associated cultural power of the House of Orange-Nassau'.[112] Equally, Mary's use of East Asian textiles in dress also asserted the power of the English via the EIC, who had come to dominate textile trade by the 1690s.

While some historians have commented that Mary's bills show that she 'enjoyed' and had a 'passion' for fashion, and her accounts record that she did spend vast sums of money on rich clothing, her interest in clothing and fashion extended beyond mere enjoyment.[113] As Julie Farguson reminds us, 'the most significant component in royal ceremonial culture was the monarch's body'.[114] Mary understood that she could use her physical appearance for political ends in public ceremonies. This was particularly important because William's frequent absences on military campaigns on the continent meant that at times she had to rule independently, proving herself to be a popular and capable queen regent and political leader.[115] Thus, unlike any of the Stuart queens before her, who were all consorts, Mary's clothing needed to materially manifest her power as a co-ruling queen regnant. Magnificent dress was also required to legitimize her rule, which was still challenged by her father's court-in-exile. As such, her wardrobe shows not only awareness of the latest fashions and styles, but also of the need to project a strong Stuart–Orange-Nassau identity.

French styles universally popular amongst the Dutch and English elites dominated Mary II's wardrobe.[116] Bills dated between 1690 and 1694 show that in England, the queen wore mantos, morning and night gowns, petticoats and stiff-bodied gowns made from silks, wools and cottons (see Appendix II).[117] In the six months before her death, she commissioned at least thirty-one mantua gowns.[118] These mantos were worn over bodies and stays and their accompanying petticoats were decorated with a variety of trims and accessories, reflecting the types of embellishment seen in fashion prints at the time. In addition to silver and gold trims and embroidery, Mary owned vast amounts of jewellery and would have looked, quite literally, radiant, when fully clothed. In addition to jewellery worn on the body, such as necklaces, lockets, rings and earrings made of pearls, diamonds and other precious stones, the queen also had jewellery made to be worn on her clothing (see Appendix III). Jewellery bills and inventories record decorative 'stars', 'diamond breast jewel[s]' and 'jewels for a Gown, of which have colour'd diamonds in the middle' (see Fig. 1.16). Stately jewels befitting her status as queen regent are also mentioned, including 'A George of Eleven Diamonds', referring to a St George insignia of the Order of the Garter. Others were more practical. The queen had diamond loops and buttons worn on the sleeves and cuffs of mantos, 'Diamond Tags for Bodys' that would have been attached to lacings, and diamond buckles and emerald clasps.[119]

The contents of Mary's Robes accounts read like the satirical pamphlet *Mundus muliebris: or, The ladies dressing-room unlock'd* (1690). This may not be a coincidence. Written by Mary Evelyn, it was edited and published by her father John Evelyn after her death in 1685. Readers of this satire, structured as a guide to women's fashions, were taken on a 'voyage to Maryland; or, the Ladies Dressing-Room'.[120] Here 'Maryland' acted as a double entendre referring to English colonies in North America and to the queen's own dressing room, and, given the timing of its writing and publication, it could refer to either Mary of Modena or Mary II.[121] The pamphlet lists, in verse, an inventory of fashionable goods that made up the fashionable woman's dressing room, and it was intended as a criticism of the materialism of fashionable women, including those at court. In doing so, it highlights the connections between court dress and fashions in the wider marketplace, showing just how much the market and emerging fashion cycle influenced royal dress by the end of the seventeenth-century.

Popular prints of Mary and her sister Anne (see Fig. 3.8 and Fig. 5.7), that borrowed from the visual rhetoric of the new genre of fashion prints, also reinforced this connection.[122] A Dutch mezzotint showing William III leaving for England to take part in the Glorious Revolution of 1688 depicts Mary in a French style known as a 'sultane' (see Fig. 1.14). This was a style of manto inspired by Ottoman dress, and the accounts of other elite women in England, such as Elizabeth Seymour, the Duchess of Somerset, record that their dressmakers were making 'sultanes' for them in this same year.[123] However,

Fig. 1.14 *Jacob Gole,* Prince William III says goodbye to his wife Mary, Princess of Orange, before going to England to help the Protestants, c. *1688–93, engraving and mezzotint. Rijksmuseum Amsterdam, RP-P-1952-646.*

rather than taken from life, the gown in this Dutch mezzotint has been copied almost exactly from a French fashion print that was also published in 1688 (see Fig. 1.15).

The use of this fashion print in this political scene not only implies that similar styles derived from France's fashion marketplace were worn at court in The Hague but also demonstrates how depictions of royalty were increasingly influenced by the fashion press too. While fashion prints influenced Mary's depiction before 1689, popular images produced during her reign in England almost always show her in her coronation robes, emphasizing her legitimacy as queen regnant.[124] However, one widely distributed print of Mary at the theatre also depicts her in the latest fashions. She wears a striped mantua gown, holds a fan and has a high wired headdress known as a commode that is covered with top knots made from lace and ribbons (see Fig. 1.16).

While the print connected the queen with the fashions of the wider marketplace, the portrait that it is based on also signalled her dynastic connections. In her analysis of this portrait, Aileen Ribeiro

Fig. 1.15 *Jean Dieu de Saint-Jean,* Femme de qualité en Sultane *[Woman of quality in Sultane gown], 1688, engraving. Musée Carnavalet, Histoire de Paris, G.4764.*

observed that the queen's mantua gown has touches of orange which signified her political and personal allegiance to the house of Orange-Nassau.[125] Certainly, an earlier portrait of Mary painted in 1677 when she was betrothed to William of Orange also depicted her in orange undress (see Fig. 1.17). When William entered London after the Glorious Revolution of 1688, he was also greeted by people wearing orange ribbons.[126] However, while portraits utilized the colour orange for sartorial politics, orange did not dominate Mary's wardrobe. Brown was the most common colour for her mantos in the

Fig. 1.16 *After a painting by Jan van der Vaart, Mary II, c. 1688–1725, mezzotint. Rijksmuseum Amsterdam, RP-P-1904-1350. The mantua gown worn by the queen in this portrait bears a striking resemblance to a surviving gown from the 1690s now in the collection of the Metropolitan Museum of Art, New York (see Fig. 4.14).*

Fig. 1.17 *Peter Lely,* Queen Mary II, c. *1677, oil on canvas. National Portrait Gallery, NPG 6214.*

surviving bills, closely followed by black, copper and grey. Reds of various shades (red, crimson and scarlet) and greens were also common in her morning and night gowns. Orange only appears in the bills once in relation to gowns. However, the queen did order orange-coloured fabrics from several different mercers in the year preceding her death. These may have been used to make petticoats (their colours are not recorded) and furnishings, or they may have been intended for gowns not started due to the queen's premature death.

Additionally, although she was married to a Prince of Orange, frequently wearing orange clothing in England would not have been advantageous for the queen. After several Anglo-Dutch wars, anti-Dutch sentiments were still common amongst the wider population and William was disliked by different political factions at court. Mary also embodied the continuity of the Stuart line and, given her young age, it was still hoped that she would give birth to a Stuart heir.[127] Thus, it was the Anglo-French styles of the Stuart courts and wider fashion marketplace that are most highlighted by her wardrobe accounts. Any further evolution in Mary II's sartorial politics was cut short when she died suddenly of smallpox at Kensington Palace on 28 December 1694 at the age of thirty-two. Her widower William III ruled for eight more years as sole monarch until his death in March 1702. After this, the Stuart throne passed to Mary's sister, Anne, who was crowned on 23 April 1702.

While Mary had moved to the Dutch Republic at age fifteen, her younger sister Anne had remained at the Stuart court in London where she had frequent contact with her father and his new wife Mary of Modena, as well as her uncle Charles II and Catherine of Braganza. She married the Protestant Prince George of Denmark, brother to King Christian V, who was naturalized as an English subject and remained devoted to her throughout his life.[128] After her marriage in 1683, Anne was styled as 'Princess of Denmark' (see Fig. 1.18). During the 1680s, she began to grow suspicious of her father's increased Catholicism and supported her sister and brother-in-law during the Glorious Revolution. She is well known for her personal life, which included a close but turbulent friendship with her 'favourite', Sarah Churchill, the Duchess of Marlborough. Their friendship would not only shape much of her life and reign, but led to periods of estrangement from her sister Mary. Anne also had seventeen pregnancies in seventeen years. Ten of these pregnancies resulted in births (five live births and five stillborn) and only one child, Prince William, Duke of Gloucester, lived past the age of three. However, he died in 1700 aged eleven, and the Stuarts were once again left without an heir.[129]

Until recently, Anne, and her consort George, have been frequently overlooked in studies of court culture, art and ceremony. R. O. Bucholz has argued the queen's shy nature, ill health and prudishness made her court unattractive to artists, courtiers and politicians, and that her reign had little impact on the fashion world as it 'became an isolated and esoteric corner of it'.[130] Kevin Sharpe has gone further to argue that Anne made the 'least visual impression' of all the Stuarts.[131] However, the last Stuart queen was not indifferent to the visual arts and the ways that it could be used as a tool to assert her political power and authority. During her reign her image was widely circulated through 'paint, print and medals' and projected in courtly ceremonies, much of which remained ephemeral.[132]

Anne, like her sister Mary, was also keenly aware of the need to use dress to assert her place in society. Her coronation portraits and the bills relating to the clothing depicted in them demonstrate that on these occasions she cared a great deal about her appearance and often wore 'rich gown[s] and petty coat[s] of cloth of gold brocade' to enhance her magnificence as monarch (see Fig. 0.1).[133] While the financial situation inherited by Anne gave her a much smaller allowance than sovereigns before

Fig. 1.18 *Jan van der Vaardt and Willem Wissing,* Queen Anne, when Princess of Denmark, *c. 1685, oil on canvas. National Galleries Scotland, PG 939. Public Domain via Wikimedia.*

her, an examination of her Office of the Robes accounts demonstrates a thriving institution abreast of the latest fashions sold and made by multiple suppliers (see Appendix I, Table 6).[134] The accounts also show a changed fashion marketplace where new, fashionable commodities were more widely available at lower prices.[135] This, coupled with a cultural turn towards propriety, elegance and cadence, which often manifested in simplicity, as well as the thrift of her Mistress of the Robes (see Chapter 2), means that less money spent in her Office of the Robes should not necessarily be equated with a court in decline.[136]

At the start of Anne's reign her clothing largely adhered to the popular fashions of the time, meaning that she was far from the dull dowdy queen (real or imagined) that is so often claimed. Gone are any mention of stiff-bodied gowns that had still been worn by her sister a decade prior. Instead, her clothing consisted primarily of mantua gowns and loose gowns of various types, which would have resembled those depicted in a French print from 1704 (see Fig. 1.19). Petticoats were worn with all these garments and account for the single largest category of dress items in her accounts. These garments were often trimmed with furbelows, which were also common on her mantua gowns, mirroring fashions of the period.[137] Breaking from earlier trends, her Office of the Robes commissioned only female mantua-makers and petticoat-makers (see Chapter 4).

Anne also embraced new fashions during her time as queen. She was the first Stuart queen to have a new fashionable stay-maker, a Frenchman named Antoine Cousein.[138] In 1708, Anne's household bills also mentioned whalebone petticoats made by her petticoat-maker, Susannah Young, and this was around the same time that 'new-fashioned Petticoats' began to be mentioned in the press.[139] These were hoop petticoats, structured underskirts that were round and large in circumference like earlier Spanish farthingales and made from whalebone or cane hoops. Between April 1710 and January 1711, the queen received eighteen of these hooped petticoats made with 'border, whalebone, & ribbon for binding' from her petticoat maker.[140] Anne's love of the mantua gown, which was articulated in letters she wrote during the 1690s (see Chapter 2), and her early adoption of the hoop petticoat demonstrates that she was keen to take on new, cutting-edge styles.[141]

Anne's embrace of the hoop petticoat – a seemingly English invention that did not reach France until 1718 – also leads to the next major theme that arises in her wardrobe: its relative Englishness compared to all other queens so far discussed.[142] As Bucholz has articulated, Anne was the first Stuart who could 'legitimately revel in her Englishness, for she was the first of her house born in England of an English mother and raised virtually the whole of her youth there.'[143] She was also the first monarch to rule Great Britain after the Act of Union in 1707. Unlike her sister Mary, she had not lived away from the English court as a consort and, although she was married to Prince George of Denmark, they were not co-rulers. Her wardrobe was influenced by French fashions – as all English fashions had been for a least forty years – and she did import some East Indian furnishings from Dutch merchants, like her sister. However, her artisans and suppliers tended to be more English than those of her predecessors (see Appendix I).

Anne's tendency to shy away from ostentatious French styles is also due to the political situation during her reign. From the very beginning, Anne was required to define herself and her identity in the aftermath of the Glorious Revolution. Much of this revolved around distancing herself from her Francophile Catholic father, reinforcing her Anglican faith and working closely with Parliament, while

Fig. 1.19 *Bernard Picart,* Woman Resting on a lounge, *1704, etching. Rijksmuseum Amsterdam, RP-P-OB-51.792. This print depicts fashionable mantua gowns and petticoats with furbelows, as well as loose informal gowns.*

also maintaining royal traditions.[144] She also had to navigate increasingly complicated and hostile politics between the two leading political parties that had emerged out of the Popish Plot and Exclusion Crisis: the Whigs and the Tories.[145] The Whigs support base came from the nobility, gentry and middling sorts with commercial interests who supported a constitutional monarchy but who were generally opposed to the court's corruption and foreign policies; notably, they were anti-French. Alternatively, the Tories supported the divine right of monarchy and the interests of the Anglican Church. Throughout Anne's reign, England, and then Great Britain, continued to be involved in protracted warfare with France, which had begun under William and Mary, who discontinued the Francophile policies of the previous kings. England was thus involved in a continental power struggle between the competing dynasties of the Spanish Habsburgs and French Bourbons between 1689 and 1697 and again in the period 1702–13.[146] Although Anne did purchase some French goods during her reign, an English-born queen who was actively seen to follow French styles after so many years of war with France was unlikely to have been met with positivity.

Politics and religion also factored in how artisans were patronized. French artisans in Catherine, Mary and Anne's accounts were much more likely to be French Huguenots or their descendants.

Catherine and Mary's tailor Peter Lombard, Anne's embroiderers the Ganerons and Le Contes, as well as her glovers the Huguenys, were all connected to French Protestant churches in London.[147] Other political and commercial interests at the turn of the eighteenth century also influenced the queen's wardrobe choices. Anne owned stock in the EIC, income from which was used to fund her privy purse, and she was fond of the cotton and silk textiles that the EIC imported.[148] Bills dating to 1701–2 contained charges for garments such as 'a red white & green Indian Callico night gown lined with an Indian green Cheyney [Chinese] taffeta' and 'a green & gold straw atlas night-gown lined with a Scarlet Indian Crape'.[149] The mercer also supplied 'black broad Persian' fabrics.[150] Like Mary before her, Anne's use of such fabrics in her clothing may have lent itself to the promotion of English mercantile interests in the East Indies. However, this was not to last.

In Michaelmas of 1701 it was declared by Parliament that 'all wrought silks, Bengals and stuffs, mixed with silk' from 'Persia, China or East India' and 'all printed calicoes, and all painted, dyed or stained there, shall be locked up in warehouses appointed by the commissioners of the customs, till re-exported'.[151] This proclamation, now known as the Calico Act of 1701, was a response to unrest caused by woollen and silk weavers who claimed these EIC textile imports had devastated their manufacturing industries. Five years later, Parliament also banned 'French alamodes, lustrings, ribbons, and laces'.[152] While both these laws were regularly defied – smuggling of these banned commodities thrived – Anne as sovereign appears to have mostly followed them, as East Indies textiles are rarely mentioned after 1703.[153]

After these bans, the queen's clothing was largely made from European satins, taffetas, Norwich crapes, brocades, damasks and 'stuffs' that are described as 'flowered with several colours' or with 'red and blue and figures'.[154] Outside of periods of mourning, where the colour purple dominated, the most common colours in Anne's wardrobe were greens (including goslin and olive), reds (including scarlet, cherry and pink) and blues, usually in combination with yellows (including brimstone and straw), blacks, grey, gold and silver. Patterns were described as striped, flowered, figured, chequered and changeable.[155] 'Figured' silks in the queen's accounts could refer to 'bizzare' silks such as the salmon-coloured silk of a British mantua dated to 1708 (see Fig. 1.20). Woven in Spitalfields in London, as well as in France, Italy, Spain and the Dutch Republic, these silks featured asymmetrical, bold, colourful designs with exotic plants or motifs inspired by Asian textiles.[156] During the first five years of her reign, Queen Anne's clothing was incredibly colourful and reflected the shift, noted by John Styles, 'towards lighter, more colourful, and more highly patterned fabrics' in the final years of the seventeenth century.[157]

The latter half of Anne's reign was shaped by her health. She was often too ill with gout to participate in public events. During bouts of the illness it was noted by some contemporary observers that her dress was 'negligent'.[158] In letters between the queen and her Mistress of the Robes, Sarah Churchill, Anne lamented that her affliction prevented her from wearing certain fashions as she 'had a mind to

Fig. 1.20 *Mantua gown of salmon-coloured bizarre silk, c. 1708, British. Metropolitan Museum of Art New York, 1991.6.1a, b.*

be fine too & in order to be so I intended to have two diamond buttons & loops upon each sleeves . . . [but] Heavy cloths are so uneasy on me' due to gout.[159] It seems that Anne also avoided restrictive clothing during much of her reign; there is a conspicuous absence of waistcoats in the queen's accounts even though this garment was still widely worn. Anne's health likely accounts for this, as these garments had a tighter sleeve that would have caused the queen discomfort with her gout. Anne was therefore lucky that mantos and loose gowns made from lightweight silks were in fashion at this time.

As the years progressed and the queen's health declined, her choice of clothing veered more towards the informal and comfortable, whilst still being made from fashionable silks. In the years 1702–4, Anne commissioned seventy-one mantua gowns and forty-one nightgowns from her mantua-maker. However, by the period 1708–11, she was consuming more informal gowns (thirty-eight morning, night, wadded and bed gowns) than mantua gowns (thirty-one). Most significantly, bedgowns began to appear more frequently in the last years of her accounts, pointing to the debilitating effects of gout and other ill-health on the queen; she was unable to walk for at least six months in 1713.[160] Despite her dress in her final years being determined by her illnesses, during much of her reign Anne mixed an interest in the latest fashions with her need to harness material magnificence to promote English interests and ceremonial protocols, and thus to bolster her rights as a Stuart queen regnant.

Conclusions

Queen Anne died on 1 August 1714 after a year of severe health issues that included a stroke. She was the last Stuart to rule the kingdoms of England, Scotland and Great Britain. After her death, the British throne passed to the Stuart's German cousins, the Hanoverians, with George I ushering in a new century of Georgian rule (see Fig. 1.21). Analysing the dress of the Stuart queens allows us to understand how these women used clothing to express their, often foreign, backgrounds, their royal magnificence, legitimacy and power. It also allows us to see how commercial interests that changed the fashion marketplace during the Stuart period influenced royal and other elite dress.

The dress of the early Stuart queens was characterized by the influence of their natal courts, with both Anna and Henrietta Maria strategically employing the use of Danish or French fashions, as well as symbolism in their dress relating to their families, to advance political ambitions and agendas. By the second half of the seventeenth century, rapid cultural, political and economic change, particularly the cultural dominance of French styles emanating from both the streets of Paris and the court of Louis XIV, and the rise of global trade, had a tremendous influence on Stuart dress and the artisans who provided it. While dress was still used strategically in sartorial politics, market forces also began to dictate much of what the Stuart queens wore: dress from the natal courts of Catherine of Braganza and Mary of Modena was rarely employed like it had been by previous consorts.

Fig. 1.21 *John Faber,* Portrait of King William II, Queen Mary II, Queen Anne and King George I, *c. 1699–1756, mezzotint. Rijksmuseum Amsterdam, RP-P-1906-2341.*

By the reigns of the English-born queens regnant, the Stuart sisters Mary and Anne, court dress was fully entrenched in London's fashion marketplace as styles emanating from the streets of Paris and of London, such as the sultane and the hoop petticoat, became common fixtures in their wardrobes, and they themselves were depicted in popular prints influenced by the fashion press. Both sisters used their engagement with clothing to bolster their claims to the throne and to engage with their political allies. For Mary, it was important that she balance her Stuart and Orange-Nassau identities, and for Anne, her identity as queen of England and then Great Britain meant that she trod a careful line between engaging with French fashions and promoting English styles and artisans. The accounts of both sisters also show wardrobes primarily driven by market forces and commercial interests, including the patronage of a vast array of tradespeople (see Appendix I, Tables 5 and 6). The last Stuart queens were therefore both trendsetters and trend chasers. While those at court were still leaders of fashion, as Chapter 2 will discuss, by the early eighteenth century they were also followers of the commercial marketplace that was increasingly influenced by global trade and novelty, as Chapters 3 to 5 explore.

2

Managing: The Office of the Robes and the work of the Mistress of the Robes

The Office of the Robes was the administrative sub-department of the queen's household responsible for managing some of her most valuable resources: clothing and accessories. Those attached to the Office of the Robes in both the king and queen's households had daily contact with the royal family and their closest confidants. Despite this, there has been surprisingly little attention paid to the role of those who managed these departments for the Stuart queens and the daily activities they undertook in this office.[1] Historians have often categorized, intentionally or simply through lack of detailed examination, posts within the royal household as sinecures: honorary positions with attached salaries that did not actually involve any real work.[2] However, transcriptions of hundreds of archival documents from the households of the Stuart queens show that this is simply not true. As Cathleen Sarti has argued, 'women were often key figures in acquiring resources and managing them, for themselves as well as for their (royal) families and their courts'.[3] While many women who held roles associated with the Bedchamber and the Robes came from privileged elite backgrounds, their attendance on the queen involved the exchange of labour and services for monetary compensation, as well as patronage, titles, lands and other forms of reimbursement.[4]

This chapter argues that women in the Stuart queens' household were highly materially literate managers who worked for wages in the Office of the Robes. In addition to being a 'large bureaucratic machine designed to procure and maintain the apparatus of magnificence essential to royal life', as Malcom Smuts has articulated, premodern courts should be understood as economic units that contained powerful female 'economic agents'.[5] In the queens' household, these women organized, dictated and carried out the day-to-day tasks and finances. Such work was crucial to the functioning of the bedchamber and other spaces, as well as the Office of the Robes which contained much of their moveable wealth, and thus, magnificence. Positions such as the Mistress of the Robes utilized aristocratic women's training and knowledge of household management and their experience in overseeing vast teams of servants. Such responsibilities and work within the Office of the Robes gave women access not only to the high ranks of service in the royal household that were well remunerated, but also to vast powers and intimate access to the queen. These roles also gave women a sense of self and of purpose beyond their families, allowing them to forge successful careers at court. Unlike the king's household where their male counterparts often mixed this work with political or military endeavours, inevitably making their roles more intermittent, many Mistresses of the Robes had long careers in their offices.

Crucially, the Office of the Robes relied on the connections of these elite court women with those in the fashion marketplace and their knowledge of the latest fashion retailers and trends. Such material literacy was honed through their own consumption habits and their established networks. As this chapter shows, Mistresses of the Robes such as Sarah Churchill, Duchess of Marlborough, were acknowledged fashion leaders who advised the queen and many others on the latest styles. The Mistress of the Robes was also crucial in vetting and choosing the best and most fashionable tradespeople. As subsequent chapters demonstrate, several Mistresses of the Robes were clients of fashionable milliners and mantua-makers whom they helped to promote as royal tradespeople. Therefore, the work required by the Office of the Robes not only allowed elite women to gain power and influence at court, but also helped these women dictate fashion both inside and outside the court, and their patronage played a crucial role in supporting the rise of women's work in the fashion marketplace.

The Mistresses of the Robes and their office

The Mistress of the Robes was one of the most senior positions within the queen's household. Under the Stuarts the title of this position varied between 'Mistress of the Robes' and 'Lady of Her Majesty's Robes'. The work carried out by this office is best described by the warrant that granted Lady Audrey Walsingham the office of 'Lady of Her Majesties Robes' to Anna of Denmark in 1603. It outlined that as 'keeper of our Robes, and of all things to our Said Robes and apparel of our [the queen's] person', Walsingham had the 'power and authority' to

> . . . buy and provide for us all Stuffs of gold, Silver, And tinsel or Silks, or of any other nature And qualities whatsoever, which for our Said Robes and apparel the ornament of our person shall from time to time be needful, and the same to convert into apparel according to our discretion: And we do give also power and authority at her discretion to make choice, and admit as well Taylors, Embroiderers, Haberdashers or any other inferior officers, which for our said Robes shall be necessary to be retained: Willing and commanding that none be used in and about our said Robes, or have access unto them but at her choice and liking.[6]

The job of the Mistress of the Robes was therefore to source, purchase and inventory textiles, garments, accessories and furnishings for the queen; to select and instruct tradespeople; to check clothing for quality and mistakes; and, alongside the Secretary and Treasurer, to oversee the payment of those supplying the Robes.

This position invested vast amounts of trust and power into one person, and the women who occupied this role very much considered their work as integral to the queen's household. In the early eighteenth century, Sarah Churchill, Duchess of Marlborough, specifically referred to the work she undertook in the Robes as 'management', implying that it was a job that involved the organization of many people, goods and administrative structures.[7] Subordinate to the Mistress of the Robes were other elite women such as the Mistress of the Sweet Coffers and members of the Bedchamber such as dressers (discussed in Chapter 5), as well as those of lower social and occupational status in the Office of the Robes including yeomen, clerks, surveyors, grooms, pages, brushers and necessary women (see Fig. 0.4).[8]

It is under the Stuart queens that the Mistress of the Robes was consolidated as a dedicated household position. Queen Elizabeth I did not have this role in her household. Her clothing, as well as furnishings, liveries and materials needed for ceremonies such as the Royal Maundy, were dealt with by the Wardrobe of Robes, which was a sub-department of the Great Wardrobe.[9] With no separate Office of the Robes solely dedicated to the queen's clothing, it was various members of her female Privy Chamber staff that liaised with clerical and administrative staff in the Wardrobe of the Robes and performed duties such as taking delivery of items and arranging payments for artisans. The management of Elizabeth's clothing has been labelled a 'fairly casual system' that lacked central management during her reign.[10] In the late sixteenth-century Scottish court, Anna of Denmark had a dedicated Master of the Wardrobe, a Danish man named Søren Jensen, who oversaw the management of her clothing.[11] The Stuart kings also had Masters of the Robes in their households.[12] The pre-existing administrative structures of the Scottish court therefore informed the structure of Anna of Denmark's English household. However, the decision to change the most senior position in the Office of the Robes from Master to Mistress may have been a compromise to appease Anna's new English gentlewomen, many of whom had done similar work for her Tudor predecessor.

Indeed, for most of the seventeenth century the Mistress of the Robes was a position occupied by women who held other important offices, such as the Groom of the Stole (who supervised the queen's private rooms and bedchamber staff), the First Lady of the Bedchamber (who assisted in dressing, guarded access to the bedchamber and provided companionship) and the Keeper of the Privy Purse (who oversaw the queen's private funds that were not accountable to the Lord Chamberlain).[13] While the creation of a Mistress of the Robes at the English court was certainly a Scottish, and possibly also a Danish, practice introduced by the Stuarts, there was no direct equivalent of this office in other European courts at this time. In Sweden, the *hovmästarinnan* or Mistress of the Court who ran the queen's household was more akin to the Groom of the Stole or First Lady of the Bedchamber, and in the Habsburg court of Vienna there was a High Court Stewardess who managed the household and its staff as well as the clothing and jewellery inventories.[14] It is in France that we find the most comparable position, of the *dame d'atour*, who ranked below the *dame d'honneur*, or First Lady, and she was responsible for the queen's wardrobe, jewellery and dressing.[15] The dedicated household position of the Mistress of the Robes therefore seems to have been particular to the Stuart courts of Scotland and England, illustrating the importance placed on clothing and its management by the Stuarts.

The duty of the Mistress of the Robes in managing vast amounts of moveable wealth in the form of clothing, accessories and furnishings required the appointment of women of suitable backgrounds and the importance this office evolved over time (see Table 2.1). At first, the position does not appear to have been a particularly high office. Although well connected, Anna of Denmark's Lady of the Robes, Audrey Walsingham (née Shelton), was only the wife of a knight, Sir Thomas Walsingham.[16] Unlike later Mistresses of the Robes, Lady Walsingham was also not part of the queen's innermost household Bedchamber. Instead, she was simply part of the Privy Chamber.[17] However, she had previously served as Lady of the Bedchamber to Elizabeth I and during this time it is likely that she liaised frequently with the Wardrobe of the Robes. This suggests that she obtained such an office based on her prior experience managing the Tudor queen's clothing and her trustworthiness rather than simply her closeness to the queen.[18] The queen clearly trusted Lady Walsingham. When the Venetian ambassador Antonio Foscarini described his final audience with Anna of Denmark at Greenwich Palace in December 1615, the queen, who was 'most richly and extraordinarily arrayed, wearing jewels of inestimable price', would only allow her 'Mistress of the Robes and the Secretary Rizzardo' to remain in the gallery during the meeting.[19]

While Anna's Mistress of the Robes was given her role due to previous experience and trust, subsequent Mistresses of the Robes were placed for political reasons. Susan Feilding (née Villiers), Countess of Denbigh, was the sister of James I and Charles I's favourite George Villiers, Duke of Buckingham (see Fig. 2.1). Buckingham's position as royal favourite and Gentleman of the Bedchamber, and later Lord High Admiral, enabled the Villiers family to acquire many titles and household offices under the early Stuart kings.[20] This made the Villiers and their extended networks extremely powerful at the early seventeenth-century court. It is perhaps unsurprising then that the Countess of Denbigh, or 'Sue Denbigh' as she called herself, would come to occupy such an office. However, her placement was not easy. Buckingham and the king had tried multiple times to position women from the Villiers family in Henrietta Maria's household. In July 1625, after the new queen's arrival in England, the Duke of Buckingham was described as wanting to 'introduce his wife, sister, and niece into the queen's chamber, as ladies of the bedchamber' but this was refused as they were not Catholic.[21] A year later the king again presented Susan and others to the queen, asking her to receive them as ladies of the bedchamber, but she again refused as 'she would never have confidence with those ladies'.[22]

The Countess of Denbigh was eventually appointed as a Lady of the Bedchamber and Mistress of the Robes in 1626 after the dismissal of the queen's French household.[23] While she was originally placed in

Table 2.1 Mistresses of the Robes to the Stuart queens

Queen	Name of Mistress of the Robes	Duration	Other positions held
Anna of Denmark	Lady Audrey Walsingham (née Shelton)	1603–19	
Henrietta Maria	Susan Feilding (née Villiers), Countess of Denbigh	1626–52	First Lady of the Bedchamber Groom of the Stole
	Elizabeth Boyle (née Feilding), Countess of Guildford	1652–67	
Catherine of Braganza	Barbara Howard (née Villiers), Countess of Suffolk	1662–81	First Lady of the Bedchamber Groom of the Stole Keeper of the Privy Purse
	Isabella Bennet (née van Nassau-Beverweert), Countess of Arlington	1681–1705	Groom of the Stole Keeper of the Privy purse
Mary of Modena	Penelope Mordaunt (née O'Brien), Countess of Peterborough	1685–8	Groom of the Stole
Mary II	Elizabeth Stanley (née Butler), Countess of Derby	1689–94	Groom of the Stole
Queen Anne	Sarah Churchill (née Jennings), Duchess of Marlborough	1702–11	First Lady of the Bedchamber Groom of the Stole Keeper of the Privy Purse
	Elizabeth Seymour (née Percy), Duchess of Somerset	1711–14	First Lady of the Bedchamber Groom of the Stole

the queen's household by her brother, over time she developed a close relationship with the queen and did gain her confidence and trust. In an undated letter from the early 1630s, she wrote to her husband, William Feilding, Earl of Denbigh, to say that 'the best news I can send to you is that I hold a good portion of my Mistress the queen's favour'.[24] By 1639 she was undertaking 'secret service for the Queen's Majesty' too.[25] After her death, in exile in Paris where she had followed Henrietta Maria in 1652, the Countess of Denbigh's daughter, Elizabeth Boyle (née Feilding), Countess of Guildford, became Henrietta Maria's second Mistress of the Robes and served until her death in 1667.[26]

The influence of the Villiers family on the queen's household continued under Catherine of Braganza, as the Countess of Denbigh's niece Barbara Howard (née Villiers), Countess of Suffolk, was appointed to several key offices, including the Mistress of the Robes in 1662 (see Fig. 2.2).[27] Aptitude

Fig. 2.1 *British School,* The Family of the 1st Duke of Buckingham *(1592–1628), 1628, oil on canvas. Royal Collection Trust, RCIN 402607. The Countess of Denbigh is seated on the far left.*

for the role of Mistress of the Robes in combination with trustworthiness and good standing were all important. In this case, the continued influence of the Villiers family at court likely contributed to the Countess of Suffolk being ultimately chosen for the role. After the death of the Countess of Suffolk in 1680, the influence of the Villiers family on the queens' households waned. In its place a new trend emerged, as members of prominent Anglo-Dutch families were instead given positions.

A Lady of the Bedchamber, Isabella Bennet (née van Nassau-Beverweert), Countess of Arlington, was appointed as the queen's Lady of the Robes in 1681 (see Fig. 2.3). Dutch by birth, she was the daughter of General-Major Louis of van Nassau-Beverweert, who was the illegitimate son of Maurice of Nassau, Prince of Orange, and ambassador to England. In 1665, Isabella married Henry Bennet, Earl of Arlington.[28] Henry had lived in exile with Charles and James Stuart during the 1650s and when the monarchy was restored to the throne, he was granted the office of Keeper of the Privy Purse in the king's household. Isabella appears to have been the ideal candidate for the position of Lady of the Robes. She had been a long-time Lady of the Bedchamber with apartments located at Whitehall next to the queen's chambers and the Office of the Robes (see Chapter 5).

While the brief reign of Mary of Modena saw Penelope Mordaunt (née O'Brien), Countess of Peterborough, sworn in as Groom of the Stole and Mistress of the Robes, after the Glorious Revolution in 1688 the Peterboroughs were stripped of their offices.[29] The new queen regnant Mary II chose

Fig. 2.2 *Attributed to Remigius van Leemput,* Barbara Howard, Countess of Suffolk *(1622–81), c. 1675, oil on panel. Royal Collection Trust, RCIN 402555.*

Fig. 2.3: *After Sir Peter Lely, published by Alexander Browne,* Isabella Bennett, Countess of Arlington, *c. 1684, mezzotint.*

Fig. 2.4 *Robert Williams, after Willem Wissing, published by Edward Cooper,* Elizabeth Stanley, Countess of Derby, *late 17th century, mezzotint. National Portrait Gallery, NPG D31006.*

Elizabeth Stanley (née Butler), Countess of Derby, as her Lady of the Robes and Groom of the Stole (see Fig. 2.4). She was the niece of the Countess of Arlington, whose sister had also married an Englishman.[30] The Countess of Derby's Dutch heritage and her late husband's military service in the Dutch Republic in the campaigns of William II of Orange influenced her appointment in the new Anglo-Dutch royal court created under William and Mary.[31] She likely also received some form of mentorship from both her aunt the Countess of Arlington and her mother the Countess of Ossory, both of whom had served as a lady-in-waiting to Catherine of Braganza.

The reign of Queen Anne represented yet another trend: the appointment of favourites and close friends to office. In 1702, Sarah Churchill (née Jennings), Duchess of Marlborough, was placed in several key offices, including that of the Mistress of the Robes (see Fig. 2.5).[32] Probably the most famous and influential of all the women in this position, and one who took full advantage of the power that offices in the queen's household could bestow, she had risen through the ranks from an impoverished gentry family to become the queen's friend and favourite. Sarah was the daughter of a Member of Parliament

Fig. 2.5 *After Godfrey Kneller,* Sarah Churchill, Duchess of Marlborough, c. *1702, oil on canvas. National Portrait Gallery, NPG 3634. They key at the duchess's side represents the key to her offices in Queen Anne's household.*

Fig. 2.6 *John Closterman*, Elizabeth Seymour, Duchess of Somerset (1667–1722), and her son, Algernon Seymour, Earl of Hertford, later 7th Duke of Somerset (1684–1750), c. *1690, oil on canvas. Petworth House and Park, West Sussex, NT 486184.*

who had gained the favour of James, Duke of York (future James II). Through this favour she was appointed as a maid of honour to Mary of Modena, when Duchess of York, in 1673. While in the York household she became the close friend and confident of Lady Anne and was made a countess and Lady of her Bedchamber when Anne's own household (as Princess of Denmark) was established in 1683.

As this chapter will show, Sarah was a formidable and extremely capable household manager as well as a leader of fashion. She also embodied the complex nature of the household offices: while they were given to women of high-standing and involved everyday practical work, they were also predicated on maintaining a good relationship with the queen. This was demonstrated in 1711, when Sarah was dramatically dismissed from her offices after her relationship with the queen deteriorated. Replacing her in several offices was another trusted friend to the queen, Elizabeth Seymour (née Percy), Duchess of Somerset (see Fig. 2.6).[33] Somerset served in this role until the queen's death in 1714.

For much of the Stuart period, the appointment of the Mistress of the Robes appears to have been dictated by family connections, in the case of the Villiers; political alignment, in the case of Anglo-Dutch families; and friendship and trust, in the case of the Duchess of Marlborough. However, these appointments are also reflective of kinship networks that trained aristocratic women, as well as men, for work in the royal courts, something which has been termed 'dynasties of service'.[34] The Countess of Denbigh must have been schooled by male relatives who had held the same office in the king's Office of the Robes, such as her husband the Earl of Denbigh who had been the Master of the Great Wardrobe in 1622. Similarly, the Countess of Suffolk and the Countess of Derby both had aunts who had held the position of Mistress of the Robes in previous queens' households, and the Duchess of Marlborough's husband, John Churchill, had served as a Master of the Robes to James, Duke of York (later James II), between stints of military service during the 1670s.[35] Thus, these women had probably been trained for such positions by family members before their appointment.

Over the course of the seventeenth century the importance of the work and status of women appointed as the Mistress of the Robes also increased. In Anna of Denmark's household, the Mistress of the Robes did not have responsibility for the queen's jewellery. Instead, Anna's household had a Keeper of the Jewels, and her first keeper, Catherine Howard (née Knyvett), Countess of Suffolk, had previously held the position in Elizabeth I's household (see Fig. 2.7).[36] At the end of Anna's reign the position of Keeper of the Jewels ceased to exist. Instead, the care of jewels was entrusted to different attendants under different queens. In Henrietta Maria's household, male Clerks of the Jewel Coffers appear to have taken on more prominent roles.[37] When Mary II died in 1694, her jewels were recorded as being in the care of her Mistress of the Robes (see Appendix III), and jewellery belonging to Queen Anne was kept in 'the closet at Kensington' under the supervision of her Groom of the Stole and Mistress of the Robes.[38] Thus, over time the Mistress of the Robes took on the responsibility of keeping other precious and expensive goods such as jewellery.

The aristocratic rank of the Mistress of the Robes also increased, from ladies to countesses and finally to duchesses, the latter setting a trend for subsequent queens of England who often went on to appoint women of this rank to the role. Over the course of the Stuart period, the salary earned by the Mistress of the Robes also increased. For much of the seventeenth century, the Mistress of the Robes earned an annual salary of £300–400, which was £100–200 less than the annual salary of £500 received by the king's Master of the Robes.[39] Such compensation was not just monetary though. Meals and lodgings, as well as gifts of clothing, old and new, from the queen were commonly provided. Anna of Denmark regularly gave away clothing from her own Robes and Henrietta Maria had clothing made for those in her household including the Countess of Denbigh, who received a mantle and a 'head dressing' in 1632.[40] After the death of the queen, those in high offices were usually entitled to her

Fig. 2.7 *William Larkin,* Katherine Howard, Countess of Suffolk, *c. 1614–18, oil on canvas. English Heritage, Kenwood, 88019158.*

personal effects: for example, the Duchess of Somerset had the right to Queen Anne's old clothing and furnishings after her death in 1714.[41]

After 1660, the pay received by the Mistress of the Robes increased. The Countess of Arlington, the Duchess of Marlborough and the Duchess of Somerset were all paid £600.[42] There are several possible reasons for this. Arlington's high pay was likely due to the First Lady of the Bedchamber position being integrated under the title of Mistress of the Robes in Catherine of Braganza's household.[43] The Duchess of Marlborough's position as royal favourite in the household of a sole-reigning queen regnant may also have increased her salary, and by extension Somerset's. The increased importance placed on the morning *levée*, a ceremony imported from France during the reign of Charles II where the king or queen received guests while being dressed, may also have increased the importance of the women and men in these positions in the royal households.[44] A similar shift took place in the King's Office of the Robes too, as the social positions of Masters of the Robes increased from viscounts to earls. Above all, the increase in duties, status and salary demonstrates that women's work as the Mistress of the Robes was becoming more valued under the later Stuart queens, particularly those who were queen regnant, bringing them on a par with that of her male counterparts in the king's household. It is this work – financial management and material literacy – and the way it shaped the Robes, the fashion marketplace and women's careers at court and beyond that the remainder of this chapter examines.

The management and finances of the Office of the Robes

The position of Mistress of the Robes was given to aristocratic women of good standing within the court; however, it was not an idle office. As discussed in the introduction to this book, management skills, along with literacy and accounting skills, were taught to aristocratic and gentry women from a young age, as they were expected to marry and manage large numbers of servants and sizable estates with considerable resources. Good household management was therefore vital to private and public communities and economies. Elite women were expected to be financially literate too. Samuel Pepys recalled in his diary on 3 October 1667 that he had spoken with Mary of Modena's Mistress of the Robes, the Countess of Peterborough, about her husband's pension which had ceased to be paid due to debts and bad financial arrangements made 'without her knowledge'. He described her plan to 'force them to take their money again, and release her husband of those hard terms', calling her 'a very wise woman'.[45] Sarah Churchill, Duchess of Marlborough, has been described as 'one of the most influential public investors' of the Financial Revolution and her 'public financial knowledge translated to her domestic affairs', as her papers show that her husband, who was often away on campaign, left all their financial matters to his wife.[46] As Amy M. Froide has argued, the duchess did not regard such achievements as extraordinary, as she 'expected a certain level of financial aptitude from women of her station'. Indeed, her letters described financial accounting as one of the most desirable traits in an aristocratic wife.[47]

Management of the Office of the Robes came with the combined responsibility of managing and distributing vast sums of money, people and goods. As Erin Griffey has shown, Henrietta Maria spent 'extravagantly on luxury goods' and even after her household was restructured and spending reigned in, she could regularly spend over £4,000 per annum on clothing.[48] In the first year of her reign in England, Anna of Denmark's Office of the Robes spent more than £12,700 and Mary of Modena regularly spent £6,425 in her Robes per year, with £8,371 spent in the first twelve months of her reign alone.[49] Catherine of Braganza spent slightly less by the end of their tenure, with her Office of the Robes' expenses calculated at £2,500 per annum in 1681, and it was claimed that Queen Anne spent only £32,050 on her Office of the Robes in nine years (roughly £3,500 per annum).[50] If assessments of previous Robes accounts are to be believed, then this was a particularly small sum for a reigning sovereign. Mary II purportedly spent an astonishing £12,000 in one year of her reign and £11,000 in another, while £8,000 a year was regularly spent in Anne's Robes when she was princess.[51] The management skills of the Mistress of the Robes were therefore crucial to the smooth running of this administrative department. Unlike a familial household, where women often could not, in theory, 'control expenditure, make contracts or incur debts without her husband's permission', the Mistress of the Robes could do all these things, with little oversight, accounting only to the Treasurer and Vice Chamberlain who appear to have usually deferred to her judgement.[52]

By paying attention to the language used in the bills, we can examine the roles that women in the Robes, as well as the queen, played in its daily running. In addition to appointing tradespeople, the Mistress of the Robes was also responsible for signing off on their work. In 1603 an embroidered waistcoat was delivered 'for her Majesty's use to the Lady Walsingham' in the Office of the Robes by a woman named Livia White. In the entry for payment to White, it was noted that 'her bill [was] vouched by the said Lady Walsingham viewed by the Officers of her Majesty's Wardrobe of Robes and seen and allowed by the Lord Chamberlain and Vice Chamberlain to her Majesty'.[53] Similar 'diverse parcels of wares for her Majesty's use' were delivered to Walsingham by a variety of artisans during her time as Lady of the Robes.[54] Not only did Walsingham receive the goods, but she was also expected to sign off on the payments made to artisans, thereby vouching that both the quality of their work was suitable and that their bills were accurate.

Anna of Denmark's accounts also record other women in the household receiving and arranging for the payment of goods, indicating that practices of the preceding Tudor queen had not been fully abandoned. In December 1603 the silkwoman Hester Le Telier delivered 'diverse parcels of Lawn cambric needlework purls bone lace and such like' to 'Mrs Jane Dromond for her majesty's use & service'. Drummond vouched for the goods and facilitated payment.[55] The queen's accounts also demonstrate the need for a competent Mistress of the Robes – family connections could only get you so far. In June 1603 a milliner named Marie Cooke delivered to the Lady Bridgett Markham, a Privy Chamber woman, diverse 'parcels of Stuffs and wares' for 'her Majesties use and service'.[56] This bill was allowed, 'signed by the said Lady Markham', and paid. Unfortunately, it appears that Markham was not as adept at this role usually performed by Walsingham, as Cooke later alleged that 'Lady Markham did her wrong in the making and delivering up of her Bill' and she was underpaid. Cooke was later given the additional amount owing to her in December 1604.[57]

The Mistress of the Robes became a much more centralized role during Henrietta Maria's reign. While a handful of women appear frequently in Anna's accounts receiving and checking goods and then approving payment, material traces left by the Countess of Denbigh in the form of her signature show her to have checked the hundreds of loose artisans' bills that have survived from Henrietta Maria's household. Considering the vast sums that the queen spent on clothing and furnishings, this represents a significant amount of Denbigh's time. Phrases such as 'The sum allowed to be paid' with her signature 'Su Denbigh' occur regularly (see Fig. 2.8). The bills of Catherine of Braganza and Mary II followed similar patterns, with the signatures 'I Arlington' and 'E Derby' appearing below any abatements (see Fig. 2.9). Statements such as 'the particulars above mentioned amounting to' was 'work done for Her Majesty by the order of' the Mistress of the Robes were also common (see Fig. 2.10). These bills were drawn up by clerks or yeomen in the Robes when goods such as fabrics, completed garments or accessories were delivered, likely dictated by the tradesperson or transcribed from their written notes, as most appear to have been written by the same few hands.[58]

These statements and the subsequent chain of signatures show that bills could not be passed on to be paid without the endorsement of the Mistress of the Robes. The Duchess of Marlborough wrote of her time in the Robes that to 'prevent all mistakes and abuses' she made sure to sign 'the tradesmen bills at the same time they delivered their goods'.[59] However, she was also known to spend long stretches of time away from the queen at her estates.[60] In that case it is unclear whether deliveries only took place when she was at court or whether her Yeoman of the Robes, who received goods and handled the physical payment of the tradesmen, informed the Mistress of the Robes of their accuracy. The Duchess of Marlborough certainly signed off on bills and even dictated the price that the Robes would pay craftspeople. A bill from the Huguenot glover Stephen (Étienne) Hugueny in 1703 was reduced from £13 8s. 6d. by Marlborough, who wrote underneath 'thirteen pound' followed by her signature. The hand of the yeoman then recorded thirteen pounds as the amount later paid.[61] Another note from her privy purse papers requested that 'vouchers' be brought to the duchess's lodgings so that she could settle the accounts.[62]

Many deliveries for Catherine of Braganza were 'carried into the Robes, & delivered into ye Custody of Mr [David] Rowlands' her Yeoman of the Robes.[63] The Yeoman of the Robes was a position usually given to those of middling status and they oversaw daily activities within the Office of the Robes. Such activities included receiving fabrics and trims from suppliers; weighing and measuring them to ensure the correct amounts were received; and then distributing them to makers who then delivered finished garments into the Robes.[64] They also helped to organize the transport, storage and cleaning of goods (see Chapter 5), bought stationary required for their account-keeping and supervised lower ranked Robes staff. Sometimes this Yeoman position was combined with another; for example, Anna of

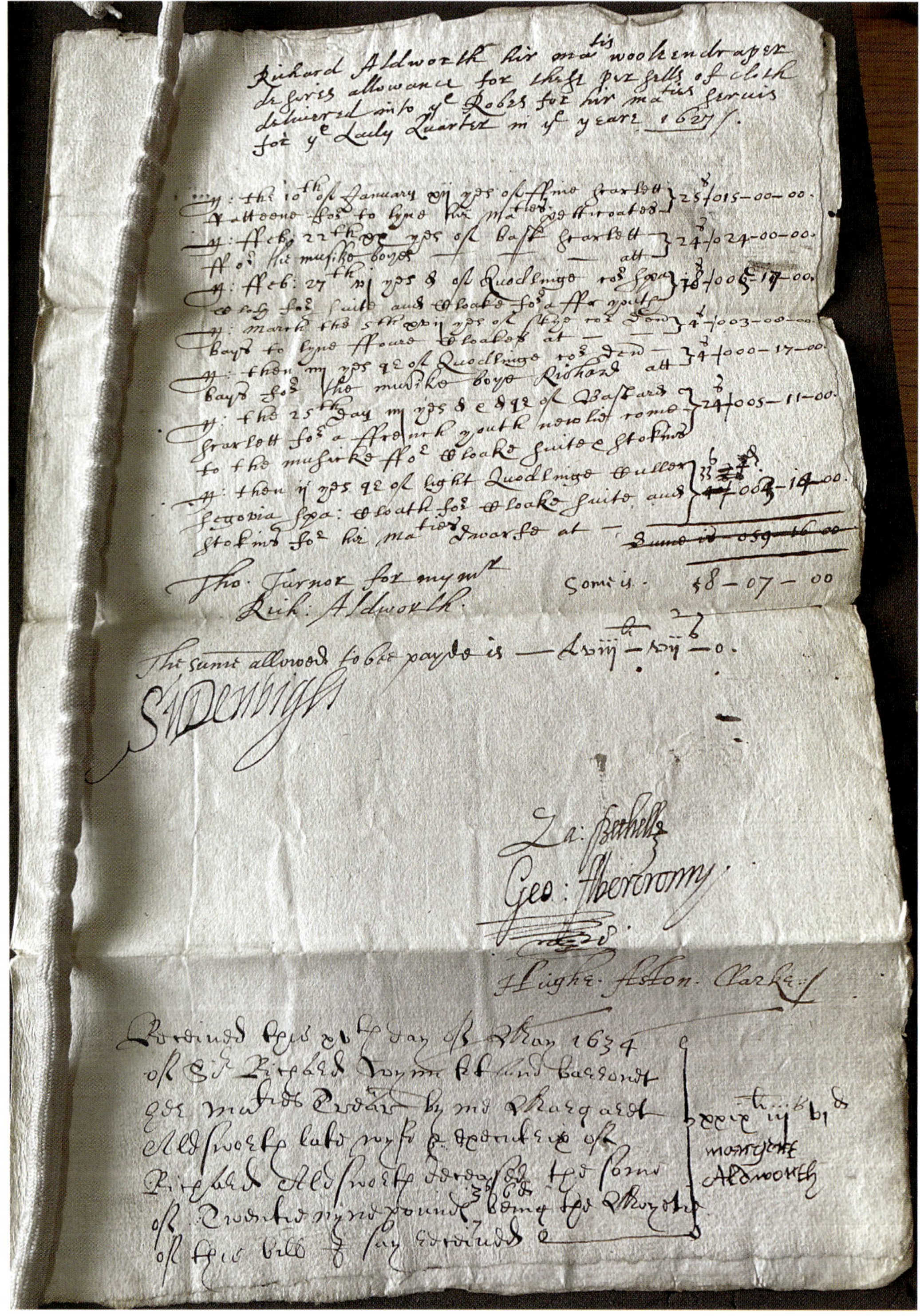

Fig. 2.8 *Bill of Richard Aldworth, woollen draper, signed by his widow Margaret Aldworth, Lady Quarter, 1627. The National Archives of the UK, LR 5/64.*

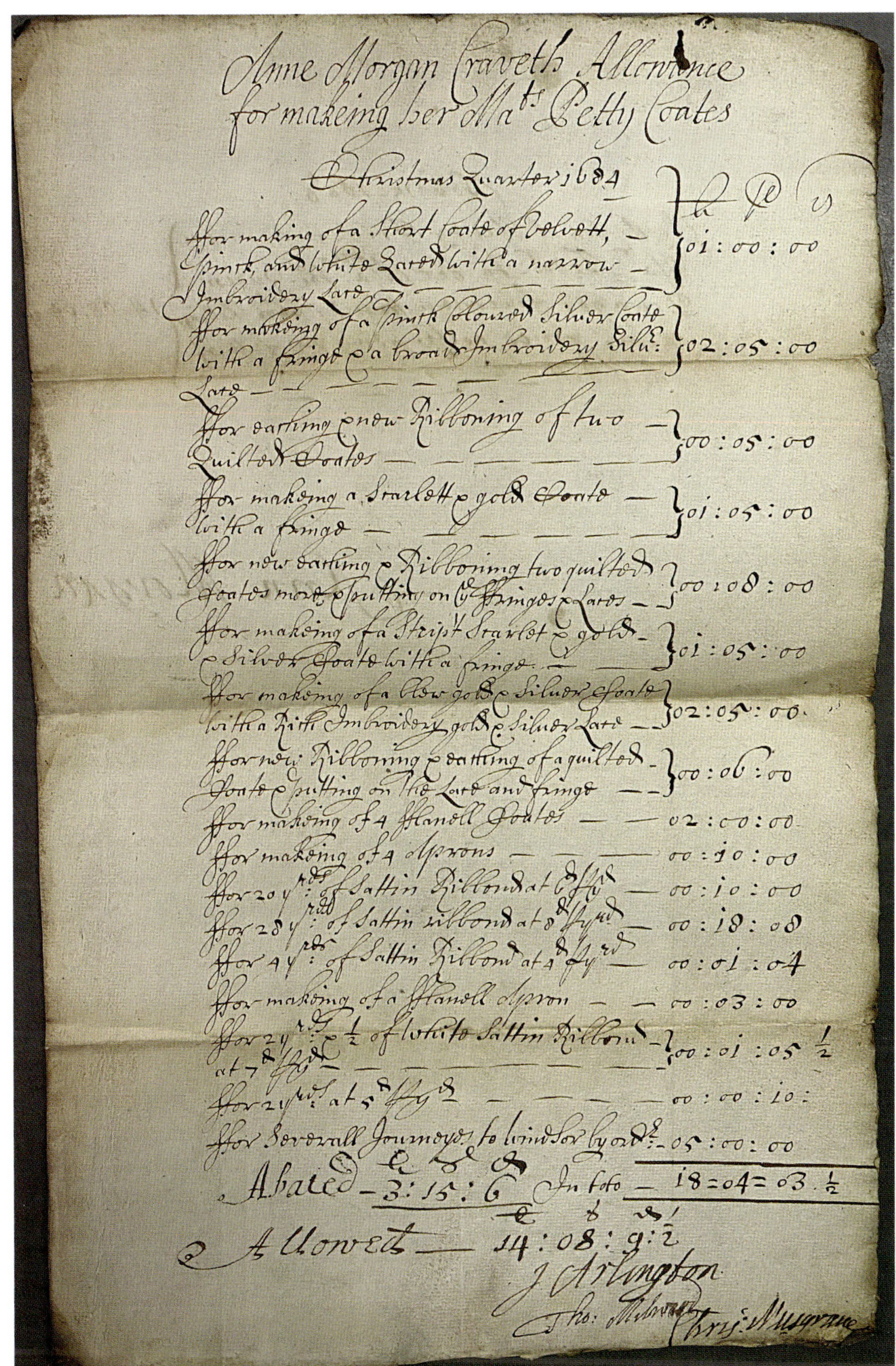

Fig. 2.9 *Bill of Anne Morgan for making her Majesty's petticoats, Christmas Quarter, 1684. The National Archives of the UK, LR 5/76.*

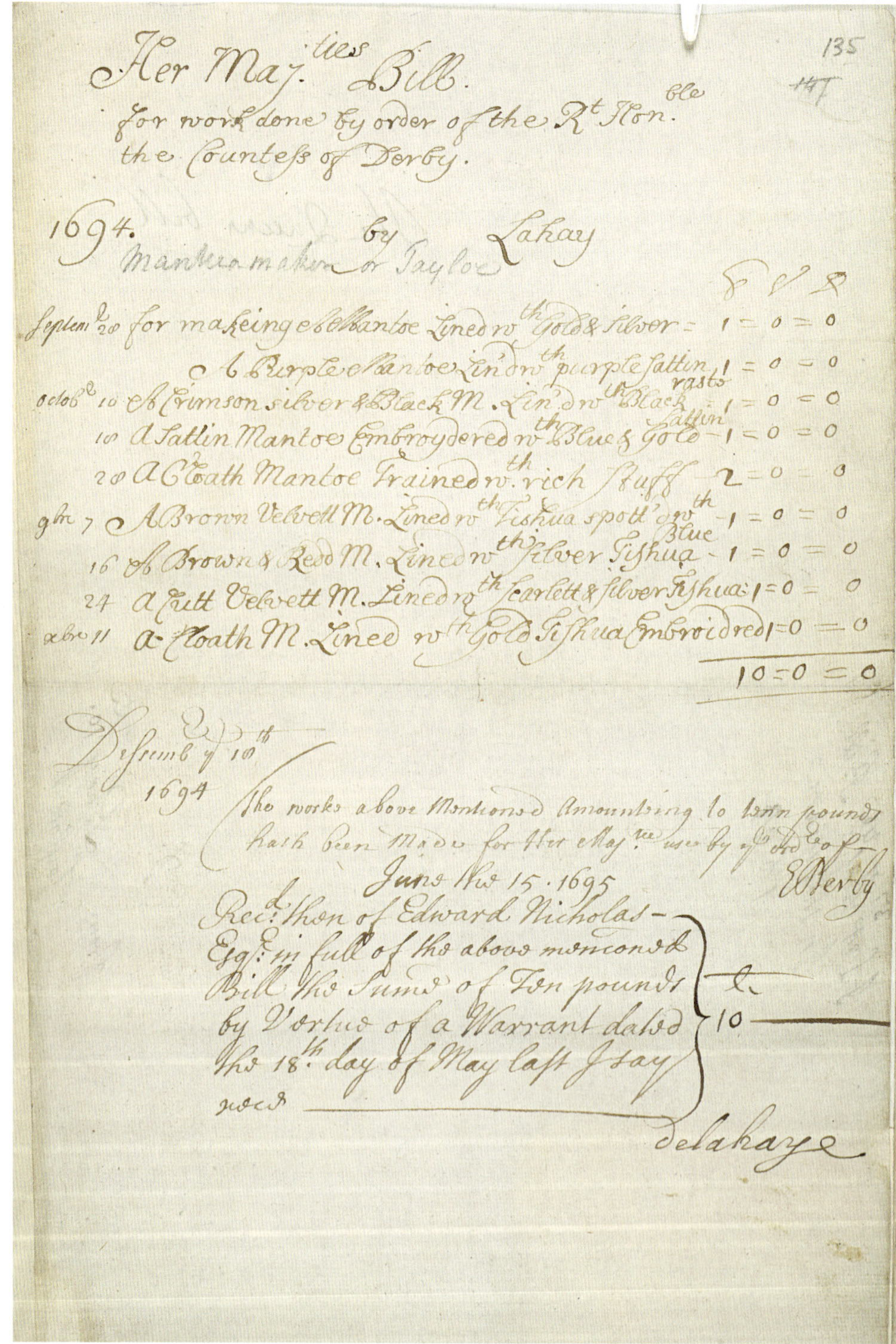

Fig. 2.10 *Bill of La Hay for work done by order of the Right Honourable Countess of Derby, 1694. The British Library, Add MS 5751 A, fol. 135.*

Denmark's Yeoman of the Robes was also her tailor James Duncane, while Henrietta Maria's tailor George Gelin was promoted from Groom of the Robes to a Yeomen in 1638.[65] They worked alongside the clerk and providitor major and all accounted to the Mistress of the Robes who signed off on their wages and other payments.[66] In 1632 the Clerk of the Robes Hugh Ashton sought additional payment for taking on the provider's duties as 'by reason of his long sickness was not able to intend any thing but his health'. This, the request noted, was 'allowed by the Countess of Denbigh'.[67]

Traditionally, the role of Yeoman had always been held by a man. However, when the Duchess of Marlborough was made Mistress of the Robes in 1702, she appointed a woman named Rachel Thomas to this position. This novel appointment of a woman was reflected in the occupational labels given to her. Marlborough later called her 'chief of the robes', while payments were made out to her 'in place of ye yeoman of the Robes'.[68] While little is known of Rachel's background, she appears to have come from middling status and several Robes staff including the waiters and grooms, as well as the starcher Elizabeth Abrahall, had previously worked in the Marlborough household. The duchess appears to have chosen them due to her 'long experience' with them and her trust in their knowledge and abilities.[69] Clearly Rachel had both. She arranged payments for various staff and her record keeping was extensive: it is she who transcribed all the loose bills into the ledgers that have survived. Similarly, Mary II's First Lady of the Bedchamber and Keeper of the Privy Purse – a Dutch woman named Anna van Goltstein who had come to England from The Hague in 1689 – also assisted in the Robes. In her roles she took delivery of many items but did not order payment, which was the job of the Mistress of the Robes. After Mary's death in 1694, Goltstein made summaries of debts owed by the queen's privy purse to various suppliers in the Dutch Republic and of salary arrears owed to servants.

Although Rachel Thomas and Anna van Goltstein were women, their ability to manage accounts in the Robes was unquestioned; these activities formed part of general tasks that elite and non-elite women alike commonly performed in an unpaid capacity in diverse households around the country. Indeed, women from business and merchant families often undertook double entry bookkeeping, managed assets, performed and made economic decisions in both households and in businesses.[70] Although the Duchess of Marlborough later claimed that she paid Rachel Thomas with 'old clothes and other little advantages', household accounts show that she actually received a yearly salary of £200, which is roughly what other male yeoman had received for this position.[71] Rachel's good service and expertise were acknowledged when the duchess was removed from office, as she was retained in her position by the next Mistress of the Robes, the Duchess of Somerset.[72] Outside the court, the Duchess of Somerset had her own stewards who looked after the finances of her own household, and a Mrs Felton was tasked specifically with 'keeping her Grace the Dutchess of Somerset's Robe[s]'.[73] Although the Mistress of the Robes was a position occupied by elite women in the queen's household, less affluent women around the country therefore carried out similar tasks on a daily basis in other households.

Once the Mistress of the Robes had signed off the bills, these documents were sent to others in the queen's household for 'Examination & Consideration'. A combination of signatures by different quills from the clerk, surveyor and providitor major of the Robes, and sometimes even the Vice or Lord Chamberlain, appear on loose bills from Henrietta Maria and Catherine of Braganza's households. It was only after all these signatures had been received that the bill was sent to the queen's treasurer and receiver general for payment. When the artisan received payment, they signed off the bill under a paragraph acknowledging how much they were paid and for what (see Fig. 2.10). In this way, these bills, with their multiple signatures, corrections and marginalia, are also important material sources that show tangible physical signs of the engagement of the Mistress of the Robes, Robes attendants and tradespeople with the Office of the Robes and the movement of paperwork around the household.

While making or supplying for the royal household came with prestige, many historians have noted that tradespeople and servants could wait quite a long time for payment and that some were never paid at all.[74] Papers drawn up after Mary of Modena's exile show that when she fled England, her household owed tradespeople that supplied her Office of the Robes at least £2,272, and many of these bills were still being chased in the early eighteenth century.[75] The sums dictated by tradespeople were also often recalculated and they were paid less than what they had charged. The accounts of Henrietta Maria, Catherine of Braganza and Mary II demonstrate that in normal circumstances payment for work could take anywhere from a couple of months to a couple of years. This could be longer if the work was not billed straight away. Before Mary II's death, the tailor Peter Lombard submitted a bill for work done as far back as 1690 – it was signed off by the Mistress of the Robes on 18 December 1694 and he did not receive payment until 15 June 1695.[76]

Special attention was also paid at times to clearing debts owed. In 1626 the Countess of Denbigh certified a claim by a Dr Cademan for money owed, writing that the queen acknowledged Cademan's account 'to be a due debt'.[77] In 1687 a warrant was signed by Catherine of Braganza requesting that her treasurer pay the Countess of Arlington funds so that she could 'clear arrears' consisting of outstanding bills from tradespeople.[78] Queen Anne's tradespeople were paid the fastest – usually within six months – likely owing to the new system brought in under the Duchess of Marlborough, discussed below. In the middle of Anne's reign, her mantua-maker often received payment of her bills within two months of the last billing item.[79]

The vast powers given to the Mistress of the Robes are most evidenced by reforms undertaken by the Duchess of Marlborough. The duchess, as others have noted, was an 'excellent business manager' who dealt with many affairs, including political, monetary and household, relating to both the court and her own estates.[80] She even referred to the work she undertook in the Robes as 'management' and during her tenure she did what managers do best by restructuring how commissions were given and the nature of the attachment of tradespeople to the queen's Office of the Robes. In the first half of the century most artisans and suppliers were patronized 'in-ordinary', meaning they were appointed to specific trade positions by the Mistress of the Robes (or Master in the king's household) and the Lord Chamberlain and others swore them in.[81] While in this position they submitted quarterly bills to the Office of the Robes for work completed. This arrangement was not necessarily exclusive on the side of the supplier, as many who submitted quarterly bills to the queens' household also supplied others at court.[82] However, it gave them guaranteed business. Some tradespeople, such as Anna's tailor James Duncane, did hold exclusive arrangements with the queen's household through letters patent.[83] Others, such as tailors, seamstresses and shoemakers, were officially part of the household itself, entitling them to annual wages and pensions.[84]

Catherine of Braganza's household accounts show that by the 1680s the Office of the Robes had already begun to patronize a wider variety of 'extra-ordinary' artisans, usually female dressmakers and milliners, on a commission-by-commission basis (see Chapter 4). As Fig. 2.11 demonstrates, there had been a steady increase in suppliers to the royal wardrobe since the reign of Anna of Denmark, and makers, although more prone to changes or dips in numbers, also increased over time, particularly dramatically between the reigns of Catherine of Braganza and Queen Anne.[85]

Part of this was to do with the increased variety of consumer goods available during the latter half of the seventeenth century and the tradespeople who sold them, as will be explored in Chapters 3 and 4. However, under the Duchess of Marlborough the commission-by-commission arrangement became standard, and the number of tradespeople patronized by the court expanded even more. She refused to designate any tradespeople in-ordinary since

> . . . in the preceding reigns, the tradesmen gave money to serve the crown, which brought in great sums to the Masters of the Robes, but at the same time obliged the tradesman to charge extravagant prices for their goods, a privilege which could hardly be disputed with them, considering the sums they had given for the custom, and the accidents that they were always exposed to by the death of the PRINCE, or the death or removal of the Master of the Robes. But the tradesman whom I made use of had nothing of this to plead; They gave no money to serve the crown nor were they put to any expense, not so much as the customary one poundage; they were paid regularly, ran no manner of hazard and had no more trouble in serving the QUEEN than in serving a common customer . . .[86]

In implementing this system, which the Duchess of Marlborough claimed was 'was quite a new practice in the court', she effectively prevented the buying of royal appointments by tradespeople.[87] It vastly increased the number of artisans patronized by the Robes and allowed them to seek business and clients elsewhere in the fashion marketplace, which many of them did (see Appendix I).

While the decision to restrict exclusive royal appointments of artisans and suppliers in Anne's reign was clearly a financial one, likely due to the poor health of the royal coffers that she inherited, it is also indicative of the Duchess of Marlborough's knowledge of the diversity of London's fashion and textile marketplace at the turn of the eighteenth century. The world of consumption had expanded with

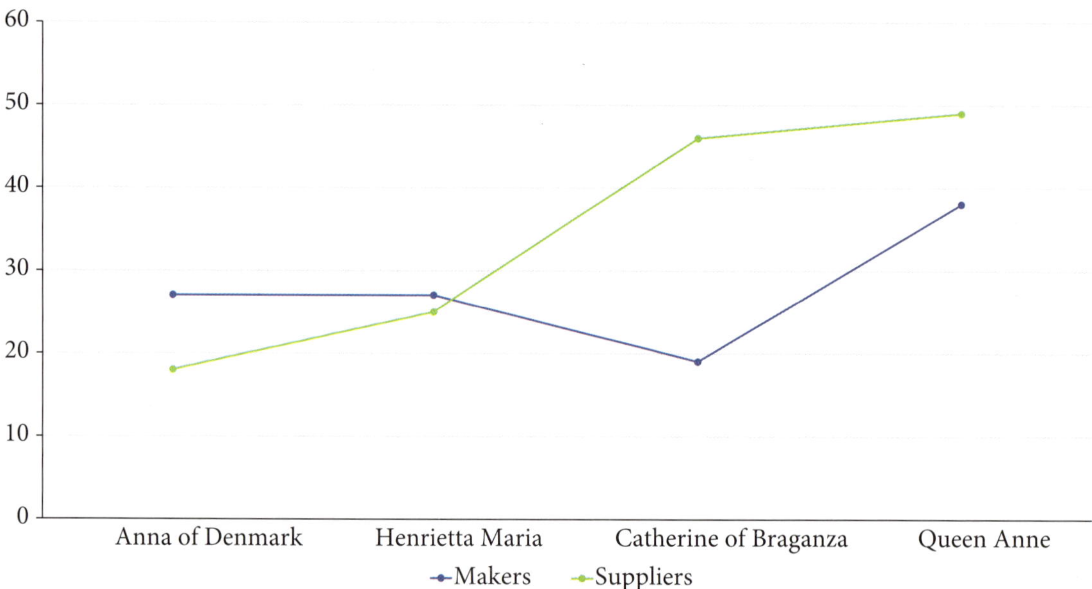

Fig. 2.11 *The growth of makers and suppliers patronized by the Office of the Robes under the Stuart queens. Data Source: Appendix I.*

Europe's exploitation of foreign labour and trade markets, giving rise to a larger range of goods at diverse price points. In response, traditional roles within the garment trades began to shift to meet ever-changing fashion and consumer demands, as subsequent chapters will show. Limiting oneself to one official maker or supplier therefore limited choice and risked the queen falling behind the fashions.

By her direction: material literacy, fashionability and shopping

Clothing was one of the primary ways that female monarchs expressed their backgrounds, their royal magnificence, legitimacy and power. However, as John Styles and Amanda Vickery have stated, 'history has had it in for the female consumer'.[88] Since antiquity, classical philosophers, and then Christian moralists, placed men and women at opposing ends of the shopping spectrum. Men's role was positive; they were rational and the producers of things. Women on the other hand were framed as materialistic and more likely to be cast negatively as consumers. In fact, discussions of women and fashion during the early modern period were littered with critiques of vanity or weakness; men who spent too much on clothing were foolish whereas women showed their covetous nature and the inferiority of their sex, just as Eve had been tempted by the apple.[89] Yet browsing, shopping and interacting with makers and suppliers was central to building a key skill that enabled the economical running of households and finances: material literacy.

Material literacy refers to the ability to 'decode and interpret' material things:[90] that is, to have an understanding of the qualities and properties of certain textiles, or an understanding of how things should be constructed, even if the consumer does not possess the making skills themselves.[91] As Serena Dyer has argued, acknowledging the presence of material literacy, particularly among female consumers and wearers of clothing, collapses the 'division between people who made things and people who bought things' as well as the aforementioned gendered 'producer/consumer binary'.[92] The responsibility of the Mistress of the Robes for appointing tradespeople and signing off on the goods they delivered demonstrates the cruciality of material literacy for elite women in the royal household. They were required to use both their financial and material literacies to check all incoming deliveries for quality and accuracy, to ensure that the queen not only got what she wanted but so that artisans did not overcharge or otherwise 'abuse' the Office of the Robes.

Mistresses of the Robes were also required to have good taste in fashion – if not be leaders of it – with an understanding of both the expectations for a queen's attire and her individual preferences. In the Office of the Robes where the crown spent vast sums of money on clothing, accessories and furnishings, a so-called feminine interest in and desire to consume expensive well-made material goods was not a negative thing. If anything, the experiences of court women allowed the Robes to make informed decisions about which tradespeople to patronize. Rather than just having an 'obsession with the appearance of potential ladies-in-waiting' because it was crucial for them to have a 'collective identity' that represented their female ruler, women in the queen's household were expected to be both fashionable and material literate to help dress their monarch and promote her court, thus facilitating her royal magnificence and power.[93] The Office of the Robes accounts demonstrate that the material literacy of the Mistress of the Robes and her subordinates can generally be characterized in three ways: shopping for the queen, facilitating the queen's purchases and giving fashion advice.

English courtiers played vital roles in helping to establish relationships between Anna of Denmark's newly formed English household and English artisans. The week after Anna's arrival in London in June 1603, Lady Bridget Markham bought several goods from different milliners, haberdashers, hosiers, silkmen and sempsters.[94] Anna of Denmark also inherited the vast wardrobe of her predecessor and in that same year she instructed Lady Walsingham and the Countess of Suffolk to 'take of the late Queen's best apparel out of the Tower at their discretion' for a Christmas masque.[95] The Mistress of the Robes and Keeper of the Jewels were given this task, to literally 'shop' the old Tudor queen's wardrobe, because Anna trusted them to make the best choice based on their offices, their material literacy and their familiarity with Elizabeth's clothing.

Other women in the Robes shopped for the queen using their own networks of international contacts and suppliers. Henrietta Maria acquired fabrics and garments through her tailors and bedchamber staff when they visited France.[96] In 1702 the Duchess of Marlborough billed the Robes for things she had bought for Queen Anne 'beyond the sea' in France and the Dutch Republic. Items included a 'rich manto out of France' that cost an incredible £130 and a 'French fan', as well as fabrics and trims such as 'all sorts of linen', 'Dutch Atlas', 'white Dutch velvet for a manto & petticoat' and silver and gold lace.[97] Catherine of Braganza also regularly used the women of her household for shopping. In the early 1680s her First Dresser, Lady Frances Bellings, the wife of her secretary, Sir Richard Bellings, arranged for several French garments and accessories to be sent to the queen. Papers record that the couple bought ells of textiles such as velvet, satin and taffetas, trims such as silk ribbons, gold and silver lace and fringe. Accessories such as 'chamois perfumed gloves', hoods, scarfs, combs, 'papers of black patches', fans of various types and false hair pieces were also purchased. The Bellings also paid a Parisian tailor and his wife, Monsieur and Madame Renault, £650 for embroidered velvet gowns, sleeves, bodies, petticoats and mantuas 'in the French style', as well as a Venetian gown and a Spanish petticoat. All these goods were sent back to England via Calais and London's Customs House, where import duties were charged.[98]

The Mistress of the Robes was also vital to childbed preparations for which textile elements – clean furnishings and cloths, as well as clothing for mother and child – were not only essential to health but part of the ritual of childbirth in early modern Europe.[99] In 1606, for the birth of Anna's last child, Sophia, Lady Walsingham received a payment of £200 for 'provision of Linen and other necessities' as well as 'fine bone laces of Sundry sizes' for the 'use of the Queens Majesty in childbed, as [well as] for her highness child'. These included cambric, lawn and holland for veils, sheets, shirts, kerchiefs, crosscloths, neckcloths, swaddle bands, 'bibbs', ruffles and 'such like for the child' made by the seamstresses and embroiderers.[100] Fine flannel for a 'blanket for the Child' and Milan fustian for a 'little waistcoat for the Child' were also bought. In addition to linen necessities, Lady Walsingham sourced luxurious materials befitting the birth of a royal child. Velvet, satin and plush fabrics for a 'bearing mantle for the child' and white satins and taffetas for two waistcoats for the queen were acquired. She was also reimbursed for velvet, satin, taffeta and scarlet fabrics, silver fringe and 'silver diamond lace with plate and purle' for the baby's cradle.[101]

Princess Sophia died one day after her birth and did not use these items, but the time invested in their preparation speak to both the importance of royal births and to the trust invested in Walsingham to procure them. The Countess of Denbigh also played a crucial role in sourcing Henrietta Maria's childbed linens and lying-ins, as she signed several warrants for goods relating to the queen's multiple births.[102] As the First Lady of the Bedchamber, Denbigh had also obtained money to pay 'physicians, surgeons, midwives, and others as have done service about the Queen during her lying-in' after the stillbirth of the queen's first son the previous year.[103]

The Countess of Denbigh also regularly shopped for gifts that were given to others by the queen. In 1629 she was paid for 'buying a rich bedstead and furniture for the King' and in 1631 she took control of the purchasing of 'several diamond rings delivered for new year's gifts' on behalf of the queen from the goldsmith William Ward.[104] She even imparted advice on what others should gift the queen. In a letter to her son Basil Feilding, who was soon to leave Venice, she advised that as he planned to 'bring the queen a present' it should 'be of Essences because those countries where you now are yield the best in the world'.[105] The stakes of early modern gift giving were high, and having the queen's Mistress of the Robes advise one on what to buy the queen, in this case perfume, would surely ingratiate them in her favour.

Observations about Henrietta Maria's 'exacting preferences', both in relation to the furnishings for her births and her clothing, raises questions about how the Mistress of the Robes mediated the queen's wishes when commissioning clothing.[106] Certainly, it appears that the queen had very strong opinions about what she wanted and sometimes instructed tradespeople directly. Griffey has noted several instances where 'the queen's own agency in such decisions appears unambiguously': several commands were not only given explicitly 'by her direction' but desirable items were sometimes delivered directly to her rather than going through the Office of the Robes. There are even instances where the queen refused to pay tradespeople who submitted bills without 'her explicit direction'.[107] Henrietta Maria's tailor and pattern cutter regularly travelled to her various residences to make her clothing by her command.[108] Other queens, while perhaps not as exacting as Henrietta, regularly had the opportunity to verbally outline their preferences to their artisans. Queen Anne's mantua-maker hired coaches to Windsor and Kensington palaces 'by the queens orders' so that the queen could 'try' her gowns.[109] It was also noted that tradespeople servicing Catherine of Braganza's Robes were paid 'by her majesties command'.[110] Even if a queen knew exactly what she wanted, it was the role of those in the Robes to facilitate such visits and to ensure that all the different elements came together to make an outfit.

Queens sometimes even went shopping themselves. Anna of Denmark shopped in person at the Royal Exchange in 1618 and drew large crowds when doing so.[111] In 1639 the milliners Joseph Atkinson and Walter Gorestellow were described as requesting adjacent shops on the south side of the Royal Exchange, as if 'her Majesty appeared in person diverse times to the shops' and they were not located together, it would have shown disrespect.[112] Seventeenth-century Exchanges, or Galleries as they were known in France, consisted of rows of small shops (usually only 5 feet wide) that were clustered around circuits of walkways where shoppers could browse.[113] When shopping, the Stuart queens or the Mistress of the Robes would have been accompanied by their ladies, such outings to the Exchange likely mirroring a satirical scene by Abraham Bosse of French courtiers shopping in his *Galerie du Palais* print (see Fig. 2.12). A cavalier on the left of the image is depicted buying books, while courtiers are being wooed by a gallant standing in front of a *mercier* or haberdasher's stall selling masks, gloves, fans, ribbons, roses and other goods. Finally, on the right a *lingère* or seamstress sells linen goods such as collars cuffs and shirts.

Maria Hayward has argued that the Gentlemen of the Robes were integral to the development and dissemination of Stuart style in the kings' households and several men in this position were known to have been well dressed and well connected to the best tradespeople in both England and Scotland.[114]

Fig. 2.12 *Abraham Bosse,* Galerie du Palais, c. *1637–8, etching/engraving. Rijksmuseum Amsterdam, RP-P-OB-42.103.*

Examining the networks of clients among the tradespeople who served the Stuart queens reveals that bedchamber women and the Mistress of the Robes also played a key role in promoting female fashions both within the court and beyond, particularly via the relationships they cultivated with makers and suppliers such as mantua-makers and milliners. These connections frequently resulted in these artisans being recommended at court. In 1667, Catherine of Braganza purchased a petticoat from a 'Madame Lorene' on the recommendation of a 'Lady Garrett' who was a member of the queen's bedchamber.[115] The Countess of Arlington's daughter, the Duchess of Grafton (see Fig. 4.21), and a 'maid of honour' were clients of the mantua-makers Mary Alexander and Jane Heath a few years before they began to make garments for the queen. These women were likely later commissioned for Catherine of Braganza on Arlington's recommendation (see Chapter 4).[116]

The detailed household accounts of the final Stuart Mistress of the Robes, Elizabeth Seymour, reveal that she patronized many of the same tradespeople as the Stuart queens (see Appendix I, Tables 3–6). Her accounts cover the period 1679–1719, when she was both the Countess of Ogle and then Duchess of Somerset. While some tradespeople such as the famous milliner Elizabeth Graydon (discussed in Chapter 3) were clearly shared favourites amongst elite women at the court, others only appear in Queen Anne's records after Somerset was appointed as Mistress of the Robes in 1711. The mantua-maker Anne Massey, who had made mantos, loose gowns and petticoats for the duchess since 1698, and became her regular dressmaker after 1703, began to supply the queen with petticoats and pockets after 1712.[117] Peter and Priscilla Motteux, who ran a fashionable India House (see Chapter 3), also began to supply the Office of the Robes with East Indies goods in 1712. The Duchess of Somerset had been their client since at least 1700.[118] Thus, for these tradespeople, it was the queen's new Mistress of the Robes – who had been their long-standing customer – who secured their patronage.

It was extremely important for the Mistress of the Robes both to know fashion and to be fashionable. This was made apparent in the first meeting between Catherine of Braganza and her Mistress of the Robes, the Countess of Suffolk, when she disembarked in Portsmouth in 1662. Catherine received her gentlewomen and appointed Suffolk to 'come and put her in that habit they thought would be most pleasing to the King'. The Earl of Sandwich, who recalled this interaction, noted that 'I doubt not but when they shall have done their parts, she will appear to much more advantage and very well to the King's contentment.'[119] Thus, even before the Mistress of the Robes was to learn Catherine's tastes, she was expected to understand the latest fashions of court and the nuanced preferences of the king, and then attire her new queen accordingly.

The Duchess of Marlborough was not only made the Mistress of the Robes because of her friendship with Anne or because she was an astute household manager; she was also a fashionable woman whom others, including the queen, looked up to. Sarah was a key member of the *beau monde*, a group of urban, metropolitan elites who dictated the world of fashion at the turn of the eighteenth century.[120] Letters in her private papers are full of references to contemporary fashion, prominent tradespeople and praise for her dress. Other elite women frequently asked Sarah for advice on the latest fashions. Princess Anne wrote to Sarah in 1697 asking her opinion on a new style of manto that she wished to wear to a birthday party for William III, stating that 'there are people that will find fault . . . for one must expect every new thing will be disliked at first'.[121] A year later, Lady Frances Bathurst wrote to Sarah that 'I want a manto and petticoat most mightily, and do very much wish you would have bought me one, for I cannot please myself in this great affair.'[122] In another letter, Lady Anabella Howard thanked Sarah for a pattern for nightclothes and wrote that 'You may like or dislike your own things, [but] you are one of those that all the rest of the world like your dress of all kinds be it what it will' (see Fig. 2.13).[123] The duchess was clearly a fashion leader with discerning tastes whom others looked up to.

Fig. 2.13 *John Smith, after Godfrey Kneller,* Portrait of Anabella, Lady Howard, c. *1693–1742, mezzotint. Rijksmuseum Amsterdam, RP-P-OB-32.767.*

Sarah also cultivated networks among other elite women who helped her shop for goods. In 1709 the Countess of Portland sent silk fabric samples to Sarah from the Netherlands, and in 1720 the Countess of Pembroke wrote that she had 'bespoke your Grace's Hoop Petticoat just the same as mine & you will have it at the beginning of the next week'.[124] Sarah also frequently assisted her friends in buying goods from specific tradespeople years before she was appointed as Mistress of the Robes. In

1697, Lady Bathurst thanked her for procuring her some lace and praised her eye for 'good quality', writing that

> . . . you will believe me, when I assure you, I never had such a Pennyworth in my Life, but I cannot say you have bought it Like a Merchant, for there is very few would bestow much pains to buy cheap for a friend, though they can for themselves, it is so fine and handsome if in deed Madam I should have been very well pleased if it had Cost more.[125]

These letters reveal that elite women commonly exchanged fashion advice, and they used their material literacy in textiles, garments and other goods to shop both for themselves and for others. Additionally, the letters showcase the frequent praise Sarah received for her good eye and ability to get a bargain, both attributes that made her well suited to managing the Robes.

Ultimately, it was the Duchess of Marlborough's assertion of her fashion knowledge over the queen that led to the beginning of the end of her place at court. On the way to St Paul's Cathedral for a thanksgiving service to celebrate the Victory of Oudenarde in August 1708, Sarah noticed that Anne was not wearing the jewels that she had laid out for her. With their relationship increasingly strained and thinking that her rival for the queen's affections, Abigail Masham (née Hill), had interfered, Sarah lashed out at the queen and they began to bicker in front of the gathered crowds. In a later letter to the queen she wrote that their argument was because 'when I had taken so much pains to put your jewels in a way that I thought you would like, Abigail could make you refuse to wear them in so shocking a manner'.[126] Sarah perceived Anne's wearing of less magnificent jewels as not only a slight against her family, as Sarah's husband, the Duke of Marlborough had led the English forces to Victory at Oudenarde, but also a sign of her increasing decline from favour and importance; the queen was beginning to take fashion advice from another 'favourite' who was not her Mistress of the Robes.

Elite women's careers? Work and identity

The threat posed by Lady Abigail Marsham to the Duchess of Marlborough, not just as a replacement for the queen's favourite but also someone from whom she took advice about clothing, demonstrates the important role that the Mistress of the Robes played for the Stuart queens. They not only oversaw the business of the Robes, but were expected to have their fingers on the pulse of fashion, balancing both the queen's tastes, the latest styles and the demands of how to appropriately project royal magnificence. While their work was vital to clothing the Stuart queens, it also became a defining element of their own sense of identity. The idea of an occupational identity or career is a slippery concept in this period. Working lives were marked by frequent job changes and interruptions. Women were often not given occupational titles even if they carried out the same duties as their male counterparts (see Chapter 4). However, the broader idea of 'working identities' has recently been explored by a range of scholars to illuminate how work informed early modern people's identities, with some finding that a sense of self gained from work, in the broadest sense, could be more powerful than social status.[127] At the royal household, work could often blur identities: was one a peeress or a Mistress of the Robes? As I will explore later in Chapter 5, tradeswomen such as silkwomen and seamstresses often occupied places within the royal household too, again blurring the boundaries between tradesperson and courtier, the court and the city. While I do not mean to suggest that social hierarchies were collapsed in the royal household – they were not – work in the Office of the Robes could give elite women a sense of identity beyond that of their families or their titles.

Barbara J. Harris has labelled aristocratic women's expected roles within their own households and those of others as 'careers', arguing that if such women were successful in this work, then they were rewarded with power, prestige and wealth 'as in all careers'.[128] This also extended to their work in the queen's household. Indeed, the establishment of a new household activated, as Leeds Barroll has articulated of Anna of Denmark's in 1603, 'a number of ambitious and talented noble women' to vie for a place.[129] Such positions were also hotly contested when the monarchy was restored. This was noted by Lord Northumberland, who wrote to the Earl of Leicester stating that 'My Lady of Suffolk is declared first lady of the bed-chamber [and Mistress of the Robes] to Her Majesty, at which the Duchess of Richmond and Countess of Portland, both pretenders to the office, are displeased.'[130] Who would gain such roles was clearly topical, and many elite women, including countesses and duchesses, vied for this position at court due to the monetary benefits that came from undertaking such work, but also because of the 'career' prospects.

Elite women in the royal household were able to work their way up the career ladder; the Countess of Arlington and Duchess of Somerset were both Ladies of the Bedchamber before being promoted to Mistress of the Robes. The men who served as the Master of the Robes in the king's household were often called away for military campaigns or other political and diplomatic business, meaning that women's roles within the queen's household were more stable. The Mistress of the Robes usually held her role either until her own death or the death of her queen. At most, a queen had two Mistresses of the Robes during her reign, whereas a king often had three or four Masters of the Robes.[131] Thus, a court appointment in the Office of the Robes was much more central to elite women's working identities than it was to their male counterparts in the king's household.

An office such as the Mistress of the Robes or Groom of the Stole in the queen's household, particularly under a queen regnant, also gave elite women power and influence that they were unable to hold elsewhere in society. Appointments to low offices were under their direct control. Letters to the Duchess of Marlborough frequently enquired about appointments to household positions and those who penned them sought to ingratiate themselves with her for social advantage.[132] The Mistress of the Robes was also frequently called on to advocate on behalf of others. Anna of Denmark's Mistress of the Robes, Lady Walsingham, was described as passing on important information relating to a petition on money matters made by women of Anna's bedchamber in 1612.[133] In 1637, Hugh Ashton, Clerk of the Robes, requested from the Countess of Denbigh a suit of livery equal to that of the surveyor, or if this was not possible, that she might 'move the Queen to bestow a suit of clothes upon him as a bounty'.[134] John Evelyn also made several references in his diary to the Countess of Arlington lobbying King Charles II and Queen Catherine on others' behalf. [135] In these cases, access to the monarch was believed to translate to personal influence, although this was not always necessarily the case.

The Duchess of Marlborough's tenure as Mistress of the Robes and the circumstances surrounding her loss of this office, and how she reflected on them later in her life, demonstrates the way that her work in the royal household was central to her identity as an elite woman. By 1710 Queen Anne and Sarah's complex relationship had deteriorated completely. Increasingly they argued over politics, matters of state and the influence of Abigail Masham, and Anne grew weary of Sarah's forceful and often dismissive personality.[136] Sarah began to spend longer periods of time away from court and, finally, in January 1711, after the election of a Tory government (the Marlboroughs were Whigs and enjoyed much protection from them), Sarah was stripped of her offices and forced to return the keys that signified her position at court (see Fig. 2.5). She was replaced in her offices by the Duchess of Somerset – who supposedly did not want them due to the amount of work they involved – and Lady Masham, the latter being made Keeper of the Privy Purse.[137]

In 1742 Sarah published a memoir titled *An Account of the Conduct of the Dowager Duchess of Marlborough* in an attempt to improve her reputation. It refuted the many smears made against her of abusing her favour with the queen, 'obtaining unreasonable and exorbitant grants' and selling 'titles of honour and places of trust'.[138] With the help of her friend Arthur Maynwaring, and drawing on numerous letters and documents – some dating back to 1704 – as well as writings she composed after her dismissal in 1711, Sarah sought to justify the decisions she made during her tenure as Mistress of the Robes, a role she held alongside the Keeper of the Privy Purse and Groom of the Stole.[139] To do so, she provided many copies of records and expenditure made in the Office of the Robes in Anne's time and during the reigns of those queens before her.

One of the primary arguments Sarah put forward to refute the 'libels' about her behaviour while in Office and to justify her good character was her excellent management skills in the Robes. She wrote that all her accounts

> . . . for the whole nine years in which I served the QUEEN in that office, were passed in the *exchequer* with greatest regularity; and that, in passing them, I produced acquaintances for every sum to the value of twenty shillings paid to any tradesman; which was such a method of exactness as had never before been used by any master or mistress of the Robes.[140]

Going further, Sarah compared her account keeping to that of other Mistresses of the Robes, such as the Countess of Derby and Flower Backhouse, Countess of Clarendon, who was Mistress of the Robes for Anne when she was Princess of Denmark. Her papers show that she had also obtained a copy of accounts kept by the kings' Masters of the Robes for the period 1662–99.[141] Sarah concluded that in comparison to all who had preceded her, she had 'saved her [the queen] a vast sum of money'. She had spent over £9,000 less per year than the Countess of Derby did for Mary II and £6,000 less than the Countess of Clarendon. Overall, she claimed to have saved the Robes between £80,000 and £100,000 under her management and, given the exactness of the accounts she reproduced and the lack of debate about them amongst her detractors, it is possible that this was the case.[142]

Another accusation that Sarah faced, presumably from tradespeople who had wished to buy a place in-ordinary in the Office of the Robes, was that she had not clothed the queen appropriately during her time as Mistress of the Robes. Addressing this in an early draft of her memoir, she wrote that

> . . . some people to be revenged of me for not letting them cheat, have said she was not fine enough for a queen, but it would have been ridiculous with her person & of her age to have been otherwise dressed, besides her limbs neve[r] so weakened with the gout for many years, that she could not ensure heavy clothes, & she really had everything that was handsome or proper for her.[143]

Sarah's assertion that she had clothed the queen appropriately is backed up not only by the accounts themselves, as discussed in Chapter 1, but also the letters between the queen and Sarah confirming that gout made it hard for Anne to wear many heavy clothes. As the letters from other elite women show, Sarah clearly understood fashion and knew how a queen should dress, but was bound by the physical limitations of Anne's ill health.

Perhaps the most significant parts of the early drafts written by the duchess that did not make it into her memoir, were those based on a letter she had written in the final months of 1710 to the queen's doctor, Sir David Hamilton, who was acting as intermediary between the two women. The letter was in response to a piece published by the author Jonathan Swift in *The Examiner* on the 23 November 1710 that compared the duchess to a lady's maid who 'sunk' large sums of money from her mistress into 'her own pockets'.[144] In defence of her conduct at court, Sarah appealed to her excellent management skills in office:

> [T]he Queen must know that I have always taken such care . . . & though no subject to any account I have all the vouchers as clear & perfect as those for the robes, of which the account is public, & who ever will take the pains to look into it, & compare it with any former Queens I am persuaded will not find it to my disadvantage, & whether I was an expensive favourite, her Majesty best knows . . . Mrs Morley [Queen Anne] has acknowledged my care & frugality in her service, those in which she has pressed me to accept of advantages which I have refused, & those in which she has said her business would never be well done unless she had a Mrs Freeman [Sarah] in every office . . .[145]

To Sarah, her ability to manage the Office of the Robes well was key to her sense of self. She had been a reliable and financially literate Mistress of the Robes who, regardless of her personal quarrels with the queen and her expensive maintenance as favourite, had kept a well-administered and financially robust office. In essence, when it came to her dismissal from court – which was due to personal and political reasons rather than any failings in her work – the duchess sought to be remembered more for her working identity as the careful and honest manager that she was, rather than the court intrigues or personal failings that she had in her friendship with the queen.

Conclusions

The position of Mistress of the Robes was a prestigious yet demanding role that required daily work in the Office of the Robes. Primarily given to peeresses from influential court families, over time, the office and its remuneration grew in importance, with appointees rising from ladies to duchesses. At its core, the role required the Mistress to be a competent manager with financial and material literacy, skills that were taught to elite women – who were expected to run their own household estates – from an early age. As the Mistress of the Robes, elite women were able to extend their household knowledge to a court context, managing vast sums of money, overseeing staff, commissioning tradespeople and approving their work.

The role required the queen's trust and confidence and, above all, an understanding of her personal tastes as well as the latest fashions. These women not only offered fashion advice but also exercised good judgment in sourcing goods from the most fashionable tradespeople in London, who, as the next two chapters will show, were increasingly female suppliers and makers. Through changes they made to the Office of the Robes and the interactions with tradespeople, Mistresses of the Robes also responded to the rapidly changing fashions of the seventeenth century, using their material literacy to navigate an increasingly dynamic marketplace.

The power, influence and work of the Mistress of the Robes is best exemplified by Sarah Churchill, the Duchess of Marlborough. Her detailed letters and memoir demonstrate that her work in her offices helped to define her sense of identity, and she used evidence of her good management in the Robes to defend her reputation. Employment in the Office of the Robes therefore provided elite women with an identity and career that extended beyond their family names and noble titles, and in this office they not only influenced what the queen wore but also influenced the wider fashion marketplace, as subsequent chapters will demonstrate.

3

Selling: Fashion retailers, milliners and their social networks

Letters in the private papers of the Mistress of the Robes Sarah Churchill, Duchess of Marlborough, are full of references to tradespeople in addition to contemporary fashions and praise for her discerning tastes. These letters capture snippets of the informal networks of fashion communication at the time, as elite women frequently discussed who was buying what and from whom. Names such as 'Mrs Graydon', 'Mrs Devet' and 'Mrs How' appear frequently in these letters.[1] But who were these women? The casualness in which their names are mentioned indicates that they were well known in their time. However, it is the names and stories of those who created elite fashions and royal magnificence that are rarely explored, while the stories of their famous clientele often live on and form the focus of historical studies. Tracing these names through the accounts of the Office of the Robes and other archival sources allows us to correct this imbalance and learn more about the entangled relationship between the rise of tradeswomen in London and the influence of the court.

As outlined in the introduction to this book, over the course of the seventeenth century the retailing marketplace of London, and Europe more broadly, began to change as the consumer and retail revolutions led to an increase in the availability of globally and locally sourced small goods used in the household. While much retail work at this time was low-paid and low-skilled, among the growing commercial networks of retailers and merchants, women began to dominate a high status and skilled profession: millinery.[2] Female milliners specialized in retailing fashionable accessories, trims and fabrics, selling them primarily to other women. The distinctions between making and selling for milliners is murky, as many milliners were also experienced makers. However, unlike seamstresses, mantua-makers and petticoat-makers who worked in their homes or in workshops, the women discussed in this chapter were first and foremost retailers with public premises, making them the highly visible faces of women's fashion.

By the mid-eighteenth century, millinery was described as a 'considerable Trade, in the Shop-keeping Way, carried on by Women', and it remained so well into the nineteenth and twentieth centuries.[3] However, the question of how women began to dominate this trade in the seventeenth century has not been explored. Scholars have shown that during the eighteenth century English milliners and the closely related French *marchandes de modes* shared several key features: they usually came from middling or gentry backgrounds, they carefully crafted a sense of exclusivity and status around their businesses, and they relied on familial and female networks within the fashion trades to be successful.[4] Such characteristics are, as this chapter will show, all ones that were pioneered by female milliners in seventeenth-century London. New retail opportunities offered by increases in global trade and the consumer revolution in the seventeenth century allowed women to build up wealth and power within the fashion marketplace and amongst their elite patrons.[5] In particular, female milliners capitalized on new trends such as busy decoration in fashion and the desire of London consumers for novelties emanating from France and the East Indies.

This chapter charts the growth of these female retailers and fashion merchants in London by using the Stuart queens' Office of the Robes accounts, alongside private correspondence, court cases and business records. These sources not only demonstrate the court's investment in and support of commercial activities, including global trade, but also the increasing accessibility of luxury goods to a more general London clientele during the seventeenth century. While male suppliers often depended on membership in London's Companies to leverage their networking, patronage and credit potential, particularly in the first half of the century, many women utilized word-of-mouth connections with other women, including those at court such as the Mistress of the Robes, and they relied on inventing and reinventing 'famous' public personas and premises in popular shopping districts.[6]

These female milliners became their brand: their skill at retailing fashion accessories relied on their abilities to create an air of novelty and celebrity around themselves and their shops. Many forged family enterprises that spanned multiple generations of suppliers, highlighting the significance of familial and social networks to women's work in these spaces. The increased opportunity for women to make their livelihoods, fortunes and names allowed some of them to not only entertain queens and correspond with powerful courtiers but in one case their work may have even helped to facilitate the overthrow of a king.

Suppliers to the early Stuart queens and their networks

During the seventeenth century vast networks of suppliers, that is, tradespeople who sold wares not made by themselves, serviced the royal court in London, selling goods such as textiles, trims, accessories and decorative furnishings. Makers of bespoke garments, discussed in the next chapter, were also integral and often worked in tandem with these retailers and merchants. Few of these early suppliers were women, and even fewer still were women working independently of their husbands. There are only two female suppliers who appear in Anna of Denmark's accounts, a milliner and a widow of a haberdasher, and in the surviving bills from Henrietta Maria's Robes there were only three women, all of whom were widows of fabric suppliers (Appendix I, Tables 1–2). Instead, it was tradesmen selling textiles and ornamental trims who dominated the accounts and commanded the largest bills at this time. This was due to the nature of the goods they sold, yards of expensive fabrics and ornamentation that were the costliest component of any garment, rather than makers who usually just charged for their labour. In 1617, the silk mercer Thomas Woodward submitted a bill for £1,024 20s. 2d. to Anna of Denmark's Office of the Robes, ten times as much as the Lord Chamberlain Robert Sidney, Earl of Leicester, was paid for his service that same year.[7] When it came to Henrietta Maria's suppliers, the silk mercers Richard Miller and Rice Williams and silkman Benjamin Henshawe commanded payments of up to £1,500 annually.[8] The dominance of men as suppliers, although challenged in the second half of the century as more women began to enter specific areas of the retail marketplace, relied on two factors: available capital and guild membership. Both these elements ensured that it was overwhelmingly men who controlled the lines of supply and access to merchant networks in the first half of the century.

As discussed in the previous chapter, the tradespeople who served the early Stuart queens were usually appointed in-ordinary, meaning that they received annual salaries and other privileges from the royal household, rather than being patronized on a commission-by-commission basis. While it was a great honour to be appointed as a royal supplier, being paid on time by elite clients was frequently a problem, and if credit was extended and remained unpaid, it could often leave the merchant or retailer in financial difficulties.[9] Thus, the main suppliers of the early Stuarts, especially those who dealt in silks and silk trims, needed to have, and clearly did have, as Erin Griffey has also shown, 'significant financial resources'.[10] Caroline Hibbard has found that some of these suppliers, particularly mercers, often acted as royal creditors, making them financially very important in elite circles.[11] The cloth merchant and mercer Baptist Hicks leveraged his connections to the courts of Elizabeth I and then James I to grow his business and amass large amounts of wealth. He often extended credit to the Great Wardrobe and was knighted by James I in 1603, made a baronet in 1620 and then elevated to the peerage in 1628. Through his extensive business dealings, he was able to effectively buy his way into the landed gentry and he served as a Member of Parliament throughout the 1620s.[12]

Several suppliers to the early Stuart queens, including Hicks, were members of London's Livery Companies (see Appendix I), and their social and professional networks reveal the importance of Company membership. In the early seventeenth century the City of London, defined by the square mile of the old city centre, was the retail hub of the capital. In the City, many tradespeople were located within or close to the Royal Exchange (see Fig. 3.1), which had been opened by Elizabeth I in 1571, or nearby in Cheapside, which was the ceremonial and commercial centre that served as a main thoroughfare connecting the court and City.[13] To work within the City of London, one needed to be an apprentice or freeman of a guild, known as a Livery Company. By the seventeenth century there were dozens of Companies in London and the twelve largest had considerable political power as their Liverymen played a key part in electing sheriffs, mayors and Members of Parliament for the City of London. Breaking with traditions still honoured elsewhere in England, by the early seventeenth century the custom of London allowed anyone who had served an apprenticeship to practice any trade irrespective of their Livery Company, so the name of the Company is not necessarily indicative of the trade practised by all its members.[14]

One extremely wealthy and influential silkman shared by both Anna of Denmark and Henrietta Maria, as well as other members of the royal family, was Benjamin Henshawe. Benjamin was the son of Thomas Henshawe, also a silkman, and both supplied the royal household with fabrics, trimmings and lace. Malcolm Smuts has estimated that Benjamin had supplied £45,000 worth of goods to James I and Anna of Denmark between 1616 and 1618, and some of this was still being paid off in 1625.[15] Benjamin Henshawe was a prominent member of the Merchant Taylors Company of London and played an important role in London's politics, serving at one point as one of the City's captains.[16] Others used the citizenship gained through these institutions to serve as Aldermen of the City of London; the mercer Sir William Stone became an Alderman of the City of London in 1605 and a

Fig. 3.1 *Wenceslaus Hollar,* Royal Exchange, *1647, etching. Metropolitan Museum of Art New York, 29.102.128.*

Master of the Clothworkers Company in 1606. The woollen draper George Wyn was elected an Alderman of the City of London in 1650 through his membership of the Mercers Company.[17] Anna of Denmark's silkman Sir William Acton was also active in City politics. Not only was he a leading member of the English East India Company, but as a prominent participant in the Merchant Taylors Company he was elected as an Alderman and Sheriff of the City of London in 1628. He is known to have lent large sums of money to Charles I and, due to his royalist views, he was passed over for Lord Mayor of London in 1640 as tensions flared in the lead-up to the outbreak of the Civil Wars.[18]

The opportunities offered by Company membership, knighthoods for royal service and membership of corporations, such as the East India Company, were not extended to female suppliers. While seamstresses and silkwomen could ply their trades in London without Company membership (see Chapter 4), until the mid-seventeenth century it was uncommon for women to be apprenticed or made free of these Companies. Although some exceptions do exist, for the most part these guilds, like others in Europe, sought to maintain the privileges of their (mostly) male members.[19] Opportunities for formal participation in most craft guilds around Europe, and certainly within England, was therefore often confined to those who were the widows of deceased members. Laura Gowing has argued that by carrying on their husband's trade after his death, these women played 'an established role' in London's Companies; however, as Clare Haru Crowston has noted of widowed mistresses in Europe more generally, the privileges inherited from their husbands often came with 'significant limitations'.[20] In the London Companies, these limitations included the inability to be elected to ranks within the organization and therefore to participate in politics.

Yet widows were able to leverage the social and business connections of their husbands in other ways. In the period 1616–17, the widow Hester Onslow delivered wares to Anna of Denmark's Office of the Robes after the death of her husband, the haberdasher George Onslowe.[21] In 1631, Margaret Ward also began to supply Henrietta Maria's Office of the Robes with linen fabrics after the death of her husband, the linen draper Gilbert Ward. She appears to have gone into partnership with John Hunt who then eventually replaced her.[22] After the death of her husband, the woollen draper Richard Aldworth, another widow named Margaret Aldworth took payment for an outstanding bill, signing as follows: 'Mistress Margaret Aldworth late wife & executrix of Richard Aldworth deceased' (see Fig. 2.8).[23] The use of the title 'Mistress' here indicates that Margaret had taken over the running of the business and possibly even her husband's apprentices, as a mistress was an established woman of means who was skilled and who taught or governed servants or apprentices; she could be single, married or widowed.[24] By 1630 her son, also named Richard and who could not have been more than twenty years of age, began submitting woollen draper's bills to the Robes.[25] It therefore appears that Margaret had managed the trade until her son could take over.

Another woman who managed her husband's business after his death was Anna Henshawe, the widow of the aforementioned Benjamin Henshawe. After Benjamin's death in 1631, Anna signed off payments for many of his bills. By 1632, she even began to submit bills in her own name and then in partnership with William Geere.[26] Many years later, during the 1650s, both Henshawe and Geere were still chasing thousands of pounds in debts owed to them by the crown.[27] While these widows were clearly capable of carrying on these trades and were expected to do so if their husbands died, once their sons or others took over, they often stepped back and resumed their unrecorded duties within the businesses. Thus, while their status as wives allowed them to leverage inherited rights and connections, it still reinforced their presence in the fashion marketplace as being one that was always connected to their relationships with men.

Changing shopping locations, busy decoration and evolving trades

During the seventeenth century, fashionable shopping districts shifted from Cheapside and the Royal Exchange in the City of London to hubs located in the West End and Middlesex. These shopping spaces were close to royal residences such as the Palace of Whitehall and the Palace of Westminster, where Parliament met, as well as to townhouses of the nobility and gentry who resided in the West End during the London season.[28] These new shopping locations included the New Exchange, opened in the Strand by King James I in 1609, Pall Mall in Westminster, and Charring Cross and Covent Garden in St Martin-in-the-Fields (see Fig. 3.2). By 1630, all sorts of luxury goods were sold at the New Exchange and it became a hub for courtiers who frequented the principal residence of Queen Henrietta Maria at Somerset House.[29] The restoration of St James's Palace by Charles II and the creation of new royal residences, such as Kensington Palace by Mary II and William III in 1689, also established the West End, known as the 'town', as a place where fashionable Londoners mingled; promenading in St James's Park and Hyde Park became established activities for the elite at this time (see Fig. 3.3). This change was particularly noticeable after the Great Fire of London in 1666 when significant amounts of the old City were destroyed or substantially damaged, including the Royal Exchange. Despite incentives given by the City of London to stay, many tradespeople did not.[30] This marked a shift towards fashionable centres of elite consumption in the West End that would continue into the eighteenth and nineteenth centuries.

The changing shopping landscape of seventeenth-century London is apparent in the bills of the Stuart queens. During the reigns of Anna of Denmark and Henrietta Maria, most of their tradespeople worked in the City of London. While a number of suppliers of the later Stuart queens still retained Company memberships, many began to trade from new locations in the West End, where the Companies had no jurisdiction (see Appendix I, Tables 3–6). Most tradespeople in the early queens' accounts were craftspeople, that is, makers of goods.[31] However, by the end of the century, suppliers and retailers,

Fig. 3.2 *'A Map of the Parish of St. Martins in the Fields, Taken from the Last Survey', from* A survey of the cities of London and Westminster . . . Corrected, improved, and very much enlarged in the year 1720 by John Strype *(1754–5). Metropolitan Museum of Art New York, 52.519.193(1-2).*

Fig. 3.3 *After Marco Ricci,* View of the Mall in Saint James's Park, *after 1709–10, oil on canvas. National Gallery of Art Washington D.C., 1970.17.132.*

tradespeople selling wares usually made by others, began to dominate. This signalled a shift to trends observed in the eighteenth century, whereby 'most shops sold goods made at a distance'.[32] Indeed, while the total number of makers exceeded those of suppliers in Anna of Denmark's accounts and were roughly even in Henrietta Maria's, in the accounts of the later Stuart queens the total number of suppliers outnumbered makers (see Fig. 2.11). The trajectory of female suppliers was not the same as female makers. While women makers came to outnumber men in key areas of clothing production during the reign of Queen Anne (see Fig. 0.3), female suppliers never rivalled their male counterparts in the royal household accounts (see Fig. 3.4).[33] Much of this was related to issues with women's access to capital required in the cloth and merchant trades, and due to the growing number of women in specific areas such as millinery, which, while influential, was only one segment of the retail marketplace.

The area that saw the highest concentration of female suppliers was in the sale of small wares (see Appendix I). In the reigns of Anna of Denmark and Henrietta Maria, their male haberdashers supplied the Robes with hats, hat bands, fans, plumes, garters, roses, gloves, points, girdles and some silk fabrics, as well as other goods to care for clothing such as brushes.[34] By the reign of Catherine of Braganza, her 'haberdasher of small wares' Matthew Bowman was only patronized for small goods to assist with dressing or caring for clothing, such as pins, needles, laces, powder, combs and brushes.[35] No references to 'haberdashers' appear in the accounts of Mary II or Anne. The millinery trade also underwent change, as more and more women took up this profession in the final decades of the seventeenth century. It has been suggested that female milliners probably derived from mantua-makers.[36] However, while women began to dominate millinery around the same time that mantua-makers began to appear, and while they both shared several skillsets derived from seamstresses, millinery had been an established trade practised by men since the sixteenth century.

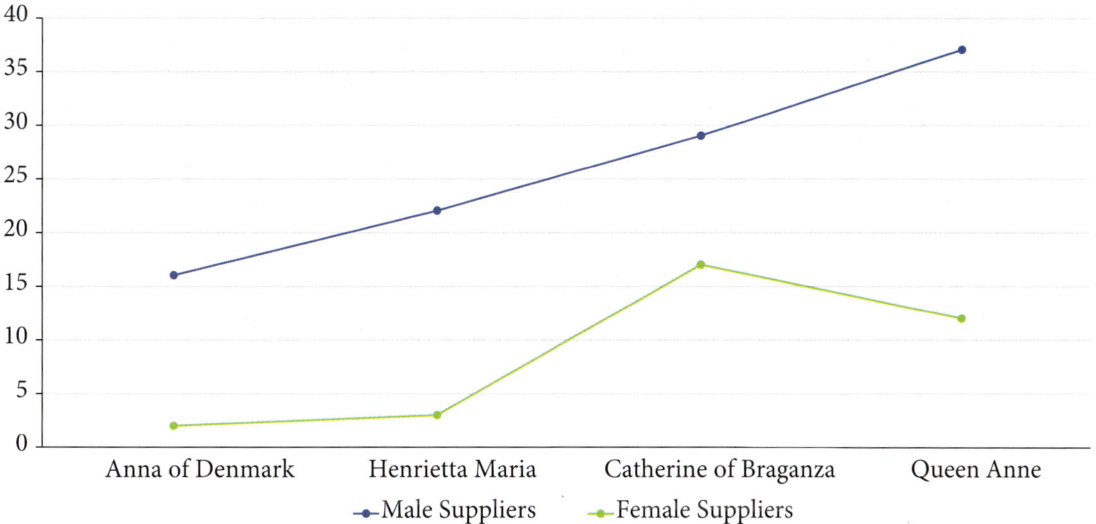

Fig. 3.4 *Gender of suppliers in the Queens' Office of the Robes accounts, 1603–1714. Data source: Appendix I.*

The name 'milliner' likely derived from sellers of luxury goods made in Milan.[37] In Anna of Denmark's accounts her milliners Richard Crawshaw, Thomas Cooke and his wife Marie Cooke sold goods such as ribbons, pins, lace, fans, garters and fine linens and silks.[38] Henrietta Maria's milliners Joseph Atkinson and Humphrey Bradbourne sold pieces of silk fabric, ribbons of various colours and types, lace, hats and hatstrings, gloves, garters, girdles, points and roses (see Fig. 3.5).[39] The early Stuart queens' accounts contain only one female milliner, the aforementioned Marie Cooke who worked alongside her husband. However, by the 1680s there were several female milliners working as individual traders in Catherine of Braganza's accounts, and by the reign of Queen Anne the only male milliners in her accounts were those from prominent millinery families headed by women, such as the Cherets and Langrishes.

The increased presence of women in fashion retail trades that sold small wares during this period has also been observed in continental Europe.[40] Many women worked as haberdashers in European cities from the late sixteenth century onwards.[41] In France, *rubanières*, women who specialized in selling ribbons, also began to appear in the seventeenth century and they were depicted by the French engraver Nicolas de Larmessin's series *Les costumes grotesques et les métiers*, which showed various tradespeople dressed in the goods they sold (see Fig. 3.6). The print suggests that in addition to ribbons, *rubanières* also sold scarves, stomachers, aprons, kerchiefs, masks and fans – all goods supplied by English milliners too. This period also witnessed the emergence of the *marchande de modes* (fashion

Fig. 3.5 *Wenceslaus Hollar,* Still-life with a group of muffs, a pair of gloves, fans, mask and two kerchiefs, *1647, etching. Metropolitan Museum of Art New York, 17.34.9.*

Fig. 3.6 *Nicolas de Larmessin,* La Rubanière *[The Ribbon Seller], 1696, engraving. Bibliothèque nationale de France, département Estampes et photographie, RESERVE FOL-QB-201 (71).*

merchant) in Paris, a woman who adorned gowns with trims and made and sold items for the head and shoulders.[42] These female occupations grew out of associated male trades including that of the *marchand mercier*, a merchant who sold wholesale and retail goods, usually those used in clothing, and many fashion merchants were married to *merciers*.[43] Unlike France, English women working as milliners did not receive a separate trade name to their male counterparts. English men and women also patronized milliners of both genders. However, the second half of the seventeenth century did mark a shift in identity for the millinery trades, which over time came to be associated with women's clothing and women's work.

The emergence of the French fashion system that prized novelty and change has been credited with facilitating the rise of the *marchande de modes* in Paris.[44] Novelty also played a key role in the development of the female milliner in London. From 1670 onwards, there was a desire for what Jane Ashelford has termed 'busy surface decoration' in dress, and during this period suppliers of lace, fringe and ribbon commanded huge bills from the Stuart queens.[45] When Mary II died in December 1694, yearly bills submitted by her laceman Thomas Moreton and her milliner Thomas Cheret totalled £1,526 and £1,321, respectively.[46] Fashionable clothing required copious amounts of ribbons, fringes, braids, tassels and lace of various sorts, as well as embroidery. For men, these adornments included large amounts of buttons, lace and ribbons, as is visible on the suit worn by Sir John Corbet of Adderley in his portrait of 1676 by John Michael Wright (see Fig. 3.7).

In women's dress, it was the petticoat that bore much of this ornamental trim. In 1687, one petticoat of white satin made for Catherine of Braganza was decorated with 'thread fringe', 'thread galoon' and 'large riband', and in 1694 several yards of fringe, tassels, galoon, lace and 'foot' were supplied for petticoats and mantos for Mary II.[47] Fashion prints, including one of Anne Stuart when she was princess of Denmark, help visualize this ornamentation (see Fig. 3.8). Although this image likely exaggerated Anne's beauty and style – produced in Paris it shares many similarities with French works of the time that combined portraits of well-known women with fashion prints – letters from Anne at this time show her fondness for the newest fashions.[48] The Princess's petticoat is decorated with various types of lace (see Fig. 3.9) and fringe (see Fig. 3.10), and elite women's accounts from the period indicate that much of this would have been a metallic lace made with gold and silver threads.

The love of such ornamentation in dress soon attracted all sorts of retailers, many of whom were women.[49] Female milliners and *marchandes de modes* were valued most for 'their style, imagination and invention', and busy decoration, which could be easily removed and replaced on the surface of clothing, helped to facilitate their work.[50] The queens' milliners are recorded as selling yards of ribbons of all sorts and colours, lace, tassels and various lengths of silk fabrics. Although there is no evidence from the bills that English milliners of the seventeenth century applied these trims, like the *marchandes de modes* of the eighteenth century did, they certainly would have offered advice on the most fashionable types of surface decorations to purchase. Some milliners commanded large sums; however, other women are regularly recorded in the Stuart queens and kings' accounts as selling small amounts of silk, ribbons and lace (see Appendix I), with some perhaps being the English equivalent of *rubanières*.[51]

Busy decoration also extended beyond the ornamentation of garments to an ever-increasing variety of fashion accessories. Female milliners sold 'suits for the head' (see Fig. 3.11) and fontanges

Fig. 3.7 *John Michael Wright,* Sir John Corbet of Adderley, 3rd Baronet, *c. 1673–6, oil on canvas. Yale Center for British Art, Paul Mellon Fund, and Friends of British Art Fund, B1992.3.*

(see Fig. 3.8), both headdresses supported by wire that were decorated with lace and ribbons 'as if their heads were milliners shops'.[52] Various styles of hoods were also sold. These accessories wrapped around the head and tied underneath the chin or at the neck and they were ubiquitous women's garments in the seventeenth and early eighteenth centuries. They feature regularly in artworks depicting everyday life in England (see Fig. 3.3) and the Dutch Republic (see Fig. 4.1), as well as in French fashion prints (see Fig. 1.9). Styles of hoods ranged from plain examples, usually made of white or black silk or gauze for elite women, to those of linen, as well as numerous French styles of various descriptions.

Fig. 3.8 *Henri Bonnart,* La Princesse de Dannemark *[The Princess of Denmark], c. 1688–1702, engraving with etching. Royal Collection Trust, RCIN 603398. Anne wears a fashionable mantua gown and highly embellished petticoat. Her outfit is accessorized with a fontange, fur scarf, muff and fan.*

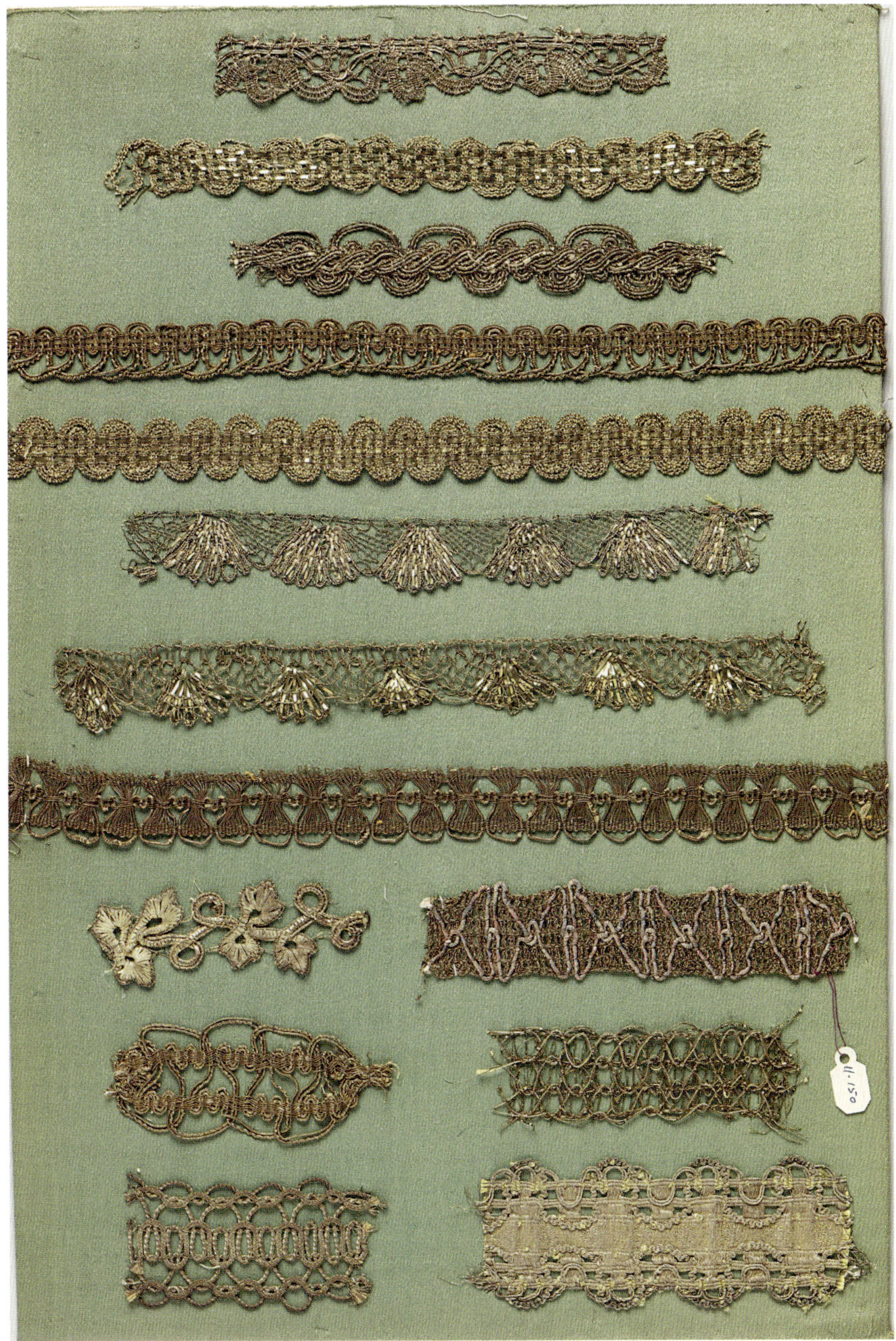

Fig. 3.9 *Fragments of metal lace and braid trims, 17th century, French. Museum of Art, Rhode Island School of Design, 11.142.*

Fig. 3.10 *Silk and metal thread fringe, 18th century, European. Metropolitan Museum of Art New York, 36.90.2047.*

Until recently, no examples of these common fashion accessories were thought to have survived. This was until the wreck of the royal frigate HMS *Gloucester* was discovered off the Norfolk coast. Travelling in a convoy of ships, the *Gloucester* had sunk on 6 May 1682 while taking James, Duke of York, to Scotland to fetch his pregnant wife Mary of Modena and his daughter Lady Anne (later Queen Anne).[53] This significant British maritime find unearthed several chests full of clothing and personal belongings including two silk petticoats (see Fig. 4.9), a silk hood, a silk gorget and a pair of women's shoes, all of which show evidence of wear. The silk hood has survived in a remarkable condition (see Fig. 3.12).[54] Its large, baggy shape indicates that it could have been worn over an elaborate hairstyle or 'suit' of head clothes. Depending on the style and height of the hair, the front edges of the circular hood would have folded back multiple times to frame the face, and it was tied at the neck by the 'ties or flaps', referring to the long edges on either side. The back of the hood was pleated and tightly gathered into a circle that rested at the base of the skull, as is visible in paintings from the period.[55]

Other small goods such as linen ruffles and silk scarves were also sold, and in some cases the bills note that these goods were made by the milliners themselves; in 1703 the milliner Mrs Langrish charged for 'making the purple Scarfe'.[56] Silk masks of various types, usually made from black velvet or satin, were also worn to protect the skin from the sun and wind, as well as to conceal appearances (see Fig. 3.5).[57] The large amounts of fine linen and silk items provided by milliners suggests that many of these women had worked as seamstresses before venturing into millinery, and it also signals the continuity of the earlier female profession of silkwoman under a different name (see Chapter 4). The husband-and-wife team

Fig. 3.11 *Nicolas Arnoult,* Femme de qualité en habit D'esté *[Woman of quality, in summer dress], from* Recueil des modes de la cour de France, *1687, hand-coloured engraving. Los Angeles County Museum of Art, M.2002.57.67. This French fashion print depicts a variety of accessories supplied by milliners. The woman wears a suit of headclothes of linen and ribbons with a cornet (a laced cap with hanging lappets). She holds a fan in one gloved hand and a mask in the other, and on her face are black paper patches.*

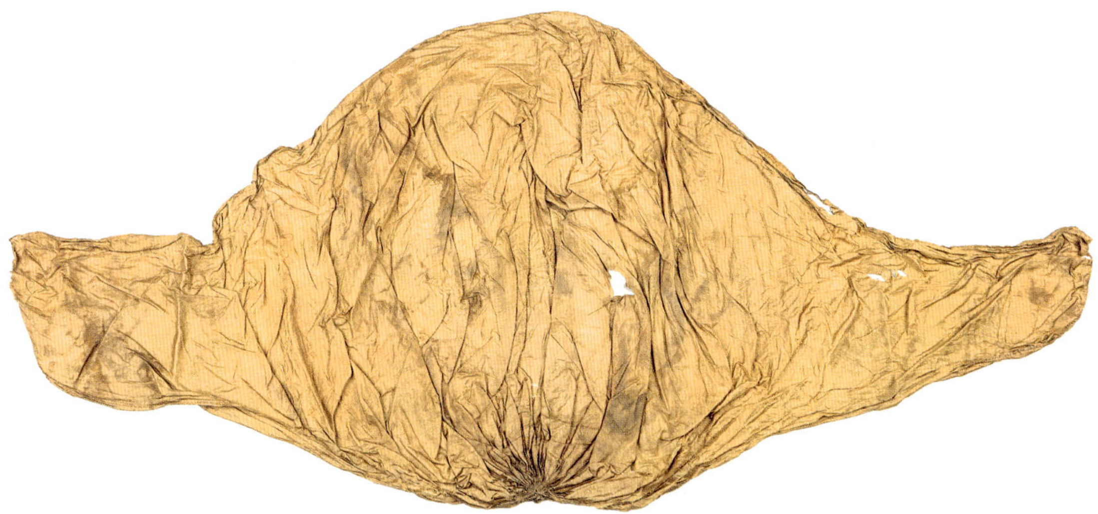

Fig. 3.12 *Silk hood, recovered from the wreck of HMS* Gloucester, *c. 1670–82. The hood would have originally been white but has discoloured due to centuries submerged under water in the wreck.*

Dorothy and Abraham Speckard both worked together to supply Elizabeth I and Anna of Denmark's Robes with goods. However, Dorothy was named a silkwoman and Abraham a milliner. This suggests a significant overlap between these two trades that eventually merged into one. At the very least, popular milliners must have had teams of seamstresses working for them making such goods.

While milliners both made and sold linen and silk items, they also vended a wide array of goods made by others. Fur and feather items, which had previously been supplied by furriers, skinners and feather dressers to the early Stuart queens, were now sourced from milliners who sold fur and feather muffs, tippets and palatines. Milliners also became the primary suppliers of goods such as fans and gloves, which they sourced from fan-makers and glove-makers. Other beauty products, including cosmetics and skincare, were also sold by milliners (see Chapter 5). This reshaped the types of trades recorded in the queens' household accounts, as female milliners soon began to replace more specialized tradespeople as they became a one-stop-shop for fashionable accessories and trims.

Female milliners, French novelties and East Indies goods in the late seventeenth century

In the bustling and competitive fashion marketplace of late seventeenth-century London, the milliner's ability to vend the latest novelties and to stay at the forefront of fashion was key to their rise and success. Two trends emerge in the Stuart queens' accounts: the influence of French goods and increased imports from the East Indies. As explored in Chapter 1, by the late seventeenth century French fashion had a firm grasp on elite tastes and some English commentators referred to the French as 'the Milliners of Europe'.[58] The Parisian fashion industry was quite advanced, and numerous specialized artisans, merchants and shopkeepers existed. Prints, periodicals and fashion dolls also spread news of French goods far and wide.[59] Demand soon grew in London and at the court among both men and women for trims and accessories that were fashionable in Paris. In 1671, the writer John Evelyn was displeased that Catherine of Braganza was 'so much governed by an ignorant Frenchwoman' named 'Madame de Boord', whom he described as a 'peddling woman' that 'used to bring petticoats and fans, and baubles, out of France to the Ladies'.[60] Catherine's privy purse accounts show that she did indeed purchase several of these things from a 'Madame de Bord' between 1670 and 1677.[61] Another French milliner, named Jeanne Ferand, is also recorded as selling fans, purses, gloves, lace trims, 'French ribbon[s]' and French 'tuberose gloves' to several Stuart queens and other elite women.[62] Several of the tradespeople who dealt in millinery goods or other small wares in the later Stuart queens' accounts were of French origin (see Appendix I).

It is no surprise then that workshops and retail premises that catered for the making and dissemination of French goods were set up in London. Many were located in Charing Cross, which came to be referred to by some as 'Petty France'.[63] However, one popular millinery establishment was Madame Cheret's 'French shop' in the Piazza in Covent Garden (see Fig. 3.13).[64] On Wednesday, 27 January 1664 Samuel Pepys wrote in his diary that 'my wife and I took [a] coach and to Covent

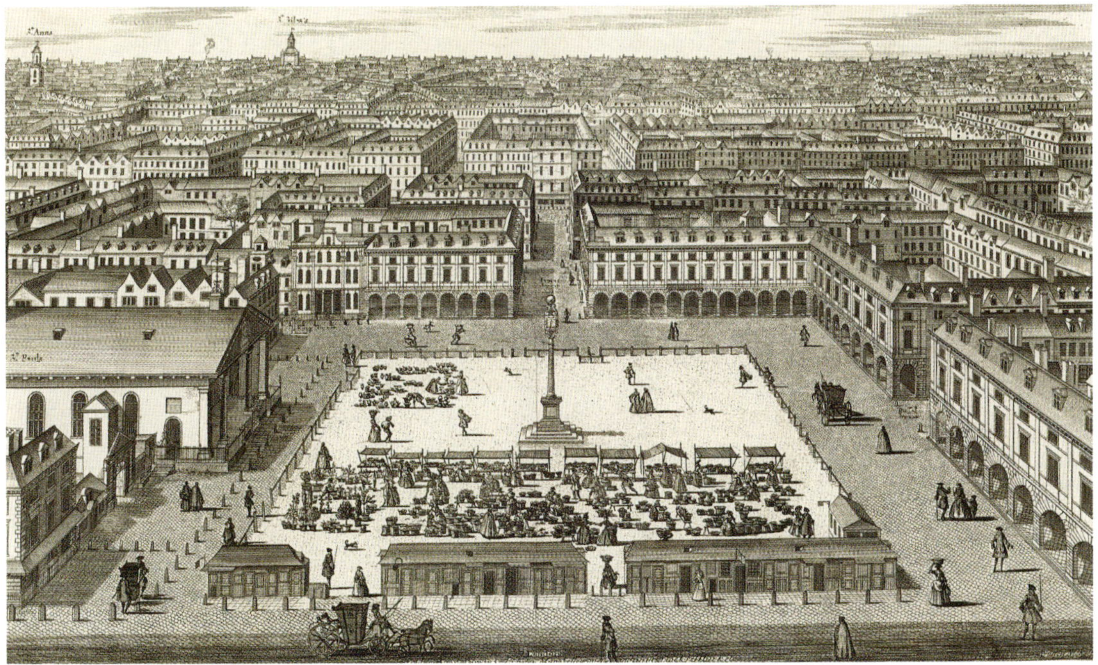

Fig. 3.13 Covent Garden, from London Described; or Perspective Views and Elevations of Noted Buildings, *c. 1720–31, etching and engraving. Rijksmuseum Amsterdam, RP-P-1918-1716.*

Garden, to buy a mask at the French House, Madame Charett's, for my wife'.[65] Madame Cheret was Marie Cheret, a name that also appears frequently in Catherine of Braganza's Privy Purse accounts between 1666 and 1679, as well as in the papers of Charles II, the Duchess of Lauderdale and the Earls of Northumberland during the same period.[66] Three other Cherets also appear in the records of the Stuart queens: Thomas, George and Susana, and all were milliners. Thomas and George appear to have been the sons of Marie Cheret, and Susana was George's wife.[67] They continued to carry on the family business in James Street in Covent Garden into the eighteenth century.[68]

Bills relating to thirty years of the Cheret's trade have survived and demonstrate that they sold a plethora of general millenary wares.[69] These included general trims and fabrics, as well as headwear such as caps, head suits, hoods and fontanges, which they charged for 'making', likely by seamstresses working for the shop. The Cherets also supplied goods to chief mourners at the funeral of Mary II, such as black veils, headclothes and crape tippets.[70] Fashion accessories made up the bulk of their goods: masks, girdles, tippets, muffs, buckles, fans and garters. Being a 'French shop', goods either in the French style or imports from France were also frequently mentioned, including scented 'French shammoy [chamois] gloves', '*à la mode*' scarfs, small French sweets called '*nonpareilles*' and numerous types of 'French hoods', 'French love hoods' and the bizarrely named '*prisioneére* hoods'.[71] Many milliners, including the Cherets, also sold French flowered gauze hoods which may have looked like the one worn by a woman believed to be Marie Anne de La Trémoille, Princesse des Ursins (see Fig. 3.14).[72]

References to French shops like the one owned by the Cherets also survive in literature from the period. In *The English mounsieur a comedy* (1674), a character enters a 'French shop' in London. The shopkeeper boasts that they can show her 'the Rarity of France' and that they had 'all the rarest things of Paris, the smell of the Orange Jessemy, Violet and Rose, all grow in my Gloves and Essences as natural as upon the trees'.[73] Around the same time this play was being performed, the Cherets sold dozens of these orange and jasmine gloves to the Earls of Northumberland and their family.[74] A typical French shop in London may have looked something like the imagined boutique of 1678 in the *Extraordinaire du Mercure galant* (see Fig. 3.15). The supplement certainly depicts and describes many of the accessories sold by the Cherets, including ribbon, palatines of *point de France* lace and crape (numbers 4 and 5 in the image), gloves with ribbons and bows (6), lace and braids (8) and cuffs of gauze and lace with bows of ribbon (9 and 10).

The barrister William Petyt specifically blamed the increase in French shops on French Huguenot refugees, lamenting that the Dutch had 'let in the French Protestants by a Toleration, and carefully Superintended the Increase of their Manufactures'. As a result, the

> . . . French Shop came to have more things of Delicacy and Variety, it drew in more Customers, and the English amongst the rest; and as a great part of Trade is driven in Fantastical Dresses, and Toys of many sorts, the French took care to provide an Abundance, with which they gulled the rest of the World.[75]

Fig. 3.14 *Attributed to René-Antoine Houasse,* Presumed portrait of Marie Anne de La Trémoille, princesse des Ursins, c. *1670, oil on canvas. Chantilly, musée Condé, PE 339.*

Fig. 3.15 *Jean Lepautre, after Jean Berain,* Interior of a boutique in Paris *(detail), from* Extraordinaire du Mercure galant, *1678, etching. Rijksmuseum Amsterdam, BI-1895-3793-127.*

This treatise conveniently blamed French Huguenot refugees for wider fears about the economic reforms of Louis XIV and Jean-Baptiste Colbert that strengthened French manufacturing and challenged English trade. Several tradespeople in London during the late seventeenth century were Huguenots. However, not all sold French goods.

At the turn of the eighteenth century, the Huguenot playwright-turned-retailer Peter Motteux, and his wife Priscilla, sold Indian muslins and silks, porcelain, Japan lacquerware, fans and 'coloured China bottles' to fashionable elites in London, including Queen Anne, from their shop in Leadenhall Street.[76] Conveniently located near East India House and warehouses, Peter and Priscilla ran what was known at the time as an Indian house: a shop that sold East Indies goods.[77] During the late seventeenth century, the trade in 'India goods' by the English East India Company (EIC) and the Dutch East India

Company (VOC) boomed.[78] While lacquerware and porcelain were used to decorate spaces within the home (see Fig. 5.5), East Indies textiles were used in both household furnishings and clothing. In addition to plain muslins and calicoes from India, brightly coloured cotton chintz fabrics, while less common, were sought after as they imitated the designs of silk fabric but were also washable, colourfast, and, above all, more affordable (see Fig. 3.16).[79] East Indies silks, on the other hand, came from India, China or the Middle East. During the seventeenth century, the EIC imported cargoes of Chinese silks from Canton and Indian silks from Surat, which had connections to silk factories along the western coast of India and Persia.[80] East Indies silks were often described as very colourful and containing 'flowered' or 'striped' patterns, and they appealed to wealthy middling and elite consumers who used them in gowns and petticoats (see Chapter 4). Plain damasks and taffetas were also used by embroiderers, and examples of these silks have survived in the papers of an English free merchant named John Scattergood who was stationed in Madras in India but also traded to China (see Fig. 3.17). [81]

Fig. 3.16 *Bed hanging of painted and dyed cotton chintz, probably made on the Coromandel Coast, Southeast India, c. 1680–1700, from Ashburnham House, Sussex. Cooper Hewitt, Smithsonian Design Museum, New York. 1953-123-1-a/h.*

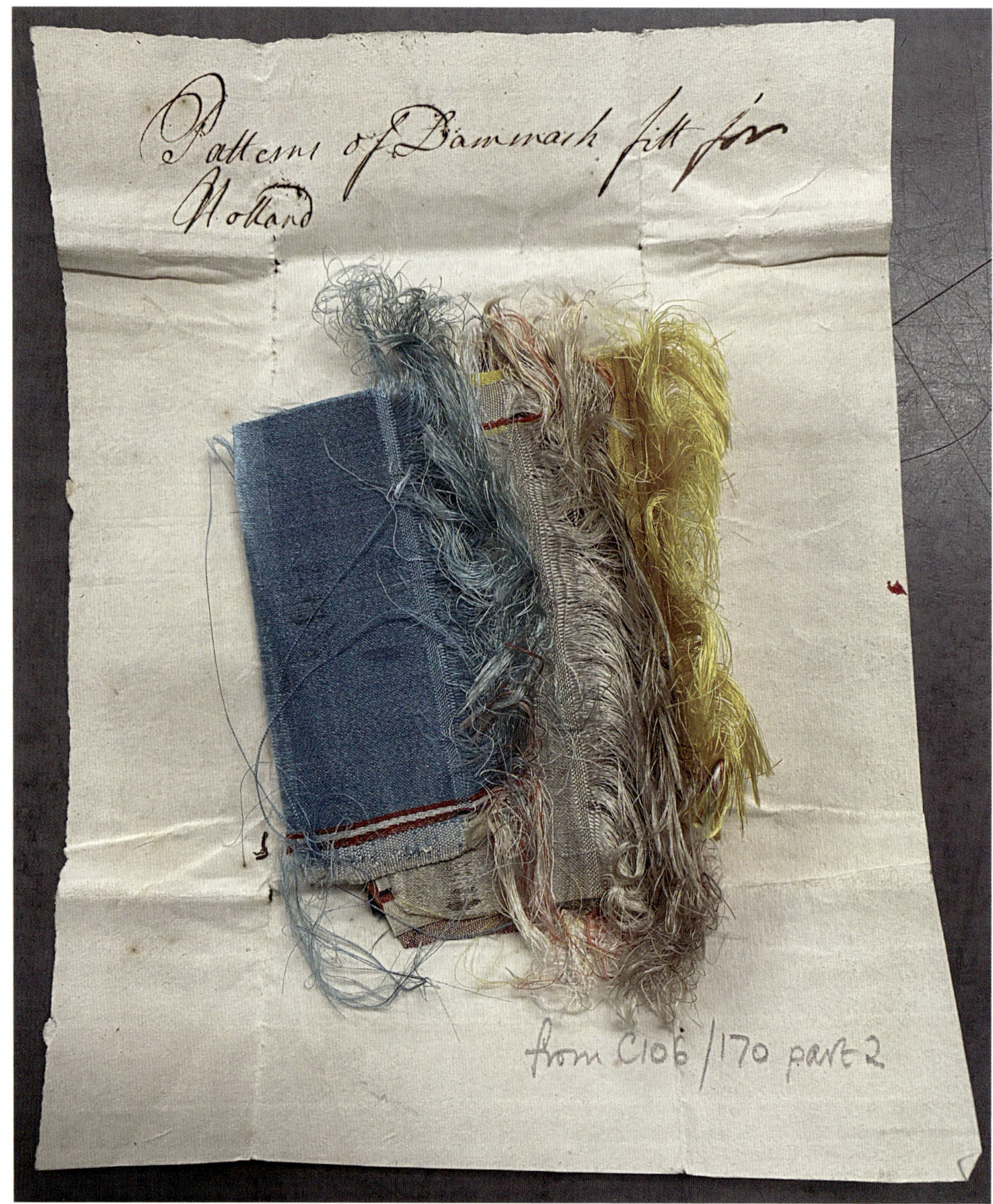

Fig. 3.17 *Silk Damasks from the workshop or firm of Deng wen hao (鄧文号), China, c. 1701–10, in the papers of John Scattergood. The National Archives of the UK, C 106/170, part 2. Although manufactured in China, these damasks were known at the time as 'Indian' damask due to their importation via East Indies merchants. By the time these samples were obtained by Scattergood, likely after the Indian cotton and silk bans of 1701, they were intended for export to continental Europe.*

Female retailers played a vital role in vending these textiles and other goods, particularly to elite female clients. In the final quarter of the seventeenth century frequent references to 'Indian Women' who owned 'Indian houses' began to appear and in popular literature they were depicted as having 'the newest things' that had 'never saw this side of the World yet'.[82] In this context, Indian women did not refer to women of South-Asian heritage. Rather, the term referred to women who sold goods from the East Indies. The appearance of Indian women as characters in several plays reveals that they were exclusive retailers of the times and that they primarily supplied elite clients with exotic novelties that marked them as in the latest fashion.[83] As such, these women became popular figureheads of global expansion, exotic trade and fashionability at a time when England was forging powerful trade networks and laying the groundwork for colonial expansion in South East Asia and the Indian subcontinent.

One real Indian woman was an unnamed merchant-retailer who supplied the Restoration court. Dating to 1682, the inventory of this unknown 'Testatrix' recorded the goods for sale in her warehouse, which included furnishings such as calico curtains, quilts and bed hangings, porcelain tableware, lacquer furniture (screens, tables and boxes), gemstones and jewellery, as well as textiles like 'flowered Atlas', 'cuttanees', 'longees', and 'several remnants of silk and calicoes'. Ready-made garments made from these East Indies textiles were also recorded. The end of the probate contains a list of debtors, of whom twenty-three were women out of a total of twenty-nine, including many courtiers such as Barbara Palmer, Duchess of Cleveland, Louise de Kérouaille, Duchess of Portsmouth, and the Duchesses of Richmond, Southampton and Monmouth.[84]

Between the years 1676 and 1710, another woman, named Mary Devet, with the assistance of her sister Elizabeth Devet, her daughter Sarah Craddock and granddaughter Joanna Tombs, supplied both millinery and East Indies goods to Catherine of Braganza, Mary II, Queen Anne and the Duchess of Somerset.[85] Sarah Churchill, Duchess of Marlborough, later recalled that Mrs Devet and Mrs Tombs 'kept Indian shops', and advertisements show that Devet was located in Mincing Lane in the City of London close to East India House.[86] In an undated letter, likely from the early 1700s, Frances Jones, Countess of Scarbrough, wrote to Sarah that 'I shall have the pleasure of being with you tomorrow . . . I do not fear a journey into the city, and I will be ready to go to Mrs Devets or where you please', indicating that such houses were fashionable places where elite women shopped and mingled (see Fig. 3.18).[87] In addition to selling millinery goods such as linen textiles and accessories, lace and small goods for infants, Mary and her daughters also sold a variety of Indian textiles such as plain and printed muslins, striped and chequered calicoes, 'turkey silks', atlas and 'Persians', 'camels hair' cloth and turkey handkerchiefs. They also vended goods such as lacquer boxes, 'Chiney' (chinaware) and pounds of 'Keyzer', 'Imperial' and 'Green' Tea.[88]

It is unclear if the Devets would have called themselves Indian women; occupational titles are often not given in their accounts and there is much overlap in their bills with the work of the milliner.

Fig. 3.18 *Studio of William Wissing,* Frances, Countess of Scarborough, *late 17th century, oil on canvas. Lacock, Wiltshire, NT 996324.*

However, we know from other women that East Indies goods often formed a key part of their millinery businesses. A 'Mrs Taylor Milliner' sold Chinese porcelain and lacquer screens to the Duke and Duchess of Lauderdale in the 1670s, and Mary Pyke, whose fashionable millinery shop occupied a large retail space in the Royal Exchange, vended Indian cottons and silks.[89] In 1696, Pyke put her name to a petition from 'Shopkeepers and warehouse keepers trading in silks and painted calicos' submitted to the House of Lords in response to unrest caused by wool merchants and silk weavers who opposed EIC textile imports, claiming that bans on East Indies goods would deprive them of 'the greatest part of their livelihood'.[90]

Selling Indian textiles like calico, muslin and silk was a natural extension for milliners who already specialized in making or selling small goods from fine linens and silks. These fabrics were also cheaper to buy, both wholesale and retail, than European equivalents. Between 1687 and 1695, Indian satin and Persians in the queens' accounts cost 5 shillings per yard, while Florence satin and Italian damasks and taffetas cost 11–12 shillings per yard.[91] European silks in these bills cost nearly double that of Indian silks. The same can be observed for linens and cottons. In 1688, the linen draper Matthias Cupper charged between 2 and 5 shillings per yard for muslin and 2–4 shillings per yard for calicoes, compared to 7–13 shillings per yard for different types of European cambric and holland linens.[92] This also reflects trends seen elsewhere in Europe, such as in the Dutch Republic, where women were also highly concentrated in less capital-intensive trades; as the supply of East Indies textiles increased and prices dropped, more women with less capital, could invest in the stock to partake in these retail trades.[93] Although female suppliers would never come to outnumber male suppliers in the queens' accounts (see Fig. 3.4), likely due to these issues of capital that constrained them, their presence in the fashion marketplace was now impossible to overlook.

Milliners, Indian women and their social networks

By the end of the seventeenth century, the milliner became the go-to for all manner of fashionable trims, accessories and textiles. There were differences between milliners: some tended to sell linen and silk goods for the head and neck, some sold haberdashery and ornamental trims, while others again specialized in fashionable accessories. Others made their fortunes by selling French or East Indies goods. Not all milliners were female. Elite men often continued to patronize male milliners and the Cherets had male and female family members who worked side-by-side in their French shop in Covent Garden. Millinery was not a one-size-fits-all business and this accounts for why elite women often had several milliners who supplied them with different types of wares (see Appendix I). For female milliners at the top of the marketplace who serviced elite patrons, there was a notable shift away from reliance on the guilds to form business and social networks during the later seventeenth century, as male retailers still did.[94] While the success of some milliners depended on their ability to secure prime retail spaces in places such as the Royal Exchange, and thus foot traffic, others rested on familial and social connections.[95]

Two millinery families, the Langrishes and the Burtons, were tied by blood and marriage. The success of Deborah Burton, who had a shop in 'the Exchange' and then 'at the Holy Lamb in the Strand', forged a family of milliners.[96] Her son Francis became a milliner and one of her daughters Deborah married another milliner named William Tuer in 1684. Tuer appears frequently in the accounts of Mary II and the Duchess of Somerset during the final decades of the seventeenth century.[97] Deborah's other daughter, Judith, also married a milliner named Barrell Langrish whose father was also in the trade.[98] During their marriage, Judith continued to help her mother Deborah in the Burtons' shop, as well assisting in her husband's own business. Barrell's ailing finances were also regularly propped up by his mother-in-law and his father.[99] Judith and Barrell's son Thomas also became a milliner. Clients of the Burtons and Langrishes included Catherine of Braganza, the Duchess of Marlborough, the Duchess of Somerset and Queen Anne (see Appendix I). Deborah's reputation and long-running business was key to their success in the fashion marketplace and when this matriarch died in 1711, she left behind several properties in the City of London, stocks in the Bank of England and hundreds of pounds in ready money to her children.[100]

Contrary to associations of millinery with ill repute in popular literature, a trope which Gowing has noted 'laid a malicious undercurrent to women's work in fashion shops' throughout the seventeenth and eighteenth centuries, several studies have found that from the mid-seventeenth century onwards it was common for girls apprenticed into the millinery trades to come from respectable families of the gentry or wealthy merchants.[101] This reflects the increasing tendency for the gentry and nobility to pursue commercial wealth and enterprise during the seventeenth century. It also follows trends observed of suppliers to the early Stuart queens who came from or intermarried into the gentry. Such backgrounds were advantageous for tradespeople cornering the top tiers of the market. For female milliners, a genteel background was crucial to building relationships with their wealthy female clients, especially those of the nobility. Milliners also needed to look and act the part to inspire their customers to browse their wares or to spend their money in their shops.[102]

Genteel backgrounds, education and manners, combined with a savvy sense of style and an air of exclusivity, were therefore crucial for milliners dealing with elite clients and allowed many of them to command huge sums in their bills. For example, in 1683, Elizabeth Graydon received several payments from the Robes of Lady Anne (later Queen Anne) amounting to a total of £986.[103] These desirable qualities in a milliner may also explain why, by the time of Queen Anne, almost all her milliners were female: it was much easier for women to establish a relationship with their clients if they were the same gender, and vice-versa. Yet, all these things could lead to infamy too. As Zara Kesterton has argued of Marie-Jeanne 'Rose' Bertin, the famed fashion merchant of Marie Antoinette, contemporary interest in female milliners and *marchandes de modes* was not just directed at their 'fashion creations' but also their relationships with elite women, and their behaviour was subject to public comment as well.[104] This was also the case in late seventeenth-century London, when a trip taken by Mary II to the theatre and then to the shops 'furnished the town with discourse for near a month'.[105]

Daniel Finch, Earl of Nottingham, penned a letter recounting an evening on 28 May 1689 when Queen Mary II attended the playhouse in Dorset Garden to watch *The Spanish Friar* by John Dryden. This play was controversial at the time, not only because James II had 'forbid it' due to the plot that concerned the usurpation of the Spanish throne, but also due to some still viewing Mary II and her Dutch husband William III as usurpers of the English throne during the Glorious Revolution. After the play, which caused the queen to 'hold up her fan, and often look behind her, and call for her palatine and hood, and anything she could next think of' to avoid the gazes of her fellow spectators who heckled the actors and commented on the usurping elements of the plot, a scene that may have inspired the print of Mary in Fig. 1.16, Nottingham described the queen going shopping.[106] He recalled:

> She dined with Mrs Graydons, the famous woman in the Mall, that sells fine Ribbons and headdresses; from thence she went to the Jew's, that sells Indian things; to Mrs Ferguson's, De Vett's, Mrs Harrison's, and other Indian houses; but not to Mrs Potter's, though in her way . . .[107]

Many of the tradespeople visited by the queen on this occasion have already been discussed. The 'Jew' and 'De Vett' were almost certainly Solomon de Medina and Mary Devet, and Mary Ferguson and Jane Harrison also appear in Mary's accounts selling East Indies goods (see Appendix I, Table 5).

The social networks and reputations of the other women mentioned by the Earl of Nottingham – Elizabeth Graydon and Jane Potter – are the focus of the final part of this chapter. Both women were connected to the royal courts and both found themselves involved in the lives and intrigues of their elite clients. Unlike male social climbers such as the aforementioned cloth merchant Baptist Hicks, who used his connections to the court to receive a knighthood and entry to the peerage, these opportunities were not available to tradeswomen in seventeenth-century England. Still, by examining the careers forged by these women we can see how they were able to leverage their work in the fashion trades to achieve fame, fortune and powerful social connections for their families. However, such meteoric rises could also lead to spectacular downfalls too.

The 'famous woman in the Mall' mentioned by the Earl of Nottingham was a milliner named Elizabeth Graydon. Elizabeth had a long career, and her bills span the accounts of all four later Stuart queens. Little is known of her early life, but, given her later social connections, it is likely that she came from a wealthy middling or gentry family. Her husband Robert's background is also unclear. However, at one point he may have been a customhouse officer who searched ships for unentered goods at the Port of London.[108] Robert was almost certainly the brother of Captain John Graydon, a vice-admiral in the English navy who was active from at least 1680.[109] John commanded many ships in battle during the Nine Years War and the War of the Spanish Succession, and he was appointed as Governor of Newfoundland briefly in 1701. After a period of unsatisfactory service as commander-in-chief in the West Indies in 1703, John, now given the title 'Esquire', was dismissed from service and by 1704 had retired from the navy to Fordwich in Kent.[110] While his later years were spent quietly in Kent, his life as a commander of several royal naval ships that fought in important battles saw him move in quite elite social circles, and his social capital was clearly high enough to warrant the creation of a portrait by the court painter Godfrey Kneller in 1703. This portrait appears to have been housed in a royal residence before being donated to the Greenwich Hospital Collection by King George IV in 1824.[111]

Whether or not her brother-in-law's reputation was the key to Elizabeth's connections to the court remains unknown. However, what is clear is that her shop was located somewhere at the eastern end of Pall Mall (see Fig. 3.19), placing her close to all the royal palaces. She first began to supply millinery

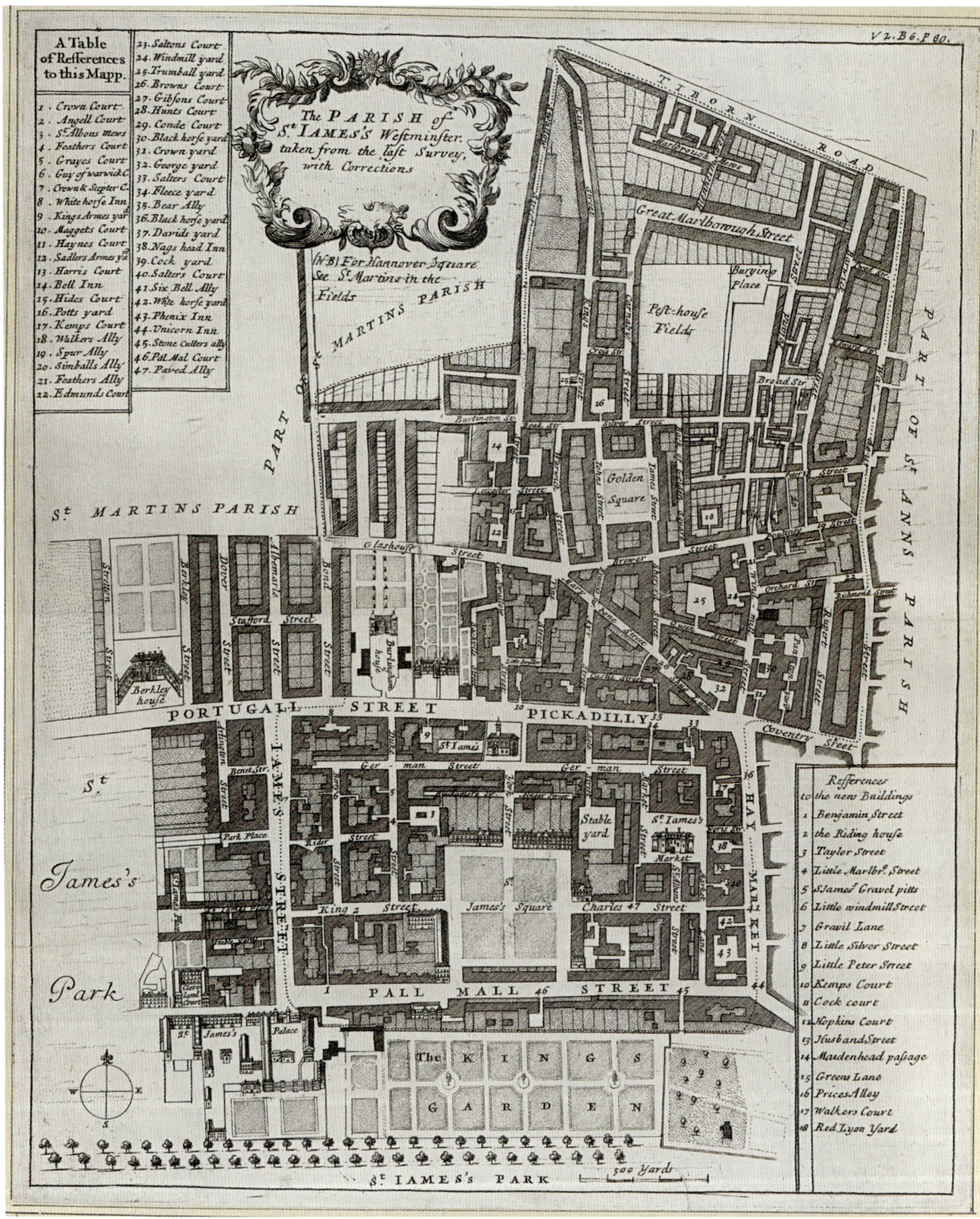

Fig. 3.19 *After Richard Bloome,* The parish of St. James's, Westminster, taken from the last survey with corrections, 1685, *reproduced in 1720. British Library, Maps.Crace.12.3.*

goods to Lady Anne (later Queen Anne) around 1682 and to Catherine of Braganza in 1686.[112] Unlike the Langrishes who sold general millinery wares, the Cherets who imported French goods, and the Devets who specialized in East Indies imports, the bulk of Elizabeth's products during the 1680s were, as the Earl of Nottingham's letter noted, headwear. This headwear was made from fine linens, silks and ribbons and included coifs and suits 'for the head', sorties and cornets. Elizabeth's bills also made frequent references to silk hoods, such as the aforementioned example from the HMS *Gloucester* shipwreck (see Fig. 3.12), often with matching scarves.[113]

Two court cases involving Elizabeth Graydon reveal much about the life and business of a successful milliner in the late seventeenth century. Both these cases, along with others explored in this book, were the result of breakdowns in the culture of credit that existed at this time. The early modern economy was a credit economy. Almost all buying and selling was done, as Craig Muldrew has articulated, 'on the basis of verbal promises or informal notes' and it was expected that the balance of such debts would be paid at regular intervals.[114] The more social credit that one had, the more sales credit they could accumulate. A well-known or well-dressed customer who was perceived to be wealthy would be extended a larger credit note than those who were not. However, misjudgements on behalf of the retailer, or untrustworthiness on behalf of the consumer, often led to breakdowns in this credit system and to litigation over unpaid debts.[115] Such was the case in 1692 when Elizabeth and Robert Graydon appear as plaintiffs in a dispute over unpaid debts owed by the estate of Sir John Coryton, 2nd Baronet, to several tradespeople in Covent Garden, Middlesex and the Royal Exchange. Although both Elizabeth and her husband are mentioned, details of the case claimed that it was actually 'Elizabeth Graydon, being a Sole trader from your orator her husband' who was owed a sum of sixteen pounds.[116] Thus, this court case reveals that at this time, Elizabeth Graydon was trading in the capacity of *feme sole*.

In 1701 another court case over money matters involved Elizabeth and Robert Graydon.[117] This time Elizabeth, a recent widow, was a defendant against the mercers William Sherrard, Paul Clowdesley and Richard Cooper, all of whom also appear in the Stuart queens' accounts (see Appendix I). These mercers claimed that Robert had bought several wares from them on credit and that debts of thirteen pounds had not been settled when he died. By this time, no mention of Elizabeth's *feme sole* status was made. However, in some cases women who ran their businesses independently of their husbands might choose to be *feme couverte* under the law, as it gave them the legal flexibility to rely on their husband's economic backing, to involve him in legal action or to manipulate women's 'poorly defined position' in the courts.[118] It is also possible that during the nine-year period between these court cases Elizabeth abandoned her *feme sole* status and that her business was subsumed legally under her husband's name. However, considering that in cases where one spouse owed debtors it was common for creditors to come after the other's assets, the mercers may have in fact been coming after Robert Graydon's probate for debts that Elizabeth owed to them.[119] Perhaps in this case, Elizabeth was happy to be known as a *feme couverte*, rather than them bring her own business into legal disrepute.

Regardless of Elizabeth's legal status, her bills from the 1690s show that her millinery business was very much her own and that her husband had limited involvement; it is always Elizabeth who is identified as the person commissioned for goods and receiving payment. Attached to the 1701 court documents were bills of evidence listing 115 clients, only eleven of whom were men (see Appendix IV). These clients had combined outstanding debts totalling over £3,600.[120] The names on this list reveal Elizabeth's extensive connections by this time. They included Frances Stuart and Anne Lennox, both Duchesses of Richmond, Mary Villiers, Duchess of Buckingham, Elizabeth Monck, Duchess of Albemarle, Mary and Jane Howard, both Duchesses of Norfolk, Mary Butler, Duchess of Ormonde, Elizabeth Seymour, Duchess of Somerset, Hortense Mancini, Duchess of Mazarin (see Fig. 4.22) and other lesser-known courtiers such as Flower Backhouse, Countess of Clarendon (who had been Anne's Mistress of the Robes before she became queen). Many other clients were the wives, daughters and sisters of some of the most powerful men in England, such as politicians, governors and nobles. Others had influential female connections; a 'Mrs Jennings' was likely a relative of Sarah Churchill (née Jennings). Others such as 'Mrs Howard' and 'Mrs South' have no immediate indication of privilege or power, and they owed only a few pounds each to Graydon.

Debts outstanding ranged from £250 owed by Dorothy Ferrers, Countess of Arran, and £240 owed by Letitia Isabella Smith, Countess of Radnor, to £1 13s. owed by Lady Anne Popham, the wife of English politician Alexander Popham. While some of these debts were probably in the middle of being settled, others were clearly much older. The 'Queen' is listed as a debtor owing £55 5s. This 'queen' is unlikely to have been Mary II, as her records show that Elizabeth Graydon's bills were paid after her death.[121] Mary of Modena was also a client, and as she fled to France during the Glorious Revolution in 1688 it is possible that this debt belonged to her. Other Jacobite women who fled to France are also mentioned as debtors, such as Lady Elizabeth Delaval and Lady Anne Wheatley, wife of the Earl of Dumbarton. In these cases, it is unlikely that their credit was ever resolved, as both women died in exile. The Graydons also owed money to others, including to mercers 'Henry and Richard Cooper & Partners'. Wages were also owed to 'Mrs Pedley & other workwomen' who were employed by Elizabeth in her millinery shop making and selling goods such as ribbons, 'edgings', wire, ermine, fabrics including 'small satins', gauzes, crape, muslin, as well as accessories such as fans, patches, necklaces, love ribbon and masks.

A queen dining with a mere milliner may seem strange to us now, however, eighteenth-century milliners often acted as 'a bridge between classes'.[122] Indeed, according to Nottingham, when the king reprimanded Mary II for dining with Graydon and later visiting a 'wise woman' who told fortunes, she replied saying that 'she had done nothing but what the late queen had done'.[123] Such relationships between elite women, their milliners and other non-elite tradeswomen was therefore not unusual. Through their work, which saw them become the public face of fashion, these women were able to gain access to those of higher social status and to those in power.

One woman who does not appear as a debtor in the 1701 case, but with whom Elizabeth Graydon had a relationship, was Sarah Churchill, Countess (later Duchess) of Marlborough (see Fig. 3.20). It is unclear how Elizabeth and Sarah became acquainted. Sarah was a Lady of the Bedchamber to Lady Anne around the time that Elizabeth first began to supply her household with millinery wares. By 1690, Elizabeth was also supplying Sarah and her daughters with goods.[124] In a letter composed sometime between 1692 and 1697, Henrietta Churchill wrote to her mother about the comings and

Fig. 3.20 *John Smith, after Godfrey Kneller,* Portrait of Sarah Churchill, c. *1678–1742, print. Rijksmuseum Amsterdam, RP-P-OB-32.799.*

goings of their Holywell House and asked 'but if my Dear Mama pleases I would not have her desire Mrs Graydon, nor nobody else to come to St Albans, for Several reasons I will give you, when I see you'.[125] This letter implied that Elizabeth Graydon was a frequent visitor to the Marlboroughs' St Albans estate, which, given its distance from London, likely required an overnight stay. While Graydon may have visited St Albans to dine and sell goods to the Marlborough girls, Sarah and Elizabeth also exchanged letters. It was not uncommon for milliners to have written correspondence with their clients; later eighteenth-century women such as Sabine Winn often had extensive correspondence with tradespeople, including her London milliner.[126] However, Sarah and Elizabeth's correspondence went beyond discussions of fashion purchases – it also involved family and politics.

A personal letter from Elizabeth Graydon to Sarah Churchill, dated 1 November 1694 and sent from London to the Marlboroughs' residence at Holywell House in St Albans, has survived. The letter begins by speaking of the 'wrong turn this business has taken after so fair a prospect'.[127] What the business was is unclear, but it appears to have involved both women as Elizabeth went on to write that 'the pleasure I have had by seeing your Ladyship's kindness to us all in this business quite takes away the sense of the loss' and that she was deeply afflicted by Sarah's 'generous sincerity' being met 'with undue returns'. The business appears to have involved Francis Godolphin, son of Sidney Godolphin, First Lord of the Treasury, as Elizabeth also wrote that 'I must know Lord Godolphin is hearty in prospect, because your Ladyship believes it, whom I take to be the very best Judge of truth and plain dealing I ever knew'. Several letters in Sarah's papers from the early 1690s refer to Lord Godolphin and his marriage prospects, as he was a desirable young bachelor.[128] Being a 'hearty in prospect' perhaps refers to Sarah's plans for nominating her daughter as a potential match, which would eventually happen when Henrietta Churchill married Francis Godolphin in 1698.

It also appears that perhaps Sarah, and by extension Godolphin, had lent weight and stepped into a matter involving the Graydons, as Elizabeth also noted that she 'humbly beg you will pardon the frequent troubles given by' her family who all possessed 'gratitude and affection' for the countess. Regardless of what had occurred, Elizabeth wrote of her gratitude for living 'in the Fruition' of Sarah's 'Favour and influence', which gave her protection against 'every misfortune'. Such sentiments were more than just grovelling; the letter also suggests that Elizabeth had come to rely on her good relationship with Sarah in her business. This was due to Sarah's well-connected nature and her fashion sense which, as previously discussed, was sought by Princess Anne and others. To receive support from the Countess of Marlborough and Lord Godolphin meant that Elizabeth Graydon was not only familiar with those in the elite *beau monde* social circles of London, but that she knew them well enough for them to help her family.

Living in the fruition of the Duchess of Marlborough's 'favour and influence' eventually sealed Elizabeth Graydon's fate at the royal court and speaks to the influence that elite women had on the rise and fall of tradeswomen in the fashion marketplace. Alongside the Langrishes, Elizabeth was one of the primary milliners who supplied Queen Anne at the beginning of her reign (see Appendix I). However, as Sarah's influence at court began to wane, the amount of goods purchased by the Robes from Elizabeth began to decrease. At the same time, the bills of another milliner named Mary Wilkins began to rise.[129] By 1710, Elizabeth Graydon no longer appeared in Queen Anne's Office of the Robes, and I have found no mention of her after 1714 when it was noted that a 'Journey Woman of Mrs Graydon's' was in Scotland Yard.[130]

The final woman mentioned in the Earl of Nottingham's letter and whose popularity and subsequent demise was tied to the royal court was Jane Potter. Jane had begun her career as a milliner selling 'laces, gloves, Ribbons, fans & such other things', but by 1680 she traded as a *feme sole* merchant dealing in East Indies goods such as tea, porcelain and Indian textiles.[131] Little is known about Jane and her husband George Potter. Some documents list 'Gent' after George's name, indicating that they may have been from the gentry. However, it was increasingly common by this period for a tradesman or a merchant with good connections and accomplishments, refined manners and wealth to be labelled a gentleman.[132] Regardless of her background, Jane was a social climber who used her retail success to make favourable social connections. In the early 1680s, she played matchmaker to one of the wealthiest and most sought-after young heiresses in late Stuart society, Lady Elizabeth Percy, who would later become Queen Anne's second Mistress of the Robes (see Fig. 3.21).

In March 1679, at the age of only twelve, Elizabeth married fifteen-year-old Henry Cavendish, Earl of Ogle. However, just over a year later, Henry died. After this, fourteen-year-old Elizabeth was wed to the thirty-three-year-old wealthy politician and landowner Thomas Thynne of Longleat in Wiltshire. The marriage does not seem to have been a happy one, and a short time later Elizabeth fled to the Netherlands and attempted to separate from Thynne. However, a separation was not required because in February 1682 Thynne was murdered in his coach in Pall Mall by assassins hired by the Swedish Count Karl Johann von Königsmark, who was infatuated with Elizabeth and wanted to marry her. Elizabeth denied any involvement with the plot to kill her husband and six months later she went on to marry again, becoming Elizabeth Seymour, Duchess of Somerset.[133]

Many years later, in 1688, Jane and George Potter pursued the executors of the will of Thomas Thynne, arguing that his estate owed them money due to the role they had played in the couple's secret marriage. They claimed that they were acquainted with both Thomas and Elizabeth, as by 1681 Jane was 'selling & trading in Indian silks & other commodities [to] several persons of quality [who] used to come or meet at their house, sometimes to buy & other time to raffle for the same'.[134] Although the executors of Thynne's will, John Hall and John Keene, stated that Jane was pretending to be 'intimately acquainted' with Elizabeth, bills in Elizabeth's papers show that she was a customer of Jane's at the time and it is very likely that Thynne was too.[135] A key intermediary was a Mrs Philadelphia Stanhope, whom the Potter's claimed had been their former lodger. A 'Mrs Stanhope' was certainly employed in the household of Elizabeth Seymour as a steward for most of the 1680s, and her name appears on bills

Fig. 3.21 *Peter Lely,* Lady Elizabeth Percy, Countess of Ogle, *c. 1679–80, oil on canvas. Royal Collection Trust, RCIN 402856.*

as the recipient of goods from Potter, acting in much the same way as the Mistress of the Robes in the royal household.[136]

The Potters claimed that Jane had told Thomas that she 'could be very instrumental in promoting & procuring a marriage' between him and Elizabeth, and they 'did much encourage the said Thomas Thynne to endeavour to accomplish the same'.[137] Shops were a place where men and women could meet and mingle. That Indian houses were used for such purposes was made explicit in many sources that mention them. A 1693 play, *The player's tragedy*, referenced the lure of the Indian House for female shoppers and warned of the gallants who frequented these establishments.[138] In a letter of June 1712, Indian houses were described by Lady Mary Wortley Montagu as 'too public, nor at all proper for a long conversation', emphasizing the hazards of meeting her future husband in such a public place while courting.[139] To encourage the match, Jane Potter claimed that she had been 'obliged to give presents to several persons' close to both parties, such as Mrs Stanhope. As such, she entered into a bond of £1,000 with Thomas Thynne, with the expectation that he would pay her £500 if the marriage should happen.[140] However, Thynne died before it could be paid, resulting in the case that was later brought by the Potters against his estate.

The court case dragged on until at least 1695, even after the death of George Potter, and by this time it was finally acknowledged by Thynne's executors that the Potters had played a role in the marriage negotiations.[141] Eventually, the bond was deemed void and the case thrown out as the court declared 'such Contracts concerning Marriages' to be 'of dangerous Consequences, and not to be allowed'.[142] However, the many documents this dispute created reveal that Jane Potter was a social climber who used the connections that she had made with persons of 'quality' through her business to gain financially, and almost certainly, socially too. The case also reveals the interconnected nature of these women and their fashion networks – a former lodger with Potter went on to become a long-time household servant to the Duchess of Somerset, who in turn went on to become a Mistress of the Robes in the household of Queen Anne.

Jane Potter's ambitious social climbing would eventually lead to her downfall. In the letter penned by the Earl of Nottingham, he went on to say that Mary II did not visit Mrs Potter's India house on her shopping trip, though her premises was on her way. He wrote that this,

> . . . caused Mrs Potter to say, that she might as well have hoped for that honour as others, considering that the whole design of bringing the queen and king was managed at her house, and the consultations held there; so that she might as well have thrown away a little money in rafling there, as well as at the other houses . . .[143]

Jane Potter was annoyed that the queen did not patronize her shop and publicly voiced her dismay, stating that she and her Indian house had played a key role in plotting the Glorious Revolution, as the 'consultations [were] held there'. It appears that Indian houses were not just shops or places where couples could court, but establishments like the coffee houses of the period: places where people would come to drink new, fashionable and stimulating beverages such as tea and engage in politics.[144]

The social aspects of Indian houses, and the social roles women played as hostesses, are emphasized in descriptions of these venues. In 1718, a letter to *The Spectator* complained of customers who came to Indian Houses where 'women officiate' and did not buy anything, preferring to only drink pots of tea.[145] In the 1697 play *The innocent mistress a comedy*, the character Sir Charles remarks that 'I have an Entertainment of excellent Musick promised me this afternoon, you know I cannot have it at home, so I have borrowed some Apartments of obliging Mrs. Bantum, the Indian Woman, and will try to prevail with the Ladies to come.'[146] Presumably these 'apartments' were somewhere within the shop. The probate inventory of the aforementioned unidentified testatrix who died in 1682 provides a glimpse of what apartments in an Indian house looked like. In addition to a 'China room' and a kitchen full of utensils for boiling and serving tea, her house contained a parlour with several large and small tables. Hanging on the wall were 'small India Pictures', and there was 'one Globe' of the world in the room too.[147] This room was very much a display of worldly connections to the East Indies and to elite clientele. Perhaps it looked something like the rooms of the dolls' house of Petronella Oortman, which depicts the interiors of a middle/upper-class household in late seventeenth-century Amsterdam, filled with East-Indies goods such as lacquerware furniture, porcelain and textiles (see Fig. 3.22).

Fig. 3.22 *Dolls' house of Petronella Oortman (detail), c. 1686–1710. Rijksmuseum Amsterdam, BK-NM-1010. The contents of this doll house reflect the interiors of middle/upper-class households in late seventeenth-century Amsterdam, filled with East-Indies goods. Its contents were made to scale using authentic materials. The doll house was assembled by Petronella Oortman, the wife of merchant Johannes Brandt. The kitchen contains miniature porcelain wares made in China and Japan; a lacquerware cabinet stands in the bedroom to the bottom-right; and Indian chintz furnishes several rooms.*

Meeting in secret to plot espionage or coups or write political documents in public meeting places such as taverns was not unusual in the seventeenth century.[148] According to the Earl of Nottingham, Jane Potter was certainly acquainted with one of the key plotters of the Glorious Revolution, the so-called 'immortal seven' who wrote and signed the letter that was sent to William and Mary, inviting them to invade England. He went on to write that 'my lord Devonshire has got Mrs Potter to be laundress', presumably in his household. Devonshire was almost certainly William Cavendish, Duke of Devonshire, a member of the immortal seven who wrote the letter to William and Mary. If Nottingham's letter is true, it shows the power those female retailers with vast social connections and popular premises, which were often associated with shopping, frivolity and novelty – making them ideal for political intrigues – had in the late seventeenth century. It was Jane's work as a milliner and then Indian woman that saw her move in the same social circles as the immortal seven.

Jane Potter's supposed involvement with the plot to bring Mary and William to England, which sparked the Glorious Revolution, did not win her many favours with the queen. After noting her new position as a laundress, Nottingham went on to say that 'she [Potter] has not much countenance of the queen, her daughter still keeping the Indian house her mother had'.[149] Certainly, all the other Indian women mentioned in this letter – except Jane Potter – appear in Mary II's surviving household accounts. Perhaps Mary II had been made aware of Jane's reputation with the Thynne marriage or her ambitious social climbing? Or, like her experience at the theatre, might the queen have wished to remain detached from the circumstances that put her on the throne? This is unclear. What we do know is that Jane Potter died in Saint James Westminster, Middlesex in 1698. Her will indicates that she was quite wealthy and well connected due to her trade in millinery and East Indies goods. The executors of her will were peers, politicians and 'Gentlemen'. Her estate, worth thousands of pounds, was to be divided up between her two daughters, Elizabeth and Mary, one of whom, as noted by Nottingham, continued to run her Indian House.[150] Like Mary Devet, whose daughter Sarah Craddock also worked in her Indian House, for the Potters this business was a family affair passed from mother to daughter(s).

For these women, their work was about more than just providing for their families. The reputations and connections they were able to foster through their businesses gave them social prestige and power within the fashion marketplace and within the court. In the case of the Glorious Revolution, Jane Potter also claimed that it gave her a stake in national politics. However, the continued success of their businesses also hinged on their ability to remain in favour, or, in the case of Elizabeth Graydon, for their main patron to remain a royal favourite. Thus, fame and business success was fickle and required a successful milliner to be adept at cultivating the right types of relationships with the right types of people.

Conclusions

The evolving fashion marketplace of the Stuart period saw the growth of women in key trades such as millinery. However, the success of the female milliner by the early eighteenth century was not an inevitability. The early Stuart accounts show that textile and fashion retail trades were initially dominated by tradesmen who leveraged their connections to London's Companies and international trade networks, to build wealth and influence, often becoming key figures in City politics and creditors to the monarchy.

Over the seventeenth century, the fashion marketplace shifted geographically and demographically. As shopping districts moved to the West End, closer to the fashion-hungry court, and tradespeople began operating outside the control of London's traditional Companies, female milliners with fashionable shopping premises established themselves as essential suppliers of fashionable small wares. Driven by busy decoration, novelty in French fashion and the desire for the latest goods from the East Indies, by the late seventeenth century milliners expanded their roles, acting as one-stop shops for fashionable consumers, especially other women.

Although women never outnumbered men among royal suppliers, their growing and well-known presence reshaped the marketplace. Their success was more than just economic. As the visible faces of fashion, their work also brought them social prestige and advancement and, in some cases, allowed them to partake in significant political events of the time such as the Glorious Revolution. Such success, though, was not without risks. The cases of tradeswomen such as Elizabeth Graydon and Jane Potter emphasize how closely tied their fortunes were to the patronage and support of their elite female clients, many of whom were influential court women such as the Mistress of the Robes. The stories of the women to be found in the Stuart queens' accounts demonstrates the business savvy of early successful milliners who fostered the right connections among the court to build family enterprises in the fashion marketplace.

4

Making: Seamstresses, silkwomen and the rise of the mantua-maker

The creation of garments for the Stuart queens required the use of many materials and the labour of many hands. Fabrics, trimmings and haberdashery were usually purchased by the Office of the Robes before being distributed to a smaller number of makers who worked with their needles to turn these supplies into both every-day and fashionable dress.[1] The seventeenth century marked a profound shift in making practices in England as garments went from primarily being made by seamstresses and generalist tailors to a diverse array of specialists by the end of the century, in both bespoke and ready-made forms. Significantly, the role that women played as makers of clothing was permanently altered. Royal household papers bore witness to this transition. Not only do these documents contain many references to women who made their living via their needles, but they show that by the early eighteenth century, women dominated the making of elite women's clothing and accessories (see Fig. 0.3). Generally, for much of the sixteenth and seventeenth centuries outer dress was made by male-dominated professions such as tailoring. However, during the seventeenth century significant numbers of women began to expand their work into making outerwear for other women. This gave rise to the mantua-maker, a female profession that carried on throughout the eighteenth, nineteenth and twentieth centuries.[2] Like the milliner, the origins of the mantua-maker and their training in seventeenth-century England is still somewhat obscure.

Clare Haru Crowston's ground-breaking study of the female *couturières* guilds in late seventeenth-century France has often been cited when discussing the mantua-maker in the English context. Her study shows that women in Aix-en-Provence, Paris and Rouen won the right to form their own guilds and to make most women's outer clothing, including the mantua gown, during the 1670s.[3] Unlike France, many English guilds did not formally acknowledge the apprenticing and involvement of female mantua-makers. John Styles has noted that during the 1690s the York Merchant Tailors Guild tried to prevent mantua-makers from working in the city, rallying support from other towns, including Newcastle and Hull, but they were unsuccessful.[4] Pam Inder has examined other regional guilds, such as those in Bristol and Chester, who also sought to limit women's participation in the making of female dress at the turn of the eighteenth century.[5] While many English guilds sought to exclude women who were not widows carrying on the business of a former male member, the pragmatic need to retain paying Company members appears to have paved the way for the formal apprenticing of girls in trades such as tailoring in London by the mid-seventeenth century, and by the early eighteenth century, many women worked outside the city and the control of its guilds. Thus, the birth of the mantua-maker in England occurred in quite different circumstances to those in France.

This chapter complicates neat ideas about women's triumph over the tailoring guilds by using the Stuart queens' household accounts to reassess this significant transition in women's work during the seventeenth century. The Office of the Robes was a dynamic institution that responded to changes in the fashion marketplace in London. At a time when studies have shown that many women faced a hostile reception by English guilds and traditional male spaces attempted to limit female participation in the making of clothing, the royal household accounts demonstrate that there were many female makers in London, both English and French, who were patronized by the Stuart queens and other elite women. I refer to all these tradeswomen collectively using the modern term *female dressmakers*, although, as this chapter will show, they had varied training backgrounds and diverse trade identities at the time.

The queens' accounts demonstrate the rise of these women in the fashion marketplace and the ambiguous occupational identities they held as they competed for patronage alongside tailors. These women relied on their knowledge and training in seamstressing, tailoring and other needlecrafts, as well as the patronage of elite women, for their initial success and the eventual solidification of their place in the eighteenth-century fashion marketplace. Significantly, this chapter also shows the pivotal role that migrant French *couturières* played in training the first generation of English mantua-makers. This forces us to rethink the gendered skills associated with different professions, the role of skilled female migrants in London's marketplace and the influence of women makers on not only the clothing of the Stuart queens, but seventeenth-century English fashions more widely.

Seamstresses, silkwomen and embroiderers to the Stuart queens

Work in the fashion trades formed the occupational identities of many men, and formal patterns of training and work were often heavily guarded and regulated by institutions such as guilds. Informally, though, women had always played a significant role in making clothing for people in medieval and early modern England. Women often performed domestic needlework and made body and household linens for their families or employers.[6] They also worked alongside male family members in textile-related trades, could be employed to do piecework or sew ready-made wares and even took over tailoring businesses as widows.[7] When women did work professionally making clothing (that is, as a skilled artisan working for payment) the trade title usually ascribed to them was seamstress. The seamstress was a woman who worked primarily with linen sewing underclothes such as shifts, accessories that clothed the neck and head, such as those sold by milliners, as well as household linens (see Fig. 4.1). Another skilled trade for women was that of the silkwoman. Silkwomen appear in English records from the fourteenth to early seventeenth centuries. They often worked individually, or alongside male relatives who identified as either silkmen or mercers, to make and supply items of silk

Fig. 4.1 *Wallerant Vaillant,* The Seamstress, *c. 1658–77, print. Rijksmuseum Amsterdam, RP-P 1910-6822.*

such as *passementerie* and certain types of haberdashery, as well as fine linen and silk accessories for the head, neck and wrists.[8] Many of these women worked in the home, a space they claimed cultivated the 'natural, divinely-ordained and ethically nurturing work of women', which allowed them to circumvent the London guild system.[9]

In contrast to these female professions, the tailor was usually male and made outer garments from wool, silk and leather. Both trades were essential for clothing the early modern body but took on fundamentally different roles that required unique skillsets. The seamstress was skilled at using small, sturdy stitches that could withstand the harsh washing of linen at the time. She did not work with paper patterns; rather, she divided, folded and cut lengths of fabric into the required shapes for garments and household goods.[10] Tailoring, on the other hand, required a knowledge of complex pattern cutting and the shaping of non-fabric materials such as pasteboard, whalebone and horsehair.[11] These trades also sat unevenly in the fashion marketplace: tailoring required a formal apprenticeship and membership of a guild, while seamstresses and silkwomen, although skilled, did not undertake formal apprenticeships and did not have their own guilds.

These differing trade identities are assumed to have been quite rigid: silkwomen and seamstresses were always female and tailors always male, and they were defined by the types of wares that they made. However, as Susan North has noted, information about silkwomen and seamstresses is 'sparse' as their professions lacked the 'official documentation associated with the occupations of men' such as apprenticeship and guild records.[12] The queens' accounts not only provide more information about the work of silkwomen and seamstresses in the seventeenth century, but they also nuance these trade descriptions and reveal the ambiguity between men and women's work in the fashion trades of London at this time.

Before the mid-seventeenth century, most female makers in the royal household accounts were described as seamstresses or silkwomen, and these women both made and mended clothing (see Chapter 5). Anna of Denmark had several seamstresses during her reign, including 'Elizabeth Price of London Seamster' and a woman named Dorothy Speckard.[13] While their itemized bills submitted to Anna of Denmark's Robes have not survived, it is possible to infer what these women made as Speckard had previously worked in Elizabeth I's Great Wardrobe in the period 1601–3. There she was recorded as making smocks, cauls, handkerchiefs, veils, ruffs and rebato wires, and sleeves decorated with needlework and cutwork, as well as washing and starching items (see Fig. 4.2).[14] It seems that Speckard also carried out similar work for Anna, as she is noted to have made, starched and mended linen sheets and other necessities for the queen's childbed.[15] Trying to ascribe a single trade identity to Dorothy Speckard is difficult, as in the queen's accounts she is sometimes labelled a seamstress and other times she is named a silkwoman. Anne Sutton has observed that 'silkwomen rarely called themselves silkwomen' and this may account for the varying descriptions given of Dorothy in the accounts.[16] The royal accounts demonstrate that as commissioned makers, the professional identities of silkwomen

Fig. 4.2 *Embroidered coif of linen worked with silk and metal thread and spangles, c. 1600–30, British. Metropolitan Museum of Art New York, 64.101.1242.*

and seamstresses were quite malleable, with much overlap in the types of garments they made. Thus, the goods that she supplied to the queen's household at any given time seem to have dictated how she was recorded.

The goods supplied by another silkwoman, named Hester le Telier, also demonstrates the overlap in the work of the seamstress and silkwoman. In addition to 'lawn cambric', she also supplied 'needlework purles bone lace and [other] such like'.[17] Anna's accounts also mention a woman named Livia White, 'widow', who supplied the queen with a fashionable embroidered waistcoat of cambric linen 'wrought with gold and silver' and 'a petticoat of white Taffeta embroidered all over with gold, silver, and Sundry coloured Silkes'.[18] Intricately embroidered waistcoats were very characteristic of late Elizabethan and Jacobean fashions, and the one mentioned in White's bill probably resembled a slightly later example now held by the Museum of Fine Arts in Boston (see Fig. 4.3). White could have been an embroiderer, or she could have been a silkwoman who both made and embroidered waistcoats and petticoats.[19]

Fig. 4.3 *Woman's waistcoat of linen embroidered with metallic threads and spangles and decorated with metallic bobbin lace, c. 1610–15, English. The Elizabeth Day McCormick Collection, Museum of Fine Arts Boston, 43.243.*

During the reign of Henrietta Maria, the trade title of 'silkwoman' disappeared, although 'silkman' was retained and used to describe suppliers of fine silk fabrics.[20] However, women continued to carry on this type of work. A Frenchwoman named Madame Du Val Cocquilliere regularly delivered 'morning head dressings', linen mantles, coifs, girdles and lengths of starched cypress to the queen's Robes during the 1630s.[21] By the late seventeenth century, as discussed in Chapter 3, this work would form a key part of the trade of the female milliner. Lacewomen such as Katherine Mulys, who supplied Lady Anne, Mary II, William III and others, was also described as supplying fine laces and 'needlework strings', as well as making up cuffs and sleeves that contained these elements, much like earlier silkwomen had done.[22]

Embroidery, which was also done by silkwomen, was a professional trade controlled by the Company of Broderers in the early seventeenth century. Those named as embroiderers in the early Stuart queens' accounts were always men; however, as the seventeenth century progressed, more women began to enter this trade with the encouragement of elite women. Mary II's accounts contain the reference to a female embroiderer, named Elizabeth Lee.[23] Such a position being given to a woman may have been due to the queen herself; in 1696 it was claimed that Mary II had given 'great Encouragement to all kind of Works with the Needle' and supported the employment of women in these trades.[24] During the reign of Queen Anne all of her embroiderers were women, reflecting not only a change in the demographics of the profession but also likely the queen's personal preference that encouraged the work of these women, as her sister had done (see Appendix I, Table 6). Thus, although the trade of the silkwoman disappeared by the mid-seventeenth century, their practices did not. Instead, these skillsets were continued by seamstresses or taken up by female milliners and embroiderers.

While guild records, literature and other published texts overwhelmingly cast the job of working with linen as women's work, both Elizabeth I and Anna of Denmark's accounts show that at the turn of the seventeenth century, men could do this work too.[25] Roger Mountague, the husband of Elizabeth I's silkwoman Alice Mountague, and silkman to James I, was also described as making linen smocks and coifs, in addition to silk headwear and garters for the Tudor queen.[26] Anna's accounts also record payment to a Mr Francis Britaine, 'sempster', although a record of what he made has not survived.[27] Besides these references, there are no other male sempsters that appear in the accounts. By the reign of Queen Henrietta Maria, only women such as Alice Waggit and Ann Davenport who worked with linen were named as seamstresses.[28] The Stuart kings also employed female seamstresses to make their linens. However, the presence of Montague and Britaine highlight that we should be wary of making rigid assumptions about the gendered natures of trades.

Throughout her nearly thirty-year stay in England as consort and then dowager, Catherine of Braganza had several seamstresses who made and mended her clothing, such as Mrs Hemden and Barbara Anna de Calvaert.[29] Calvaert's bills reveal what was typically made by a seamstress for elite women by the 1680s. This ranged from basic everyday undergarments, such as shifts and socks, to accessories including bands, ruffles and *engageantes*, handkerchiefs, aprons and night rails, and even fashionable headwear also sold by milliners, such as coifs, cornets, night caps, surtouts and 'suits of head clothes' (see Fig. 3.11). Household linens such as towels, pillowbears and sheets were also made.[30] All these objects were made from linen or cotton fabrics delivered into the Office of the Robes by the linen draper Matthias Cupper.[31] Linen goods such as cornets, pinners and coifs were also supplied by the laceman William Rutland, who had a shop at the Royal Exchange. Given the nature of Rutland's business selling different types of lace, he presumably had his own team of seamstresses working for him.[32]

Fig. 4.4 *Bernard Picart,* Five women wearing the latest fontange fashions, *1703, etching. Rijksmuseum Amsterdam, RP-P-1944-435.*

In the early eighteenth century, women who were explicitly named as seamstresses in the household accounts of Queen Anne and other courtiers still dealt exclusively with linen goods.[33] Mary Godde and a 'Mrs Duran' both made linen shifts and smocks, nightclothes, ruffles, cuffs, tuckers and sleeves, as well as 'heads' for the queen. 'Heads', which were commonly mentioned alongside charges for 'starching' and 'wires', referred to the fashionable *fontange* or top-knot headdress (see Fig. 4.4).[34] This headdress was a defining accessory of the period and consisted of a linen cap trimmed with lace and ribbons with two hanging lappets that were supported by a wire frame known as a *commode*. These long lappets are visible in the previously discussed portrait of Mary II (see Fig. 1.16). All those explicitly named as seamstresses in the queens' accounts during the seventeenth century were therefore women who primarily made linen goods. However, there were several women whose occupation was not labelled in the accounts and this, as the follow section argues, is likely due to the expanding repertoire of garments that women began to make in the final quarter of the seventeenth century.

Later women makers and their ambiguous occupational identities

In England, all of Anna of Denmark's gowns were made by her master tailor, James Duncane, from 1603 until at least 1617. Henrietta Maria's outer clothing was also made by her two male tailors: George Gelin, who came with her from France in 1625; and Jacques Bardou, who took over in 1636 (see Appendix I, Tables 1–2). However, by the 1680s traditional modes of production began to change as the firm line between seamstress and tailor began to blur. In 1688, Randle Holme remarked that 'very often the Seamster occupieth the room and place of a Taylor in furnishing the Nobility and Gentry with such conveniences as serve the whole body, especially in the Summer season'.[35] This statement by Holme likely refers to the mantua-maker who had begun to make new, fashionable loose gowns and mantos (see Fig. 4.5). The queen's accounts show that alongside tailors, and eventually without them, women were beginning to make this new style of gown, as well as a variety of other outer garments that had previously been associated with the work of the male tailor. All these women were referred to in the household accounts as 'Mrs', the prefix standing for Mistress, here referring to social rather than marital status, indicating she taught or governed servants or apprentices.[36] It is tempting to call these women mantua-makers, and, indeed, they did make everything that Robert Campbell later noted in the eighteenth century was 'her [the mantua-maker's] business'.[37] However, unlike silkwomen, seamstresses and tailors, or even female retailers such as milliners, in many of their bills these women were not given occupational labels.[38]

One of Catherine of Braganza's dressmakers, a French woman named Mary Mandove, exemplifies this ambiguity. While the garments she made have not survived, her material presence in the Office of

Fig. 4.5 *Dieu de Saint Jean,* Femme de qualité en deshabille desté *[Woman of quality in informal summer dress],* c. 1676–83, hand-coloured etching. Rijksmuseum Amsterdam, RP-P-2009-1098. *This gown is similar to those featured in the* Extraordinaire du Mercure galant *as the latest fashion for spring 1678.*

the Robes was left via her bills, which list not only what she made but give her name in her own hand, as her signature in French-style script reads *Marie Mandou* (see Fig. 4.6). In the queen's accounts, her occupational title is never specified. This is despite, or maybe because of, the fact that she made a wide range of garments for the queen (see Fig. 4.7). While one bill does note that she was a maker of 'mantos', it does not specifically label her a mantua-maker.[39] Another document, a debenture recording

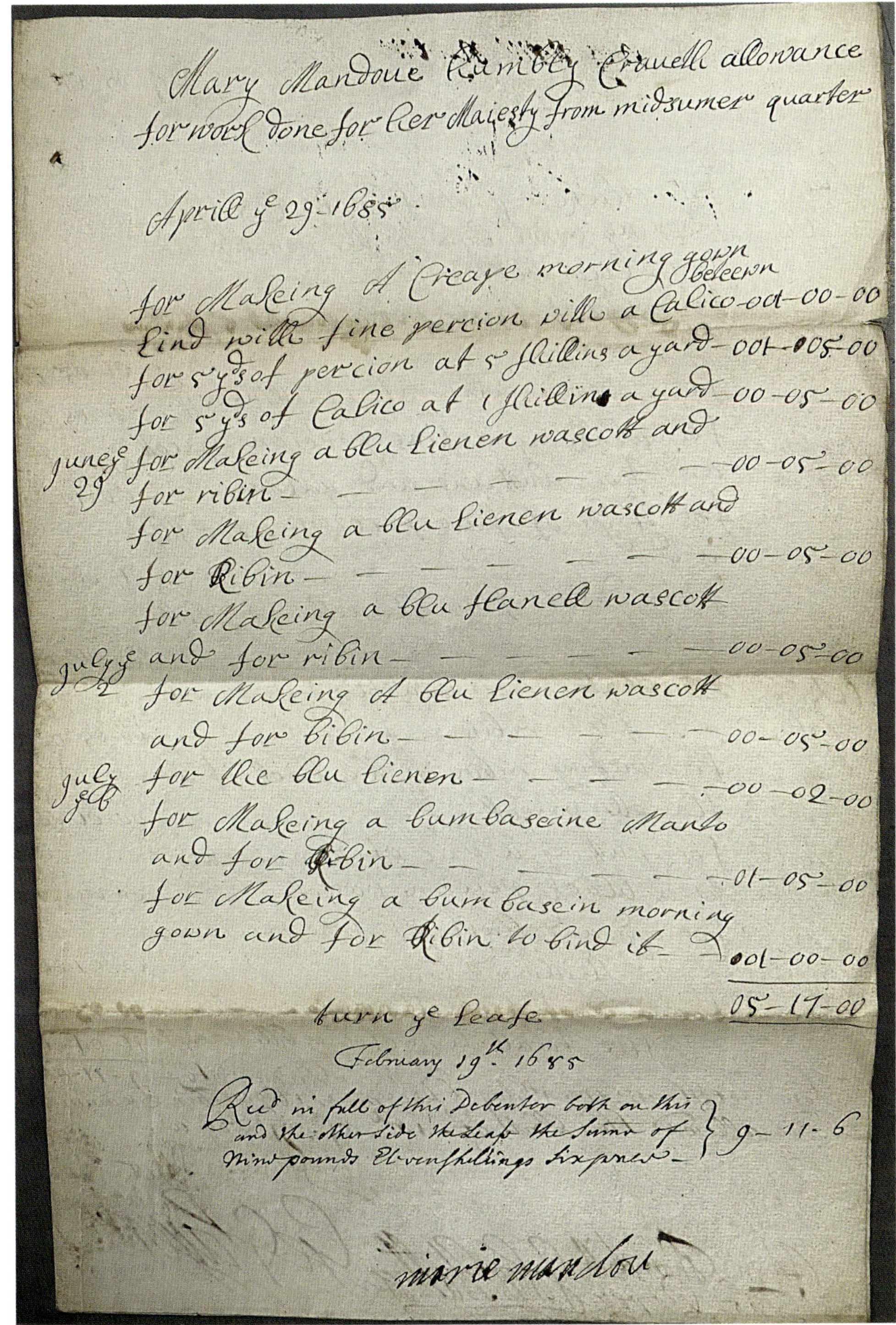

Fig. 4.6 *Bill from Mary Mandove with her signature (Marie Mandou), Midsummer Quarter, 1685. The National Archives of the UK, LR 5/76.*

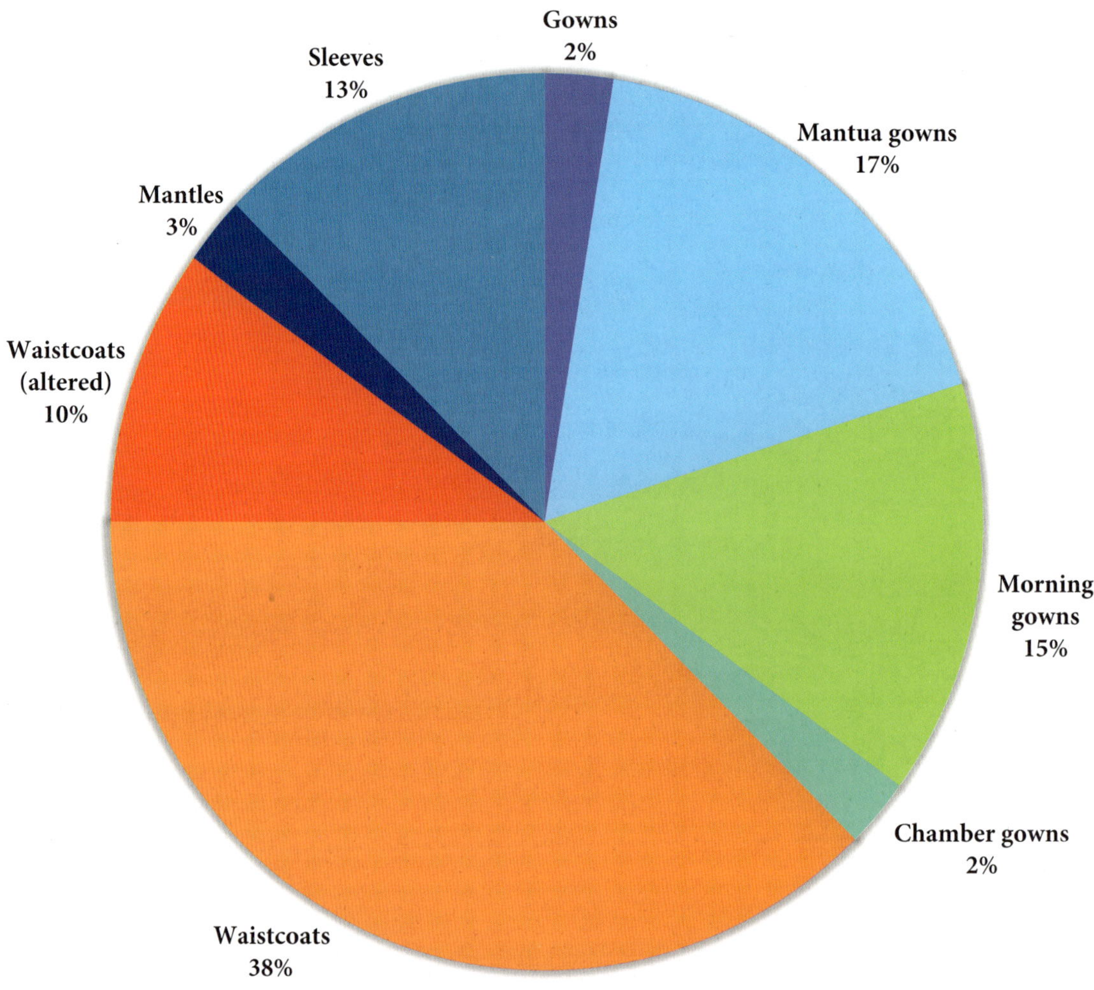

Fig. 4.7 *Garments made by Mary Mandove for Catherine of Braganza, 1684–6. Data source: TNA: LR 5/76–79.*

sums owed to tradesmen, called her a 'tailor'.[40] Additionally, in Edward Chamberlayne's *Present State of England* (1684) it was noted that in the queen's household there was a 'Mrs Mary Mandove' who was an 'Indian Gown-maker'. Indian gowns were made for the Stuart kings by their tailors, and by the 1670s shops run by Indian gown-makers, usually men, also began to appear in London. One such gown-maker was Edward Gunn, who stocked men's gowns, women's 'gowns', morning gowns, waistcoats, mantles and petticoats when he died in 1672.[41] Mary's bills show that while she did supply East Indies textiles and make morning and chamber gowns, which likely resembled a miniature example on the fashion doll known as 'Lady Clapham', now in the Victoria and Albert Museum (see Fig. 4.8), such gowns were not the main staple of her work for the queen.[42]

Fig. 4.8 *Doll's Undress Gown of Italian or French salmon pink satin with a floral pattern, lined with blue Chinese silk damask, c. 1690–1700, English. Victoria and Albert Museum London, T.846Q-1974. At the time of its making, this garment could have been called a morning or night gown, a chamber gown or an Indian Gown.*

The ambiguity surrounding Mary's occupational title, and her making of a variety of garments associated with both male and female trades, demonstrates the flexible nature of women's artisanal identities during the final decades of the seventeenth century. This was a time when women began to make garments that had previously been associated with tailoring, and so they did not fit neatly into pre-existing trade descriptions.[43] During the 1680s, Catherine of Braganza's Robes patronized another French woman, named Jane Heath (*Jeanne Haite*), who was, at least once, explicitly referred to as a mantua-maker. Two other women with ambiguous occupational identities were also employed to make Catherine's outer clothing. The first was another French woman, named Mary Alexander, who made waistcoats for the queen.[44] The second was an Englishwoman, named Anne Morgan, who regularly made 'her Majesty's Petty Coates' and aprons and supplied yards of ribbons (see Fig. 2.9). Although Morgan's occupational title is not given in her bills, she was also labelled a 'tailor' in a summary of debts owed to tradespeople in 1684.[45] Another woman explicitly named as a 'tailor' was an Englishwoman named Ellen Becker, who was patronized by Queen Mary II.[46] Like Morgan, Becker appears to have specialized in making petticoats. As explained in Chapter 1, petticoats were one of the most numerous garments in all the later Stuart queen's wardrobes; one of Becker's bills detailing work completed for Mary II between April and December 1694 contains forty petticoats and nothing else.[47]

By the middle of the eighteenth century, the making of petticoats was the job of the mantua-maker.[48] However, in the later Stuart queens' accounts, these garments were made by seamstresses, tailors, dressmakers and, increasingly, those who were labelled petticoat-makers. There is some evidence from earlier in the seventeenth century which suggests that petticoat-making had been a specialization within the tailoring trade, and later in the eighteenth-century there are some references to men who specialized in this too.[49] The royal accounts make clear, though, that it was not until the late seventeenth century that 'petticoat-maker' became an established trade identity for women. This was likely due to the nature of outer petticoats worn with gowns during this period.

By the second half of the seventeenth century, petticoats were comparatively simple garments to construct. They were made from panels of fabrics that were joined together and pleated or gathered into a waistband that was tied or fastened at the back. A surviving petticoat made of floral silk damask that was recovered from HMS *Gloucester*, which sank in 1682, gives an idea of what this garment may have looked like in the early 1680s, and it is constructed according to the above description (see Fig. 4.9).

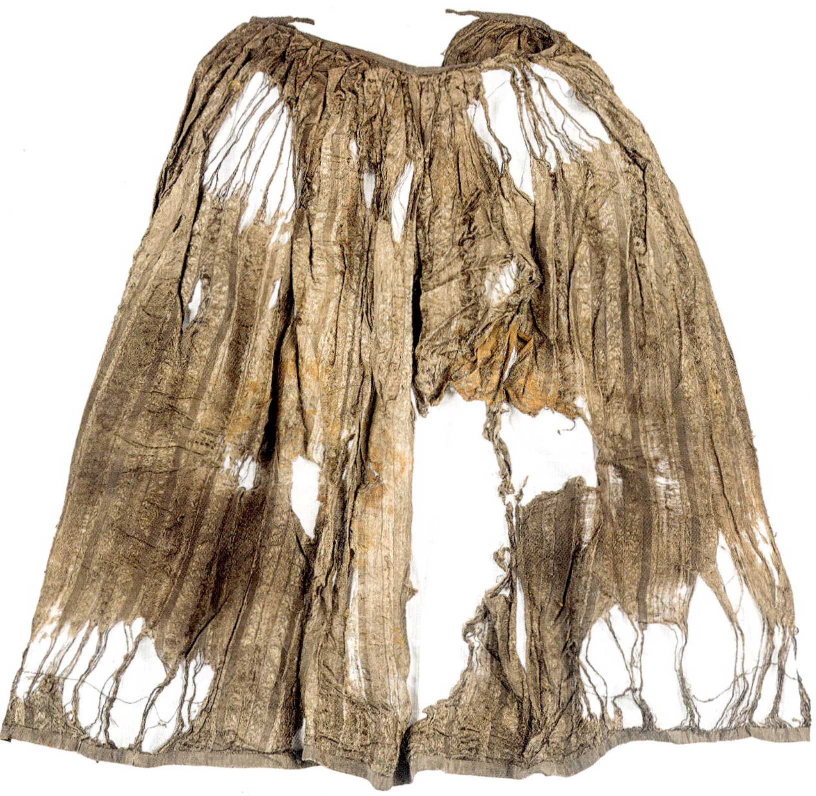

Fig. 4.9 *Petticoat of floral silk damask, recovered from the wreck of HMS* Gloucester, c. *1670–82, English.*

While the construction of petticoats was relatively straightforward, these items of clothing often carried much of the busy decoration of the period. The effigy of the famous Stuart court beauty, Frances Stuart, Duchess of Richmond and Lennox, who died in 1702, is clothed in five petticoats (see Fig. 4.10). These range from, in order of layers, a petticoat of flannel, then worsted, then silk, then worsted and, finally, an outer petticoat of silk tabby brocade decorated with metallic lace and braid.[50] The petticoat-maker not only produced numerous types of petticoats, but they quilted and trimmed them too.[51] In her bills, Anne Morgan is often described as altering petticoats by 'putting on the Lace and fringe' as well as 'ribanding' them, meaning to decorate or adorn with ribbons. As explained in the previous chapter, petticoats at this time were highly ornamented with yards of trims, and the application of these decorations would have taken just as long, if not longer, than the actual construction of the garment itself (see Fig. 3.9).

Some early dressmakers and petticoat-makers were involved in millinery and related trades. The dressmaker Mary Alexander also supplied Catherine of Braganza with ribbon, gloves, buttons and garters.[52] Details from a court case in 1684 involving Alexander reveals that in addition to making clothing, she had also ventured into the 'buying, selling and bartering of all goods and Commodities', just like those female retailers explored in the previous chapter.[53] These records show the crossovers between many fashion trades, as the training and business ambitions of some women saw them dabble in multiple practices. This was an evolving space where these women defied categories that had divided the clothing trades – often along gendered lines – in the earlier part of the Stuart period.

The effigy of Frances Stuart is dressed in the robes that the duchess wore to Queen Anne's coronation that same year. While the crimson robes are typical of such garments, her petticoat shows the fashions of the early eighteenth century: it is made from silk tabby brocade and appears to be an early type of bizarre silk. It is trimmed with metallic bobbin lace and woven metallic braid. Original ruffles or engageants made by seamstresses are also visible around the bottom of her elbow-length sleeves.

It was not until Queen Anne's reign that the title 'petticoat-maker' was regularly used and that this female occupational identity was solidified. This was due to two reasons: the aforementioned decoration of petticoats and also the rise of the stiffened hoop petticoat that required specialized skills and materials.[54] During her twelve-year reign, Queen Anne had two petticoat-makers.[55] The first was Elizabeth Banks, who held the position until her death in 1705.[56] Banks was replaced by a woman named Susannah Hawker. Records from the Office of the Robes document a significant life event for Susannah and one that can often make the lives of female artisans hard to trace in the historical record: her marriage. In a transcription for a bill dated 1710, the yeoman had noted, 'Mrs Hawkers bill – now Mrs Young'.[57] Westminster marriage records confirm that on 10 July 1710 a 'Mrs Susanna Hocker' had married John Young of Middlesex at Knightsbridge Holy Trinity, which was close to Kensington Palace, where she made regular trips to the queen. On 10 June 1714 their daughter Susanna Young was baptized, but the infant's death was recorded a week later.[58] Common life-changing events for women

Fig. 4.10 *Funeral effigy of Frances Stuart, Duchess of Richmond and Lennox, 1702, Westminster Abbey.*

such as marriage, reproduction and the loss of a child clearly did not affect their business or occupational identities. Susannah continued to work for the Office of the Robes and her last period of work for the queen was from July 1713 to July 1714, before the queen's death on 1 August 1714.[59]

By the beginning of Queen Anne's reign in 1702, the place of the mantua-maker had also been cemented within fashionable society and the royal court. During her reign, the queen had a 'manto maker' named Anne Clifton. Little has survived of Anne's early life. It is not clear where she received her training, whether she was formally apprenticed or to whom. Where we can begin to trace her career is from the point of her marriage; in 1670 Anne Follensbee married Thomas Clifton at St James's church, Clerkenwell, Islington.[60] While Thomas is recorded in 1702 as accepting payment from the Office of the Robes on Anne's behalf, guild and probate records indicate that he may have actually been a tallow chandler in the Bowyer's Company of London. Her husband's professional identity clearly did not restrict Anne's work as a mantua-maker; it is plausible that she traded using *feme sole* status, as many others like her did. Thomas's will, made upon his death in 1710, shows that at this time they resided in St Martin-in-the-Fields in Middlesex, which was close to Whitehall and St James's Palace, and they were surrounded by neighbours and friends who were also involved in the fashion trades, such as tailors and shoemakers.[61]

The emergence of 'petticoat-makers' and 'mantua-makers' in the final decade of the seventeenth century marks a significant shift in the recognition of women's artisanal identities, as their skilled labour began to be labelled and distinguished beyond the general designation of seamstress. Across early modern Europe, men were more likely to be identified by their work; this shows how, both socially and economically, work officially defined the public lives of men much more than women. Anna Bellavitis has remarked that 'women's activities were often defined in terms of "doing" rather than "being"', attesting to the transient nature of paid work for women, who often balanced it with family responsibilities.[62] Tawny Paul has also observed that while work provided 'a central component of masculine selfhood' in the early modern period, 'occupational plurality was the norm' and it was common for individuals within households to diversify work and income streams.[63] As the tables in Appendix I demonstrate, women were much more likely to be recorded as being paid 'for work done', 'for making' or 'for goods', compared to men who were usually labelled as tailors, hosiers, haberdashers, mercers and so forth.[64]

Now we must consider that the way that the Office of the Robes chose to describe these artisans and how they described themselves might have differed. This is especially true in accounts like those of Queen Anne, where bills were transcribed into a separate manuscript, which is what has survived. Still, this speaks to the late Stuart period as one of great transformation and flux in London, and in Northwestern Europe more widely. One where a changing consumer culture saw a great increase in the variety and sheer amount of goods available, as well as the prevalence of ready-made clothing and the influx of women into trades in both official and unofficial capacities. This irreparably changed patterns of work within the fashion marketplace and led to the modern consumer culture of the eighteenth and nineteenth centuries. By 1702, Queen Anne's primary dressmakers were always labelled 'petticoat-makers' and 'mantua-makers'. Significantly, this shows that this work was not just a thing women did, but that by the early eighteenth century it was a recognized female professional identity that was given an occupational title, in the same way that seamstress was, or that silkwoman had been during the sixteenth century.

Changing patterns of work in the Robes and in the City

The papers in the Office of the Robes capture a subset of suppliers and makers within London's fashion marketplace who serviced networks of elite clients in the growing West End. As discussed in the previous chapter, although tradeswomen were increasingly permitted to be apprenticed in London's Companies, they were still treated differently to male members and given fewer rights.[65] For Queen Anne's dressmakers, Anne Clifton and Susannah Young, Company membership and a location in the old City would have held little appeal and so they based themselves in Middlesex, close to Kensington Palace where the queen usually resided while in London. These dressmakers would have been able to reach the palaces of Whitehall, St James's and Somerset House on foot. As such, their bills only ever claimed compensation for carriage travel to those residences further afield, such as Hampton Court and Windsor, when they did fittings or delivered goods.[66]

During the seventeenth century, English makers, particularly those who catered to elite clientele, increasingly competed with French artisans, many of whom were part of the growing diaspora of skilled French Huguenots who fled France during the reign of Louis XIV. The Office of the Robes accounts record several foreign artisans. Queens such as Henrietta Maria had employed French tailors and she placed them outside the traditional square-mile of London's Companies and their control; for example, George Gelin was recorded as 'dwelling in the Strand' in 1631.[67] Catherine of Braganza also patronized several London-based French artisans in addition to sourcing items directly from France. Her tailor during the 1670s appears to have been French, as he was referred to as 'Luis Roche' or 'La Roche' in the accounts.[68] By the 1680s, she had a Huguenot tailor, Peter Lombard, who resided in St Martin-in-the-Fields, and her French dressmakers Jane Heath and Mary Alexander also lived in St Martin-in-the-Fields and the parish of St Paul in Covent Garden, respectively (see Fig. 3.2).

By the 1670s, several 'French Taylors & other Foreigners' had set up shop in the City of London and its surrounds, much to the opposition of native-born makers.[69] English guilds, including London's livery companies, had traditionally been hostile to foreign 'alien' tradespeople, particularly in times of economic distress. Migrants were often denied admission into the Companies, or, if they were admitted, they were rarely given the same privileges as English artisans.[70] Thus, it is unsurprising that many migrant artisans appear to have resided, whether by choice or necessity, outside the traditional City mile and outside of the record-keeping practices of the Livery Companies. However, through the

Office of the Robes accounts we can begin to build a fuller picture of the work of tradespeople usually excluded by the Livery Companies, such as women and migrants.

While women's work, both within and outside the guilds, was beginning to become more 'structured, regulated and valued' in London during the late seventeenth century, female dressmakers did not fully displace tailors until the reign of Queen Anne.[71] The tailor Peter Lombard is predominately recorded as making and altering petticoats, 'under bodies' (stays) and older-style gowns with stiffened bodices for Catherine of Braganza. Although Lombard still made most of the queen's clothing, the majority of mantos, morning gowns and waistcoats were made by the queen's female dressmakers (see Fig. 4.11). In fact, it was Jane Heath, the only dressmaker in Catherine's accounts to be referred to explicitly as a 'manto maker', who made almost all the queen's mantos, as well as some nightgowns. Additionally, cloaks and 'gowns', likely mantos or loose gowns, made of flowered silks, calicoes and Florence sarcenet were also supplied by a 'John Barne Gownman' in 1686.[72] This demonstrates that a range of tradespeople, both men and women, were plying their needles in the making of mantos during the final decades of the seventeenth century.

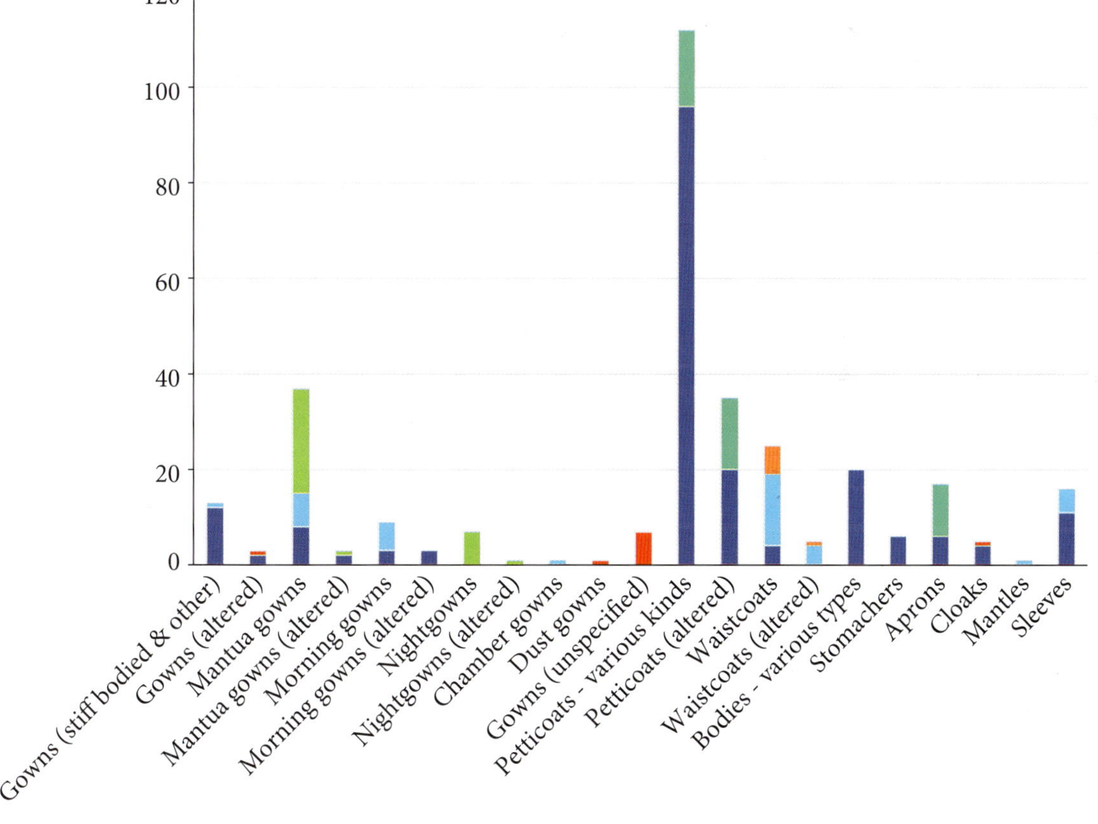

Fig. 4.11 *Garments made for Catherine of Braganza between 1 October 1684 and 31 March 1688. Data source: TNA: LR 5/76–84.*

The making of petticoats was also shared, as both the tailor Peter Lombard and dressmaker Anne Morgan made these garments for Catherine of Braganza. Morgan was often employed to alter quilted petticoats and to make flannel petticoats. Conversely, Lombard primarily constructed and altered plain petticoats and he also made quilted petticoats. Both, however, made silk petticoats that were trimmed with 'fringe', 'rich embroidery' and 'silver lace', although Lombard's were more usually made as part of a whole outfit that he provided.[73] Mary II's female tailor, Ellen Becker, also shared the making of the queen's garments with her other tailors Gerard (Bert) Small, La Hay and Lombard, as well as the embroiderer Elizabeth Lee. Becker was the only female dressmaker in Mary's surviving accounts, and she is also the only artisan who made elaborately decorated petticoats of silk.[74]

By the early eighteenth century, gendered patterns of work in the Robes had altered dramatically. Most of Queen Anne's fashionable outerwear was made by female mantua-makers and petticoat-makers (see Appendix I, Table 6). Other ceremonial dress such as coronation and Parliament robes, as well as widow's weeds, were also made by a dressmaker named Anne Howe.[75] In fact, the only male makers in Queen Anne's accounts were the stay-makers Antoine Cousein and Mr Gazain, a profession that remained male-dominated until the early nineteenth century. Distinct eighteenth-century patterns of gendered work within the clothing trades had therefore emerged by the end of the Stuart period in England.

It may be tempting to assume that all female dressmakers were paid less than their male counterparts and this is why they posed such a threat to male tailoring guilds. However, where comparisons can be drawn in the queens' accounts, it appears that their dressmakers were paid roughly the same amount as tailors.[76] In June 1687, Jane Heath and Peter Lombard both made mantos for Catherine of Braganza.[77] Heath charged £1 for her labour and Lombard charged £1 5s. for his. However, Lombard's charge also included labour for making a petticoat, which he often valued separately at 5s. in his bills. Both therefore charged £1 for their labour. Mary II's tailor Bert Small charged £1 for making mantos and an extra 3s. for those with 'buttons & loops', as did La Hay.[78]

Buttons and loops (looped cord) were parts of early mantua gowns that held up the gathered train of the gown and secured loose shoulder and cuff pleats, as is visible on a surviving mantua gown dating from 1695–1720 in the National Museum of Copenhagen (see Fig. 4.12).[79] They could also be made from precious gemstones and gold or silver by jewellers; an inventory of Mary II's jewels recorded 'Forty six Loops, and eighteen buttons of Diamonds' in 1694 (see Appendix III).[80]

The mantua-maker Anne Clifton charged £1 for making mantos and between 6d. and 2s. for buttons and loops for Queen Anne at the start of her reign.[81] However, by 1710, Clifton was regularly charging £2 for mantua gowns, such as 'one manto – purple paduasoy – lin'd in the body'.[82] The description of adding lining to the body (bodice) was a new addition to Clifton's bills and it signalled a new way of constructing these gowns. Indeed, the bodices of surviving mantua gowns dated before 1710 tend to be unlined or only partially lined. By the 1730s it was common for all types of mantua

Fig. 4.12 *Detail of loop and button of Mantua Gown of green and gold silk brocade, c. 1695–1720, Danish. Nationalmuseet Danmark, 242786.*

gowns to have lined bodices.[83] Lining in the bodices of mantua gowns only became common in Anne's accounts after 1710, and it appears that mantua-makers at this time began to charge more for this additional, more time-consuming step. Other construction techniques that began to incur an extra charge during Anne's reign included 'new Robing a green & yellow satin manto', referring to replacing or altering the folds on the front-opening edges of the mantua gown, which Clifton also charged an additional 2s. 6d. for.[84] We can therefore trace the evolving styles of these gowns through the charges listed in these accounts.

When it came to morning gowns, nightgowns and chamber gowns, prices charged for making were roughly the same during the 1680s but fell substantially after that. In midsummer 1685, both Mandove and Lombard submitted bills to the queen's household requesting payment for making morning gowns of 'Persian'. Each morning gown came to a total of £3 – £2 in costs for the materials and £1 each for labour.[85] In 1694, Mary II's tailor charged only 15s. for 'making a morning night gown with green flowers' and the same again for 'making a waded nightgown with white & gold flowers', although the silk wad cost an additional £3.[86] By the reign of Queen Anne, Anne Clifton charged around 8s. for making nightgowns and 15s. for morning gowns.[87] It appears that the prices charged for making these garments by the early eighteenth century were not just dictated by the gender and occupational identity of the maker. Instead, they were also related to changing styles and complexities of construction. Similarly, Anne Morgan and Peter Lombard charged between 5s. and £5 5s. to make petticoats during the 1680s. Ellen Becker usually charged £1 10s. for 'making a coat' in the 1690s, and by the early eighteenth century the charges for making petticoats by Elizabeth Banks ranged from 10s. to £1 6s., depending on the style.[88] This decline in labour costs is probably partly attributable to changing styles of petticoats too, as they became less ornately decorated with trimmings such as fringe and tassels at the start of the eighteenth century, and so took less time to make.

Throughout history and even in modern times, female-dominated occupations tend to be lower paid; there was certainly no shortage of poorly paid female labourers who made cheap ready-made clothing or military slops during the late seventeenth century and eighteenth century.[89] Judith Bennett has noted that 'the history of women's work suggests that women were clustered in low skilled, low-status, low-paying occupations in 1200 as in 1900'.[90] However, we must be careful about simplifying or claiming universality in these observations, as this data from the queens' household accounts demonstrates. While being female was the biggest factor that determined the work and low wages of poor younger women, the group examined here, though not elite themselves, clearly belonged to a more exclusive tier of maker within London's fashion marketplace and they were able to leverage their connections to elite patrons and charge premium prices for their services.

Further investigation into some of the dressmakers named in the queens' accounts certainly shows that they had extensive networks of patrons. Diana de Marly has argued that late seventeenth-century suppliers such as milliners, mercers, silkmen, hosiers and others 'were able to dominate their fields by capturing a wide range of aristocratic patronage', whereas makers such as tailors and dressmakers tended to have 'but one noble client'.[91] While it is certainly true that milliners, by nature of their trade – as retailers with public shops – could capture a larger share of customers and reach levels of fame discussed in the previous chapter, the queens' tailors and dressmakers were also patronized by others. The tailor Peter Lombard made clothing for many elite women, such as the Countess of Marlborough, the Duchess of Somerset and Lady Anne (later Queen Anne), as well as Catherine of Braganza and Mary II. When it came to mantua-makers and petticoat-makers, networks of female clients were crucial to their financial success. In Paris, many *couturières* did not operate public shops; instead they relied on 'word-of-mouth to acquire clients'.[92] One such woman was Madame du Creux at Rue Traversine, whose reputation was noted by the *Mercure galant* as she made mantua gowns 'like they make them at Court' and dressed 'the largest part of the people of the first quality'.[93] The same was also true in London.

Court records relating to the breakdown of a business partnership between royal dressmakers Mary Alexander and Jane Heath (discussed in detail in the next section) reveal that, like the milliner Elizabeth Graydon, they had several clients of different social classes. Noble clients included Mary of Modena, then Duchess of York, and the Duchesses of Mazarin, Somerset, Grafton, Norfolk and Buckingham, as well as the Countesses of Marlborough, Clarendon, Northampton, Northumberland, Chesterfield and Oxford. Women in Catherine of Braganza's household such as 'Lady Diaz' and a 'maid of honour' are also mentioned. Others were the relatives of prominent London figures such as 'Mrs Duntan', likely the wife of the famous bookseller and author John Dunton, and Lady Jeffreys, the wife of Judge George Jeffreys. A substantial number of clients were simply referred to by 'Mrs', 'Madam' or 'Widow', sometimes accompanied by descriptions of where they lived, such as 'Mrs Foster in St Martins Lane' and 'Mrs Prais of the Park'. In addition to gowns made directly for their clients, work journals also recorded gowns made for others through intermediaries, such as a 'Striped Indian manto for Mrs Bilson's friend', an 'Indian Manto to Lady Grey's sister' and 'silk Crape Manto & petticoat to Mam Walks' mother'.[94] Heath and Alexander's success was clearly due, in part, to the informal social connections they cultivated among fashionable women in London and their wider social networks.

Having garments made on recommendation was common at this time. For dressmakers, their all-female clientele and the hours they spent with them in fittings was also part of their appeal. Such fittings were integral to the making of clothing and would have resembled the scene presented in a French engraving by Nicolas Arnoult from 1692, which praised the skill and style of the *couturière* and the garments she made (see Fig. 4.13). The dressmaker on the right measures her client with a piece of tape while the other dressmaker on the left takes a gown out of a box, presumably to test the fit. While the dressmakers of elite women do not seem to have formed the same kind of social friendships with their customers as milliners did – I have found no evidence of mantua-makers dining with the queen – they did have close access to their clients during the hours they spent fitting them. In 1709, the Countess of Scarborough wrote to the Duchess of Marlborough that 'Mrs How' had 'told me a week ago' that Marlborough would plan to be at 'the Lodge' where her letter was delivered.[95] Dressmakers such as Anne Howe therefore acted not only as fashion makers, but also as informal go-betweens in information exchange between their elite clients.

Yet these fashionable dressmakers did not just have elite clients, so another part of their appeal among the aspirational sorts was their elite connections. Popular literature certainly made these connections clear. In an imagined conversation between two contemporary 'ladies', one asked the

Fig. 4.13 *Nicolas Arnoult,* La Bonne Couturierre *[The Good Couturière], 1692, etching with engraving. The caption reads 'Was there ever a more skilful female worker: / I give good style to my garments / Appearing at court or staying in town, / Madame, you will attract many lovers.'*

other why she needed the 'Indian Woman, the Tire-Woman, the Mantua-Woman, the Sempstress and the Jeweller' when they were all 'unnecessary People', as one could buy things 'Cheaper, and with less Trouble at the Shops'. To which the second lady replied that without them 'no Body [would] think me well dressed'.[96] As previously noted, Mary Alexander and Jane Heath's business journals demonstrate that they were not picky about clients.[97] If a woman could afford it, they would make her a gown.

Amounts charged for gowns varied. They usually charged between 10s. and 15s. for making mantua gowns and 7s. to 10s. for nightgowns. Titled and non-titled women alike often paid the same prices for the same types of garments. Lady Sarah Churchill and a 'Mrs Cooke' were both charged 15s. for lustring mantos trimmed with lace, and all women regularly paid the same to have plain mantos and nightgowns made. This reinforces the regular connections between the court and the city that have been discussed in all the chapters of this book. The royal court was not divorced from the fashion marketplace, and by the later Stuart period one did not need to be a courtier to have gowns made by the queens' dressmakers.

There are some instances when Alexander and Heath appear to have charged their aristocratic clients significantly more for the same type of garment. By the mid-1680s, Heath regularly commanded fees of £1 for mantos made for Catherine of Braganza. It is possible that dressmakers billed the queens' household for more, simply because they knew that it would pay more. Sarah Churchill later noted that it was common for royal tradespeople to charge the queen double what they offered other elite clients.[98] It is also possible that, as Crowston has noted of French tradeswomen, these women charged the Office of the Robes more because they knew the bill would be reduced, which was common, or because it often took so long for their bills to be paid that they incorporated interest into the price.[99] However, the higher prices may also have been due to the complexity of the garment construction itself.

There are only four £1 charges in Alexander and Heath's work journal, and these were for mantos made for the Duchesses of Grafton, Mazarin and Norfolk, and Lady Rutland. In the descriptions given of these mantos there is no indication of why they cost so much more. However, as such journals relied on very basic descriptions – 'a brick-coloured tissue manto', or 'blue satin Manto lined with black trimmed with point' – that were designed to recall detailed information in the mind of the maker, it is likely that these mantos were somehow different in construction to others and so required more labour.[100] It is also possible that these were mantos intended to be worn at court and thus required more detailed attention to construction and materials, which came with an the additional price tag.

The French background of dressmakers such as Mary Alexander, Jane Heath and Mary Mandove were part of their appeal. However competent London makers were, after the Restoration of the monarchy in 1660, and especially in Francophile court circles, they were always 'outclassed' by French artisans.[101] The clothing accounts of Elizabeth Seymour, Duchess of Somerset, during the 1680s demonstrate the differences in the charges of French and English dressmakers based on their backgrounds and reputations. While her English dressmakers charged roughly 8s. for mantos, 6s. for morning gowns and 5s. for petticoats, the French mantua-maker Jane Heath commanded between 10s. to 15s. for mantos, 8s. for nightgowns and between 5s. and 12s. for petticoats.[102] Mary Alexander charged somewhere in between, 12s. for mantos and 8s. for chamber gowns, presumably due to her

French origins and connections to the royal court.[103] This shows clearly that being a royal dressmaker, and secondly a French dressmaker, allowed one to charge a premium for her services.

This was still the case in the early eighteenth century when *The Ladies Catechism* (1703), which claimed to be 'useful for all Eminent Females' that would 'attain to the Dignity of the mode', described a character who preferred French mantua-makers. When asked why she would give a Frenchwoman three guineas to make a mantua when 'an English woman would be glad of one, and perhaps do it as well', the Lady replies 'only for the name of having it made by a French Woman'.[104] The ability to boast about having one's gown made by a Frenchwoman was therefore worth the extra price. The queens' household accounts, and other sources that relate to their dressmakers, therefore demonstrate that there was a tier of London dressmaker who, despite gender, could charge roughly the same as male tailors. This was due to a multitude of factors, including networks of elite clientele, word-of-mouth and reputation, and, above all, their French background and training. It is the training and skills of these women, particularly by French *couturières*, that the next section explores.

The skills, training and working relationships of early mantua-makers

The overlapping work of those who made the later Stuart queens' clothing calls into question the skills of early dressmakers and the long-held belief that mantua-makers in England were solely derived from seamstresses. Many theorize that mantuas were the creation of seamstresses who began to expand their skills from making loose undergarments of linen to relaxed, less structured chamber robes, morning gowns and night gowns, and then to mantua gowns of silk. Janet Arnold, Norah Waugh and Anne Buck have all suggested that in England seamstresses became mantua-makers.[105] Avril Hart has written that early mantua-makers 'had no tailoring expertise at this time, their knowledge of construction came from their experience with making simple T-shaped garments' usually associated with the seamstress, such as shifts.[106] The work of Rebecca Morrison and the School of Historical Dress has also suggested that early eighteenth-century mantua gowns were likely constructed using pattern folding and cutting techniques common to the methods of seamstresses, rather than those pattern-making techniques utilized by tailors.[107] Thus, these loose garments not only complemented the pre-existing skill sets of seamstresses but these women, by taking over the production of women's outer garments, liberated their female customers from the heavily tailored boned bodices of the 1660s.[108]

However, many of the earliest sources that mention mantua gowns in England indicate that they were first made by tailors, not female seamstresses seeking to save women from the yoke of male tailoring. This is unsurprising, as such patterns of work reflected the gendered divisions of labour within the garment trades up to that point. In 1706, Isobel Wood gave evidence in front of the Durham tailoring guild in defence of her mantua-maker daughter, stating that she could recall that her former mistress, the wife of a Clerk to the Spicery in the service of Charles II, 'had her first Manto made by a Frenchman' during the 1670s, and noted that mantos were 'usually made both by tailors and women, but the women exceed the tailors'.[109] In 1682, Catherine of Braganza had two mantos made by a French tailor named Monsieur Renault which were brought back to England by her secretary, Sir Richard Bellings.[110] Even English tailors were early makers of mantua gowns; in 1673 Elizabeth Maitland, Duchess of Lauderdale, had a 'purple and white Manteau, lined and edged with black' made by her tailor, John Ferguson.[111] As the previous breakdown of work in the Robes also shows, royal tailors also made mantos for Catherine of Braganza and Mary II (see Fig. 2.10).

It is unlikely that tailors would have used the techniques of folding and cutting textiles like seamstresses when making mantos. Indeed, the different approaches taken when making these gowns appear to have been at the heart of criticism of tailors in the 1706 Durham proceedings, as another woman, Mary Mitford, claimed that most tailors did 'not under stand the art of Manto-making so well as women' which often led to mantos being 'spoiled' by them.[112] Just as trade identities were ambiguous and multifaceted, ways of making these new gowns also varied at this time. In their rush to translate and make the new and latest fashions out of France, tailors and seamstresses alike would have drawn on their pre-existing skills with varying levels of success. Some gowns were probably constructed using tailoring methods and others by the flat-lay patterning of seamstresses.

As there are very few surviving examples of mantos from the seventeenth century, it is impossible to be sure about common construction methods from the material record alone. However, some surviving gowns, such as the brown wool example at the MET (see Fig. 4.14), appear to use a mixture of tailoring and mantua-making techniques.[113] To investigate the origins of the fashionable mantua-maker and her skills in England, we must look beyond the simple narratives of seamstresses becoming mantua-makers and examine the specific context of women's changing place as makers in London. By attentively reading for making practices in bills submitted to the Office of the Robes, as well as examining wider training practices, it is clear that the knowledge and skill of seamstresses, tailors and French *couturières* were all integral to the development of the mantua-making trade in London.

Recent studies by Sarah Birt and Laura Gowing have found that girls were being apprenticed into traditional male trades like tailoring in London in the mid to late seventeenth-century, much earlier than previously thought. At least forty-nine girls were apprenticed to tailors and four girls to body-makers in the Merchant Taylors Company in the period 1658–88.[114] Although the presence of these women was often minimized in the guild paperwork, other sources show that once they had served their apprenticeship, many began their own businesses in tailoring-related trades. Martha Pillah worked for herself, 'making and mending Men's Clothes', and Anna Cowell worked as a 'Childs Coate

Fig. 4.14 *Mantua gown made from wool and embroidered with silver-gilt thread, late 17th century, English. Metropolitan Museum of Art New York, 33.54a–c.*

Maker' after her freedom in 1681.[115] Both women had been apprenticed to tailors in London and both would have learned to make all manner of men's, women's and children's clothing, as well as acquiring skills such as pattern-making and cutting. It is possible that like these women, Mary II's 'tailor' Ellen Becker had also trained under a tailor before specializing in making petticoats.

Husband and wife partnerships were also common. For example, in 1691 Elizabeth Thomas petitioned for freedom to trade in the City, citing that she had been trained by a tailor in the Drapers' Company and had worked alongside her first husband, a merchant tailor, and since his death had 'used, carried on, and exercised the said Trade of Tailor in the City of London'.[116] It was not unknown for widows to take over the business and train new apprentices with the skills that they had learned working alongside their late husbands.[117] Seamstresses and dressmakers married to tailors often kept shops next to their husbands too.[118] Henrietta Maria's accounts list an Alice Waggit, seamstress, and a Thomas Waggit, tailor, who made clothing for the queen's servants.[119] In the eighteenth century many mantua-makers in England and Scotland were the wives of tailors.[120] Others offered dual services: a husband and wife, stay-maker and mantua-maker, duo who provided both services to their clients are mentioned in a letter between two gentry women in Norfolk in 1700.[121] In such situations, there was bound to be overlap in the skills acquired. Indeed, even when a woman did not hold a business separately to her tailor husband, the very nature of clothing production meant female members of the household would have undertaken some forms of tailoring work. In 1601, Jane Damport of St Botolph Aldgate was described as 'sitting at work' in her husband's tailoring shop.[122] The binary between men's work as tailors and women's work as seamstresses stressed in written literature was, and likely always had been, quite fluid.

Materials and techniques utilized by tailors were certainly employed by the queens' dressmakers. John Styles has observed that between the late sixteenth century and late seventeenth century there was a dramatic shift away from 'heavy, short-staple woollen cloth' and heavy silks traditionally used by tailors towards lightweight worsteds wools ('stuffs, serges, tammies, mohair'), light silks, mixed fibres and then cotton.[123] The ability to use lightweight textiles that were similar to the linen fabrics many women were used to sewing has been suggested as a reason for women transitioning easily into the mantua-making trades. Tailors such as Peter Lombard were more frequently recorded as making mantuas from 'cloth', denoting a heavier type of wool fabric, compared to the dressmakers who were more likely to use silks of all kinds, cottons and 'stuffs'. Certainly, the queens' dressmakers frequently used Indian satins and damasks, Chinese taffetas and calicoes in mantos, petticoats and loose gowns before their banning in 1701–2.[124] Mary Alexander and Jane Heath are even recorded as making mantos from flowered and plain 'mousseline' or muslin too.[125] However, it should be stressed that Lombard also used these lightweight fabrics and the mantua-maker Heath is also recorded as using 'black cloth' on several occasions.[126] Thus, it is hard to make such clear-cut distinctions between the fabrics that tailors used and those that mantua-makers used at this time in the queen's accounts, even if the way that later mantos were constructed – draping, pleating, gathering – lent itself more to lightweight cottons and silks.

During the late seventeenth century, mantos and other loose gowns were often lined with a contrasting fabric. The manto of patterned ivory silk damask worn by the doll named Lady Clapham in the Victoria and Albert Museum is lined with a contrasting pink silk taffeta (see Fig. 4.15). Such contrasting lining fabrics would have been visible on the out-turned robings and cuffs of these gowns and when the skirts were bustled up, as is demonstrated by a recreation of Lady Clapham's manto (see Fig. 4.16).[127] While Clapham's lining fabric was left plain, bills in the queens' accounts frequently referred to 'pinking' the lining. For instance, in December 1687 Heath made a 'Purple Brocade

Fig. 4.15 *Doll's Mantua of silk damask, possibly Chinese, lined with silk taffeta, c. 1690–1700, English. Victoria and Albert Museum London, T.846E-1974.*

Nightgown lined with brown lustring' and a 'Brown flow[ered] Manto lined with black Lustring' for Catherine of Braganza. Under both entries, she listed a separate charge for 'Pinking the Lutestring' linings.[128] Anne Clifton's services were similarly described. In 1702, she charged 6s. 6d. for 'pinking 12 yds 1/2 of lutestring to line it [a manto] through with'.[129] Pinking referred to the process of using specialist metal punches to create small, decorative cuts in the fabric – a decorative technique often used in earlier seventeenth-century dress.[130] Henrietta Maria's embroiderer and pattern cutter, Charles Genty, frequently pinked and printed fabrics to be used in the queen's clothing.[131] Pinking required much skill and expertise, as mistakes could quickly ruin expensive fabric.

Pinking the lining may seem unusual to those more familiar with eighteenth-century mantua-making techniques, where this technique was only utilized on the edge of fabric trims. However, pinking the linings of garments was common during the seventeenth century. The linings of several coats and waistcoats made for Charles II were pinked by a specialist pinker named Robert Prichard.[132] A woman's loose gown dating to 1610–20 demonstrates how decorative pinked linings looked, as the garment contains a pinked silk taffeta lining (see Fig. 4.17). This decorative technique was also common in France. In 1678 the *Extraordinaire du Mercure galant* noted that mantuas in Paris were also being lined

Fig. 4.16 *Reconstruction of the Lady Clapham doll's mantua gown. Made by Rebecca Morrison, Michelle Barker, Sarah Bendall, Serena Dyer, Brooke Welborn and Elisabeth Gernerd at the Making Historical Dress Festival, 12–14 September 2024, De Montfort University, Leicester.*

with pinked taffetas.[133] When the skirts of mantos were bustled up revealing the lining layer, this pinking would have created a striking visual effect. While mantua-makers like Jane Heath charged extra for pinking, work journals from her partnership with Mary Alexander show that she also outsourced some work to professionals as payments to 'the Pinker in Newport Street' and 'the Pinker in Henrietta Street' were also made.[134] In Queen Anne's accounts a woman named Mrs Talbot was labelled a 'racer' and paid for 'pinking' and 'racing' yards of satin fabric.[135] Thus, this common construction technique was borrowed from tailoring and incorporated into the earliest iterations of the manto.

Mantua-makers also made garments traditionally associated with tailoring, such as waistcoats. There was little change to the general shape and style of waistcoats during the seventeenth century and

Fig. 4.17 *The pinked lining of a woman's gown of Italian mulberry-coloured velvet and silk taffeta lining, c. 1610–20, English. Victoria and Albert Museum London, 178-1900.*

they were worn by both common women as everyday wear and elite women as informal wear. Waistcoats were made of multiple pattern pieces that needed to be carefully drawn out and cut to fit, rather than draped on the body. Pattern cutting was a highly skilled and risky part of clothing production, as mistakes could waste fabric or lead to issues with fit and finish. For these reasons, patternmaking was more commonly associated with the tailoring trades. This is made apparent in the *Habit de Tailleur* engraving by Nicolas de Larmessin which depicts a tailor cutting pattern pieces for women's stays and men's coats out of fabric (see Fig. 4.18). Henrietta Maria's waistcoats were cut and made by her French cutter and tailor. However, by the time of Catherine of Braganza, Mary Mandove and Mary Alexander were the preferred providers of these garments.[136] Nearly half of the garments that Mandove made for the queen were waistcoats (see Fig. 4.7), and she supplied this garment in vastly greater numbers than the tailor Lombard in the same years.[137] This gives further weight to the idea that rigid distinctions drawn between male and female makers in the late seventeenth century are too simplistic and that the matter was much more complicated and varied than has previously been recognized.

While the skills of early dressmakers likely derived from the melting pot of training opportunities that opened up for women in the mid-late seventeenth century, the influence of French *couturières*

Fig. 4.18 *Nicolas de Larmessin,* Habit de Tailleur *[Clothes of the Tailor], from the series* Fancy Trade Costumes, *c. 1695–6, engraving. Bibliothèque nationale de France, Hennin, 6247. The plate depicts a stylized tailor whose dress is constructed from the tools of his work. It shows complex pattern cutting to be one of the defining characteristics of the tailoring trade.*

cannot be understated. The array of garments made by the French dressmaker Mary Mandove for Catherine of Braganza largely conformed to the French statutes of the *couturière* guilds of Paris. These decrees specified that after 1675 women in their guild were permitted to make chamber gowns, petticoats and mantua gowns, as well as waistcoats, hungerlines and different types of lightly boned bodies and stays (see Fig. 4.19).[138] They were not permitted, however, to make court gowns with highly stiffened bodices (see Fig. 4.20), such as those made by the tailor Peter Lombard. Garments such as waistcoats, hungerlines and bodies required more complex construction than is usually associated with the folding, cutting and draping of linen by seamstresses. This suggests that Parisian women had

Fig. 4.19 Madame de Soissons en Robe de Chambre *[Madame de Soissons in a Chamber Gown], late 17th century, French. Bibliothèque nationale de France, département Arsenal, ARS EST-368 (266). Madame wears a chamber gown over a camisole, which was a lightweight unboned bodice, and petticoat, all garments made by French couturières after 1675.*

long been adopting the making methods and techniques of tailors before they were allowed to form their own guild. In fact, the varied skills of French *couturières* earned them the occupational title of *Sarta* in Italy, which in English translated to 'a woman Taylour', and may account for why the label 'tailor' was given to Mandove in some household accounts.[139]

The breakdown of the working partnership between royal dressmakers Mary Alexander and Jane Heath gives us a fascinating glimpse into the skills and ambitions of two migrant French *couturières* working in London during the late seventeenth century.[140] Descriptions of their trade were recorded in a 1684 court case that Mary brought against Jane for lost revenue and costs associated with the

Fig. 4.20: *Nicolas Arnoult,* Marie Anne fille légitimée de France, *daughter of Louis XIV, c. 1685, hand-coloured etching with engraving, French. Rijksmuseum Amsterdam, RP-P-2016-8-2. The bodice (Corps de Robes) of this court gown would have been structured with whalebone. Female dressmakers in France were not permitted to make this style.*

deterioration of their 'co-partnership'. The depositions given by both parties provide insightful details about the training of both women, and demonstrates the mobility facilitated by women's skilled labour. Several years before the court case, Mary had brought Jane and her husband Francis 'out of France' so that Jane could instruct Mary and her two daughters in the 'Art & trade of making of mantua or manto gowns & vests [waistcoats]'.[141] Mary was also a French 'alien' who had married an Englishman and lived in London for many years.[142] She appears to have been a milliner before trying her hand at mantua-making, as in 1676 she sold ribbons and gloves to Catherine of Braganza.[143] By 1679 Mary was making petticoats, mantos, chamber gowns and camisoles (lightweight bodices) for the Countess of Ogle, all garments that Parisian *couturières* were permitted to make under the 1675 statutes, indicating that it is probably around this time that Jane Heath had begun to instruct her in this art.[144]

When it came to learning how to make mantos, it is not necessarily the case that a seamstress or tailor could just adapt their making without instruction.[145] Far from being 'less qualified artisans' than tailors and who performed a craft that 'called for no great technical skill', as some scholars have suggested, French *couturières* were widely recognized and sought after for their expertise and skills.[146] Clearly it was not enough just to study a gown brought over from France or to try to communicate such making knowledge via letter. Mantua-making knowledge, like most craft knowledge, was tacit and required the expert maker herself to be brought over from France to instruct those wishing to learn. To be the one who brought a skilled *couturière* from France was also a savvy business decision by Mary Alexander, as the previously discussed work journal with dozens of client orders makes clear.

Mary was not happy just being taught the art of mantua-making by Jane and she soon began to ask 'at length' to enter a partnership with her. Due to the laws of couverture in England, Mary sought approval for this arrangement from Jane's husband Francis. However, he refused to agree to the partnership without the consent of his wife, as he claimed that he 'understood nothing of the said trade' as he was a periwig-maker. In his deposition, Francis claimed that his wife Jane was 'very expert in the making' of mantos and vests, and, although he himself was a skilled craftsperson, it is clear that it was Jane's trade that had led the couple to migrate to London from France. Francis also claimed that through her work Jane 'had great acquaintance with many persons of great quality who he knows would employ his wife', and so Jane did not need Mary to help her maintain a customer base in London. It is unclear from the court case whether these acquaintances had been made before her coming to England, and thus whether her reputation in France was also well known, or if such acquaintances had been made once her expert mantua-making abilities became known after she emigrated.

Transcribed work journals provided as bills of evidence in the court case show that by 1684 Alexander and Heath certainly had many noble clients, such as the Duchess of Grafton (see Fig. 4.21), daughter of the queen's Mistress of the Robes, the Countess of Arlington, and others in the household of Anne, Princess of Denmark (later Queen Anne), including the Countess of Clarendon and 'Lady Churchill' (later Duchess of Marlborough). Their workshop also attracted French émigrés in London, such as Charles II's French-Italian mistress Hortense Mancini, Duchess of Mazarin (see Fig. 4.22) and her daughter Marie-Charlotte de La Porte-Mazarin, Marquise de Richelieu, who lived for a time with her mother.[147] When the Marquise de Richelieu commissioned a 'crape manto and petticoat' from Alexander and Heath in May 1684, likely on the recommendation of her mother, she and her husband were freshly arrived from France, having only entered England a month before.[148] The Duchess of Mazarin was later credited by English women as bringing 'the garb of Mantos with her' and popularizing them at the English court.[149] While mantua gowns in Catherine of Braganza's records predate Mazarin's arrive in

Fig. 4.21 *John Smith, after Godfrey Kneller,* Portrait of Isabella Fitzroy, The Duchess of Grafton, c. *1677–98, mezzotint. Rijksmuseum Amsterdam, RP-P-OB-32.754.*

England in 1675, the duchess was clearly an arbiter of fashion, particularly French styles. Counting her among their customers therefore must have been a huge boost for Alexander and Heath, and supports the claim that Jane Heath was an expert *couturière* who attracted many influential customers.

Depositions in the court case also reveal that the Heaths were hesitant to enter into any agreement with Mary Alexander due to her reputation. Francis noted in his deposition that Mary 'had but very few customers having lost many customers of what she formerly had had'. Why Mary had lost such customers is unclear. However, their hesitation reiterates how important a good reputation was for makers in the fashion marketplace who wished to gain and maintain elite clients and the types of success that could come from their patronage. While initially hesitant, the Heaths agreed to Mary's proposal on the condition that she would 'take care and look after the household affairs'. In exchange,

Fig. 4.22 *Jacob Ferdinand Voet,* Portrait of Hortense Mancini, Duchesse Mazarin, as Aphrodite, c. *1675, oil on canvas. Private Collection.*

Jane would continue to train Mary and her daughters and would bring her 'many and great customers' to their business.

Mary Alexander rented a property in Covent Garden for a term of seven years off Henry Cope, a mercer who also supplied Catherine of Braganza. She paid rent on the property, which she occupied with her two daughters, some servants and a housekeeper, while the Heaths agreed to occupy only one chamber. They would share the workspaces and 'equally bear all other charges' for domestic servants and tools, and other 'goods & commodities' used in mantua-making. It was agreed that all gains and losses would be split in equal halves between the two parties and that a 'true & just book of

Accounts or journal books' would be kept. Detailed entries of all work ordered, made and delivered was to be kept in these work journals and Mary, Jane and Francis agreed 'at all time [to] have free access' to them.[150]

In their Covent Garden workshop, Mary Alexander and Jane Heath worked alongside their apprentices and workwomen making mantos, petticoats and nightgowns for several women, including those famous court figures previously mentioned. Between April and June 1684, their work journal, which was transcribed and submitted in bills of evidence to the court, recorded that the duo made and altered 154 mantos and nightgowns for at least ninety different women, totalling £79 16s. 6d. in labour costs alone.[151] Tasks such as embroidery and some pinking were frequently outsourced to other artisans (usually other women).[152] Although mantos were not as time consuming to construct as the stiff-bodied gowns of the period, this is still a huge number of garments to be created in such a small amount of time and indicates that they must have had several journeywomen labouring for them. Indeed, the court case mentions a 'head workwoman' and others who worked with Mary and Jane in the art of mantua-making.[153]

While the partnership was profitable, things soon began to sour under the roof they all shared in Covent Garden. It appears that Mary and her daughters were less than diligent in helping Jane with the actual making of gowns, and it is certainly clear from both parties that Mary and Francis did not get along. As the relationship deteriorated the Heaths began to make and sell garments to others outside of the partnership. This was not a charge that they denied. Instead, in his deposition, Francis stated that he believed there was never any agreement between the partners prohibiting Jane from selling mantos or other things on the side. He claimed their co-partnership was only for making 'mantuas, manto gowns and vests' for customers who commissioned gowns from the co-partnership. The Heaths, it appears, may also have been taking special commissions or selling ready-made gowns behind Mary Alexander's back.[154]

Unfortunately, the final ruling in this legal case has not survived. After 1684, Catherine of Braganza and the Duchess of Somerset's papers show that Mary Alexander and Jane Heath were still working for many of their former clients, albeit trading separately. Jane, being the 'very expert' *couturière* who had trained and worked in France, appears to have been more successful than Mary: she was more likely to be commissioned for making mantos and she commanded a much higher price for her work. The court case between these women gives us an unparallelled view of the complex working relationships between early mantua-makers in seventeenth-century London. Their trade was clearly one where competition ran high, and the skills and work of French *couturières* was immensely sought after, by both clients and other makers wishing to learn the trade.

By the early eighteenth century, English mantua-makers exhibited many of the same skills shown by earlier French *couturières*, and it was these female migrants who trained and passed their knowledge onto English makers. In addition to training Mary Alexander, her daughters and other 'workwomen' in the art of mantua-making during their business relationship, Jane Heath also took on other apprentices while working independently, training a new generation of English mantua-makers using the knowledge and skills she had gained in France. Her bills in the Robes accounts of Catherine of Braganza and the Duchess of Somerset were often signed off 'by the Order' of her Mistress 'Mrs Jane Heath' by an apprentice or journeywoman mantua-maker named Mary Blurton.[155] No details of Blurton's apprenticeship arrangement with Heath have been located. However, in 1690 a Mary Blurton married a John 'Laforte' (also recorded as Laforce) in Holy Trinity Church, Knightsbridge. They are documented as paying taxes at the 'Exchange Court' in St Martin-in-the-Fields for the following four decades. In 1720 'Mary Laforce of St Martins in the fields', whose occupation was a 'mantua-maker', took Elizabeth Piggot as an apprentice to learn the art and trade of mantua-making, which Heath had taught to her.[156] Thus, by the turn of the eighteenth century the skills of the *couturière* had been learned by English mantua-makers who continued to pass them on to further generations of dressmakers.

Conclusions

Records left by the households of the Stuart queens show that women makers were not only vital in creating Stuart queenly magnificence, but also in shaping the changing fashion marketplace of London during the seventeenth century. Women had always been patronized by the queens' households as seamstresses and silkwomen. However, the emergence of the female professional identities of 'petticoat-makers' and 'mantua-makers' marks an important shift in the acknowledgement of women's artisanal identities during the final decade of the seventeenth century. The influence and training of early English dressmakers by French *couturières* was integral to this shift, and the dominance of successful female dressmakers in elite circles who were not paid substantially less than their male counterparts also indicates that forms of female social capital gave them clout in the fashion marketplace, just like milliners.

Royal household records and other sources that document the work of these royal dressmakers, such as court cases or bills sent to other elite women, also show the vital importance of elite women's patronage to the success of women-makers in the fashion marketplace. One could not simply rely on skills: the leading tier of mantua-maker also depended on persons of quality to both patronize their workshops and recommend their wares to other women. The court case involving Mary Alexander and Jane Heath, which details their working relationship and their numerous clients, demonstrates this. The work of the French *couturières* was clearly desired in London both amongst elite women and those non-elite women who aspired to and had the money to dress in the latest fashions from France. Highly skilled French women also migrated to London for work opportunities, sometimes bringing their husbands with them, and these *couturières* were integral to training the first generation of English mantua-makers.

The records of the Stuart queens provide information about the work and lives of women who do not appear in those guild records usually employed by historians to detail the history of women's artisanal work. These records challenge neat gender distinctions between dressmakers and tailors and the simple narrative that seamstresses became mantua-makers. They show that women made a wide range of clothing during the seventeenth century and that their identities and skills were challenged and reinterpreted before entering the eighteenth century as the better-known mantua-maker.

5

Caring: Maintaining clothing and appearances in the care economy of the royal household

After clothing was delivered into the Office of the Robes, it was passed to teams of Robes officers, bedchamber women and servants who identified and kept track of items, stored, cleaned and mended garments, as well as physically assisted the queen to dress. As outlined in Chapter 1, clothing was a form of stored wealth. It visually projected the magnificence of a ruler and the wealth and stability of the crown. Thus, caring for clothing extended the life of a garment and the substantial investment of money, materials and labour that had gone into its creation. This chapter explores what happened to clothing in the Office of the Robes, both before and after the acts of wearing. It takes a wide approach to the theme of caring; I am interested not just in the care for clothing but also care for the body through dressing practices, including cosmetics, skincare and hairstyling.

The early modern care economy generated vast amounts of paid and unpaid work for women.[1] Urban and rural households in seventeenth-century England were heavily dependent on the labour of servants and at any given time around '60 per cent of 15- to 24-year-olds worked in service'.[2] Many of these servants were live-in domestic workers, usually single women, who performed household tasks such as cleaning and laundry.[3] As Charmian Mansell has noted in her study of female servants in early modern England, these women were vital to underpinning the early modern economy and home; however, they have left 'few traces in the archives'.[4] Elite household accounts are one place where records of such work have survived.

The basic tasks of storing, dressing, mending and laundering were performed throughout early modern England by women of all backgrounds in all sorts of households. The work that took place in the royal household can help us to understand how clothing was cared for in households of various sizes around the country. My aim here is not to collapse the experiences of elite women at court into those of general domestic servants. However, tucked amongst invoices for goods from tradespeople are bills for work performed in the wardrobes, dressing rooms and laundries by elite and non-elite women alike, as well as information about goods purchased to perform care work and the wages paid, that can reveal more information about domestic labour during this period.

This chapter highlights the consistent role that women played in the household during the long seventeenth century, particularly in relation to the caring for clothing and the dressing of bodies. While some of these 'care' positions in the queens' households were exclusive to women, such as those of bedchamber women, dressers, and tirewomen, other roles like seamstress and laundress were designated as women's work across all royal households, including the kings'. The need for skilled tradeswomen such as seamstresses and starchers, as well as positions that were always considered a woman's job, such as that of laundresses, enabled women to obtain important and well-renumerated positions at court. Some tradeswomen used their training and skills in the fashion marketplace to enter service in the royal household, and others helped to establish 'dynasties of service' which gave birth to multiple generations of laundresses, starchers and seamstresses who served the Stuarts. Opportunities that care work relating to clothing presented could therefore enable social mobilities and blur the boundaries between the marketplace and the court, and between hierarchies of status. Above all, care work for clothing within the royal household also offered women who were not from the peerage meaningful careers.

Storing clothing: wardrobes, the Mistress of the Sweet Coffers and the dressing room

The primary site of the Office of the Robes for Anna of Denmark, Henrietta Maria and Catherine of Braganza was Somerset House in London (see Fig. 5.1). Conveniently located close to the royal palaces of St James's and Whitehall, which remained the primary residences of the Stuart kings, Somerset House was also ideally situated near the shops of the City of London and the Strand. Initially gifted to Anna of Denmark when James I ascended the English throne in 1603, the house was extensively remodelled during her reign to include an east wing and new staterooms, and it was later renamed Denmark House in her honour.[5] When Henrietta Maria took up residence in 1626, Somerset House was already well stocked with clothing and furnishings that had belonged to Anna and previous Tudor monarchs. The new queen undertook her own renovations to the river side of the palace, including her apartments, chapel and closet. During the English Civil Wars and Interregnum (1642–60), Somerset House was repurposed as the headquarters of the parliamentary army and many of its contents were sold off. Following the Restoration of Charles II in 1660, Henrietta Maria returned to the house, though it was in need of substantial repair. She lived there only five years and returned to France in 1665, where she remained until her death in 1669.[6]

Fig. 5.1 *Cornelis Bol,* The Thames from Somerset House, *c. 1650, oil on canvas. Dulwich Picture Gallery, DPG360.*

After this, Somerset House was given to Catherine of Braganza, although it did not become her primary residence until after the death of Charles II in 1685. Prior to this, while maintaining a wardrobe at Somerset House, Catherine spent most of her time at Whitehall Palace.[7] A 1680 map of Whitehall shows that Catherine's wardrobe occupied four rooms on the south side of the palace, next to the Stone Gallery (see Fig. 5.2). These wardrobe spaces were situated next to another four rooms occupied by the Countess of Suffolk, who was her Mistress of the Robes from 1671 to 1681. The apartments of Charlotte Killigrew, Mistress of the Sweet Coffers, who oversaw the storage of clothing, were also nearby, as were those of Lady Arlington who became the Mistress of the Robes in 1681.

What did these wardrobe spaces look like? An inventory of Somerset House drawn up in 1619 after the death of Anna of Denmark gives some indication. Firstly, the inventory records yards of fabric stored in the wardrobe, likely ready to give to tradespeople commissioned to make them into clothing and furnishings. It specifies that 'Remaining in the Robes' were goods such as 'One whole piece of Tawny satin brocaded with gold in flowers' and 'One whole piece of russet satin flowered with white silk in branches'. Trimmings such as 'silk fringe of several Colours', gold and silver fringe and spangles were also stored in these rooms. Garments, including clothing that had belonged to Henry VIII and Elizabeth I, were located in trunks in rooms labelled as the 'wardrobe', the 'long wardrobe', the 'Robes' and 'the room beyond the little Bedchamber'.[8] Robe rooms were multifunctional spaces often containing other furnishings unrelated to the storage of clothing; for instance, Queen Anne's Robe

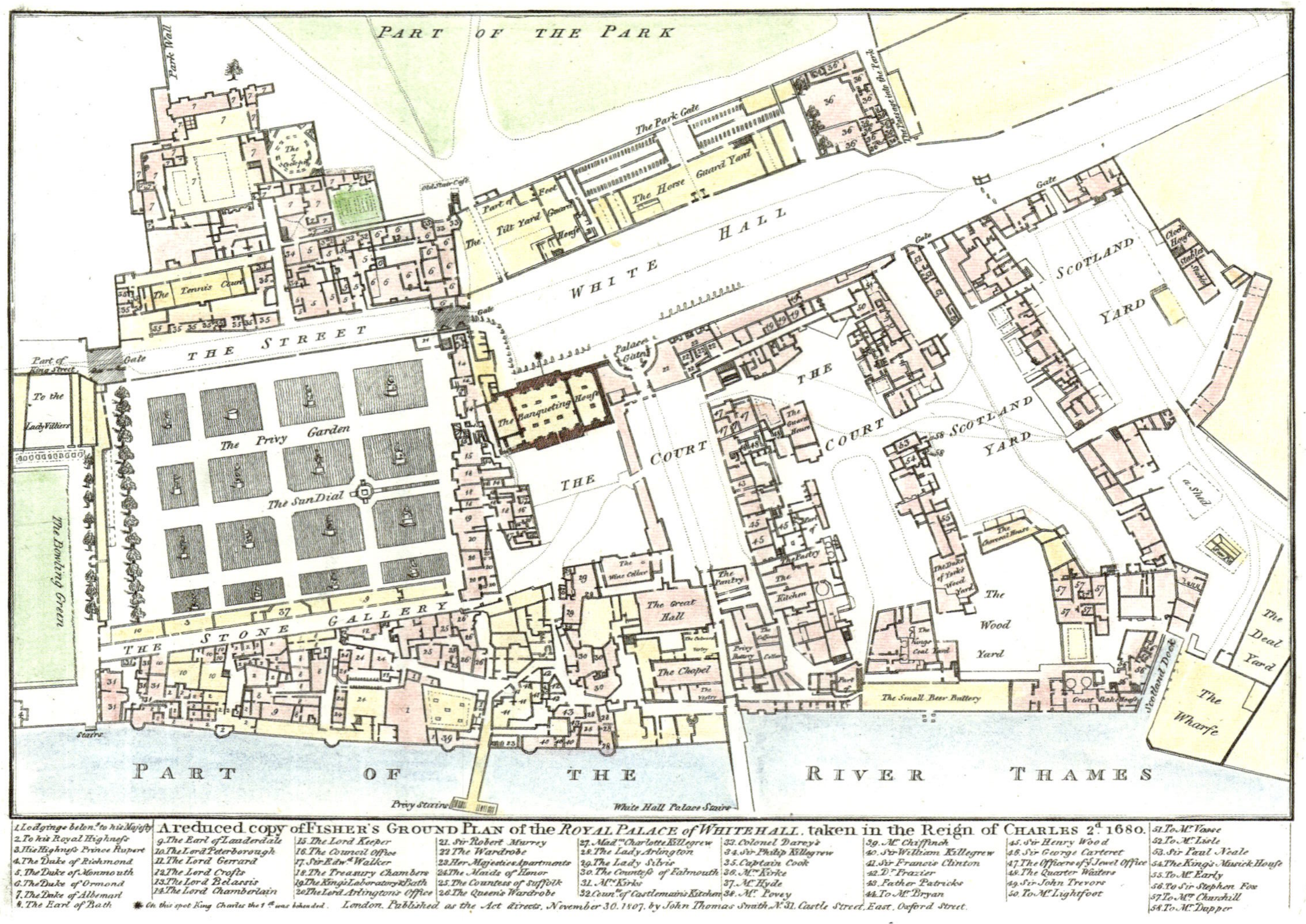

Fig. 5.2 *John Smith*, Fisher's Plan of the Royal Palace of Whitehall in 1680, *1807. The queen's apartments were on the river to the left of the Privy Stairs.*

rooms at St James's contained beds.[9] These spaces were cared for by a variety of servants and housekeepers, both male and female, who swept floors, changed mats, cleaned furnishings and hangings and made sure that these spaces were free from pests that might damage delicate textiles.[10]

Somerset House remained part of Catherine of Braganza's jointure until 1705, after which it was granted to Queen Anne, though she chose not to use it.[11] Instead, the clothing of the later Stuart queens was kept in wardrobes at their primary palaces of Whitehall, St James's and Kensington. Throughout the Stuart period, clothing was moved between the many residences kept by the royal family in London and its surrounds, a task managed by numerous staff employed in the Office of the Robes. In February 1608, a warrant appointed Gentleman Ushers in Anna of Denmark's household to 'keep account' of all the queen's clothing and to 'have a provident care of them'. Marginal notes in an inventory compiled by these Ushers between 1608 and 1611 documented the movement of the queen's clothing between royal residences such as Somerset House, Hampton Court, Greenwich Palace and Whitehall.[12] Henrietta Maria's Mistress of the Robes, Susan Feilding, Countess of Denbigh, also helped to facilitate the movement of goods from the Great Wardrobe to the queen's household.[13] Entries from other Robes attendants confirm that they were personally responsible for the transportation of the queens' clothing. In September 1694, Mary II's Page of the Robes John Keydel noted that several chests 'out of Holland' were discharged at Customs House and under his supervision taken to Whitehall and Kensington palaces.[14] In 1703, Yeoman Rachel Thomas billed the Robes for organizing the 'carriage of 3 petticoats & 3 night gowns from London to Windsor' in 'deal boxes' in June, and then in September she paid for 'the carriage of [the] Queens mourning linen' to the spa town of Bath where Anne had gone to take the waters.[15] Deal (pine) boxes and leather trunks are mentioned in various accounts from tradespeople and those within the Office of the Robes, indicating that these were the preferred containers in which to transport these expensive textile goods.

In the queen's household, elite women such as the Mistress of the Sweet Coffers were also responsible for the storage of clothing. In 1663, the new Mistress of the Sweet Coffers Charlotte Killigrew submitted a report to the Lord Chamberlain, Edward Montagu, Earl of Manchester, that described her role in detail. This report was necessary because the function of her office, prominent under earlier Stuart queens, had been partially forgotten following the monarchy's restoration in 1660. Based on her 'perusal of several papers' and discussions with older women, such as the former laundress and seamstress Elizabeth Elliot (discussed below), who could recall the duties of those who had served in this role under the early Stuart queens, Killigrew wrote:

> We do find that the Keeper of the Sweet Coffers to the Queens Majesty ought of right to have the keeping of her Majesty's Gloves, Feathers, Fanns, Hats and Feathers, all manner of ribbons for fans and scarves and Small looking glasses, all manner of perfumes, perfumed pockets, sweet powders and masks, muffs and Sweete Bags likewise the keeping of all Sweet waters and all presents.[16]

This was not a particularly high-paying role. While the Mistress of the Robes could receive a salary of £300 in the 1670s, the Mistress of the Sweet Coffers received only £20 13s. 4d. However, the office did come with prestige such as lodgings at court close to the queens' apartments and the Robes spaces themselves, as well as servants, horses and carts with livery.[17]

The Mistress of the Sweet Coffers was a new position implemented under the Stuarts in 1603; such a title does not exist in the papers of Elizabeth I. Like the Mistress of the Robes, women who held this position were both members of the bedchamber and the Office of the Robes.[18] It was a position given to elite women of moderate status. Anna of Denmark's Mistress was Elizabeth Carey (née Trevannion), Countess of Monmouth, while the women who served this role in the households of Henrietta Maria and Catherine of Braganza – Thomazine Carew, Charlotte Killigrew and Frances Bellings – were all the wives of knights who held other important positions at court.[19] The bills of the Stuart queens show that while the Mistress of the Sweet Coffers sometimes accepted deliveries, her main duty was to supervise the storage of clothing and accessories in the scented chests located in the wardrobe rooms. As Killigrew noted elsewhere, she was also in charge of buying perfumed gloves 'for her Majesties Service'.[20] Henrietta Maria's Mistress of the Sweet Coffers, Dame Thomazine Carew, regularly purchased dozens of white gloves for the Office of the Robes.[21] It is unclear how these were used. Were they used by Robes staff to handle clothing? Or were they solely worn by the queen? The gifting of perfumed gloves was a common practice in early modern courts and used by elite women such as queens consort to 'cultivate political influence' or in acts of diplomacy.[22] So it is possible that Carew's role was also to buy and distribute these tokens of favour. Frustratingly, the accounts do not give us an answer to this question.

By the reigns of Mary II and Queen Anne, the Mistress of the Sweet Coffers ceased to be a position in their households. The reasons for this are unclear. A Master of the Sweet Coffers was not a position in the king's household, even though clothing was stored in a similar manner.[23] As Mary and Anne were both queens regnant, perhaps they felt it was not necessary to have this dedicated role common in a consort's household within their own. Instead, this role was taken up by other attendants in the household who had previously been under the instruction of the Mistress of the Sweet Coffers, such as grooms, pages and brushers, as well as the yeoman of the robes, bedchamber women and necessary women.

The connections between the Mistress of the Sweet Coffers and the storage of clothing become apparent when we consider that heavily perfumed (sweet) chambers, including wardrobes, were a defining element of royal spaces. As Holly Dugan has argued, 'Royalty had its own aroma' and 'elaborate and sumptuous displays of power that defined royal dress' included 'scenting rituals as well as sensory symbolism', linked to both health and performances of power.[24] Royal clothing was not just stored in musty old chests; it was expected to carry the scent of authority. This was achieved by perfuming the clothing itself and storing it in sweet smelling coffers. Several references to scented coffers, chests and trunks made specially for clothing exist in the Robes accounts. In 1628, the Coffer-maker Henry Lenger delivered several chests into Henrietta Maria's 'Robes and Bedchamber', including one 'made of seasoned Boards covered with hide leather and strongly bound with partitions in it for hats'.[25] In 1685, three trunks covered in Russia leather lined with sarcenet and 'quilted with perfume' were delivered for Mary of Modena, and it was specified that two of the trunks had 'Drawers and partitions' for the storage of garments and accessories.[26]

One trunk of red Russia leather with drawers and partitions bearing the monogram of William and Mary has survived (see Fig. 5.3). It consists of a compartment above three drawers, each with a separate lock. Although the trunk is now lined with paper, it would originally have been covered with perfumed silk like many of the bills describe. A surviving chest bearing the monogram 'KR' with a crown for Catherine of Braganza has also survived, complete with its red quilted silk interiors. Perfuming manuals from the period explain that to scent these storage boxes, the silk lining was laid over 'a Bed of Cotton' that had been well perfumed, then quilted and cut to line the inside.[27] Baskets lined with perfumed silk were also used to 'keep Ladies cloths in' during the seventeenth century, and several references to these quilted baskets feature in the accounts of the later Stuart queens.[28]

Fig. 5.3 *Trunk of softwood, covered with leather, metal fittings and studs, 1680–1700, English. Victoria and Albert Museum London, 497-1894.*

Before being stored in these chests and baskets, garments were placed in specially made bags. A 'bag for night gear of yellow satin embroidered' was recorded in 1619 and a 'Cloak bag of black Cloth' in 1709.[29] Large pieces of fabric called toylets or twillets were also wrapped around garments in these chests. Twillets were made by a variety of tradespeople including seamstresses and tailors, including George Gelin who made 'taffeta Twillets' and Peter Lombard who made 'great sarsenet twillets' for the garments they supplied.[30] In 1708, the petticoat-maker Susannah Hawker also made 'a black toylet for the parliament Robes'.[31] Old sheets, curtains and table cloths were also used for this purpose, as Daniel Tompson, a chamber keeper, asked for an allowance for washing these items 'used about her Majesty's apparel in the Robes' in the early 1630s.[32] Such storage methods were common in kings' households too.[33]

As the name suggests, the chests and trunks under the supervision of the Mistress of the Sweet Coffers were also filled with perfumed 'sweet' bags that made clothing smell good and protected against insect damage. A 'red leather guilt Chest in the Wardrobes' in 1619 contained a 'Sweete bag of white Tinsel embroidered with silk' and another 'sweet bag of white satin embroidered' alongside garments and soft furnishings.[34] Sweet bags were small bags that contained powders made from a variety of perfuming agents (see Fig. 5.4). These included amber, musk, orris, civet and ambergris, mixed with ground herbs or dried flowers such as sandalwood, cloves, rosemary, marjoram, rose,

Fig. 5.4 *Embroidered Sweet Bag, c. late 16th century, British. Metropolitan Museum of Art New York, 1986.300.1.*

jasmine, violet, lavender and orange flowers, and then combined with starch or another white powder base and then placed into small bags or the linings of royal chests and trunks.[35]

Sweet powders were usually supplied by perfumers and apothecaries, and the bags used to hold them were provided by seamstresses, tailors and other tradespeople. Under the supervision of the Mistress of the Sweet Coffers, these sweet bags would have been made up, changed and refilled as required. While all the examples discussed in this chapter come from the Office of the Robes, perfumery books and other manuals aimed at housewives indicate that boxes and chests perfumed with sweet bags were common in all kinds of households throughout the seventeenth century.[36]

Another space that was closely associated with the wardrobe was the attiring or dressing room. The dressing room was a chamber, usually connected to the bedroom, where one would put on clothes, style their hair and apply cosmetics or skincare. In smaller homes, it could also be the room where clothing was stored. Before the mid-seventeenth century, both women and men used rooms known as closets or attiring rooms to dress. In the 1619 inventory of Somerset House, Anna of Denmark's 'little attiring chamber close to the Gallery' was decorated with damask curtains, Flemish 'tapestry hangings' and 'three pictures of Venetian women'. It contained couch chairs and stools of crimson satin and velvet with gold lace, a looking glass in a black ebony frame, small walnut tables and an 'old footstool of needlework in flowers wrought upon Canvas'. This attiring room overlooked the yard and was connected to the clerk's rooms, the little bed chamber and the great gallery and it was still being used in 1640 by Henrietta Maria.[37]

After the mid-seventeenth century, references to 'dressing rooms' began to appear in English, coinciding with the introduction of the *levée* and *couché* (rising and retiring) dressing ceremonies that Charles II adapted from the French court.[38] The fashion for dressing rooms soon caught on and those of the middling or aspirational sorts also had these separate spaces in their homes. In 1663, Samuel Pepys mentioned his dressing room, which he was rather proud of, many times in his diary.[39] While ceremonies in the dressing room were courtly spectacles in France, English dressing rooms were slightly more private and not intended for daily public ritual. The more informal or intimate nature of the English dressing room was sometimes reflected in the location of the room itself. In the apartments built by Mary II and William III at Hampton Court, the queen's dressing room was placed next to her bedchamber at the farthest end of a series of interconnected rooms, with each one requiring more seniority in rank of household staff, or more importance on the part of a visitor, to gain access to.[40]

Dressing rooms were not just places to ready oneself but also spaces where 'women could show off their belongings', as Tita Chico has argued.[41] John Evelyn described visiting the Countess of Arlington in 1673 when she was a lady of the bedchamber. He wrote that 'she carried us up into her new dressing room at Goring House, where was a bed, two glasses, silver jars, and vases, cabinets, and other so rich furniture as I had seldom seen'. Evelyn was less than impressed, adding that 'to this excess of superfluity were we now arrived and that not only at Court, but almost universally, even to wantonness and profusion.[42] Evelyn similarly described the dressing room of Louise de Kérouaille, Duchess of Portsmouth, which was within her bedchamber:

> Here I saw the new fabric of French tapestry . . . beyond anything I had ever beheld. Some pieces had Versailles, St. Germains, and other palaces of the French King, with huntings, figures, and landscapes, exotic fowls, and all to the life rarely done. Then for Japan cabinets, screens, pendule clocks, great vases of wrought plate, tables, stands, chimney-furniture, sconces, branches, braseras, etc., all of massy silver.

In addition to this 'rich and splendid furniture', the king's mistress also positioned herself as a spectacle to be admired. When Evelyn made these observations, the duchess was 'in her morning loose garment, her maids combing her, newly out of her bed, his Majesty and the gallants standing about her'.[43]

Of note in Evelyn's description are the 'Japan' cabinets and screens that decorated this space. Goods sold by those merchants and Indian women described in Chapter 3 were crucial to decorating the dressing rooms of elite women and men during the late seventeenth century (see Fig. 5.5). In a room adjoining Anna of Denmark's attiring room at Somerset House, 'eight pieces of porcelain garnished with silver guilt' were displayed in a cabinet of crimson velvet, and a 'globe' and 'China carpet' were also recorded.[44] Over seventy years later, dressing rooms belonging to Elizabeth Seymour, the Duchess of Somerset, who was a customer of many Indian women, including Jane Potter and Mary Devet, were filled with these goods. One of the duchess's dressing rooms, either at Petworth or Northumberland House, was furnished with striped calico wall hangings from India, 'Japaned' daybeds and large cabinets with drawers and doors, presumably to store clothing and accessories.[45] In addition to these goods, during the 1690s the duchess's dressing room, bedchamber and drawing room at Northumberland House were furnished with 'dense porcelain garnitures on cabinets and overmantels', likely in imitation of Mary II's porcelain displays in her own apartments at Kensington Palace.[46] Thus, while wardrobes were practical, sweet smelling spaces used for storing and protecting clothing, dressing rooms were intimate spaces nearby designed for private retreat and also for the storage and display of the newest fashionable, decorative goods.

Getting dressed: tirewomen, dressers and the *toilette*

The centrepiece of the dressing room was the dressing table or toilet. Its name derived from the French term *toilette*, which referred to the cloth draped over the dressing table. There are several references to 'toylets' that were made for the dressing tables of the Stuart queens.[47] The use of these fabric toylets in both wardrobe and dressing spaces reinforced the connections between the practices that cared for clothing and those that cared for the body. Toilet could also refer to what we now call a vanity set, or

Fig. 5.5 *Cabinet of lacquered wood with gold and red, with mother of pearl inlay, engraved brass mounts and hinges,* c. *1670, Japan. Ham House, Surrey, NT 1139896.1. This cabinet was probably purchased by Elizabeth Maitland, Duchess of Lauderdale, and was recorded in an inventory of Ham House in 1677.*

matching receptacles and tools used for personal grooming. In 1673, John Evelyn wrote of seeing Catherine of Braganza's 'rich toilet in her dressing room' which was made 'all of massy gold, presented to her by the King, valued at £4,000'.[48] Such a set was a magnificent display of the queens' importance at court.

A scene of a lady at her *toilette* painted by Gerard ter Borch in 1660 also depicts a woman with a gold toilet and may give some indication as to what was in Catherine's elaborate set, including a mirror, containers, a gold dish and a candlestick (see Fig. 5.6). Depictions of elite women sitting at their dressing tables in loose gowns formed a popular type of genre art during this period, particularly in the Dutch Republic and France. Printmakers even depicted Mary II in such a scene (see Fig. 5.7).

Fig. 5.6 *Gerard ter Borch,* Lady at Her Toilette, *c. 1660, oil on canvas. Detroit Institute of Arts, 65.10.*

Although printed in 1694, the scene depicts Mary when she was Princess of Orange, sitting at a dressing table covered in several toylets, applying a paper patch.

Paper patches, or *mouches* as they were colloquially known in France, were used to conceal blemishes such as pimples or smallpox scars, or simply to make a fashion statement. These black paper patches came in the shape of circles, stars, moons and hearts, among others, and were wetted and placed on the face as depicted in the etching. Although moralists often associated patches with ill repute, due to their connections to sex workers who supposedly used them to conceal syphilis sores, Catherine of Braganza, Mary II and Queen Anne all bought these patches from their milliners, demonstrating their universal appeal amongst the fashionable elite.[49] These patches were usually kept in ornate boxes placed on the dressing table. In 1694, Mary II's Huguenot jeweller James Seheult

Fig. 5.7 *Antoine Trouvain,* Marie Anne Stuard Princesse d'Orange *[Mary Anne Stuart, Princess of Orange], 1694, etching. Rijksmuseum Amsterdam, RP-P-1906-2660.*

submitted a bill for 'a gold patch box with an Agate Stone Cover' amounting to £10.[50] Another gold-and-enamelled box set with diamonds containing Mary's monogram has survived in the Royal Collection (see Fig. 5.8).

In addition to patch boxes and mirrors, Fig. 5.7 also depicts a container filled with glass bottles containing skincare or cosmetics. Colour cosmetics were occasionally used; Anna of Denmark is known to have used red ointment on her lips and some face recipes with lead, mercury and talc that would have imparted a slight red and white colour, respectively.[51] Although it is very likely that the later Stuart queens wore some type of cosmetics, due to their associations with both beauty and health, I have found no mention of them in their Robes accounts. Recipe books containing cosmetic formulas

Fig. 5.8 *Queen Mary II's patch box of enamel, gold and diamonds,* c. *1694. Royal Collection Trust, RCIN 19133.*

had been widely circulated throughout Europe since at least the sixteenth century, and books such as the *Queens Closet Opened* (1656) even purported to be transcribed from Henrietta Maria's own recipe books by one of her servants.[52] Thus, it is possible that many beauty remedies used by the later Stuart queens were created or adapted in their household using these recipes.

Depicted in many scenes of women at their *toilette* are the servants who dressed elite women. The roles of gentlewomen and domestic servants in dressing practices were repeated in other elite and even middling households throughout England. In 1675, Anne Clifford, Dowager Countess of Dorset, Pembroke and Montgomery, had two gentlewomen 'that waits upon me', and even Samuel and Elisabeth Pepys had maids that helped them dress.[53] Much of this was to do with status, but it was also practical. Dressing in the Stuart period involved pinning, lacing, tying and arranging multiple layers of clothing together and onto the body. Many of these actions were difficult for the wearer to do themselves, especially once garments were on the body.[54] Queens, who wore some of the most elaborate outfits of the time, were therefore dressed by a team of bedchamber personnel overseen by the Groom of the Stole and First Lady of the Bedchamber, positions often combined with the Mistress of the Robes. As Abigail Masham later recalled, bedchamber women would retrieve and pass linens to one of the bedchamber ladies to place on the queen's body. The Page of the Backstairs would bring in water for the queen to wash herself, then the 'women' would assist in putting on outer garments while the Lady watched on. Sometimes the Lady of the Bedchamber would give the queen her final accessories, such as a fan. Assisting all these women were other 'Necessary Women', who were non-elite domestic servants.[55]

The main difference between *Ladies* of the bedchamber and *Women* of the bedchamber was status. *Ladies* tended to be from the nobility – marchionesses, countesses and duchesses – while *Women* were not of the peerage but usually the wives of knights or women of the gentry. Ladies were also paid more: Mary II's Ladies had salaries of £500 per year, while her Women were given between £200 and £300 (see Table 5.1).[56] Some bedchamber women were specifically referred to as 'dressers', emphasizing the importance of the queens' clothing. Mary of Modena had a First Dresser, Madam Dawson, and a Second Dresser, Madam Bromley.[57] Some could have several. Catherine of Braganza increased the

Table 5.1 The women of Mary II's bedchamber, 1689–94[60]

Position	Name	Wage per year (£)
Lady of the Robes	Elizabeth Stanley, Countess of Derby	400
Groom of the Stole	Elizabeth Stanley, Countess of Derby	800
Ladies of the Bedchamber	Mary, Countess of Dorset and Middlesex	500
	Ann, Countess of Nottingham	500
	Bridget, Countess of Plymouth	500
	Frances, Countess of Scarborough	500
	Frances, Countess of Wiltshire	500
	Gartrude, Marchioness of Halifax	500
	Frances, Marchioness of Winchester	500
First Woman of the Bedchamber and Keeper of the Privy Purse	Mrs Anna van Goltstein	300
Women of the Bedchamber	Mrs Dorothy Cason	200
	Mrs Cary (Mary) Jesson	200
	Mrs Martha Lockhart	200
	Mrs Agnes Vygh	200

(continued)

Table 5.1 Continued

Position	Name	Wage per year (£)
	Mrs Rachel Wyndham	200
Maids of Honour	Mrs Mary Berkley	200
	Mrs Mary Compton	200
	Mrs Eleonora Franklin	200
	Mrs Stuart Walburt Howard	200
	Mrs Ann Greville	200
	Mrs Elizabeth Mohan	200
	Mrs Jane Martha Temple	200
	Mrs Henrietta Villiers	200
Seamstress	Mrs Dorothy Ireland	60
Starcher	Mrs Dorothy Ireland	40
Laundresses	Mrs Elizabeth Worthington and three maids	260
Necessary Women	Elizabeth Wiele	50
	Margaret Wood	44
A Woman to Clean the Privy Chamber	Ann Duhurst	30

number of dressers in her household between 1671 and 1684 from eight to fifteen.[58] It was common for the queens' dressers to be women who had come with them from their natal courts. In 1663, Jane de La Gard and Dona Helena were listed as dressers for Catherine of Braganza, and Henrietta Maria de Vaullett and Jane de L'Espernanche were 'dressers to the Queen Mother' during the brief few years that Henrietta Maria spent back in England after the Restoration.[59] Having women from their home countries with whom they could converse in their natal languages was probably comforting for many consorts, particularly because the act of dressing for a queen could be quite time consuming.

One woman described in 1747 as a 'Prime Minister at the Toylet', who armed women with the dangerous weapons of 'nice curls' and 'ringlets', was the tirewoman.[61] Tirewomen 'dressed' the hair, their name deriving from headdresses known as 'tires', which was itself derived from 'tire room' or 'attiring room'. Throughout the seventeenth century this was a predominately female trade. Natasha Korda has shown that in the world of the early modern theatre, tirewomen 'specialized in the manufacture, adornment, and arrangement of head-attires', periwigs and hairpieces, as well as accessories such as 'ruffs, cuffs, bands (and the wires used to support them), points, laces, and fans'.[62] Tirewomen could therefore be both makers of hairpieces, headwear and linen accessories, as well as hair stylists who dressed the head with these accessories. Tirewomen who worked on the early modern stage appear to have specialized in making headpieces and laundering, starching and setting linen goods. However, in the Stuart queens' accounts they were primarily responsible for 'Dress[ing] in the Hair, when in Fashion, and when out, to cut the Hair, and Dress the Head'.[63]

Several tirewomen appear in the accounts of the early Stuart queens. Perhaps the best known is French Huguenot Marie Mountjoy who, with her husband Christopher, rented a tenement above their shop on the corner of Silver and Monkwell streets in Cripplegate to the playwright William Shakespeare in the period 1602–4.[64] During this time, Marie supplied many goods for Anna's court masques. In 1603, she billed the queen's Office of the Robes for a 'helmet for her Majesty and diverse Trimmings for the Ladies of her Majesty's masque at Twelvetide'.[65] Henrietta Maria's tirewoman Blanche Browne also billed the Robes for 'dressing' the queen's head for masques and for making headdresses described as 'wings'.[66] However, these women were not only called on for elaborate court performances. Marie Mountjoy also supplied 'necessaries belonging to Her Highness' Robes and other ornaments' between November 1604 and March 1605.[67] Tire-making was a family business for the Mountjoys; court records relating to a lawsuit involving the couple refer to Christopher as a 'tyer maker' too. The Mountjoy's only daughter, also named Marie, and her husband Stephen Belott were also trained in the trade.[68] Although the laws of couverture have obscured Marie and her daughter's part in the business in tax and legal records, Marie was the face of their trade in the queen's accounts. She dressed the heads of courtiers, while her husband worked behind the scenes making these accessories.

The tirewoman's role within the private dressing room was key to women's long-term success in this trade, as the intimacy of this space meant that elite women preferred female tirers. It was later wondered in the eighteenth century whether tirewomen made their living by acting more as intermediaries, passing on private messages between clients, than by their actual skills in trade.[69] One woman who regularly attended Anna of Denmark and her daughter Princess Elizabeth was Blanche Swansted. Several 'head attires' were found in a 'green satin box' in a room adjoining the attiring room in Somerset House in 1619 after Anna's death and it is possible that these were made by Swansted.[70] In a petition submitted to the crown in 1619, Swansted requested a pension for past services rendered and described what was expected of a tirewoman 'in-ordinary'. She wrote that at the Stuarts

> . . . first coming into this kingdom, she was sent to Edinburgh to attend upon the said queen in her profession which is to adorn the head, which service she then performed still waiting upon her Majesty unto London. And continuing that service towards her Majestie ever since, until her death having also attended her Majestie in divers Progresses.[71]

Clearly, Blanche's work as a tirewoman formed a key part of her identity. Not only did she call it a 'profession' in this petition, meaning that she viewed it as a career that required training and expertise, but in serving the queen it had taken her many places on progress, including to Scotland.

By the time that Anna of Denmark arrived in London, she preferred, as Jemma Field has argued, the 'Spanish fashion for hair piled high with narrow sides' with the remainder of the hair covered by a cap or hairpiece at the back of the head (see Fig. 1.1).[72] According to contemporary sources, after the hair was curled it would have been gathered into the desired style and 'underpropped with forks' and 'wires' that bolstered it. 'Great wreaths of gold and silver curiously wrought', referring to tires made from gold and silver wire, were then 'applied to the temples of their heads'.[73] This hairstyle was also popular with other women at court. In 1603, an unknown Scottish woman who kept a list of expenses incurred during her time in London recorded purchases of 'a tire of pearl to put on my head' valued at 30s., 'a silk tire to wear in my head' costing 10s. and 'a wire to my head with nine peaks' for 10s.[74] Tires with peaks covered in jewels appear in multiple portraits of women from the period. A portrait of Elizabeth Stuart depicts the princess wearing a tire headdress that forms round peaks threaded with pearls and inset with gems (see Fig. 5.9).

As a result of work which required constant attendance on the queen, Blanche Swansted stated in her petition that she had 'lost such customers by whom she was formerly set on work, & got her living'.[75] Her position was somewhat liminal; although she was frequently at court, she was not a member of the queen's bedchamber and did not receive allowances for diet or board as they did. Tirewomen's bills show the time-consuming nature of constantly waiting on a queen who sometimes did not require their services. One hundred years later, Queen Anne's tirewomen Mary Ducaila and Frances Baillon were regularly called to the queen's residences at Windsor, St James's and Kensington palaces. They did not always get to cut and style her hair, as their bills often requested payment for 'going to Kensington to cut ye Queens hair & coming back without cutting it' and 'for Attending to dress the Queen, and her Majesty not going'.[76] While Blanche Swansted was tirewoman in-ordinary with a wage, those who serviced the later Stuarts were commissioned on a piecework basis. Although their services were frequently required, the job also involved a lot of waiting around and they expected to be renumerated for it on account of lost business elsewhere.

Fig. 5.9 *Robert Peake the Elder,* Princess Elizabeth Stuart, Later Queen of Bohemia *(detail), c. 1606, oil on canvas. Metropolitan Museum of Art New York, 51.194.1.*

The pay received by tirewomen for their labour was more than a mantua-maker charged to make a gown, but less than many of the other tradespeople in the accounts. Over the six-year period that Ducaila served Queen Anne she charged roughly £2 3s. for cutting the queen's hair and about the same again for dressing it. In some years Ducaila made only £20 from her services and in others, such as in the first year of Queen Anne's reign, she made £64 8s. 6d. in total.[77] Ducaila had been a fashionable and sought after tirewoman for at least two decades. Her bills appear in the Duchess of Somerset's accounts in 1683, and she was paid £50 by Catherine of Braganza's household for caps, 'Towers of hair' and 'cutting of Our Hair' in the years 1686–7.[78]

The first year of Anne's reign was a particularly busy time for Ducaila, who was called to cut and style the queen's hair on many occasions for state events. In 1702, Ducaila charged £10 15s. for the 'dressing [of] her Majesty's head' on her coronation day.[79] Descriptions of the queen explain why such an occasion warranted a large sum. Celia Fiennes wrote in her travel memoir that Anne's head was

> . . . well dressed with Diamonds mixed in the hair which at the Least motion Brill'd and flamed. She wore a Crimson velvet Cap with Ermine under the Circlet, which was set with Diamonds, and on the middle a sprig of Diamonds drops transparent hung in form of a plume of feathers . . .

The queen's ladies in waiting were similarly described by Fiennes as having 'Jewels in their hair'.[80] The hairstyle that the Queen and her ladies wore on her coronation day has been preserved in a wig that adorns the effigy of Frances Stuart, Duchess of Richmond and Lennox, at Westminster Abbey (see Fig. 5.10). The wig is made from light brown hair and has an accompanying headdress made from wire, clear and red paste glass stones forming rosettes and tear-shaped drops and a small red velvet and silver gilt coronet, mirroring the description given by Fiennes.[81]

The construction of this wig is extremely useful in understanding Ducaila's bills in Anne's accounts as it is contemporary to them; before her death in October 1702, the duchess requested that her effigy be dressed in the garments she had worn to Queen Anne's coronation. The hair in the wig has been 'built up' or held up by a wire frame and false hair known as towers. Such scaffolding was satirized by John Dryden in 1693: 'With Curls, on Curls, they build her Head before; And mount it with a Formidable Tow'r'.[82] The curls that sit atop the head have been stiffened and held in position with rolls of black paper, which was a common technique.[83] Strings of paste gemstones and gold ribbons have been woven through the towers of hair on this wig, as is described in Ducaila's bills. The hairstyle created by Ducaila for the queen's attendance at the second session of her second Parliament in December 1706 called for '24 yards of gold ribbon for her Majesty's head' and '24 yards of Silver ribbon'.[84] Ribbon was not only decorative but served a practical function. In 1711, Queen Anne's tirewoman Mrs Baillon requested payment for 'black satin Ribbon to fasten the locks' and keep the hairstyle in place.[85]

Finally, conservation has shown that the Duchess of Richmond's wig has been powdered.[86] Several perfuming manuals and recipe books from the period contain information about how to make 'Powders for Hair' and several types of powders were delivered to the dressers of the Stuart queens.[87] The tirewoman Anne Tolat also delivered 'rolls twisted with ribbon', 'wires' and linen caps to Mary II's First Lady of the Bedchamber, Anna van Goltstein.[88] These deliveries indicate that hairstyling was an intensive business that involved several tradespeople and members of the household, including dressers who set up the toilette for the tirewoman and her apprentices or assistants, as is depicted in a French engraving showing a tirewoman at work (see Fig. 5.11). During her time as a bedchamber woman and dresser, Abigail Masham was described as 'a woman that combs [the Queen's head]' by her cousin the Duchess of Marlborough.[89] Thus, the women of the bedchamber probably assisted the tirewoman and also provided basic hairstyling too.

The French equivalent of the tirewoman was the *Coiffeuse* and she was also depicted in prints of trades by the engraver Nicholas de Larmessin during the 1690s (see Fig. 5.12). These prints help us to visualize many of the things described in tirewomen's accounts and are useful in understanding their work, not least because many of the later Stuarts' tirewomen were French and had possibly trained as *coiffeuses* in France.[90] Mary Ducaila's bills to the Duchess of Somerset are written in French, as are those from her husband Francis who also worked with hair as a periwig-maker.[91] After Ducaila's death

Fig. 5.10 *Wig and headdress from the funeral effigy of Frances Stuart, Duchess of Richmond and Lennox, 1702, Westminster Abbey.*

in 1708, the royal household accounts note that the tailor and stay-maker John Gazain was 'her brother & Executor' and it appears that she came from an extended family of French migrants working in the fashion trades.[92]

Larmessin's engraving reveals several tools of the *coiffeuse* and tirewoman's trade. The standing *coiffeuse* is depicted dressing a wig sitting on a dummy head, like those recorded in accounts for the Stuart queens. In 1694, the milliner Thomas Cheret supplied Mary II's Robes with 'a stand to a wooden head' on which wigs and other false hairpieces would have sat.[93] Hanging on the wall are various false hairpieces, and the *coiffeuse* on the right of the image sits stringing strands of hair onto another hairpiece soon to join them. Several false hairpieces are described in Catherine of Braganza's accounts. In 1687, the queen imported several '*tour[s]* of hair' from France, to achieve the high off-the-face hairstyles seen in front of early fontanges (see Fig. 3.11).[94] Mrs Ducaila also provided 'towers' and 'favourites' to Queen Anne, the latter being small locks of curled hair that dropped down onto the

Fig. 5.11 *Nicolas de Larmessin,* La Coiffeuse [The Tirewoman]*, late 17th century, engraving. Bibliothèque nationale de France, département Bibliothèque-musée de l'opéra, RES-926 (7). The Coiffeuses or tirewomen wear aprons with pockets, and from their waistbands hang scissors and other tools of the trade. The caption reads: 'Beneath an elegant hairstyle / One hides a number of years, / And art does not surpass nature / Except to capture lovers'.*

temples as depicted in a portrait miniature of Anne (see Fig. 5.13). These 'locks' of false hair were carefully stored and kept for later use in boxes also supplied by Ducaila.[95] Finally, padded circular rolls 'twisted' with ribbon on which all the fake hair would have been pinned and piled, as mentioned in Ducaila's bills, hang on the wall behind the *coiffeuses*, alongside metal wires used to build the hairstyle and support fontanges and ribbons.[96] These items illustrate the complexity and preparation involved in elite hairstyling at the time.

Fig. 5.12 *Nicolas de Larmessin,* La Coifeuse *[The Tirewoman], late 17th century, engraving. Bibliothèque nationale de France, département Estampes et photographie, RESERVE FOL-QB-201 (71).*

Fig. 5.13 *Charles Boit, after Godfrey Kneller,* Queen Anne, c. *1703–27, enamelled portrait miniature. Rijksmuseum Amsterdam, SK-A-4299.*

The tirewoman could also provide other essential elements of the toilet: beauty and medicinal remedies. By 1747 the tirewoman was described as creating 'natural and artificial complexions' for her clients.[97] Mrs Ducaila sold a 'bottle of maidenhair syrup' and 'Cypress powder' to the Duchess of Somerset, both of which were used for medicinal and cosmetic purposes.[98] Bottles of 'orange flower water' and 'Hungary water' were also sold to Mary II and Queen Anne by their milliners.[99] These distilled waters were used to treat medical conditions such as palsy and gout (the latter of which Anne suffered from frequently), to remove blemishes and pimples, and to wash the face and body.[100] The waters would have promoted 'good colour' and radiant skin indicative of both good health and also of high social status.[101] Thus, the role of the tirewoman was an important one in the queen's dressing room and she worked alongside women of the bedchamber and dressers to clothe the queen, style her hair and to apply cosmetics and skincare products. The presence of tradeswomen such as the tirewoman, who by the end of the century were increasingly patronized in an extra-ordinary basis, also demonstrates the permeability of the borders between the royal household and fashion marketplace at this time.

Cleaning clothing: brushers, laundresses and starchers

Dirty clothes were a fact of early modern life. Clean bodies and body linens were essential to maintaining health and communicating the state of the 'mind, morals and spirit'.[102] Perceptions of cleanliness were based on external appearances and clean clothing signalled civility and a virtuous moral character and lent itself to ideals of beauty. Washing the skin in conjunction with linen was considered essential in early modern England. Charles II and Catherine of Braganza both bathed regularly; Charles is known to have had a bathing room at Whitehall and Catherine's Wardrobe Keeper's man moved the 'Queen's bathing Tub, & all things belonging to it' in 1691.[103] As previously noted, when queens dressed, they also washed parts of their bodies with basins of water, a ritual depicted in images of the toilette (see Fig. 5.6). Cleaning also extended the life of a garment, protected one's (often large) monetary investment in their clothing and, in the case of starching items such as ruffs and collars, ensured that these garments functioned as they should when worn. Thus, the cleaning of the body and of garments were key aspects of the caring processes that this chapter examines.

The Robes and bedchamber accounts show the many types of cleaning tasks that occurred in the royal household. For much of the seventeenth century, outer garments such as gowns, waistcoats and petticoats were constructed with materials such as buckram, whalebone and pasteboard. They could be decorated with gold and silver lace, braids, coloured ribbons, tassels and other trims, and embroidered with coloured or metallic silk threads. Additionally, many silk and wool fabrics used to make clothing contained non-colourfast dyes or were pinked and stamped. As a result, none of these garments could be fully immersed in water for cleaning.[104] Instead, outer garments were usually dry cleaned using a variety of methods including shaking and airing, brushing, spot cleaning and perfuming, and brushers were employed to carry out these tasks in the Robes.

An undated petition from Mary of Modena's Brusher in the Robes, John Groce, gives an insight into these processes. He wrote that since being sworn in as Brusher after her majesty's coronation (in 1685), he 'hath been unprovided of several sorts of Brushes, Wigs, and Balls for Clothes, to take away the Spots or Stains of Oil, Tallow, wax, and Grease'. He also noted that this work required him to purchase ells of Linen cloth and 'black crape' 'for cleaning her Majesty's Clothes . . . [and] Mourning Clothes' with his own money which amounted to a 'considerable Sum' that he requested reimbursement for.[105] During the reign of Queen Anne, her Yeoman of the Robes also purchased goods such as brushes of various sizes and 'Venice, and English chalk, to get out spots'.[106] Chalk is still a method used today to remove oil or grease from clothing, and it appears that cloth was used to either rub out spots or to apply spot cleaning agents consisting of alcohols, acids and enzymes that were known to breakdown stubborn stains.[107] In addition to dry and spot cleaning, outer garments were also perfumed with sweet powders to deter insects and vermin and to keep them smelling nice. This was particularly common for furred items. Henrietta Maria's skinner, Richard Downing, aired, cleaned and mended the queen's furred robes of state in the 1630s.[108]

Not all laundry was created equal, nor were those who undertook the cleaning of clothing. While dry cleaning and perfuming were tasks undertaken by male Brushers and Grooms in the Office of the Robes, as well as tradespeople like perfumers and skinners, laundering, meaning to wash linen and cotton clothing in soapy water, was overwhelmingly a woman's job.[109] The gendered discrepancy between these household tasks is indicative of the traditional place of male and female servants in large early modern households. While food preparation, serving and room cleaning were jobs generally performed by men, laundering and nursing were considered female roles.[110] In her analysis of chores carried out by female domestic servants, Mansell found that laundry accounted for almost two-fifths of all their housework labour in early modern England.[111] This is because washing involved many steps: dirty linens needed to be sorted before they were soaped, scalded (washed in hot soapy water) and then batted and beat to remove dirt and filth. After they were rinsed, linens were wrung to 'force the water out', starched, air dried, smoothed and ironed. They may also have been treated with sweet waters, made in a similar way to sweet powders, which perfumed the linen garments before they were placed into storage chests with sweet bags.[112] These waters were usually made locally but sometimes they were imported. In 1689, Catherine of Braganza's wardrobe man Robert Paxton billed for 'Custom house Charges for a Chest of Sweet Waters from Lisbon, & bringing it to Somerset House'.[113] These waters likely fragranced the queen dowager's clothing stored at Somerset House with the aromas of her homeland.

Susan North and Carole Rawcliffe have both argued that the work of the laundress, or washerwoman as she was also known, occupies a marginal place in the historical record.[114] Laundry was a fact of life, but those women who performed this physically exhausting, time-consuming and sometimes dangerous task have rarely been acknowledged. Partly this is because of their position: most laundresses throughout history were illiterate, of low status and performed insecure and underpaid – but still vital – care work. Laundresses and washerwomen were also frequently associated with female unruliness and sex work, and, in times of disease outbreaks, they were singled out as vectors of sickness due to their handling of dirty clothing and household linens.[115] In England, as North has articulated, 'Washing appears to have been the first chore that women paid someone else to do when they had the resources and their last resort for income when all attempts to find other work failed.'[116] However, laundresses could also be highly skilled and well remunerated. The linen garments of the elite often contained delicate lace and non-colourfast silk embroidery. A good material literacy and the specialist knowledge of how to launder delicate and expensive linen goods without ruining them would therefore have been required in any elite household.[117]

In the royal household, the position of Laundress of the Body was a coveted and reputable one. The Laundresses of the Body to the Stuart queens tended to come from trusted families in service or the gentry, and they also appear to have had a much closer relationship with their female patrons than Laundresses in the kings' households. The status of these women and the labour-intensive demands of laundry raise questions about who truly got their hands wet in washing royal garments. The household accounts indicate that, while the Laundress of the Body likely understood laundering techniques, her role focused primarily on overseeing teams of non-elite servants employed as laundry maids and washerwomen. In 1661, just a few months after the marriage contract between Charles II and Catherine of Braganza was signed, the Lord Chamberlain issued a warrant for 'Mary Chiffinch to be sworn Laundress to the Queen, with power to choose laundry maids'.[118] By 1678, the next laundress Elizabeth Nun was paid £185 per year for 'her self and Three Laundry maids'.[119] Later, Mary of Modena's Laundress of the Body Elizabeth Pearse submitted a petition to the Lords of the queen's council stating that,

> She humbly prays your Lordships in consideration of the Premises, and the great expense she is at by keeping constantly three maids, and hiring a Washerwoman to help, and finding all necessary for the Laundry, to make such augmentation to her salary and settlement of Traveling Charges; as to your Lordships shall seem fit.[120]

A team of three laundry maids appears to have been typical. The households of both Henrietta Maria and Mary II also had three maids.[121] These records also suggest that there was some sort of difference in status between laundry maids and washerwomen. It is possible that washerwomen were less specialized day labourers hired, as Pearse said, 'to help' the laundry maids.

Pearse's petition also mentioned the great expense of washing and other records show that laundering materials required for a royal household were not cheap. In 1663, the 'Laundress of the Queens Table Linnen' and the 'Laundress of the Queens Body Linnen' were both given 'five shillings a day' for 'soap, Starch, Wood, Coals and other necessities' used to wash the queen's table and body linens.[122] Soap, made from a variety of plant and animal fats during this period, was essential to washing, as was lye, an alkaline agent made from wood ashes. The preparation of lye was a common task undertaken by laundresses and perhaps in the queens' households it was made using the wood specified in these bills.[123]

Unfortunately, the Stuart household accounts do not indicate where the work of the laundresses took place. King James II's laundress, Mrs Dupuy, was given ten shillings per day 'for Travelling charges', suggesting that perhaps some of the washing was done offsite, or that the Laundress consistently travelled between royal residences collecting and delivering laundry.[124] Washing required substantial amounts of water and adequate space for drying. In expansive complexes like Whitehall and Hampton

Court, the laundering and drying of linens likely took place in various locations throughout the palace; comparable buildings on the continent had large, dedicated rooms that were set aside specifically for hanging laundry.[125] It is also possible that laundry was done offsite. At the establishment of William III's household in 1689, it was stipulated that the Laundress of the Body required allowance to hire a laundry when the king was at Whitehall.[126]

A complementary and overlapping role to laundress was that of the starcher. In the queens' households, the starcher was an established position with an annual wage, boardwage and other privileges. Linen accessories such as ruffs, collars and cuffs often required starching and setting to remove wrinkles and to have the stiffness required to function as they should. Starching also added a protective layer to clothing, as stains would sit on the starch rather than seeping into the fabric, making linens easier to launder.[127] The re-starching and setting of standing ruffs and collars after every laundering required 'time, skill and knowledge' to do correctly.[128] As Korda has argued, it was these 'techniques and technologies' of starching that 'transformed the low-status labour of laundering' into a highly skilled, well paid occupation.[129] Indeed, both contemporary sources and modern recreative practice have emphasized that the starching and setting of ruffs with hot pokers was a time-consuming task that required specialist knowledge.[130]

This process is demonstrated in an earlier sixteenth-century satirical etching by Pieter van der Borcht that depicts laundresses, starchers and their clients as monkeys 'aping' the latest fashions (see Fig. 5.14). In the top-left corner customers bring in their dirty ruffs, they are laundered in tubs and hung up to dry before being covered in starch (bottom left), dried by the fireplace (bottom right) and then set in place with hot poking sticks (bottom centre).[131] Many of the items required for this process are recorded in the Stuart household accounts. Catherine of Braganza's starcher was provided with 'Coales and other necessaries' in 1663 and the laceman William Rutland supplied 'starching and mending' supplies to the Robes in 1686. This suggests that lacemen sold not only delicate lace and trims used on linen items but also the supplies used to launder them.[132] A survey of Hampton Court Palace from 1702 outlined six rooms, three garrets and a closet that were used by the starcher and seamstress for this process.[133]

Although large ruffs fell out of fashion in England by the middle of the Stuart period, many other linen items continued to require starching. During the seventeenth century the work of the starcher was so valuable that girls began to apprentice into these trades. Laura Gowing has found that girls were bound as a 'sempster and starcher' and 'starcher and cutter out of linen'.[134] In manuals that instructed servants, the skilled work of a woman who could wash and starch was contrasted with the unskilled work of laundry maids who washed only basic garments like smocks, as well as household linens.[135] Increased remuneration for such a skillset is visible in the Stuart queens' accounts. In Anna of Denmark's household, the Laundress of the Body and Starcher were often one and the same, as Susanna Greene is recorded as receiving a salary of between £20 and £40 for her role as

Fig. 5.14 *Pieter van der Borcht*, Plate 9: The Laundry, c. *1562, etching. British Museum, 1866,0407.46.*

Laundress and also requested extra payments for 'service done unto her Majesty as for Starching of her Ruffs'.[136] In 1662, Elizabeth Nun drew a salary of £60 for her work as Laundress of the Body and another salary of £60 as a starcher in Catherine of Braganza's household.[137] In Mary II's household, Dorothy Ireland also drew two separate salaries as a seamstress and starcher (see Table 5.1). By the mid-seventeenth century, starching was therefore considered a specialized skillset that required extra renumeration.

Dynasties of service and social mobility

The care economy encompassed the wardrobe, dressing and laundering spaces of the royal household. It provided paid work for many who undertook tasks considered to be low status women's work, such as storing clothing and assisting the queen in dressing, as well as laundering and starching. As this final section will show, care work in the royal household also provided social mobility.[138] This is because employment by aristocratic and royal households brought not just wages and gifts, but also social connections and other forms of patronage that enabled advancement for individuals and families. Skilled tradeswomen such as silkwomen and seamstresses were able to hold offices within the royal household because of their trade identities and they used them to their advantage. Other lower-ranking female servants such as laundresses and starchers, who in other contexts performed some of the lowest paid work in the care economy, were able to forge lifelong vocations in the royal household and, over time, many of them increasingly came from non-aristocratic families who provided 'dynasties of service' to the Stuarts.[139] The work of these women, their backgrounds and positions within the royal household, like those elite women discussed in Chapter 2, show that the royal household provided 'careers' for a variety of women, not just peeresses.

The dual role of many laundresses, seamstresses and starchers, as both tradeswomen and members of the Bedchamber, highlights the social mobility available to women who undertook this work in the royal household. At the court of Henry VIII, the seamstress was not an official office. Rather, the wives of other tradesmen informally did this work.[140] However, by the Stuart period seamstresses could be external tradeswomen commissioned on a piece-by-piece basis, or, they were salaried office holders. This is because as well as making new linen garments, seamstresses also helped to take care of clothing in the form of mending and remaking. Both the king and the queen's household had a seamstress who was paid a yearly wage for her services.[141] In the case of queens regnant, salaries paid to their seamstresses were issued by the Great Wardrobe, which oversaw all royal provisions. It was always noted of Queen Anne's seamstress Mrs Duran that her bills were 'not enter'd into the Robes account' as they were 'to be paid at the great wardrobe'.[142] This suggests that Duran was both a member of the queen's household and an in-ordinary tradeswomen in the Great Wardrobe, tending to all manner of making and mending royal clothing and provisions.

The career trajectory of the silkwoman and seamstress Dorothy Speckard demonstrates the social mobility that skilled artisanal work could give women in the royal household. As outlined in Chapter 4, Dorothy began her career as the silkwoman to Elizabeth I in the final years of the Tudor queen's reign, first appearing in her accounts in 1601. When the Stuarts took the throne in 1603, she began to work for both James I and Anna of Denmark. For her Tudor and Stuart patrons, Dorothy is described as making several silk and linen goods for the body, head, neck and wrists, doing embroidery and needlework, making household linens and furnishings, and washing and starching goods.[143] Dorothy's family origins are unclear. However, she was married to Abraham Speckard who was a wealthy milliner and merchant who also supplied the Robes of Anna of Denmark and James I.[144] Abraham may have come from a Flemish merchant family, and, like Baptist Hicks discussed in Chapter 3, his successful business and merchant trading endeavours may have allowed him to buy his way into the gentry.[145]

The good standing of the Speckards in London, and, more importantly, Dorothy's skilled trade as a silkwoman and seamstress, enabled her to transition from a place as a tradesperson in the Robes to take up a court office in Anna of Denmark's bedchamber. At some point between 1603 and 1610, Dorothy was made a Lady of the Privy Chamber, and another woman, Hester le Telier, became the queen's silkwoman in-ordinary in the Robes.[146] Chamberers at the Tudor and Jacobean courts undertook similar tasks to the dresser. They usually assisted in dressing and looked after the queen's household and body linens, small items of clothing and the storage of clothing and jewels.[147] In addition to making linen goods for the queen, the inventory of 1619 for Somerset House listed that one 'crimson Velvet Chest with a red leather Case' was in 'Mrs Speckarts charge'. Located within this chest were fourteen embroidered and needle-worked linen waistcoats, embroidered silk stockings of diverse colours, and a headcloth embroidered with the arms of Denmark and the queen's name.[148] Dorothy's trade occupation and training, which involved embroidery and needlework, as well as her work laundering and starching goods for Elizabeth I, made her an ideal chamberer in charge of caring for these goods.

Like other women who held an office in the queen's household, Dorothy was gifted old clothing by the queen as a show of thanks and remuneration. In 1610, the queen gave her a black satin gown with hanging sleeves.[149] When Anna died in 1619, Dorothy walked in the funeral procession alongside other members of the queen's privy chamber and, employing her occupational skills, made the 'large veil' that dressed the head of the funeral effigy.[150] It does not appear that the next Stuart consort, Henrietta Maria, took Dorothy into her own household, and, as a woman, she was not allowed to occupy a bedchamber position in the king's household. Nor did Charles appoint her as his seamstress. Instead, he chose Julian Elliot, who had been his seamstress while Prince of Wales, and Dorothy appears to have reverted back to her trade.[151] While Dorothy Speckard's court career was not long-lasting, it was her continued occupation and skilled work as a silkwoman and seamstress that allowed someone like her to move between the worlds of the court and the fashion marketplace.

While Dorothy Speckard was rewarded with offices in the bedchamber due to her skill with a needle and reputation as a tradeswoman, other women who undertook care work in the queen's household were elevated to that status through their personal or familial, particularly matrilineal, connections. Queen Anne's starcher Elizabeth Abrahall had previously worked in the Churchill household. She came from a trade background, perhaps a seamstress or milliner, as bills record her making pockets and head clothes in addition to starching. Sarah, Duchess of Marlborough, appointed her in the royal household due to her long experience and her trust in Elizabeth's knowledge and abilities. When she died in 1711, Elizabeth was interred in Westminster Abbey.[152] It had been intended that the daughter of Charles I's seamstress Julian Elliot, Elizabeth Elliot, would succeed her mother in her office as seamstress to the king. However, the events of the Civil War prevented this. Instead, Elizabeth was given the office of seamstress in Catherine of Braganza's household when the monarchy was restored, and she held this position from 1662 until at least 1678.[153] Her mother's long service to the Stuarts ensured Elizabeth's placement within one of the newly created royal households.

The members of the Chiffinch family embody the idea of 'dynasties of service', referring to families who held offices in the courts of successive sovereigns. The Chiffinches were not an aristocratic family. However, they are an example of how work in the royal household could lead to social mobility for many generations. While male members of the family served in various roles in the king's household, female members of the Chiffinch family created dynasties of laundresses, seamstresses and starchers to Henrietta Maria, Charles II and Catherine of Braganza. The family appears to have come from Staplehurst in Kent and had no immediate connections to the court until 1641, when the Bishop of Salisbury brought a young Thomas Chiffinch to the court of Charles I. He was soon made a Page of the Bedchamber and went on to serve the Prince of Wales (later Charles II). When the royal family fled into exile during the Civil Wars, the Chiffinches went with them. It was during their time in Paris that Thomas's wife Dorothy Chiffinch began to serve as laundress and seamstress to both Charles and his mother Henrietta Maria.[154] In 1659 she petitioned for backpay for mending Henrietta Maria's laced linen and managing Charles's laundry with a team of servants.[155] When the monarchy was restored in 1660, Thomas was made the keeper of Charles II's jewels and closet, and Dorothy was made laundress and seamstress to the king in recognition of their service during the years in exile.[156]

When Catherine of Braganza became queen in 1662, two Chiffinch family members were placed in her household. One was Thomas's brother William, who was made a Page of the Back Stairs, and the other was the previously mentioned Mary Chiffinch, who became the queen's Laundress of the Body. It is unclear how Mary was related to Thomas and William, but she was neither their wife nor daughter; perhaps she was a sister or niece. However, she was placed in this position due to family connections and Dorothy Chiffinch's role as laundress in the king's household. Mary held this position for a few years before being replaced by Elizabeth Nun, William Chiffinch's sister-in-law.[157] As previously mentioned, Elizabeth drew salaries as both a laundress and starcher.

Laundresses of the Body, seamstresses and starchers were often trusted confidants, particularly for queens. The natural processes of a woman's body – menstruation, pregnancy and childbirth – which created a greater need for linen, and the frequent washing thereof, made the Laundress of the Body to the queen especially important. As their title suggested, they not only looked after the queen's body linens, but also had intimate knowledge of the royal body and, by extension, the queens' personal lives. In 1688, Mary of Modena's laundress Elizabeth Pearse was called to testify about the birth of the Catholic heir, James Francis Edward Stuart, when rumours that the queen falsified the birth began to spread. She attested that she had been present at the birth and had 'fetched her maids, and with them took away all the foul linen, hot as they came from the Queen', and continued to launder linen stained by breastmilk in the following months.[158] In 1709, Queen Anne wrote to the Duchess of Marlborough about choosing a new seamstress and starcher, stating that, as it was a 'post that next to my bedchamber women is the nearest to my person of any of my servants', she wished to have a direct say in who was appointed.[159]

For these reasons, Elizabeth Nun appears to have had a close relationship with Catherine of Braganza. In May 1669, Samuel Pepys recalled that he went to Whitehall and dined with the Chiffinches but their dinner was interrupted when the 'Queen, as being supposed with child, fell ill, so as to call for Madam Nun, Mr. Chiffinch's sister, and one of her women'.[160] Nun remained in Catherine's household until the 1680s, when she was replaced by Catherine Sayers who does not appear to have been any relation of the Chiffinches.[161] Like the laundresses before her, Sayers probably had multiple laundry maids working beneath her, whom she managed in her position. As well as being the Laundress of the Body, during the 1680s Sayers was also a bedchamber woman, where she had additional work as a dresser and received a yearly wage of £200.[162] While the holding of both positions may lend itself to an interpretation of these offices being sinecures, it might be due to the downsizing of the queen dowager's household in the later years of her life, and in the years before her return to Portugal in 1692.

Indeed, if we return to the question of sinecures, the monopolization of certain household positions by dynasties of service has raised questions about the nature of these posts and the types of work they involved, or did not involve.[163] As previously stated, the Laundress of the Body was a managerial position. It was she who oversaw a team of laundry maids and had access to the queen's bedchambers and staff to collect dirty linens, rather than being the person who got her hands wet. However, in relation to starchers and seamstresses, these were positions that did involve skilled work that began to be formalized into recognized training via apprenticeships during this century. Thus, just because women came from families that secured several offices in the royal household does not mean that they were unskilled or did no work. Girls who wished to find work as chambermaids in elite households during this century were advised to learn how to wash and starch fine linens and lace.[164] If one came from a family of women such as the Chiffinches who were already doing these jobs, it is likely they were trained informally in the home. Jane Ireland was made seamstress and starcher in 1690 to William III, and her mother Dorothy Ireland was also Mary II's seamstress and starcher. Dorothy had been at court for several decades and during this time she likely taught her daughter the skills of her offices.[165]

This was a change from earlier in the century when women such as Dorothy Speckard, Julian Elliot and Elizabeth Abrahall worked as tradeswomen in the fashion marketplace or other households before moving into the royal bedchamber. However, the expert skills necessary for caring for delicate linen and silk items that were held by tradeswomen were still necessary. As the work of the silkwoman evolved into the trade of the female milliner (see Chapter 3), their skill with laundering continued to be utilized. The Cherets requested payment for 'washing & making a cambric [head] suit' and for washing two pairs of 'double fringed ruffles' for Mary II, and in 1710 the milliner Mary Wilkins 'made and washed' six muslin handkerchiefs for Queen Anne.[166] These references to washing and making likely refer to the act of remaking. These skilled tradespeople were entrusted with this task as metal and other colourful trimmings, as well as delicate lace, often needed to be unpicked and resewn back onto the linen or silk accessory after it had been cleaned.[167]

The fact that these types of laundering activities were often outsourced in royal households shows the value of these materials and the desire to make sure they were appropriately cared for by those with specialist knowledge of their construction. Therefore, while there were almost certainly some appointments that were sinecures as the century progressed, it is equally plausible that women from long-standing dynasties of service were trained from a young age for these officers, while particularly skilled work was outsourced to milliners.[168] The overlapping skills, training and positions held by tradeswomen in the fashion marketplace and by laundresses, seamstresses and starches in the royal household therefore reinforces the interconnected nature of the royal household and the fashion marketplace during the seventeenth century.

Conclusions

Caring for the queen's clothing and her fashionable appearance was a labour-intensive process that required various office holders, servants and tradespeople with a variety of skillsets. Examining the Stuart queens' wardrobe and dressing spaces, as well as laundries and starching rooms, makes early modern care work in relation to clothing visible, and it highlights the connections between women's work in the fashion marketplace and their work in the care economy of the household.

In wardrobe spaces dotted throughout various royal palaces, clothing was kept in perfumed coffers and trunks that were managed by the Mistress of the Sweet Coffers and other wardrobe staff. In attiring and dressing rooms located nearby, teams of bedchamber women, dressers and tirewomen played critical roles in dressing the queen, styling her hair and applying cosmetics. These spaces demonstrate the connections between the practices that cared for clothing and those that cared for the body. Dressing rooms, adorned with decorative goods sourced from global and local marketplaces, as well as the frequent presence of extra-ordinary tradeswomen such as tirewomen, also reflected the intertwined nature of the royal household and the broader marketplace.

The laundering, cleaning and maintenance of expensive clothing also demonstrates the ways that royal service allowed women who usually performed low-compensated, feminine coded care work to be well remunerated and, like their elite counterparts, have careers within the royal household. Caring for clothing and the body in the royal household enabled skilled and trusted tradeswomen such as tirewoman Blanche Swanstead to frequently move around with the court on progress, or, in the case of Dorothy Speckard, to transition into prominent court roles; it was her continued occupation as a silkwoman and seamstress that allowed her to move between the worlds of the court and the fashion marketplace.

Social mobility could also happen within the household through generations of women from dynasties of service who were trained specifically for positions relating to the care of clothing, and by extension the queen's body, within the royal household. For the Chiffinch family, their connection to several Stuart households dictated their occupational choices. While this mobility may not have always been long lasting – the Chiffinches seem to have fallen out of favour after the deaths of Charles II and Catherine of Braganza – such mobility did set them up financially and allowed them to intermarry with other well-to-do families.[169] These dynasties of service therefore created generations of laundresses, starchers and seamstresses whose work ultimately helped their family to amass wealth and advancement through their offices.

Conclusion: Women's patronage and women's work

On the 9 March 1726 in the parish of St Margaret's, Westminster, the Laundress of the Body to the final Stuart monarch, Elizabeth Atkinson, died at the age of sixty-four. At some point in the following decades, her body was interred in Westminster Abbey alongside that of her friend, Elizabeth Gates, to whom she had left her estate.[1] A plaque in the north cloister commemorates the women, and others from the Gates family:

> Near this place lies the body of Mrs Elizabeth Atkinson whose truly benevolent temper render'd her universally belov'd, and especially by the poor, whose relief was her care and constant pleasure. She had the honour to serve Her late Majesty Queen Anne during her whole reign as body-laundress . . .[2]

Queen Anne's household accounts show that Mrs Elizabeth Atkinson had indeed been her Laundress of the Body throughout her reign (1702–14). Before this, Elizabeth had been a bedchamber woman to Anne when she was Princess of Denmark, and she had cared for Anne's son, William, Duke of Gloucester. Like the Chiffinches, Elliots and Irelands, Elizabeth appears to have come from a dynasty of service family and had likely been trained up to enter service under the Stuarts.[3] Elizabeth's place in the queen's household, which involved managing laundry and other clothing, provided her with financial means and mobility. This ultimately allowed her to be buried at Westminster Abbey, near royalty and other powerful and important figures. It also gave her contact with a diverse array of people, ranging from the queen herself to Sarah Churchill, Duchess of Marlborough, other gentlemen and women and even tradeswomen in the fashion marketplace.

In her will, Elizabeth bequeathed £10 to another woman whose work and life have been discussed in this book, the mantua-maker Anne Clifton.[4] It is through their shared work for the queen's household that this bedchamber woman and this tradeswoman must have forged a friendship that saw Anne Clifton become one of the few beneficiaries of Elizabeth Atkinson's estate. The friendship between this Laundress of the Body and mantua-maker to the final Stuart queen highlights the interconnected nature of the queen's household and fashion marketplace, and the shared experiences of the women whose work with clothing saw their lives overlap.

This book has reconstructed the work that took place in relation to managing, selling, making and caring for royal and elite women's clothing to examine the nature and growth of women's work during the long seventeenth century. It has examined the strong connections between the worlds of the Stuart courts and London's fashion marketplace to show that a growing number of tradeswomen, many of whom worked outside the guilds, serviced a number of elite patrons. Through the commercial and social connections that these women established with their elite clients, such as the Mistress of the Robes and other staff in the queen's household, they forged successful careers and businesses. The work of the elite and non-elite women examined in this book rewarded them with a sense of identity and social mobility. Working for the queen's household not only formalized and compensated women's work as managers and carers for clothing, as we have seen with Robes staff, laundresses, seamstresses and starchers, but it legitimized women's trade identities as tirewomen, milliners and mantua-makers, occupations that became a mainstay of women's formal training and work for the next three centuries.

This book highlights how household accounts, and the types of sources they contain – bills, warrants for payment, receipts of wages paid, descriptions of duties, inventories and petitions – can serve as valuable datasets for reconstructing women's work tasks, recompense and social networks. These accounts offer insights that might otherwise be obscured or totally absent from other historical records usually employed to examine women's work, such as guild records or court documents, as well as personal papers and political documents that describe the lives of women within the court and royal household.

While men still dominated politics and commerce, and while it would still take several centuries for women to achieve full financial independence within the home and the workplace, these archival sources illuminate the economic agency that women could have. From elite women in the Office of the Robes, who were responsible for managing significant sums of money and overseeing the procurement of goods, to female tradespeople, who billed for their services. Beyond simply recording transactions, these papers also offer glimpses into their tastes, preferences and social interactions. These include the Stuart queens themselves, whose different backgrounds and life stages (as consort, dowager or regnant), as well as their personal tastes, shaped not only their consumption of dress and the apparatuses of material power, but also the nature of their Office of the Robes and Bedchamber, which in turn influenced their patronage of tradespeople and servants.

Not only did the consumption of royal clothing become more influenced by market forces and global trade during the seventeenth century, most significantly through the dominance of French fashions throughout Western Europe and increasing trade with the East Indies by the English and the Dutch, but the nature of tradespeople's attachment to the Office of the Robes also began to change.

Over time, fewer tradespeople were given salaried in-ordinary positions, leaving the Stuart queens and their Mistresses of the Robes free to patronize a much wider array of makers and suppliers. At the same time, offices within the Robes and Bedchamber became more prestigious and the role of Mistress of the Robes was given to higher-ranking peeresses. While high-ranking offices within the royal household have sometimes been cast as mere sinecures, this book has shown that Mistresses of the Robes, Laundresses of the Body, starchers and seamstresses undertook real work, usually managerial, and displayed financial and material literacy. These posts rewarded women in lower offices with social mobility and financial recompense that they would not have experienced elsewhere. High-ranking offices offered peeresses careers at court, similar to their male counterparts, and a sense of identity that extended beyond their family names and noble titles.

The changing nature of royal appointments, as well as economic changes in the fashion marketplace such as the waning power of the guilds, also influenced where tradespeople worked. As several sources from the period reiterate, the court was a powerful driver of fashion and one of the most significant patrons of the London marketplace. Over the course of the century, influential tradespeople, including many men and women discussed in this book, set up shop in Middlesex and the West End of London close to the royal court. This created not only a more diverse and geographically dispersed market, but one that hoped to secure patronage from those who attended court or London for the season. In this way, this book is not just about the consumption of the Stuart queens or others at court; their choices are somewhat indicative of wider changes in consumption going on in London at this time.

Importantly, the large and bureaucratic nature of aristocratic households, and especially those of the royal court, created archives that shed light on the intertwined economic activities of a range of women from across different social strata. While we tend to treat the world of court women and that of tradeswomen as different spheres, the queens' household papers record the times that these spheres intersected. In particular, the focus of this book has shown that clothing and fashion were areas that facilitated an overlap in the lives and work of these women.

Elite women within the royal household such as those in the Office of the Robes and the Bedchamber had frequent contact with tradeswomen whom they commissioned goods from. As this book has shown, sometimes these relationships extended far beyond the strictly professional. Examination of letters and court records alongside household accounts reveals that news and gossip circulated between elite women via their mantua-makers and tirewomen, and elite women visited the shops of female retailers such as milliners and Indian women to socialize. The Duchess of Marlborough hosted the milliner Elizabeth Graydon at her home in St Albans and they exchanged personal correspondence that discussed family matters and politics. The milliner-cum-Indian woman Jane Potter also played matchmaker to her elite client the Countess of Ogle (later Duchess of Somerset), and her fashionable Indian House saw her move in the same circles as those who plotted the Glorious Revolution, the latter of which she supposedly helped to facilitate. Dorothy Speckard's skill as a silkwoman enabled her to join the queen's Bedchamber with an official court office, and Queen Anne's laundress Elizabeth Atkinson left money to the queen's mantua-maker Anne Clifton, indicating that their relationship extended beyond their professional interactions within the royal household.

Through these types of relationships, tradeswomen gained access to court circles, enhanced their reputation – or, in the case of Jane Potter, damaged it – and secured work among courtiers and the growing *beau monde*. Many tradeswomen were clients of court women before the royal household began to patronize them. In some cases, these tradeswomen were clearly promoted to a royal supplier or maker through their pre-existing connection with the Mistress of the Robes. Others had several royal patrons and by the late seventeenth century it was uncommon for a tradesperson to be exclusively supplying or making for the royal household. Thus, tradesmen and tradeswomen used their connections to the royal household to boost their reputation and grow their businesses in the wider fashion marketplace.

For tradeswomen the stakes were high. This was the time when women began to enter the fashion trades in larger numbers and when their occupational identities and opportunities as petticoat-makers, mantua-makers and milliners were being realized. While significant and long-lasting changes occurred to the fashion marketplace and the guild system during the consumer and retail revolutions, which allowed women to enter the fashion trades in larger numbers and receive more formal training, it is unlikely they would have achieved such success in the seventeenth century, or at any point, without the support of their (primarily) female clientele. It is clear from looking at the relationships examined in this book that female patronage was incredibly important to the success of new female trades, and the support of fashionable elite women legitimized their increased presence in the marketplace.

Unsurprisingly then, as women's roles in the royal household expanded or became more formalized under the Stuarts, the number of female tradespeople recorded in the queen's accounts increased. Roles such as the Mistress of the Robes and Mistress of the Sweet Coffers either did not exist under the Tudors or were held by men. It was not until second half of the century that women began to, quite literally, control the queen's private purse strings as Keeper of the Privy Purse. By the end of the seventeenth century, key suppliers and makers to queens were increasingly women (see Appendix I). While the Stuart kings also patronized women, they still had their clothing made by male tailors and appeared to prefer male milliners as well. The shared social experiences of women – even those from vastly different social spheres – as well as their shared interest in female fashion must have contributed to this development. While it is hard to say for certain, it also appears that some women, such as Queen Anne and the Duchess of Marlborough, simply preferred to use female tradeswomen and staff.[5]

Sarah Churchill, Duchess of Marlborough, was the first Mistress of the Robes to appoint a woman as Yeoman of the Robes. As this study has shown, this was not necessarily due to cost. Rachel Thomas received a similar wage to her male counterpart in the king's household, and mantua-makers were paid much the same as tailors for undertaking the same work for the queens. The patronage of elite women also encouraged those lower down the social scale to consume from these tradeswomen too. Surviving court cases relating to the businesses of the milliner Elizabeth Graydon (see Appendix IV) and royal dressmakers Jane Heath and Mary Alexander indicate that they served clients from various social backgrounds and offered different wares at different price points. As the ability of women to spend their money on consumer goods and fashionable novelties increased during the industrious revolution of the seventeenth century, these women looked to women of the court and other elites to know how to spend it. As court women were switching from using tailors to fashionable mantua-makers, many of whom were French *couturières*, this influenced other women in London, as letters to the Duchess of Marlborough and popular literature from the period show. If you could afford to buy something from suppliers and makers to the queen or other fashionable court women, or those like them, why would you not? The aspirational prestige that court patronage gave to tradeswomen and the products they sold therefore influenced their success.

This book has also uncovered the overlooked role that French migrant women played in training the first generation of English mantua-makers and their influence on other female fashion trades such as millinery. The skills of French *couturières* were highly sought after in the London fashion market by both consumers and makers alike. The Frenchwoman Mary Alexander, an already established milliner-cum-dressmaker in London, brought Jane Heath and her husband from France specifically to teach her and her daughters the 'art and trade' of making mantua gowns. Their records reveal not only how these early business partnerships ran, including information about staff and journals that kept track of orders, but show that the success of *couturières* in London was closely tied to their networks of elite clientele and their ability to cater to the demand for French styles. Like *marchandes de modes* in Paris, women in England also flocked to trade in small wares and accessories. By the late seventeenth century, a significant portion of the milliners in the Stuart queens' accounts were of French origin. The entry of the names of these migrants into the royal household account books allow us a glimpse into the social and business networks that these French migrants established in London and how they influenced London's fashion marketplace.

Tradeswomen such as Elizabeth Graydon and Jane Heath clearly belonged to a more exclusive tier of maker in the fashion marketplace and so cannot be representative of all tradeswomen in London. However, the success of women like Graydon and Heath created opportunities and work for other journeywomen and workwomen who laboured in their workshops completing orders. It also provided apprenticeships for women such as Mary Blurton, who learned the trade and subsequently trained the next generation of mantua-makers. In the case of many milliners and Indian women, the businesses they successfully built provided ongoing work for generations of women and men in their families. Of course, this system was not without exploitation. Many women worked for milliners and mantua-makers for low wages, and fashion retailers such as Indian women relied on the increasing exploitation and control of peoples on the other side of the world. However, the stories of these women do shed more light on occupational training and working conditions experienced by some of the earliest female milliners, mantua-makers and related trades in England.

The Stuart period saw the rise of women as makers, retailers and consumers. Fashion was both dictated and followed by the court in various ways throughout the long seventeenth century, giving opportunities to tradespeople in an increasingly diverse London marketplace. Studying the royal household accounts and related records challenges simplistic understandings of women's work and highlights the complex interactions between women from different social classes. It collapses sometimes arbitrary distinctions between consumer and maker/supplier, and the court and the fashion marketplace. Ultimately, women's patronage was a powerful force that shaped the seventeenth-century fashion marketplace, and the support and promotion of female-dominated trades by female courtiers and fashion leaders was crucial in establishing new professional identities and opportunities for tradeswomen in London and beyond.

Appendix I: Makers and suppliers to the Stuart queens[1]

Table 1 Tradespeople to Anna of Denmark, 1603–19

Name	Gender	Trade as described in bills (as listed elsewhere)	Years active	Location and company (if known)	Also in the accounts of
William Acton	Male	Silkman	1617	Aldersgate Merchant Taylors' Company	
Francis Baker∧	Male	Shoemaker	1604–17		
Marie Barnaby	Female	Unspecified, for linen cloth	1617	St Martin-in-the-Fields	
Richard Barnaby*	Male	Widower	1617	St Martin-in-the-Fields	
Francis Blondewe∧	Male	Perfumer	1603–17		
Francis Britaine	Male	Sempster	1604		
Richard Bruneby	Male	Girdler or Milliner	1603–4		
Thomas Capp	Male	Girdler	1617		
Mistress Case	Female	Unspecified, for making of linen goods and washing childbed linen			
William Clanvile	Male	Goldsmith	1604		
Marie Cooke	Female	Milliner	1604	near Cheapside	
Thomas Cooke	Male	Milliner	1603		
William Cookesberrie	Male	Haberdasher	1604	Haberdashers' Company	Elizabeth I, James I, Prince Henry

(*continued*)

Table 1 Continued

Name	Gender	Trade as described in bills (as listed elsewhere)	Years active	Location and company (if known)	Also in the accounts of
Richard Crawshawe	Male	Milliner	1604		
Thomas Doloron	Male	Tailor	1617		
James Duncane∧	Male	Master Tailor	1603–17	City of London	
Edward Ferrers	Male	Linen draper	1603–4	Mercers' Company	
James Freeland∧	Male	Embroiderer	1603–6		
Richard French	Male	Haberdasher	1603–4	Haberdashers' Company	Elizabeth I
Hugh Griffith	Male	Hosier	1603–4		
Jane Gascard	Female	Feathermaker	1603		
Benjamin Henshawe[2]	Male	Silkman	1616–17	Milk Street Merchant Taylors' Company	James I, Princess Elizabeth Stuart, Henrietta Maria
Thomas Henshawe	Male	Silkman	1604	Milk Street	
John Harris	Male	Goldsmith	1615		
George Heriot∧	Male	Jeweller	1603–17	The Strand; Edinburgh	James VI/I
Thomas Huxley	Male	Mercer	1616–17		
Robert Hughes	Male	Farthingale-maker	1603–19	Bow Lane	
Thomas Middleton	Male	Linen draper	1604		
Marie Mountjoy	Female	Tirewoman	1603–4	Corner of Silver and Monkwell Streets in Cripplegate	
George Onslowe	Male	Haberdasher	1603–4	Parish of St Bride Haberdashers' Company	
Hester Onslowe*	Female	Haberdasher	1616–17	Parish of St Bride	

William Phillips	Male	Pinner	1604	Haberdashers' Company	
Elizabeth Price	Female	Seamstress	1604		
Christopher Shawe, Snr	Male	Embroiderer	1603–4	Broderers' Company	
Thomas Sheppard	Male	Perfumer	1603–4		
Abraham Speckard	Male	Milliner	1603–4	St Giles	
Dorothy Speckard	Female	Silkwoman and seamstress	1604–19	St Giles	Elizabeth I, James I, Charles I
William Stone, Knight	Male	Mercer	1604	Cheapside; Farringdon Without Clothworkers' Company	
Blanche Swansted	Female	Tirewoman in-ordinary	1603–19		Princess Elizabeth Stuart
Elias le Telier	Male	Husband of Hester	1603–6		
Hester le Telier∧	Female	Silkwoman	1603–6		
Christoper Weaver	Male	Weaver	1604		
Livia White*	Female	Unspecified, for embroidering waistcoats and petticoats	1604		
Thomas Wilson	Male	Shoemaker	1604		
Thomas Woodward	Male	Mercer	1615–17		
George Wyn	Male	Woollen Draper	1603–4	Mercers' Company	

* Widow or widower.
∧ Salaried artisans and suppliers named in the queen's household establishment lists.

Table 2 Tradespeople to Henrietta Maria, 1627–39

Name	Gender	Trade as described in bills (as listed elsewhere)	Years active	Location and company (if known)	Also in the accounts of
John Ager	Male	Farthingale-maker	1630–9	Bow Lane Drapers' Company	
Richard Aldworth	Male	Woollen draper	1628–32	Watling Street	
Margaret Aldworth*	Female	Woollen draper	1627–30	Watling Street	
William Ardington	Male	Pinmaker	1628–39		
Margaret Ardington	Female	Pinmaker	1630		
Joseph Atkinson	Male	Milliner	1628–39	Royal Exchange	Charles I
Robert Austin[3]	Male	Silk mercer	1637		
Jean Baptiste Ferrin	Male	Glover and perfumer	1629–37		
Jacques Bardou	Male	Tailor	1636–9	St Martin-in-the-Fields	
Edward Basse	Male	Lace seller	1630–9	near St Mary Magdalen, Milk Street Mercers' Company	Charles I
George Bennison	Male	Silkman	1627		
Edward Bradbourne	Male	Haberdasher	1631–9		Charles I
Humphrey Bradbourne	Male	Unspecified, 'Furnisher of ribbon' (milliner)	1628–39	Clothworkers' Company	Charles I
Blanche Browne	Female	Tirewoman	1630–2		
John Buckner	Male	Hosier	1628–33		
Robert Chandler	Male	Silk mercer	1628		
Ann Davenport	Female	Seamstress	1631–9		
Richard Downing	Male	Furrier / skinner	1630–9	The Strand Skinners' Company	Charles I, Charles II

Antonia DuVall	Female	Unspecified, Maker of 'mourning dressings'	1632		
Jean Fausse	Male	Shoemaker	1628–39		
George Garrett	Male	Woollen draper	1632	Castle Baynard Drapers' Company	Charles I
Charles Genty (Gentile)	Male	Embroiderer and cutter	1628–39		
William Geere	Male	Silkman	1632–39	All Hallows, Cheapside Drapers' Company	
George Gelin (Gillin)	Male	Tailor	1628–35	The Strand	
Thomas Gray	Male	Shoemaker	1628		
Sarah Gretton	Female	Tirewoman	1634–8		
Anna Henshawe*	Female	Widow	1632	Milk Street	
Benjamin Henshawe	Male	Silkman	1628–31	Milk Street Merchant Taylors' Company	Anna of Denmark, James I, Princess Elizabeth Stuart
William Honywood[4]	Male	Silk mercer	1637	Mercers' Company	
John Huguitt	Male	Farthingale maker	1627–9		
John Hunt	Male	Linen draper	1633–9		
Robert Hutchinson	Male	Perfumer	1627–37		
Arthur Knight	Male	Haberdasher	1628–39	Haberdashers' Company	Charles I
Peter Le Hue	Male	Cutter	1631		
Judith Lermitt*	Female	Feather dresser	1638–9		Charles I
Peter Lermitt	Male	Feather dresser	1626–38	Farringdon Within Haberdashers' Company	
Richard Miller[5]	Male	Silk mercer	1627–39	Drapers' Company	Charles I
Gilbert Morette [6]	Male	Tailor	1626–37		

(*continued*)

Table 2 Continued

Name	Gender	Trade as described in bills (as listed elsewhere)	Years active	Location and company (if known)	Also in the accounts of
Thomas Mount	Male	Tailor	1633		
Roger Nott	Male	Silk mercer	1633–7		Charles I
Roger Price	Male	Woollen draper	1637–9		
Thomas Robinson	Male	Hosier	1634–9		
Christopher Shaw, Jnr	Male	Embroiderer	1627	Addle Hill Broderers' Company	
Margaret Shaw*	Female	Widow	1628–34	Addle Hill	
Robert Simpson	Male	Jeweller	Before 1628		
Barbara Stevenson	Female	Seamstress	1631–9		
Matthew Sumpers	Male	Tinsell seller	1631		
Gilbert Ward	Male	Linen draper	1626–32		
Margaret Ward*	Female	Linen draper	1632–3		
William Ward[7]	Male	Silk mercer	1627–30	Drapers' Company	
William Ward	Male	Goldsmith	1630–1		
Rice Williams[8]	Male	Silk mercer	1631–9	Drapers' Company	
John Willet	Male	Silk mercer	1637		

* Widows.

Table 3 Tradespeople to Catherine of Braganza, 1662–92

Name	Gender	Trade as described in bills (as listed elsewhere)	Years active	Location and company (if known)	Also in the accounts of
Thomas Alchorne	Male	Mercer	1686–92	Westminster Painters' Company	Duchess of Lauderdale, Duchess of Somerset, Queen Mary II, William III
Mary Alexander	Female	Unspecified, for waistcoats, ribbon and gloves	1675–88	Covent Garden	Sarah Churchill, Countess of Chesterfield, Countess of Clarendon, Countess of Northampton, Countess of Northumberland, Countess of Ogle/Duchess of Somerset, Countess of Oxford, Duchess of Buckingham, Duchess of Grafton, Duchesses of Mazarin, Duchess of Norfolk, Duchess (Mary) of York & several others
Adam Bancks	Male	Woollen draper	1689–90		
Mrs Bardou	Female	Unspecified, for veils, coifs and ribbons	1666		
John Barne	Male	Gown-man	1686–8		
John Barrington	Male	Mercer	1684		
Mrs Bew	Female	Milliner	1663–75		
Madame de Bord	Female	Unspecified (pedlar)	1670–4		
Matthew Bowman	Male	Haberdasher of Small Wares	1684–90	Westminster, The Strand	
Deborah Burton	Female	Milliner	1665–88	The Exchange The Strand (by 1685)	Duchess of Somerset, Earl of Yarmouth, Lady Anne Stuart,[9] Sarah Churchill
Francis Burton	Male	Milliner	1688	Westminster (by 1720)	

(*continued*)

Table 3 Continued

Name	Gender	Trade as described in bills (as listed elsewhere)	Years active	Location and company (if known)	Also in the accounts of
Daniel Brown	Male	Skinner	1685–9		Lady Anne Stuart, Duchess of Somerset, Mary II, William III
George Caldecott	Male	Mercer	1687–8	Mercers' Company	Mary II, Queen Anne, Earl of Bedford
Barbara Anna de Calvaert∧	Female	Seamstress	1685–92	Bedchamber staff	
Nicholas Charlton∧	Male	Woollen draper	1684–7		
George Cheret	Male	Unspecified (milliner)	1685–7	Covent Garden	Lady Anne Stuart
Marie Cheret	Female	Unspecified, for French goods including hoods and gloves	1666–79	Covent Garden	Samuel and Elizabeth Pepys, Duke and Duchess of Lauderdale, Earls of Northumberland, Earl of Yarmouth, Countess of Ogle,[10] Charles II
Susana Cheret	Female	Milliner	1685–6	Covent Garden	Lady Anne Stuart, Duchess of Somerset
Paul Clowdesley & Partners	Male	Mercers	1690		Mary of Modena
Henry Cope & Partners	Male	Mercer	1686–8		Lady Anne Stuart, Duchess of Somerset, Sarah Churchill, Mary II
Matthias Cupper	Male	Linen draper	1686–90	The Strand Haberdashers' Company	Lady Anne Stuart, William III
Mrs Clark	Female	Unspecified (for shoes)	1684	The Strand	
Mrs Crane	Female	Unspecified (for a hood)	1675	Bedchamber woman	
Mary Devett	Female	Unspecified, for millinery and Indian goods	1679–88	Mincing Lane	Lady Anne Stuart, Mary II, Duchess of Somerset, Queen Anne, Sarah Churchill, Lady Scarborough

Monseuir Driplessys	Male	Unspecified, for fabrics and lace	1673–7		
Mary Ducaila	Female	Tirewoman	1686–7		Duchess of Somerset, Queen Anne
John Eaton	Male	Unspecified, for rich point lace (laceman)	1667	St. Mary le Bow Mercers' Company	Charles II, Sister of Earl of Yarmouth, Duchess of Lauderdale
Katherine Eaton	Female	Unspecified (wife of John Eaton)	1675		Charles II, Earl of Yarmouth
Jeanne Ferand	Female	Milliner	1676–87		Lady Anne Stuart, Mary of Modena
Nicholas Fownes	Male	Unspecified (mercer)	1685	Hammersmith Mercers' Company	Duchess of Lauderdale, Charles II
Peter Du Fresnoy	Male	Fringe-maker (laceman)	1685–91	Middlesex	Duchess of Somerset, Mary of Modena, Sarah Churchill
William Gostlin∧	Male	Laceman / silkman	1684–90	St Martin-in-the-Fields Haberdashers' Company	Charles II, James II, William III, Duke and Duchess of Lauderdale, Duke of Bedford, Great Wardrobe
Elizabeth Graydon	Female	Milliner	1687–9	Pall Mall	Mary of Modena, Mary II, Lady Anne Stuart, Sarah Churchill, Queen Anne, Duchess of Somerset & others (see Appendix IV)
Thomas Groome∧	Male	Shoemaker	1684–92		
Mrs Guidat	Female	Unspecified (for lace)	1675		
Mr Griffith	Male	Unspecified, for a screen for the closet	1663		

(continued)

Table 3 Continued

Name	Gender	Trade as described in bills (as listed elsewhere)	Years active	Location and company (if known)	Also in the accounts of
Jane Heath	Female	Mantua-maker	1686–8	St Martin-in-the-Fields	Duchess (Mary) of York, Duchesses of Mazarin, Duchess of Somerset, Sarah Churchill, Duchess of Grafton, Duchess of Norfolk, Duchess of Buckingham, Countess of Clarendon, Countess of Northampton, Countess of Northumberland, Countess of Chesterfield, Countess of Oxford and several others
Thomas Herbert	Male	Clockmaker and watchmaker	1675		Mary II, Sarah Churchill, William III
Mrs Hemden	Female	Seamstress	1671–9		
Francis Kynnesman	Male	Hosier	1687–8	George Street, York Buildings, St Martin-in-the-Fields	Lady Anne Stuart, Queen Mary II, Sarah Churchill, Wiliam III, Lady Russell, Earl of Rochester, Duchess of Bedford, Duke of Ormonde, Mary Evelyn
Dr Lightfoot	Male	Apothecary, for sweet powders and perfumes	1675–90		
Barrell Langrish	Male	Milliner	1678–9	The Strand	Duchess of Somerset, Lady Anne Stuart
Judith Langrish	Female	Milliner	1679	The Strand	Duchess of Somerset, Sarah Churchill, Queen Anne
Peter Lombard∧	Male	Tailor	1684–9	Villiers Street East Side, St Martin-in-the-Fields	Lady Anne Stuart, Sarah Churchill, Mary II, Duchess of Somerset
Frank Maidstone	Male	Mercer	1684		
Mary Mandove ∧	Female	Unspecified (tailor; Indian gown maker)	1678–86		

Gabriel Martin	Male	Milliner	1684–9	Under The Exchange	
Solomon de Medina	Male	Merchant (for India goods)	1687–9	Great St Helens	Lady Anne Stuart, Mary II, Duchess of Somerset, William III
Thomas Moreton & Partners	Male	Laceman	1688		Lady Anne Stuart, Mary II, Queen Anne, Wiliam III
Anne Morgan	Female	Unspecified for petticoats and aprons (tailor)	1684–6		
William Nicholas & Partners	Male	Mercers	1684–8		William III
Mr Le Noir	Male	Unspecified, for muffs	1675–89		
Mrs Pigon	Female	Unspecified, for ribbon	1675–88		
Madam Pinzon	Female	Unspecified, for ribbon	1668		
Cotton Plowdon	Male	Woollen draper	1689		
Thomas Price & Partners	Male	Woollen draper	1687–8		Charles II
Luis Roche ∧	Male	Tailor	1663–81		Duchess of Somerset
Mary Rougee	Female	Unspecified (for pieces of 'Turkie silke')	1688		Lady Anne Stuart, Sarah Churchill[11]
William Rutland	Male	Laceman or sempster	1678–88	Royal Exchange	Lady Anne Stuart, Charles II, James II, Duke of Bedford, Sister of Earl of Yarmouth, Great Wardrobe
William Sherard & Partners	Male	Mercer	1685–9		Lady Anne Stuart
Thomas Templer	Male	Hosier	1684		Charles II, Duke of Richmond and Lennox, Earls of Salisbury
Isaac Terry	Male	Unspecified, for clogs	1686–90		

(*continued*)

Table 3 Continued

Name	Gender	Trade as described in bills (as listed elsewhere)	Years active	Location and company (if known)	Also in the accounts of
Sam Tooley	Male	Unspecified, for fabrics and haberdashery	1683–5		
Michael Waring	Male	Hatter	1687		
Mr Wright	Male	Unspecified (for buttons)	1674		
Sir Edmund Wiseman & Company∧	Male	Mercer / silkman	1684–9	Paternoster Row, London Clothworkers' Company	Lady Anne Stuart, Mary of Modena, Charles II, James II, Countess of Ogle

∧ Salaried artisans and suppliers named in the queen's household establishment lists.

Table 4 Tradespeople to Mary of Modena whose bills were unpaid after 1688[12]

Name	Gender	Trade as described in bills (as listed elsewhere)	Location and company (if known)	Also in the accounts of
Nicholas Alexander	Male	Laceman		Mary II, Duchess of Somerset
Mr Aynsworth	Male	Woollen draper and linen draper	The Angel in Cornhill	
Mrs Best	Female	Seamstress		Duchess of Somerset
Mr Browne [13]	Male	Furrier		
Mr Charlton	Male	Woollen draper		Catherine of Braganza
Paul Clowdesly & Company	Male	Mercer		Catherine of Braganza
Mr Drake	Male	Milliner	The Exchange	
Jeanne Ferand	Female	Milliner		Catherine of Braganza, Lady Anne Stuart

Peter Du Fresnoy	Male	Fringe-maker	Middlesex	Catherine of Braganza, Duchess of Somerset, Sarah Churchill
Mr Goddar	Male	Embroiderer		
Elizabeth Graydon	Female	Milliner	Pall Mall	Catherine of Braganza, Lady Anne Stuart, Mary II, Sarah Churchill, Queen Anne, Duchess of Somerset & others (see Appendix IV)
John Hay	Male	Tailor		Great Wardrobe
Mr Mannock	Male	Woollen draper		
Thomas Marort	Male	Woollen draper		
Richard Rigby	Male	Mercer		William III, Sarah Churchill
Henry Roberts	Male	Shoemaker		
Edward Rouse	Male	Hosier	New Exchange	
Richard Sherrard[14]	Male	Mercer		
Frances Siegler	Female	Embroiderer		Mary II
Mr Small	Male	Unspecified (tailor)		Mary II
Edmund Wiseman	Male	Mercer	Paternoster Row, London Clothworkers' Company	Catherine of Braganza, Lady Anne Stuart, Charles II, James II, Countess of Ogle
Benjamin Wood	Male	Laceman		

Table 5 Tradespeople to Mary II, 1689–94

Name	Gender	Trade as described in bills (as listed elsewhere)	Years active	Location and company (if known)	Also in the accounts of
George Abbott	Male	Linen draper	1693		Sarah Churchill
Thomas Alchorne	Male	Mercer	1690–4	Westminster Painter's Company	Catherine of Braganza, Duchess of Lauderdale, Duchess of Somerset, William III
Nicholas Alexander	Male	Unspecified (laceman)	1690		Mary of Modena, Duchess of Somerset
Mary Bampton	Female	Unspecified	1690–1		
Robert Bampton	Male	Unspecified, for lace (laceman)	1694	The Strand	William III
Richard Beauvoir	Male	Jeweller	1690–4		Duchess of Somerset, Sarah Churchill
Ellen Becker	Female	Tailor	1690–4		Lady Anne Stuart
John Bishop [15]	Male	Unspecified, for lace and brocades (laceman)	1691–3		William III, Duchess of Somerset
Robert Blake	Male	Unspecified (draper)	1690–1		Lady Anne Stuart, Earl of Bedford
Daniel Brown	Male	Skinner	1689–94		Catherine of Braganza, Lady Anne Stuart, Duchess of Somerset, William III
Richard Brown	Male	Unspecified	1690		
Sarah Browne	Female	Comb-maker	1689–94		

George Caldecott[16]	Male	Unspecified for brocade fabrics (mercer)	1694	Ludgate Hill Mercers' Company	Catherine of Braganza, Queen Anne, Earl of Bedford
Thomas Cheret	Male	Milliner	1691–4	Covent Garden	
James Chase	Male	Unspecified	1690		
Joseph Coles	Male	Glover	1691–4		
John van Collema	Male	Unspecified, for Indian goods	1694	Green Street, near Leicester Fields, Westminster	Duchess of Somerset, Queen Anne, Queen Caroline
Richard Cooper	Male	Unspecified, for damask	1690–4		Catherine of Braganza, William III
Henry Cope	Male	Unspecified (mercer)	1690		Catherine of Braganza, Lady Anne Stuart, Duchess of Somerset, Sarah Churchill
Mr Corns	Male	Unspecified	1691		
Levena Cozen	Female	Unspecified	1689–90		
Ellis Cryer	Male	Unspecified	1690		
Aaron Dally	Male	Unspecified	1690–1		
John Deacle	Male	Unspecified (woollen draper)	1691	Drapers' Company	Wiliam III, Queen Anne
Mary Devet	Female	Unspecified, for millinery and Indian goods	1690–4	Mincing Lane	Catherine of Braganza, Lady Anne Stuart, Duchess of Somerset, Queen Anne, Sarah Churchill, Countess of Scarborough
Mary Ferguson	Female	Unspecified, for millinery and Indian goods	1690–1		Sarah Churchill, Duchess of Somerset
William Garway [17]	Male	Unspecified, for silks	1690–3		William III

(continued)

Table 5 Continued

Name	Gender	Trade as described in bills (as listed elsewhere)	Years active	Location and company (if known)	Also in the accounts of
Elizabeth Graydon	Female	Milliner	1690–4	Pall Mall	Catherine of Braganza, Mary of Modena, Lady Anne Stuart, Sarah Churchill, Queen Anne, Duchess of Somerset & others (see Appendix IV)
George Hanbury	Male	Unspecified	1691		
La Hay[18]	Unknown	Tailor	1694		
Peter [Pierre] Harache [19]	Male	Goldsmith or silversmith	1690–4	Goldsmiths' Company	Duchess of Somerset
Jane Harrison	Female	Unspecified (Indian woman or milliner)	1689–90		William III, Duchess of Somerset, Duke of Devonshire, Earl of Exeter
Stephen Harrison	Male	Unspecified			
Thomas Herbert	Male	Clockmaker and watchmaker	1691		Catherine of Braganza, Sarah Churchill, William III
Ann van der Hoeyen	Female	Unspecified, for cut glass and calico	1690–4	Princess' Laundry, Whitehall	
Charles Hooper	Male	Unspecified, for cloth	1694		
Richard Howse	Male	Unspecified	1690		
Stephen [Étienne] Hugueny	Male	Glover	1689–94	Westminster	Lady Anne Stuart, Queen Anne, Duchess of Somerset
Nathaniel James	Male	Unspecified	1689–90		

Gilbert Kirk	Male	Unspecified	1689–91		
Francis Kynnesman	Male	Hosier	1690–4	George Street, York Buildings, St Martin-in-the-Fields	Catherine of Braganza, Lady Anne Stuart, Queen Mary II, Sarah Churchill, Wiliam III, Lady Russell, Earl of Rochester, Duchess of Bedford, Duke of Ormonde, Mary Evelyn
Patrick Lamb	Male	Laceman	1694		
Elizabeth Lee	Female	Embroiderer	1692–4		
Richard Leeds & Partners	Male	Unspecified, for tissues and brocade	1694		
Peter Lombard [20]	Male	Tailor	1690–4	Villier Street East Side, St Martin-in-the-Fields	Catherine of Braganza, Lady Anne Stuart, Sarah Churchill, Duchess of Somerset
Isaac Marot [21]	Male	Unspecified, for designing silks and furnishings	1694		Earl of Montagu
Solomon de Medina	Male	Unspecified, for India goods (merchant)	1690–4	Great St Helens	Catherine of Braganza, Lady Anne Stuart, Duchess of Somerset, William III
Thomas Moreton & Partners	Male	Lacemen	1690–4		Catherine of Braganza, Lady Anne Stuart, Queen Anne, Wiliam III
Katherine Mulys	Female	Unspecified, for Indian goods and millinery wares (lacewoman)	1690	Outward Walke, St Martin-in-the-Fields	Lady Anne Stuart, Duchess of Somerset, William III

(*continued*)

Table 5 Continued

Name	Gender	Trade as described in bills (as listed elsewhere)	Years active	Location and company (if known)	Also in the accounts of
George Noble [22]	Male	Unspecified, for Indian silks and making gowns	1693–4		Queen Anne
J. [Jeremy] Peirce [23]	Male	Unspecified, for lace and brocades (laceman)	1691–4		William III
Elizabeth du Perrier	Female	Unspecified	1690–1		
Godfrey Poole	Male	Unspecified, for sweet bags, trunks, baskets	1690–4	St Martin-in-the-Fields	Lady Anne Stuart
Mary Pomeroy	Female	Unspecified, for fashion accessories	1694		
John Prince & Company	Male	Unspecified, for silk fabrics	1691–4		
David Pugh & Company	Male	Unspecified, for silk fabrics	1694		William III
Phillip La Sage	Male	Unspecified	1690		
Windsor Sandys [24]	Male	Unspecified, for brocade fabrics	1694	Ludgate Hill	Queen Anne
James Seheult	Male	Jeweller	1691–4	New Street West Side, St Martin-in-the-Fields	
Mrs Siegler	Female	Unspecified, fabrics delivered to her	1692		Mary of Modena
Gerard [Bert] Small	Male	Tailor	1690–2		Mary of Modena
Christopher Spicer	Male	Unspecified	1691		
Henry Southouse	Male	Unspecified	1691		

Thomas Sutton[25]	Male	Unspecified, for Indian silks and making gowns	1693–4		Sarah Churchill, William III
Matthew Reynolds	Male	Shoemaker	1690–4		Queen Anne, Queen Caroline
Robert Rhodes	Male	Unspecified, for silk fabrics and trims	1691–4		
Henry Robins	Male	Unspecified, for lace	1690–3		Charles II, Sarah Churchill
Matthew Talbot	Male	Unspecified	1691		
Ann Tolat	Female	Unspecified, for nightcaps and hair accessories	1694		
Thomas Tompion[26]	Male	Watchmaker and clockmaker	1690–3	Fleet Street Clockmakers' Company	Charles II
William Tuer[27]	Male	Unspecified, for millinery goods	1691	Pall Mall	Duchess of Somerset
Edward Vickers	Male	Unspecified	1690–1		
Margaret Wood	Female	Unspecified	1690		
Elizabeth Worthington ∧	Female	Laundress	1690–4		
John Wallis	Male	Unspecified, for silk fabrics	1692–4		

∧ Salaried members of household in the queen's establishments.

Table 6 Tradespeople to Queen Anne, 1702–14

Name	Gender	Trade as described in bills (as listed elsewhere)	Years active	Location and company (if known)	Also in the accounts of
Elizabeth Abrahall∧	Female	Starcher	1702–11		
Gilbert Abrahall	Male	Starcher [husband of Mrs Abahall]	1703–08		
James Alexander	Male	Mercer	1702–11	Covent Garden, Mercers' Company	
Elizabeth Atkinson∧	Female	Laundress of the Body, bills are for silk fabric and scarves	1703–14		
Richard Appleford	Male	Hosier	1702–14		
Frances Baillon	Female	Tirewoman	1709–14		
Catherine Balmier	Female	Unspecified, for combs	1702		Duchess of Somerset
Elizabeth Banks	Female	Petticoat-maker	1702–5		
Edward Bayley	Male	Unspecified, for hair camblet	1712		
Arnoldt van Beck	Male	Jeweller	1702–8	Oxindon Street West Side, St Martin-in-the-Fields	
Mrs Beckman	Female	Embroiderer	1710–11		
Mr Barrodell	Male	Mercer	1702–5		
Thomas Browne	Male	Furrier and skinner	1702–14		
Anne Bull	Female	Unspecified, for 'stuffs', linen, silk, muffs	1702–7		Queen Caroline
George Caldecott	Male	Mercer	1702–5	Ludgate Hill, Mercers' Company	Catherine of Braganza, Mary II, Earl of Bedford
Anne Clifton	Female	Mantua-maker	1702–14	St Martin-in-the-Fields	
Mrs Collins	Female	Embroiderer	1702–3		

John van Collema	Male	Unspecified, for fans (chair turner and India merchant)	1702–8	Green Street, near Leicester Fields, Westminster	Mary II, Duchess of Somerset, Queen Caroline
George Colwell	Male	Perfumer	1702–5		
Antoine Cousein	Male	Stay-maker	1702–14		
Anthony Cracherode	Male	Woollen draper	1702–5	Covent Garden, Mercers' Company	Mary II
Sarah Craddock	Female	Unspecified, for Turkey silks and Indian silks	1707–11	Mincing Lane	Duchess of Somerset, Great Wardrobe
James Davison	Male	Mercer	1702–9	Church Lane, St Martin-in-the-Fields	Great Wardrobe
John Deacle	Male	Woollen draper	1701–11	Drapers' Company	Mary II, Wiliam III
Mary Devet	Female	Unspecified, for millinery and Indian goods	1702–10	Mincing Lane	Catherine of Braganza, Lady Anne Stuart, Mary II, Duchess of Somerset, Sarah Churchill, Countess of Scarborough
Henry Dighton	Male	Perfumer	1708–14	Fleet Street, Haberdashers' Company	
Thomas Dixon	Male	Unspecified, for taffeta	1702		
Mr Douglas	Male	Glover	1702		
Mary Ducaila	Female	Tirewoman	1702–9	St Martin-in-the-Fields	Catherine of Braganza, Duchess of Somerset
Margaret Dupuis	Female	Milliner	1708–10	St James Westminster	Duchess of Somerset
Mrs Duran[t]	Female	Seamstress	1702–11		
William Elliot	Male	Laceman	1702–11	New Exchange and The Strand	William III, Earl of Montagu, Duke of Devonshire, Duke of Marlborough, Great Wardrobe

(continued)

Table 6 Continued

Name	Gender	Trade as described in bills (as listed elsewhere)	Years active	Location and company (if known)	Also in the accounts of
Mr Fielder	Male	Mercer	1707–8		Prince George of Denmark
Mr Fisher	Male	Mercer	1706–8		
Marie Ganeron	Female	Embroiderer	1709–14	Pall Mall (Spring Gardens)	Duchess of Somerset, Queen Caroline
John Gazain	Male	Tailor and stay-maker	1704	St Martins Lane, St Martin-in-the-Fields	
Mrs Godde	Female	Seamstress	1702–12		Duchess of Somerset
Robert Graham	Male	Unspecified, for Parliament robes and a portmanteau (Tailor)	1701–5		Sarah Churchill, Charles II, William III, Great Wardrobe
Elizabeth Graydon	Female	Milliner	1702–9	St Martins Lane West, St Martin-in-the-Fields	Catherine of Braganza, Lady Anne Stuart, Mary of Modena, Mary II, Sarah Churchill, Duchess of Somerset & many more (see Appendix IV)
Philip Guerin	Male	Mercer	1709–14		
Mrs Harford	Female	Unspecified, for mohair & ferrandine	1702		
Susannah Hawker (later Young)	Female	Petticoat-maker	1705–14	Westminster	
Thomas Hinchcliffe & Company	Male	Mercer	1710–14	Ludgate Hill	Queen Caroline
Anne Howe	Female	Unspecified, for royal robes and widows weeds	1702–11	Exchange Court, St Martin-in-the-Fields	Duchess of Somerset, Countess of Scarborough

Stephen [Étienne] Hugueny	Male	French glover	1702–7	Half Moon Street, St Martin-in-the-Fields	Lady Anne Stuart, Mary II, Duchess of Somerset
Mary Hunter	Female	Embroiderer	1702–14	St Martin-in-the-Fields	Great Wardrobe
John Johnson & Company	Male	Mercers	1712–14		
Judith Langrish	Female	Milliner	1704–9	Hemings Row, St Martin-in-the-Fields	Catherine of Braganza, Sarah Churchill, Duchess of Somerset
William Langrish	Male	Milliner	1712–14		
Stephen Laurat	Male	Unspecified, for damask fabric	1712–14		
Magdelen Leconte	Female	Embroiderer	1710–11	Westminster	Duchess of Somerset
William Lilly	Male	Unspecified, for combs	1712–14		
William Lovegrove	Male	Unspecified, for silk textiles and quilting	1704–9		
Henry Lupton	Male	Unspecified, for a hood	1712–14		
John Maine	Male	Unspecified, for gloves	1712		
Anne Massey	Female	Unspecified, for petticoats and pockets (mantua-maker)	1712–14		Duchess of Somerset
Mary Mirande[28]	Female	Pin-woman	1709–14		
Francis Molyneux	Male	Woollen draper	1702–14		
Anne Moore	Female	Unspecified, for making linen goods	1712–14		
Thomas Moreton	Male	Laceman	1712		Catherine of Braganza, Lady Anne Stuart, Mary II, Wiliam III

(*continued*)

Table 6 Continued

Name	Gender	Trade as described in bills (as listed elsewhere)	Years active	Location and company (if known)	Also in the accounts of
Peter Motteux[29]	Male	Unspecified, for flowered velvet (Indian goods retailer)	1712	Leadenhall Street Grocers' Company	Duchess of Somerset
Phillip Musard[30]	Male	Unspecified, for setting a diamond (jeweller)	1714	St Martin-in-the-Fields	
Mr Nash	Male	Linen draper	1703–8		
George Noble	Male	Unspecified, for silk fabric	1702	New Exchange	Mary II
Elizabeth Oxley	Female	Unspecified, for quilting	1705–11		
John Paitfield	Male	Unspecified, for mantua silk	1708		
Mr Parrot	Male	Unspecified, for damask	1702		
John Patrickson	Male	Unspecified, for stars and garters	1710–11		
Mrs Peacock	Female	Unspecified, for making linen goods	1705–6		
Mr Peirce	Male	Laceman	1706–14		Mary II
Blanche Pope	Female	Unspecified, for mantua silk	1708–9	The Strand	
Mrs Rainsford^	Female	Seamstress	1702–14		Lady Anne Stuart
Margaret Reeves	Female	Embroiderer	1703–11		
William Reynolds	Male	Shoemaker	1702–14		
Matthew Reynolds	Male	Shoemaker	1703–5		Mary II, Queen Caroline
Robert Riggs	Male	Unspecified, for needlework Indian basts	1712		
Windsor Sandys	Male	Mercer	1702–9	Ludgate Hill, Upholsterers' Company	Mary II

William Sherrard[31]	Male	Mercer	1702		Lady Anne Stuart
Thomas Smith	Male	Pinman	1702–9		
Mr Starland	Male	Unspecified, for purple cloth	1709–10		
Mrs Talbot	Female	Unspecified, for pinking and racing	1710–11		
Henry Tatlock	Male	Laceman / mercer	1704–9	Mercers' Company	Queen's stable
Mr Tonstall	Male	Mercer	1708–9		
Mrs Dinos Toumbs	Female	Unspecified, for fans	1702		Duchess of Somerset
Isaac Tully & Company	Male	Mercers	1702–12	Covent Garden	
Walter Turner	Male	Laceman	1712–14		Queen Anne
Matthew Vernon & Partners	Male	Mercers	1702–14	The Naked Boy and Seven Stars, Ludgate Hill	
Samuel Ward	Male	Glover / white glover	1702–14		
Joseph White	Male	Ribbon-weaver	1702		
Mary Wilkins	Female	Milliner	1702–14		Duchess of Somerset

∧ Salaried artisans and suppliers named in the queen's household establishment lists.

Appendix I reference list

Archives

BA: 911–1 to 911–52; BL: Add. MS 15897; BL: Add. MS 45122; BL: Add. MS 5751 A; BL: Add MS 61346; BL: Add. MS 61407; BL: Add. MS 61420–5; BL: Add. MS 61455–6; BL: Add MS 75388; BL: Add. MS 78269; BLO: MS. Rawl. C. 987; BLO: MS Eng Misc B 31; DCCH: CH37/1, fol. 167; LA: 1 WORSLEY 6–9; NAL: RC.U.21; NAL: RC.K.3–4; NWA: CH 194/7, fol. 214r; RAO: GEO/ADD/17/75; TNA: AO 1/2067/100–1; TNA: AO 1/2067/103; TNA: AO 3/919–929; TNA: C 8/298/61; TNA: C 10/364/32; TNA: LC 2/4/5; TNA: LC 9/280; TNA: LR 5/63–7; TNA: LR 5/76–94; TNA: SC 6/CHASI/1692–1705; SC 6/JASI/1639–55; TNA: SO 3/9; WSRO: PHA: 252–90; TNA: SP 14/107, fol. 121.

Online sources

'Boyd's Inhabitants of London and Boyd's Family Units, 1200–1946', *Findmypast*; 'City of London, Haberdashers, apprentices and freemen 1526–1933', *Findmypast*; 'England Marriages 1538-1973', *Findmypast*; 'Records of London's Livery Companies Online', *ROLLCO*; 'Trial of Sarah Burrows, alias Hill, Ann Dye alias Thomas, alias Whiterod (t16891009-32)', *Old Bailey Proceedings Online*, https://www.oldbaileyonline.org/record/t16891009-32; 'Westminster Rate Books 1634–1900', *Findmypast*; 'Westminster Baptisms', *Findmypast*; 'Westminster, London, England, Church of England Baptisms, Marriages and Burials, 1558–1812', *Ancestry*; 'England, Select Births and Christenings, 1538–1975', *Ancestry.com*.

Printed Works

Beaven, *The Aldermen of the City of London*, 47–75; Bruce, *CSPD: Charles I, 1635–6*, 1–21; Bucholz, *The Database of Court Officers: 1660–1837*; Churchill, *Account of the Conduct*; Edwards, *Horses and the Aristocratic Lifestyle*, 188; Franits, *Godefridus Schalcken*, 37–54; Greenstreet, 'Sir Solomon de Medina'; Griffey, 'Re-Dressing the Evidence', 8–18; Hamilton, *CSPD: Charles I, 1639–40*, 506–49; Holford, *A chat about the Broderers' Company*, 126–7; Keene and Harding, *Historical Gazetteer of London*, 48–78, 244–51; Lim, 'John van Collema'; de Marly, 'Fashionable Suppliers', 345–9; Riley and Gomme, *Survey of London: Volume 5*, 117–26; Shaw, *Calendar of Treasury Books, Volume 10*, 1073–87; Shaw, *Calendar of Treasury Books, Volume 17*, 1045–6; Shaw, *Calendar of Treasury Books, Volume 25*; Shaw, *Calendar of Treasury Books, Volume 26*, ccvii–cclvii; Shaw, *Calendar of Treasury Books, Volume 27*, clxxxix–ccxlii; Shaw, *Calendar of Treasury Books, Volume 28*, cc–cclxii; Shaw, *Calendar of Treasury Books, Volume 29*, 89–106; Sleigh-Johnson, 'The Merchant-Taylors Company of London'; Wardle, 'Seamstresses to the Stuart Kings', 16–27; Westman, 'William Elliot "the laceman"', 89–102; Yarmouth, *The Whirlpool of Misadventures*, 138.

Appendix II: Clothing and accessories of the Stuart queens[1]

Common garments, materials and accessories of the Stuart queens[2]

Table 7 Clothing and accessories of the Stuart queens

		Garments	Fabrics/Textiles	Trims	Accessories
Anna of Denmark	1603–19	Bodies (gown bodice, pair of, whalebone); doublets; farthingales (including French); gowns (including riding gowns); jerkin; kirtles; mantles; nightgowns; petticoats; safeguard; skirts (side, long, short); sleeves (hanging, long, wearing); waistcoats	**Silks:** Cloth (of gold and silver); cypress; damask; fillozella; grosgrain; sarcenet; satin (including brocade); tabine; taffeta (including Spanish, tuffed); tiffany; tinsel; velvet (including unshorn) **Wool:** Striped cloth; stuff (including Italian) **Mixed or unspecified fibres:** Camlet; plush **Linens/cottons:** Cambric; calico; canvas; holland; lawn; cobbwebb lawn **Leather/furs:** Leather (Spanish); ermine	**Lace:** Binding (silver, gold); bonelace; chain; cloud; 'heart'; open; parchment (including silver); purle; 'purled heart'; Spangled (silver); 'sprigge'; Venice **Other:** Bugles; buttons (gold, silver, fabric); buttons and loops; fringe; galloon; knots; laces; pearls; ribbons; spangles; twists **Decorative work:** Cutwork; embroidery; needlework; pinking (crosses, herringbone, French, cut and raised, cut and ravelled); printing	Beaver hat; fans; garters; gloves (Spanish); handkerchiefs; points and tags; pomander; scarves; silk stockings **Linens:** Bands (including falling); coifs; cuffs; night caps; ruffs; tires (head attires)

Henrietta Maria	1627–39	Bodies; busks; cassocks; cloaks and riding cloaks; farthingale rolls; foreparts; gowns (French, Italian); hungerlines; mantles; morning gowns; nightgowns; petticoats; simares; sleeves; stomachers; suits (with doublet and breeches); surcoat; waistcoats (including night waistcoats) **Linens (for body):** Drawers	**Silks:** Cloth (of silver and gold); grosgrain; plush; poudesoy; sarcenet; satin (including Florence); Segovia cloth; tabby; taffeta (including Florence); tinsel; Turkey grosgrain; velvet (including Jeane) **Wool:** Mohair; scarlet **Mixed fibres:** Camlet; crape; gauze; grosgrain **Linen:** Buckram; cambric; Flanders baremillion; holland; lawn **Furs/leathers:** Ermine; goat skin	**Lace:** Bonelace; Flanders work; metallic; needlelace (gold and silver); silver compass; silver parchment, silver pearl; tinsel **Other:** Buttons; fringe; knots; loops; pins (farthingale, large, round head); ribbon (including stiff, taffeta); spangles **Decorative work:** Embroidery; pinking and printing; raising	**Garters; girdles; gloves** (plain, Spanish, white); hats (beaver hats, straw hats); hose/ stockings (silk, worsted); masks; points; roses; veils **Linens:** Bands; coifs; handkerchiefs **Shoes:** Boots; shoes laced with gold or silver; slippers laced with gold or silver

(continued)

Table 7 Continued

		Garments	Fabrics/Textiles	Trims	Accessories
Catherine of Braganza	1662–90	Bodies (including embroidered, underbodies); busks; cloaks; gowns (chamber gowns, dust gowns, Indian gowns, mantua gowns, morning gowns, nightgowns, stiff-bodied gowns); mantles; petticoats; sleeves; stomachers; waistcoats **Linens (for body):** Aprons; day shifts; half shirts; 'night shifts'; night rails; night cloths and bands; ruffles; socks	**Silks:** Allamode; damask; Florence; 'flowered'; Indian satin; lutestring; manteau; pelong; Persian; poudesoy; sarcenet; satin; tabby; taffeta; 'Turkey'; velvet **Wools:** Cloth; drap de holland; drugget; flannel; grazet; prunella; serge; stuff **Mixed fibres:** Bombasin; crape; frieze; gauze; poplin **Linens:** Cambric; holland **Cottons:** Calico; muslin **Furs/leathers:** Ermine; kid leather	**Lace:** Bone chain; broad; colbertine; embroidery lace; Florence; gimp; Italian; narrow; needle; orris; point (raised, silver, Spain, Venice); unspecified lace (gold and silver) **Other:** Binding (narrow); foot (purled, tuffed); fringe (billadine, twisted); galloon (billadine, French); knots; ribbon **Decorative work:** Embroidery; pinking	Buckles; 'Carolina' hats; fans; girdles; gloves; handkerchiefs; hoods; hose; muffs; palatines; pockets; scarves; stockings (hose and stirrups); tippets (including feather, laced); veils **Linens:** Band-strings; coifs; cornets; cuffs; engageants; 'necks' (collars/bands); night bands; night caps; ruffles; 'suits of head clothes' **Shoes:** slippers and clogs (of leather, silk satin and velvet); tennis shoes

| Mary II | 1690–4 | Bodies; busks; gowns (mantua gowns, morning gowns, night gowns, stiff-bodied gowns); mantles; sleeves; stays | **Silks:**
Allamode; atlas; brocade; damask (including Venetian); flowered; gauze; Indian; lutestring; poudesoy; sarcenet (including Florence); satin; tabby; taffeta; tissue (gold and silver); velvet (uncut)

Wools:
Grazet; shagg; worsted

Mixed fibres:
Crape; gauze

Linens:
Cambric; holland

Cottons:
Knitted cottons; muslin

Furs:
Ermine; sable; squirrel | **Lace:**
Bone; broad; foot; French; Flanders; gold; narrow; needlework; point de Spain; scallop thread; silver; sludded; thread

Other:
'Chain'; fringe (corded, knotted, twine); furbelow; galoon; 'purle'; ribbons; tassels; twist

Decorative work:
Embroidery | **Buckles; fans; garters; girdles; gloves; hoods (alamode, gauze, 'snail'); hose; muffs; palatines; patches; pockets; points; scarves; tippets (feather, lace)**

Linens:
Commode and wires; day caps; night caps; pinners and sorties; ruffles; sleeves; 'suit of head clothes'

Shoes:
Sabots; broad shoes and slippers made from satin and leather |

(*continued*)

Table 7 Continued

		Garments	Fabrics/Textiles	Trims	Accessories
Queen Anne	**1701–14**	Cloaks; corset; gowns (bedgowns, mantua gowns, morning gowns, nightgowns, wadded gowns); hoop petticoats; mantles; petticoats; sleeves; stays; stomachers; weeds **Linens (for body):** Linen/cotton petticoats; shifts; sleeves; smocks	**Silks:** Atlas; brocade; cypress; damask; ducape; gauze; lutestring (including Italian); mantua (including Italian); Persian; poudesoy; sarcenet; satin (including Florence, flowered, Italian); sattenet; silks (including chequered, figured, flowered, striped); tabby; taffeta (including Chinese); tissue (silver); velvet (including Genoa); Venetian **Wools:** Cloth; mohair; serge; shaloon **Mixed fibres:** Crape (including Indian, Norwich); farindine; Marseille's cloth; poplin **Linens:** Cambric; damask; holland; lawn **Cottons:** Calico; dimity; muslin **Furs/leathers:** Ermine; shagreen	**Lace:** Bone; breed; broad; Brussels; chain; French; Mechlin; narrow; orris (silver, gold); scalloped **Ribbons:** Cambric; French; garter; George; love; narrow; satin; Spanish; taffeta **Other:** Furbelows; gold binding; pinking; ribbons; tassels **Decorative work:** Embroidered borders	Buckles; fans; girdles; handkerchiefs; hoods (various styles, including black, flowered, love, mourning, snail, spotted); hose; masks; mittens; muffs (feather, fox); paper patches; pockets; scarves; steinkirks; tippets (lace, sable, velvet); tuckers; wires (for hairstyles or headdresses) **Linens:** Cuffs; heads; hose; necks; ruffles; suits for the head; tuckers **Shoes:** Clogs (leather); shoes (cloth, corked, satin); slippers (cloth, satin)

Appendix III: A list of Queen Mary II's jewels, 1695

January 21st: 1694/5. BL: Add MS 61420

[112r]

A List of the Queens Jewells in the keeping of the Countess of Derby Groom of the Stole vizt.

No. 1.   All the Queens Rubys and Diamonds that are intermingled, as they are Specifyed in Her Majestys own List.
No. 2.   Forty Six Loops, and Eighteen Buttons of Diamonds.
No. 3.   Four Jewells for a Gowne, two of which have colour'd Diamonds in the middle.
No. 4.   Sixty Eight Pieces of Four Diamonds each.
No. 5.   Eight Loops of five Diamonds each, and Twelve of Three.
No. 6.   A Necklace of Pearls thirty seven with a Diamond Locket of a great flat stone.
No. 7.   Ten of Thirty of the Brilliant Diamond Loops of Ten Diamonds each.
    2 Ditto of Twelve Diamonds each
    2 Ditto of Eight Diamonds each
    4 Ditto of Six Diamonds each
    4 Double Ditto of Eleven Diamonds Each
No. 8.   Twelve Brilliant Diamonds in loose Collets.
No. 9.   Twenty of the Thirty Brilliant Diamonds.
No. 10.   Sixty Five Pearls.
No. 11.   Fourteen Brilliant Diamonds.
No. 12.   Forty loose Diamond Collets Great and Little.

A

[112v]

No 13.   A Jewell of Twenty Six Diamonds the Large One therein comprehended, for to be worn behind.
No. 14.   A Red diamond Ring.
    a Yellow Diamond Ring.
    an Emerald Ring.
    two Brilliant Ear Rings; Diamond.
    two Pearl Ear Rings.
No. 15.   Twelve Loose Emeralds.
No. 16.   Twelve Little Taggs with small Diamonds.
    One Piece of a Three square Diamond set about with small ones.
    One other Piece of Eight small Diamonds.
No. 17.   The Little Sancy.[1]
No. 18.   Six Diamond Buckles, and Twelve Diamond Taggs for Bodys.
No. 19.   The great Diamond Ear Rings with their Drops.
No. 20.   Two Large Diamond Loops.

No. 21.   A Diamont Buckle.
No. 22.   A George of Eleven Diamonds.
No. 23.   A Ruby Ring.
          a Conceited Ring of small Diamonds.
          One Pair of Diamond Shooe Buckles.

Appendix IV: Debts owed to Robert and Elizabeth Graydon, 1701

Sherard v Graydon. TNA: C 10/364/32. 1701.

A schedule or Inventory of all the Debts due or owing to the said Robert Graydon deceased att the time of his [   ][1] and to which the Answer refers.

[ ] Atwood	_ _ _ _ _	012; 00; 06
[La]dy Ashfield	_ _ _ _ _	002; 10; 00
[ ] Allen	_ _ _ _ _	003; 07; 00
[ ] Bensford	_ _ _ _ _	021; 00; 03
[ ] Bulteele	_ _ _ _ _	048; 03; 04½
[ ] Burton	_ _ _ _ _	005; 03; 06
[ ] Blackwell's Sister	_ _ _ _ _	003; 07; 09
[ ] Corbett	_ _ _ _ _	002; 19; 06
[La]dy Clifford	_ _ _ _ _	072; 01; 01
[Lad]y Coute	_ _ _ _ _	008; 12; 06
[Lad]y Cornbury	_ _ _ _ _	170; 17; 06
[La]dy Clarendon	_ _ _ _ _	136; 00; 00
[ ] Devaux	_ _ _ _ _	001; 00; 10
[La]dy Dunbarton	_ _ _ _ _	016; 09; 06
[ ] Dalmain	_ _ _ _ _	007; 07; 06
[La]dy Dearham	_ _ _ _ _	005; 16; 00
[La]dy Exeter	_ _ _ _ _	036; 00; 00
[La]dy Fotherly	_ _ _ _ _	011; 17; 00
[ ] Graydon	_ _ _ _ _	030; 00; 00
Mrs Humphryes	_ _ _ _ _	015; 00; 00
Lady Holmes	_ _ _ _ _	008; 07; 00
Mrs Howard	_ _ _ _ _	002; 15; 00
Lady Huntington	_ _ _ _ _	003; 06; 00
Mrs Harison	_ _ _ _ _	031; 16; 06
Mrs Jennings	_ _ _ _ _	004; 06; 00
Lady Kingston	_ _ _ _ _	086; 01; 09
Lady Lindsey	_ _ _ _ _	005; 00; 00
Lady Lloyd	_ _ _ _ _	152; 10; 00
Lady Monmouth	_ _ _ _ _	089; 18; 00
Mrs Marshall	_ _ _ _ _	003; 00; 00
Lady Melford	_ _ _ _ _	019; 17; 00
Lady Norris	_ _ _ _ _	017; 01; 03
Mrs South	_ _ _ _ _	002; 10; 00
Lady Oxford	_ _ _ _ _	049; 02; 00

Lady Ann Popham	001; 13; 00
Lady Betty Powlett	002; 08; 00
Mr Pearse	018; 09; 00
Lady Christian Rolles	006; 00; 00
Lady Radnor	240; 00; 00
Lady Scott	036; 00; 00
Mrs Scott	008; 00; 00
Mr Fredenham	070; 00; 00
Lady Tennet	005; 10; 00
Mrs Vermuden	015; 00; 00
Lady Watgrove	010; 12; 00
Lady Aaron	250; 00; 00
Duchess of Albemarle	080; 00; 00
Duchess of Buckingham	166; 15; 00
Lady Lisborne	062; 12; 00
Mrs Lowther	004; 08; 00
Duchess of Mazarine	263; 05; 06
Duchess of Norfolk Dowager	070; 03; 00
Duchess of Norfolk Junior	002; 05; 00
Duchess of Ormond	099; 14; 06
Queen	055; 05; 00
Dutchess of Richmond Dowager	118; 12; 00
Lady Sussex	012; 00; 00
Mrs Arnold	021; 16; 00
Lady Barker	010; 00; 00
Mrs Bailey	003; 03; 00
Mrs Bridgman	004; 12; 00
Lady Bellasye	002; 00; 00
Mrs Croucher	002; 10; 00
Lady Elizabeth Dallevill	018; 13; 00
Countess Dona	011; 00; 00
Mrs Harlackington	004; 05; 00
Mrs Labody	036; 00; 00
Lady Heron	039; 00; 00
Lady Eleanor Touchett	002; 16; 00
Mr Vincent	004; 10; 00
Lady Winchelsea	020; 14; 00
Mrs Whitby	009; 08; 06
Lady Wenman	001; 16; 00
Lady Atkins	001; 15; 00
Mrs Beauclais	020; 00; 00
Lady Uphiston	004; 00; 00
Mr Flumering	006; 10; 00
Lady Lovelave	001; 16; 00
Mrs Lundy	003; 00; 00
Mr Francis Needham	006; 09; 00
Lady Arabella Mercarty	050; 00; 00
Mrs Middleton	135; 07; 11
Lady Pembrooke Dowager	036; 16; 06
Lady Purbeck	[ ]5; 11; 06
Mrs Darby	[ ]
Lord Valgrave	010; [ ]

Lady Moon	_ _ _ _ _	001; 02; 00
Lady Ganesborough	_ _ _ _ _	024; 00; 00
La[ ][　]	_ _ _ _ _	021; 09; 09
La[　] Stuart	_ _ _ _ _	030; 00; 00
Lady Shrewsbury	_ _ _ _ _	031; 06; 00
Mrs Sandes	_ _ _ _ _	014; 17; 00
Mrs Boan	_ _ _ _ _	006; 00; 00
Lady Crew	_ _ _ _ _	007; 13; 00
Lady Lincolne	_ _ _ _ _	008; 19; 00
Mr Swindon	_ _ _ _ _	017; 15; 00
Sir William Holford	_ _ _ _ _	019; 15; 07
Mrs Venable	_ _ _ _ _	003; 00; 00
Mrs Wanderbank	_ _ _ _ _	001; 05; 00
Mrs Bartlet	_ _ _ _ _	002; 10; 00
Mrs Allen	_ _ _ _ _	001; 05; 00
Lady Anne Grevile	_ _ _ _ _	035; 00; 00
Lady Brookes	_ _ _ _ _	014; 00; 00
Lady Longvile	_ _ _ _ _	002; 07; 00
Lady Pettis	_ _ _ _ _	002; 00; 00
Mrs South	_ _ _ _ _	005; 15; 00
Mrs Croope	_ _ _ _ _	010; 00; 00
Mr Harvey	_ _ _ _ _	065; 00; 00
Mrs Greenvile	_ _ _ _ _	001; 15; 00
Mrs Barham	_ _ _ _ _	005; 10; 00
Dutchess of Somsersett	_ _ _ _ _	009; 00; 00
Mr Pelthey	_ _ _ _ _	040; 00; 00
Dutchess of Richmond Junior	_ _ _ _ _	035; 00; 00
Mr Vaughn	_ _ _ _ _	040; 00; 00
Mr Pankey	_ _ _ _ _	010; 00; 00

Glossary of clothing, textile and sewing terms[1]

Allamode a type of lightweight glossy silk fabric. Could also refer to something being *à la mode* or 'in fashion'.

Atlas a high-quality silk-satin from Surat.

Band a type of neck collar that could be falling or standing. Usually made of linen or silk and decorated with lace; see also *Falling band* and *Piccadilly collar*.

Band strings strings with tassels used to tie and fasten bands or ruffles.

Bengal Bengals referred to cotton or silk fabrics originating in the Bengal region of India.

Bobbin lace a type of lace made by twisting lengths of thread around pins that have been arranged in a pattern using bobbins (usually made from bone). Also known as 'Bone lace'.

Bodies a garment that covered the torso; could be outer or underwear and have detachable sleeves. Unstiffened or made from thick fabrics for most of the sixteenth century, it became more rigid and structured in the 1590s onwards, with the addition of whalebone. Predecessor of stays and corsets.

Bombasine a twilled or corded silk-wool fabric.

Bone lace see *Bobbin lace*.

Brocade a fabric made from silk with a pattern made by introducing a supplementary weft. It had the appearance of being embroidered.

Buckram a medium-heavyweight coarse fabric (usually of linen or hemp) that could be further stiffened with paste (paste buckram) or through starching.

Cambric fine quality, lightweight, plain-weave linen.

Calico a generic term for cotton fabrics imported from India. These textiles could be printed or plain.

Camisole a type of *chemisette*, which was a type of bodie (bodice) worn over the shift from shoulders to hips. Also described as a type of 'brassière'. Perhaps a forerunner of what was later known as jumps in the eighteenth century.

Camlet a lightweight fabric made from a mixture of silk, goat hair and linen. Also spelled 'chamlet' and 'chamblett'.

Canvas a durable plain weave cloth made from linen or hemp and of various weights, usually heavy.

Carolina hats hats made from either felted beaver fur or deer skin from the North American colonies.

Caul a mesh bag that was pinned over the bun or coiled hair, similar to a snood.

Chamois a soft, pliable leather originally made from the skin of the goat-antelope of the same name. It was often used in gloves.

Chemise see *Shift*.

Chintz the name given to brightly coloured, painted or printed glazed calico cloth.

Cloth cloth referred to a plain weave woollen fabric.

Cloth of gold an expensive fabric woven with threads of gold.

Cloth of silver an expensive fabric woven with threads of silver.

Coat this has several meanings during this period. For men, it was a sleeved or sleeveless outer garment worn over the doublet or later vest. For womenswear, it was usually the shortened form of the word petticoat. A child's coat could refer to an outer garment worn on the torso, or, more likely, petticoats with attached bodices, as child's coats are later mentioned in relation to stay-making.

Coif a decorative or plan linen close-fitting cap worn by women to cover their hair.

Colbertine a style of French lace resembling net work, named after the French government minister Jean-Baptiste Colbert who encouraged lace manufacturing in France.

Collar linen accessory usually trimmed with lace that sat around the neck. It could be propped upright with a Piccadil to frame the head or could lay flat. See also *Falling band*.

Commode a wire frame covered in fabric that held up and supported a topknot or fontange headdress. Often used to refer to the whole headdress by the 1690s.

Cornet the upper part of the pinner that dangled down over the cheeks.

Corset during the early eighteenth century, 'corsets' were unboned but tight sleeveless bodices, that could sometimes contain a busk. By the nineteenth century, corsets came to refer to a boned torso-shaping female undergarment.

Cotton could refer to either the cotton fibre or, before the mid-eighteenth century, a type of woollen cloth with a raised nap.

Crape a thin, transparent, crimped silk gauze or a plain-woven silk warp and worsted weft fabric used for mourning. Also spelled 'crepe'.

Crosscloth a triangular piece of fabric worn with a coif or other head covering.

Cuttanees a satin made from silk and cotton or linen from Gujarat.

Cutwork a style of linen ornamentation where small parts of the fabric were cut to form shapes and the edges were hemmed with stitches. See also *Needlework*.

Cypress a light and transparent fabric made of silk and linen fibres. Also spelled 'sipers'.

Damask a fabric woven with a reversible floral or geometric pattern that was created by bringing the weft threads to the surface. Commonly made using silk.

Doublet a sleeved upper-body garment that was worn over the shirt. Doublets were close fitting, bombast and sometimes even boned. It was originally a male garment but female doublets were popular in the Elizabethan and Jacobean periods.

Draper a dealer in cloth used in clothing, usually woollen cloth.

Drawers an undergarment resembling hose or breeches worn by men and women. In the queens' accounts they are made of linen or flannel.

Drugget a heavy wool cloth, or wool-mix cloth.

Ducape a plain-wove silk fabric.

Edgings a decorative trimming, usually lace, that was used to trim the edges or seams of a garment.

Ell a unit of measurement for fabric lengths. One English ell is equivalent to 1¼ yards (1.14 m.).

Engageants double ruffled cuffs that fell over the forearm or wrist.

Falling band a collar that lay flat around the neck. Made from a rectangular piece of linen or other fine fabric and often trimmed with bobbin lace.

Farendine a fabric made from silk and wool/hair. Also spelled 'farrenden'.

Farthingale a structured underskirt designed to hold out the petticoats and enlarge the lower half of the body. It came in various styles, including a Spanish style consisting of graduated hoops that were sewn into the underskirt, and French styles that sat around the waist, usually as rolls.

Favourites curled locks of hair on the temple or forehead.

Figured adorned with distinct shapes, forms or patterns. Could be either woven or worked into the fabric or printed using hot irons.

Fillosella a double camlet or coarse silk. See *Camlet*.

Flannel a type of woollen fabric.

Flowered to embellish with images of flowers or with flower-like patterns.

Fontange a linen cap trimmed with layers of lace and ribbons with two long hanging lappets that was supported by a wired structure known as a commode. Colloquially known as a topknot; usually called a 'head' in the queens' accounts. Common from the late 1680s until the early eighteenth century.

Forepart a decorative piece of an underskirt that was made from rich fabrics and displayed through the front opening of an outer-skirt or gown.

Frieze a course woollen cloth with a nap.

Furbelow a gathered flounce or trim on petticoats, mantua gowns and scarves. Often called a 'falballa' (from the French) in the queen's accounts. They begin to appear in the Stuart queens' accounts during the reign of Mary II, in the early 1690s.

Fustian a coarse mixed fibre fabric usually made from linen, wool and cotton.

Galloon a narrow lace, ribbon or band made from silk, gold or silver thread, and used for trimming.

Garters bands of fabric or ribbon that were tied just above or below the knees to hold up the stockings.

Gauze a thin, semi-transparent textile, usually made of silk.

Girdle a decorative cord, band or belt placed around the waist.

Gorget ambiguous term used to describe a neck covering. Could refer to a partlet, small ruff, collar or *Falling band* that covered the neck and breast. See also *Whisk*.

Gown this word had various meanings over the seventeenth century. It usually denoted a long outer garment with sleeves, worn by women and men. For much of this period, a gown for women referred to a skirt with a matching bodice, either all-in-one or separate. See also *Indian gown*, *Loose gown* and *Mantua gown*.

Grazet cheap woollen fabric that is grey in colour. Also spelled 'crazet' or 'grisette' in the accounts.

Grosgrain a type of silk fabric or ribbon that has a ribbed surface.

Guardainfante a seventeenth-century Spanish hooped skirt. Descended from the sixteenth-century Spanish farthingale, this garment was more structured around the hips and usually took on an oval rather than conical shape.

Haberdasher a dealer or retailer who sold small items related to garment making, usually trims like ribbon and lace and notions such as thread, buttons, needles, etc.

Head a part or all of the fontange headdress. Also referred to wooden dummy heads that wigs sat on.

Holland a medium-weight, plain weave, fine linen cloth, originally imported from Holland.

Hoods various styles of loose, soft head covering that were worn by women to cover their hair. During the seventeenth century these were often separate garments that tied under the chin.

Hoop petticoat a hooped underskirt made with linen or cotton and stiffened with cane or whalebone.

Hungary water a distilled water made of rosemary flowers and white wine or alcohol and used as skincare or medicinally.

Hungerline a short waistcoat of French origin that was derived from the male justacorps. In seventeenth-century women's dress it was defined by its voluminous and flowy lower half. Also spelled 'hongreline'.

Indian gown the Indian gown was a kimono-style gown made from Indian, Chinese and other East Asian or Middle Eastern silks, and worn by both men and women as informal wear at home. It was likely derived from Japanese styles that were combined with traditional European nightgowns. Later called a banyan in the eighteenth century.

Japaning see *Lacquerware*.

Jerkin a sleeveless torso-covering V-shaped garment worn over the doublet for extra warmth.

Journeywoman skilled labourers who worked for others. Derived from the French term *journée*, meaning they were paid by the day. Their work was often insecure and many journeywomen lived in the households of their employers. Also called 'workwomen'.

Kerchief a square piece of cloth that was folded and worn around the neck or head. It usually covered the neck and chest area. Also called a 'neckerchief' and a 'kercher'.

Kirtle a sleeveless dress worn under a gown. By the early seventeenth century it could be worn over a petticoat or as a substitute to a petticoat by wealthy women.

Lacquerware decorative objects and containers that were painted, carved or inlaid with materials before being covered with lacquer. Lacquering was a technique commonly used in East Asia. 'Japaning' was a European method that sought to imitate dark-coloured Japanese lacquer styles.

Lappet a long flap that hung from the pinner on either side of the head.

Lawn a very fine quality, expensive and often transparent type of linen.

Linen a fabric made from the fibres of the flax plant.

Longuins a cotton cloth from the Coromandel Coast in India. Also spelled 'longees'.

Loose gown a loose-fitting gown, with or without sleeves. Often referred to morning gowns, nightgowns or chamber gowns worn informally in the home.

Love ribbons a narrow gauze ribbon with satin stripes.

Lustring a type of glossy silk fabric, resembling taffeta. Usually spelled 'lutestring'.

Mantle a sleeveless loose cloak.

Mantua gown a gown with an unboned bodice that was constructed in one with a skirt that could be bustled. In the late seventeenth century, it typically had a pleated back, robings, cuffed sleeves and the overskirt opened in the front to expose a decorative petticoat underneath. The bodice front could be joined together or left open, showing a decorative pair of bodies, stays or stomacher underneath. Also known as a 'manto'. See also *Robings*.

Mercer a dealer in textile fabrics, especially silk and velvets. They could also dabble in haberdashery or other small goods.

Muff a tube-shaped accessory used to keep the hands warm. Often made from fur, feathers or fine fabrics.

Muslin a fine, semi-transparent cotton fabric imported from India. Known as 'mousseline' in French.

Needlework involved cutwork where the gaps were further ornamented with geometric stitching or embroidery. See also *Cutwork*.

Night rail short linen capes similar to whisks.

Palatine a woman's shoulder cape usually made of fur or lace. Before the mid-1680s it was called a tippet or sable, due to the use of the tails of those animals.

Paper patches black patches made from paper that were worn on the face, usually to conceal blemishes. Also known as 'mouches'.

Passementerie a generic term referring to trimmings made from needlework or ornamental braids made by twisting silk, silver or gold threads in the hands. It could also refer to a style of lace. Originally used to conceal seams or decorate hems.

Pasteboard a type of cardboard made from multiple layers of paper glued together.

Peaudesoy a type of ribbed or grosgrain silk fabric. Commonly spelled 'poudesway' in early modern records, the term is derived from the French 'peau de soie'.

Pelong a thin silk fabric from China.

Periwig a styled wig.

Persian a fine silk originating in Persia, noted for its strength and colour range. It was the most abundantly used silk at the time, primarily sourced through Surat.

Petticoat from around 1550 to 1660, the term 'petticoat' referred to a skirt that often, but not always, had an attached bodice (petticoat-bodies). Petticoats could be worn as outer garments with a waistcoat, or as undergarments under gowns (under-petticoat). It was commonly red and worn by women of all social ranks. From 1660 onwards, petticoat usually referred to a separate skirt worn with a waistcoat or under a mantua, or an underskirt (under-petticoat).

Philamont the colour of a dead or faded leaf, brown or yellowish brown.

Piccadilly collar a wide flat collar trimmed with lace and supported by an underproper. The term usually referred to the collar and the support. See also *Band, Collar, Rebato* and *Underproper*.

Piece refers to a loom length of cloth. It could also refer to an amount of cloth or many yards or ells, depending on the time and place.

Pile the raised surface or nap of a fabric.

Pinking to create ornamental cuts or edges in cloth or leather using a punch tool.

Pinner several meanings. Before 1680, see *Tucker*. From 1680 onwards, it referred to a type of close-fitting coif/cap with long lappets/flaps that hung down to the top of the breast or were pinned up on the head. Usually made with gauze or muslin. It was a simplified version of a fontange/topknot without a wire frame.

Plush silk, or silk-mixed, fabric with a long nap or high warp pile, similar to velvet.

Point lace a type of lace made with thread and a needle on parchment paper. Now known as needle point lace or needle lace. 'Point de France' was a type of point lace developed in late seventeenth-century France with elaborate and formal designs.

Points laces, usually of leather or ribbon tipped with aglets, that threaded through eyelet holes in garments and tied to attach them together.

Poking stick a metal rod that was heated and used to mould the pleats of a starched ruff or cuff.

Poplin a medium-weight cloth made from a fine silk warp and woolen weft, with a fine horizontal rib on the surface.

Printing refers to stamping fabric with heated tools to emboss it with a design.

Prunella a strong silk or worsted fabric, usually a coarser black version of *shaloon*.

Purle an ornamental edging made from a series of small twists and loops worked into lace, braid or net. Also a thread or cord made of twisted loops.

Rebato a wide flat collar trimmed with lace and supported by an underproper. The term usually referred to the collar and the support. See also *Band*, Other names: 'piccadill' and *Piccadilly collar*.

Robings folds of fabric on the front-opening edges of the mantua gown and its descendants.

Roses an ornamental trim made from ribbons shaped like a rose.

Ruff a gathered and starched frill worn around the neck. Ruffs were made from white linen and often decorated by expensive and intricate bobbin lace.

Ruffles deeply flounced or ruffled cuffs worn around the wrists or at the end of elbow-length sleeves.

Sable several meanings. A shoulder cape (see *Palatine*) or a hood attached to a night rail. Also a type of fan trimmed with fur.

Sad refers to a dark or deep dull colour.

Safeguard a protective overskirt worn when riding.

Sarcenet a soft, sheer twilled silk fabric that originated in Italy, used for lining garments. Also spelled 'Sarsanet'.

Satin a light-medium twill weave silk fabric with a dull back and shiny top surface.

Serge a lightweight twilled worsted fabric made from wool.

Shagg cloth with a velvet nap on one side.

Shagreen a type of untanned leather with a rough surface.

Shaloon a closely woven woollen fabric often used for linings.

Shift a basic undergarment worn by both women and men of all levels of society during the early modern period. It resembled an oversized shirt that came to the knee and was usually made from linen. It could be elaborately decorated at the cuffs or neckline, with embroidery or frills. Other names: *smock*, 'shirt', 'chemise'.

Silkman a dealer in silk fabrics.

Simare anglicization of the Italian 'zimarra'. An overgown trimmed with fur worn by women in southern Europe.

Smock earlier name for a *Shift*.

Sortie a little knot of ribbon, peeping out between the pinner and bonnet. Also spelled 'sortee'.

Spangles small round or oval pieces of flat metal, sewn onto a garment as embellishment; similar to modern sequins.

Starching refers to using starch (extracted from grains) mixed with water to form a paste that was applied to linen to stiffen it.

Stays the name given to stiffened torso-shaping female garments from the 1680s until the early nineteenth century. See also *Bodies*.

Stirrup a kind of footless stocking that has a strap that passes underneath the foot.

Stomacher a V-shaped triangular panel, sometimes elaborately decorated, that filled in the front opening of a gown, bodice or under the front laces of bodies. Stomachers could be stiffened or unstiffened.

Stuff a general term used to describe worsted woollen fabric.

Suit an ensemble of matching garments or an entire outfit.

Suit for the head an early type of headdress that would evolve into the fontange, often made from gauze with an accompanying coif. Decorated with ribbons and other trims. Also called a 'suit of head clothes'. See also *Fontange*.

Sultane a type of mantua gown trimmed with buttons and loops, inspired by Ottoman dress.

Surtout a night hood that was worn over the other headgear to protect it.

Tabby a thick type of glossy taffeta or watered silk. Commonly called Florentine or Mantua.

Tabine see *Tabby*.

Taffeta a plain woven silk with a stiff crispy texture.

Tags metal tags found on the end of laces (points) that enabled them to be easily threaded through the eyelet holes of clothing.

Tiffany a semi-transparent silk gauze.

Tinsel a cloth of silk or wool interwoven with gold or silver thread.

Tippet several meanings. Could refer to part of a hood that hung down the back or, by the seventeenth century, mostly a shoulder cape. See *Palatine*.

Tire derived from attire or (at)tiring room, it referred to a headdress worn by women from the mid-sixteenth century until the late seventeenth century. Tiremakers, tirers and tirewomen were tradespeople who made and applied the headdress.

Tissue the finest version of cloth of gold or silver that was made from very fine metallic threads.

Toilet referred to lengths of cloth or bags used to wrap clothes in storage. Also referred to a cloth that covered the dressing table or a dressing table set. Also spelled 'toilette' and 'twillet'.

Topknot see *Fontange*.

Tower false hairpiece or hair curl that sat atop the head towards the forehead in women's hairstyles. A tower of artificial hair. Also called a 'tour' in French.

Tucker a narrow piece of cloth used about the top of a woman's gown or neck to cover the chest. It was tucked into the top of the bodice.

Tufted taffeta taffeta cloth woven with raised spots (tufts) that were cut to produce a velvet pile.

Twill weave a weave characterized by its use of diagonal lines. It creates a durable, longwearing fabric.

Twillet see *Toilet.*

Underproper a stiffened support used to support a collar or ruff. It could be made from wire that was fashioned into decorative loops or pasteboard with bents or whalebone that was covered in fabric. See also *Piccadilly collar.*

Velvet a fabric with a short pile, usually made of silk in the early modern period.

Wad/Wadding raw silk or cotton fibres used as padding or as insulation in gowns and quilts.

Waistcoat a sleeved jacket-bodice that that often contained short gored 'skirts' that flared over the hips. Sometimes stiffened in the body, it was usually worn with a petticoat. Waistcoats were worn by both elite women for informal dress and by common women as everyday dress.

Warp refers to the thread or yarn that is stretched over the loom during the production of cloth; sits lengthwise in a fabric.

Weeds derived from an Old English term, during the Stuart period 'weeds' referred to garments of dark colours, usually black or purple, worn by widows during mourning.

Weft refers to the thread or yarn that is passed over and under the warp to create cloth.

Whalebone the early modern term for baleen. Keratinous plates in the mouth of baleen whales that form part of a filter-feeder system.

Whisk a plain or decorated band that tied around the neck and fell about the shoulders (falling whisk).

Worsted fabric or yarn made from a long wool fleece that was combed out before spinning. It created a lightweight, cool woollen fabric.

Image credits

Alamy

CBW / Alamy Stock Photo: Fig. 0.1.
PRISMA ARCHIVO / Alamy Stock Photo: Fig. 1.1.
incamerastock / Alamy Stock Photo1: Fig. 1.17.
Gallery Of Art / Alamy Stock Photo: Fig. 2.3.
ART Collection / Alamy Stock Photo: Fig. 2.5.
Vidimages / Alamy Stock Photo: Fig. 5.1.
Antiqua Print Gallery / Alamy Stock Photo: Fig. 5.2.

Sarah A. Bendall

© Sarah A. Bendall: Figs 0.4, 0.2.
Private collection of Sarah A. Bendall: Fig. 4.13.

Bibliothèque nationale de France

Bibliothèque nationale de France: Figs 3.6, 4.18, 4.19, 5.11, 5.12.

Bridgeman Images

© Fashion Museum Bath/Lent by the Vaughan Family Trust/Bridgeman Images: Fig. 1.7.
© British Library Board. All Rights Reserved / Bridgeman Images: Fig. 2.10.
© Chawton House Library, Hampshire, UK/Bridgeman Images: Fig. 3.18.

British Library

British Library. From the British Library archive: Fig. 3.19.

British Museum

© The Trustees of the British Museum. All rights reserved: Fig. 5.14.

Cooper Hewitt, Smithsonian Design Museum

Fig. 3.16.

Detroit Institute of Arts

Founders Society Purchase, Eleanor Clay Ford Fund, General Membership Fund, Endowment Income Fund and Special Activities Fund: Fig. 5.6.

Getty

Heritage Images / Hulton Fine Art Collection via Getty images: Fig. 2.7.
Fine Art Images/Heritage Images via Getty Images: Fig. 4.22.

Los Angeles County Museum of Art

Figs 1.10, 3.11.

Metropolitan Museum of Art New York

Purchase, Rogers Fund, Isabel Shults Fund and Irene Lewisohn Bequest, 1991: Fig. 1.20.
Gift of Junius S. Morgan, 1929: Fig. 3.1.
Rogers Fund, 1952: Fig. 3.2.
Gift of Dr. Van Horne Norrie, 1917: Fig. 3.5.
Gift of The United Piece Dye Works, 1936: Fig. 3.10.
Gift of Irwin Untermyer, 1964: Fig. 4.2.
Rogers Fund, 1952: Fig. 4.14.
Purchase, Judith and Gerson Leiber Fund, 1986: Fig. 5.4.
Gift of Kate T. Davison, in memory of her husband, Henry Pomeroy Davison, 1951: Fig. 5.9.

Musée Carnavalet, Paris

Fig. 1.15.

Museum of Art, Rhode Island School of Design

Gift of Mrs. Gustav Radeke: Fig. 3.9.

Museum of Fine Arts, Boston

© 2025 Museum of Fine Arts, Boston: Fig. 4.3.

National Archives, UK

Courtesy of National Archives of the UK: Figs 2.8, 2.9, 3.17, 4.6.

National Gallery of Art, Washington

Courtesy National Gallery of Art, Washington: Figs 1.5, 3.3.

National Museum of Denmark

CC-BY-SA: Fig. 4.12.

National Portrait Gallery, London

© National Portrait Gallery, London: Fig. 2.4.

National Trust

© National Trust Images / Matthew Hollow: Fig. 2.6.
© National Trust / Christopher Warleigh-Lack: Fig. 5.5.

Norfolk Historic Shipwrecks

© Norfolk Historic Shipwrecks Ltd.: Figs 3.12, 4.9.

Royal Collection Trust

© His Majesty King Charles III 2025: Figs 1.2, 1.3, 1.8, 1.11, 1.13, 2.1, 2.2, 3.8, 3.21, 5.8.

Rijksmuseum Amsterdam

Figs 1.9, 1.12, 1.16, 1.19, 1.21, 2.12, 2.13, 3.15, 3.20, 3.22, 4.1, 4.4, 4.20, 4.21, 5.7, 5.13.
Purchased with the support of the F. G. Waller-Fonds: Fig. 1.14.
Gift of C.P.D. Pape: Fig. 3.13.
Purchased from the F. G. Waller Fund: Fig. 4.5.

Scala

Chantilly, musée Condé. © RMN-Grand Palais /Scala : Fig. 3.14.

Victoria and Albert Museum, London

© Victoria and Albert Museum, London: Figs 4.8, 4.15, 4.17, 5.3.

Westminster Abbey

© Dean and Chapter of Westminster: Figs 4.10, 5.10.

Yale Center for British Art

Paul Mellon Fund, and Friends of British Art Fund: Fig. 3.7.

Notes

Introduction: 'She craveth allowance'

1 At her coronation and other state occasions, Queen Anne was described by eyewitnesses as wearing 'rich gown[s] and petty coat[s] of cloth of gold brocade'. BL: Add. MS 61407, fols. 10r, 14v, 19r, 22r; Celia Fiennes, *Through England on a Side Saddle: In the Time of William and Mary* (London: Field and Tuer, 1888), 255; Julie Farguson, *Visualising Protestant Monarchy: Ceremony, Art and Politics after the Glorious Revolution (1689–1714)* (Woodbridge: Boydell Press, 2021), 238–9.

2 I use 'household' here to refer to the administrative structures around the queen and her jointure, as well as those who held offices above the stairs and those servants who worked 'below the stairs'.

3 Neil McKendrick, John Brewer and J. H. Plumb, eds, *The Birth of a Consumer Society: The Commercialization of Eighteenth-Century England* (Bloomington: Indiana University Press, 1982), 9; Nancy C. Cox and Karin Dannehl, *Perceptions of Retailing in Early Modern England* (London: Routledge, 2016), 161–2. For an overview of the five proclaimed consumer revolutions, see Jan De Vries, *The Industrious Revolution: Consumer Behaviour and the Household Economy, 1650 to the Present* (Cambridge: Cambridge University Press, 2008), 4–5, 37–9.

4 Lorna Weatherill, 'The Meaning of Consumer Behaviour in Late Seventeenth- and Early Eighteenth-century England', in *Consumption and the World of Goods*, eds John Brewer and Roy Porter (London: Routledge, 1994), 206–27; De Vries, *The Industrious Revolution*, 122; Clare Haru Crowston, *Credit, Fashion, Sex: Economies of Regard in Old Regime France* (Durham, NC: Duke University Press, 2013), 143–5.

5 Sarah A. Bendall, 'Women's Dress and the Demise of the Tailoring Monopoly: Farthingale-Makers, Body-Makers and the Changing Textile Marketplace of Seventeenth-Century London', *Textile History* 52, no. 1–2 (2021): 23–55; Woodruff D. Smith, *Consumption and the Making of Respectability, 1600–1800* (London: Routledge, 2002), 3, 224–6; Keith Wrightson, *Earthly Necessities: Economic Lives in Early Modern Britain, 1470–1750* (London: Penguin, 2002), 300.

6 Danae Tankard, *Clothing in 17th-Century Provincial England* (London: Bloomsbury, 2019); Jemma Field, 'Clothing the Royal Family: The Intersection of the Court and City in Early Stuart London', in *Monarchy, the Court, and the Provincial Elite in Early Modern Europe*, ed. Peter Edwards (Leiden: Brill, 2024), 253–4; Sophie Jane Pitman, 'The Making of Clothing and the Making of London, 1560–1660' (PhD diss., University of Cambridge, 2017), 35.

7 John Styles, 'Fashion and Innovation in Early Modern Europe', in *Fashioning the Early Modern: Dress, Textiles, and Innovation in Europe, 1500–1800*, ed. Evelyn Welch (Oxford: Oxford University Press, 2017), 39; Jon Stobart, 'A History of Shopping: The Missing Link between Retail and Consumer Revolutions', *Journal of Historical Research in Marketing* 2, no. 3 (2010): 344–5.

8 Styles, 'Fashion and Innovation', 38–9, 44–47.

9 R. O. Bucholz, 'Going to Court in 1700: A Visitor's Guide', *Court historian* 5, no. 3 (2000): 181.

10 Kevin Sharpe, 'Restoration and Reconstitution: Politics, Society and Culture in the England of Charles II', in *Painted Ladies: Women at the Court of Charles II*, eds Catharine MacLeod and Julia Marciari Alexander (London: National Portrait Gallery, 2001), 18.

11 N. B. Harte, 'State Control of Dress and Social Change in Pre-Industrial England', in *Trade, Government and Economy in Pre-Industrial England*, eds D. C. Coleman and A. H. John (London: Weidenfeld & Nicolson, 1976), 148

12 Although social mobility was constant and recognized, by 'elites' I refer to those who were titled or landed, consisting of the monarchy, the aristocracy, the nobility, the gentry and those top members of the merchant class. By 'middling' I refer to merchants, successful craftspeople and educated professionals in towns and cities such as lawyers and clerks. By 'common' I refer to those people who ranked below these middling sorts and who had little wealth and no title, such as tradespeople with low incomes, the working poor such as labourers and lowly domestic servants, poor country folk, as well as vagrants. Keith Wrightson, 'The Social Order of Early-Modern England: Three Approaches', in *The World We Have Gained: Histories of Population and Social Structure*, eds Lloyd Bonfield, Richard Michael Smith, Keith Wrightson and Peter Laslett (Oxford: Blackwell, 1986), 191; Barry Coward, *The Stuart Age: England, 1603–1714, 2nd edn* (London: Longman, 1994), 44, 58; Alexandra Shepard, *Accounting for Oneself: Worth, Status, and the Social Order in Early Modern England* (Oxford: Oxford University Press, 2015), 7.

13 John Styles, *The Dress of the People: Everyday Fashion in Eighteenth-Century England* (New Haven, CT: Yale University Press, 2007), 31; Tankard, *Clothing in 17th-Century Provincial England*, 177–9; Margaret Spufford and Susan Mee, *Clothing of the Common Sort: 1570–1700* (Oxford: Oxford University Press, 2017), 255–61.

14 Richard Brathwaite, *The English Gentlewoman* (London: n.p., 1631), 21; Hannah Woolley, *The gentlewomans companion* (n.p.p.: A. Maxwell for Dorman Newman, 1673), 60. Maria Hayward has also argued that 'the middling and upper strata of London society felt' that the Restoration court was 'the driving force behind female fashion'. Maria Hayward, '"The best of Queens, the most obedient wife": Fashioning a Place for Catherine of Braganza as Consort to Charles II', in *Sartorial Politics in Early Modern Europe: Fashioning Women*, ed. Erin Griffey (Amsterdam: Amsterdam University Press, 2019), 235.

15 *Several petitions presented to the Honourable Houses of Parliament now assembled . . .* (n.p.p.: John Wright, 1641)

16 R. O. Bucholz, *The Augustan Court: Queen Anne and the Decline of Court Culture* (Stanford, CA: Stanford University Press, 1993), 241.

17 Hannah Greig has also argued that the court was not sidelined from fashionable society during this period. Hannah Greig, *The Beau Monde: Fashionable Society in Georgian London* (Oxford: Oxford University Press, 2013), 99–130.

18 Marlo Avidon's doctoral study focuses on the development of fashionable society in late seventeenth-century England by a broadly defined group of elite female consumers. Marlo Avidon, 'Elite Female Appearances and the Formation of Fashionable Society in the British Isles, 1660–1702' (PhD thesis, University of Cambridge, forthcoming).

19 Bendall, 'Women's Dress', 37–44.

20 Serena Dyer, *Labour of the Stitch: the Making and Remaking of Fashionable Georgian Dress* (Cambridge: Cambridge University Press, 2024), 9.

21 For studies on the history of women's work, see Margaret R. Hunt and Alexandra Shepard, 'Introduction: Producing Change', in *The Whole Economy: Work and Gender in Early Modern Europe*, eds Catriona Macleod,

Alexandra Shepard and Maria Ågren (Cambridge: Cambridge University Press, 2023), 4–7; Raffaella Sarti, Anna Bellavitis and Manuela Martini, 'Introduction', in *What is Work? Gender at the Crossroads of Home, Family, and Business from the Early Modern Era to the Present*, eds Raffaella Sarti, Anna Bellavitis and Manuela Martini (New York: Berghahn Books, 2018), 1–84; Deborah Simonton, *A History of European Women's Work: 1700 to the Present* (Abingdon: Taylor & Francis, 1998).

22 Alice Clark, *Working Life of Women in the Seventeenth Century*, ed. Amy Louise Erickson (London: Routledge, 1992).

23 Amy Louise Erickson, 'Eleanor Mosley and Other Milliners in the City of London Companies 1700–1750', *History Workshop Journal* 71, no. 1 (2011): 148.

24 Amy Louise Erickson, 'Married Women's Occupations in Eighteenth-Century London', *Continuity and Change* 23, no. 2 (2008): 267–307; Peter Earle, 'The Female Labour Market in London in the Late Seventeenth and Early Eighteenth Centuries', *Economic History Review* 42, no. 3 (1989): 337.

25 Mary Weisner-Hanks, 'Women's Agency: Then and Now', *Parergon* 40, no. 2 (2023): 22.

26 For an overview of these debates, see Laura Gowing, *Ingenious Trade: Women and Work in Seventeenth-Century London* (Cambridge: Cambridge University Press, 2022), 4–5; Jane Whittle and Mark Hailwood, 'The Gender Division of Labour in Early Modern England', *Economic History Review* 73, no. 1 (2020): 3–32; Earle, 'Female Labour Market', 328–53.

27 Gowing, *Ingenious Trade*, 9.

28 Hunt and Shepard, 'Introduction', 1.

29 De Vries, *Industrious Revolution*, 104–10.

30 De Vries, *Industrious Revolution*, 179; Beverly Lemire, *Global Trade and the Transformation of Consumer Cultures: The Material World Remade, C.1500–1820* (Cambridge: Cambridge University Press, 2018), 78–81.

31 Heide Wunder, *He is the Sun, She is the Moon: Women in Early Modern Germany*, trans. Thomas Dunlap (Cambridge, MA: Harvard University Press, 1998), 85–112;. Sofia Ling, Karin Hassan Jansson, Marie Lennersand, Christopher Pihl and Maria Ågren, 'Marriage and Work: Intertwined Sources of Agency and Authority', in *Making a Living, Making a Difference: Gender and Work in Early Modern European Society*, ed. Maria Ågren (Oxford: Oxford University Press, 2017), 216.

32 Hunt and Shepard, 'Introduction', 17.

33 Allyson M. Poska, 'The Case for Agentic Gender Norms for Women in Early Modern Europe', *Gender & History* 30, no. 2 (2018): 354.

34 Merry E. Wiesner-Hanks, 'Gender and Social Structures', in *Interpreting Early Modern Europe*, eds C. Scott Dixon and Beat Kümin (London: Routledge, 2020), 76.

35 Rosemarie Fiebranz, Erik Lindberg, Jonas Lindström and Maria Ågren, 'Making Verbs Count: The Research Project "Gender and Work" and Its Methodology', *Scandinavian Economic History Review* 59, no. 3 (2011): 278.

36 'Gender and Work', Uppsala Universitet, https://www.uu.se/en/research/gender-and-work.

37 Maria Ågren, 'Making Her Turn Around: The Verb-Oriented Method, the Two-Supporter Model, and the Focus on Practice', *Early Modern Women* 13, no. 1 (2018): 146.

38 Poska, 'Agentic Gender Norms', 360.

39 Weisner-Hanks, 'Women's Agency', 19.

40 Bucholz, 'Going to Court', 187–8.

41 Nadine Akkerman and Birgit Houben, 'Introduction', in *The Politics of Female Households: Ladies-in-Waiting across Early Modern Europe*, eds Nadine Akkerman and Birgit Houben (Leiden: Brill, 2013), 1.

42 Sonya Wynne, '"The Brightest Glories of the British Sphere": Women at the Court of Charles II', in *Painted Ladies: Women at the Court of Charles II*, eds Catharine MacLeod and Julia Marciari Alexander (London: National Portrait Gallery, 2001), 37. Duindam has argued that women in the queens' household 'held offices as formal as those of the male office holders'. Jeroen Duindam, 'The Politics of Female Households: Afterthoughts', in *The Politics of Female Households: Ladies-in-Waiting across Early Modern Europe*, eds Nadine Akkerman and Birgit Houben (Leiden: Brill, 2013), 367.

43 Jane Whittle and Elizabeth Griffiths, *Consumption and Gender in the Early Seventeenth-Century Household: The World of Alice Le Strange* (Oxford: Oxford University Press, 2012), 8.

44 While a comparative study of kings and queens is beyond the scope of this monograph, the household papers of the Stuart kings also contain references to many female servants and tradespeople.

45 Whittle and Griffiths, *Consumption and Gender*, 26–7.

46 Whittle and Griffiths, *Consumption and Gender*, 1–2.

47 Beverly Lemire, *The Business of Everyday Life: Gender, Practice and Social Politics in England, c.1600–1900* (Manchester: Manchester University Press, 2005), 187–8, 201–2; Whittle and Griffiths, *Consumption and Gender*, 31–2.

48 Charmain Mansell, *Female Servants in Early Modern England* (Oxford: Oxford University Press, 2024), 2.

49 Dyer, *Labour of the Stitch*; Pam Inder, *Busks, Busques and Brush-Braid: British Dressmaking in the 18th and 19th Centuries* (London: Bloomsbury, 2020); Emily Taylor, 'Gendered making and material knowledge: Tailors and mantua-makers, c. 1760–1820', in *Material Literacy in Eighteenth-Century Britain: A Nation of Makers*, eds Serena Dyer and Chloe Wigston Smith (London: Bloomsbury, 2020), 151–72; Carolyn Dowdell, '"No Small Share of Ingenuity": An object orientated analysis of eighteenth-century English dressmaking', *Costume* 55, no. 2 (2021): 186–211; Crowston, *Credit, Fashion, Sex*; Erickson, 'Eleanor Mosley', 147–72; Clare Haru Crowston, *Fabricating Women: The Seamstresses of Old Regime France, 1675–1791* (Durham, NC: Duke University Press, 2001); Elizabeth Sanderson, 'The "New Dresses": A Look at How Mantuamaking Became Established in Scotland', *Costume* 35, no.1 (2001): 14–23; Avril Hart, 'The Mantua: its Evolution and Fashionable Significance in the Seventeenth and Eighteenth Centuries', in *Defining Dress: Dress as Object, Meaning, and Identity*, ed. Amy Le Haye (Manchester: Manchester University Press, 1999), 93–103; Anne Buck, 'Mantuamakers and Milliners: Women Making and Selling Clothes in Eighteenth-Century Bedfordshire', *Bedfordshire Historical Miscellany* 72 (1993): 142–55; Deborah Simonton, 'Milliners and Marchandes de modes: Gender, Creativity and Skill in the Workplace', in *Luxury and Gender in European Towns, 1700–1914*, eds Deborah Simonton, Marjo Kaartinen and Anne Montenach (London: Routledge, 2015), 19–38.

50 Clare Crowston, 'Women, Gender, and Guilds in Early Modern Europe: An Overview of Recent Research', *International Review of Social History* 53, no. S16 (2008): 22–7.

51 Laura Gowing, 'Girls on Forms: Apprenticing Young Women in Seventeenth-Century London', *Journal of British Studies* 55, no. 3 (2016): 447–73; Sarah Birt, 'Women, Guilds and the Tailoring Trades: The Occupational Training of Merchant Taylors' Company Apprentices in Early Modern London', *London Journal* 46, no. 2 (2021): 146–64; Sarah Birt, 'A Fashionable Business: Seamstresses, Mantua-Makers, and Milliners in Seventeenth and Eighteenth Century London' (PhD diss., Birkbeck, University of London, 2021), 145; Erickson, 'Eleanor Moseley'.

52 Craig Muldrew, '"A Mutual Assent of her Mind"? Women, Debt, Litigation and Contract in Early Modern England', *History Workshop Journal* 55, 1 (2003): 49; Amy Louise Erickson, 'Coverture and Capitalism', *History Workshop Journal* 59, no. 1 (2005): 19.

53 Danielle van den Heuvel and Sheilagh Ogilvie, 'Retail Development in the Consumer Revolution: The Netherlands, C. 1670–C. 1815', *Explorations in Economic History* 50, no. 1 (2013): 69.

54 Whittle and Hailwood, 'Gender Division of Labour', 17–18.

55 Earle, 'Female Labour Market', 339–41.

56 Whittle and Hailwood, 'Gender Division of Labour', 27.

57 Widows and tirewomen are included as makers in this graph.

58 Marjorie K. McIntosh, 'The Benefits and Drawbacks of Femme Sole Status in England, 1300–1630', *Journal of British Studies* 44 (2005): 410; Anna Bellavitis, *Women's Work and Rights in Early Modern Urban Europe* (London: Palgrave Macmillan, 2016), 72. This status also existed in other European cities such as Paris, which allowed women to operate as *marchande publique* (public merchants). Crowston, *Credit, Fashion, Sex*, 143.

59 Muldrew, 'Women, Debt, Litigation and Contract', 48.

60 Political concerns and the desire to participate in City politics have been noted as the primary motivator for men joining London's Livery Companies during the eighteenth and nineteenth centuries; women were denied these political rights of freedom. L. D. Schwarz, *London in the Age of Industrialisation: Entrepreneurs, Labour Force and Living Conditions, 1700–1850* (Cambridge: Cambridge University Press, 1992), 210–16.

61 Jacob F. Field, *London, Londoners and the Great Fire of 1666: Disaster and Recovery* (London: Routledge, 2017), 103; Vanessa Harding, 'London and Middlesex in the 1660s', in *London and Middlesex 1666 Hearth Tax*, eds M. Davies et al. (London: British Record Society, 2014), 42.

62 Joseph P. Ward, *Metropolitan Communities: Trade Guilds, Identity, and Change in Early Modern London* (Stanford, CA: Stanford University Press, 1997), 27–9.

63 Gowing, *Ingenious Trade*, 1–2, 60–1.

64 Simonton, *History of European Women's Work*, 3.

65 My examination draws on methods from studies by scholars such as Janet Arnold and Maria Hayward, who have examined the household papers of Tudor and Stuart monarchs. Janet Arnold, *Queen Elizabeth I's Wardrobe Unlock'd* (Leeds: Maney, 1988); Maria Hayward, *Dress at the Court of King Henry VIII* (Leeds: Maney, 2007); Maria Hayward, *Stuart Style: Monarchy, Dress and the Scottish Male Elite* (New Haven, CT: Yale University Press, 2020). Bucholz's study of Queen Anne's court has also been influential: Bucholz, *The Augustan Court.*

66 'Independent Sub-departments: Great Wardrobe 1660–1782', in *Office-Holders in Modern Britain: Volume 11 (Revised), Court Officers, 1660–1837*, ed. R. O. Bucholz (London: University of London, 2006), *British History Online*, https://www.british-history.ac.uk/office-holders/vol11/pp146-156.

67 'Independent Sub-departments: Robes 1660–1837', in *Office-Holders in Modern Britain: Volume 11 (Revised), Court Officers, 1660–1837*, ed. R. O. Bucholz (London: University of London, 2006), *British History Online*, https://www.british-history.ac.uk/office-holders/vol11/pp135-141.

68 See the manuscripts section of my bibliography for full reference details of all the papers mentioned in this section.

69 Accounts for Anna during her time as queen of Scotland also survive; however, as this book is focused on London, these do not form a core focus of this study. NRS: E35/13-14.

70 For a more thorough overview of all Henrietta Maria's household papers, see Caroline Hibbard, '"By Our Directions and for Our Use": The Queen's Patronage of Artists and Artisans', in *Henrietta Maria: Piety, Politics and Patronage*, ed. Erin Griffey (Farnham: Ashgate, 2008), 118–20.

71 This book does not closely examine the accounts of Henrietta Maria's time in England after the Restoration as the accounts reveal little about her clothing.

72 See LA: 1 WORSLEY 6–9. Maria Hayward has also recently transcribed and examined these accounts: Maria Hayward, *The Material World of a Restoration Queen Consort: The Privy Purse Accounts of Catherine of Braganza*, Publications of the Lincoln Record Society, vol. 112 (Woodbridge: Boydell and Brewer, 2024).

73 It is unclear what happened to bills and papers from tradespeople during the period 1661–83. If they have survived, they are not located in the National Archives with Catherine's other household accounts.

74 See KKCA: AR/33/9/63-151.

75 The accounts from the Duchess of Marlborough's time as Mistress of the Robes were kept with her private papers and form part of the 'Blenheim Papers' that were acquired by the British Library.

76 Aileen Ribeiro has also noted the lack of accurate depictions of elite women's fashions and her reliance on French fashion prints. Aileen Ribeiro, *Fashion and Fiction: Dress in Art and Literature in Stuart England* (New Haven, CT: Yale University Press, 2005), 244.

77 Elizabeth Davis, 'Habit de Qualité: Seventeenth-Century French Fashion Prints as Sources for Dress History', *Dress* 40 (2014): 117–43; Marlo Avidon, '"Instructive Types" or Mere "Fancies": Assessing French Fashion Prints in the Library of Samuel Pepys', *The Seventeenth Century* 39, no. 4 (2024): 663–94.

78 Stefan Hanß has recently noted this of similar household records produced at the court of Württemberg between 1593 and 1628. Stefan Hanß, 'Gendering the Material Renaissance: Women, Industriousness and the Female Body at the Court of Württemberg', *German History* 41, no. 3 (2023): 367–99.

79 Hunt and Shepard, 'Introduction', 18.

1 Wearing: The Stuart queens and elite fashions in the long seventeenth century

1 R. Malcolm Smuts, 'Art and Material Culture of Majesty', in *The Stuart Court and Europe: Essays in Politics and Political Culture*, ed. R. Malcolm Smuts (Cambridge: Cambridge University Press, 1996), 88–9.

2 Peter Burke, *The Fortunes of the Courtier: The European Reception of Castiglione's Cortegiano* (Cambridge: Polity Press, 1995), 27.

3 Erin Griffey, *On Display: Henrietta Maria and the Materials of Magnificence at the Stuart Court* (New Haven, CT: Yale University Press, 2015), 27.

4 Erin Griffey, 'Introduction', in *Sartorial Politics in Early Modern Europe: Fashioning Women*, ed. Erin Griffey (Amsterdam: Amsterdam University Press, 2019), 15–32; Laura Oliván Santaliestra, 'Isabel of Borbón's Sartorial Politics: From French Princess to Habsburg Regent', in *Early Modern Habsburg Women*, eds Anne J. Cruz and Maria Galli Stampino (London: Routledge, 2013), 224–42.

5 Smuts, 'Art and the Material Culture of Majesty', 112; Griffey, 'Introduction', 17–18; Jemma Field, *Anna of Denmark: The Material and Visual Culture of the Stuart Courts, 1589–1619* (Manchester: Manchester University Press, 2020).

6 I use 'Anna' to refer to Anne of Denmark. This is the spelling that the queen herself preferred and I also use it to distinguish her from her great-granddaughter, Queen Anne.

7 Amy Lim, 'World of Interiors: Mary II, the Decorative Arts, and Cultural Transfer', in *Later Stuart Queens, 1660–1735: Religion, Political Culture, and Patronage*, eds Eilish Gregory and Michael C. Questier (London: Palgrave Macmillan, 2023), 177; Adam Morton, 'Introduction: Politics, Culture and Queens Consort', in *Queens Consort, Cultural Transfer and European Politics, C. 1500–1800*, eds Helen Watanabe-O'Kelly and Adam Morton (London: Routledge, 2017), 1–3.

8 Field, 'Clothing the Royal Family'; Field, *Anna of Denmark*; Jemma Field, 'The Wardrobe Goods of Anna of Denmark, Queen Consort of Scotland and England (1574–1619)', *Costume* 51, no. 1 (2017): 3–27; Jemma Field, 'A "Cipher of a and C Set on the One Syde with Diamonds": Anna of Denmark's Jewellery and the Politics of Dynastic Display', in *Sartorial Politics in Early Modern Europe: Fashioning Women*, ed. Erin Griffey (Amsterdam: Amsterdam University Press, 2019), 139–59; Jemma Field, 'Dressing a Queen: The Wardrobe of Anna of Denmark at the Scottish Court of King James VI, 1590–1603', *The Court Historian* 24, no. 2 (2019): 152–67; Michael Pearce, 'Anna of Denmark: Fashioning a Danish Court in Scotland', *The Court Historian* 24, no. 2 (2019): 138–51; Hibbard, 'The Queen's Patronage', 115–37; Griffey, *On Display*; Erin Griffey, 'Re-Dressing the Evidence: Henrietta Maria's Wardrobe Accounts, 1627–1639', *Costume* 57, no. 1 (2023): 3–30.

9 Joanna Marschner, Aileen Ribeiro, Maria Hayward and Julie Farguson have examined some aspects of the dress of Catherine of Braganza, Mary II and Queen Anne, in different parts of their reigns. However, there have been few systematic or comparative studies of their wardrobe accounts like those of the earlier Stuarts. Joanna Marschner, 'Mary II: Her Clothes and Textiles', *Costume* 34, no. 1 (2000): 44–50; Ribeiro, *Fashion and Fiction*, 240–4, 266–70, 286–94; Hayward, 'Fashioning a Place for Catherine of Braganza', 227–52; Farguson, *Visualising Protestant Monarchy*; Hayward, *Material World of a Restoration Queen Consort*, 36–9.

10 See essays in Eilish Gregory and Michael C. Questier, eds, *Later Stuart Queens, 1660–1735: Religion, Political Culture, and Patronage* (London: Palgrave Macmillan, 2023) and Susannah Lyon-Whaley, ed., *Floral Culture and the Tudor and Stuart Courts* (Amsterdam: Amsterdam University Press, 2024).

11 James was the great-great-grandson of Henry VII of England (Henry Tudor). Margaret Tudor (daughter of Henry VII and sister of Henry VIII of England) had married James IV of Scotland in 1503.

12 Leeds J. Barroll, *Anna of Denmark, Queen of England: A Cultural Biography* (Philadelphia: University of Pennsylvania Press, 2001), 5–6; Steve Murdoch, *Britain, Denmark-Norway and the House of Stuart, 1603–1660: A Diplomatic and Military Analysis* (East Linton: Tuckwell Press, 2000), 23–4; Field, 'Wardrobe Goods', 3; Field, *Anna of Denmark*, 19.

13 Field, *Anna of Denmark*, 123; Field, 'Dressing a Queen', 152; Pearce, 'Fashioning a Danish Court', 138.

14 Field, 'Wardrobe Goods', 4; Lauren Working, 'Anna of Denmark (1574–1619)', in *Lives in Transit in Early Modern England*, ed. Nandini Das (Amsterdam: Amsterdam University Press, 2022), 47–54.

15 In Scotland, Anna had a Danish tailor, Paul Rey, until 1591, and then Scottish tailors, Peter Rannald, Peter Sanderson and William Simpson, after this. Pearce, 'Fashioning a Danish Court', 141; Field, 'Dressing a Queen', 155–7.

16 Field, 'Dressing a Queen', 153–5; Pearce, 'Fashioning a Danish Court', 142.

17 Field, 'Dressing a Queen', 159; Arnold, *Queen Elizabeth's Wardrobe*, 115–18.

18 Field, 'Anna of Denmark', 123–4.

19 Barroll, *Anna of Denmark*, 8; Field, 'Wardrobe Goods', 4; Field, *Anna of Denmark*, 19.

20 Linen accessories such as cuffs and standing collars decorated with lace are not recorded in this inventory. CUL: Dd 1.26; Field, 'Wardrobe goods', 7.

21 CUL: Dd 1.26, fols. 6v, 7r, 8v, 20v.

22 Field, 'Wardrobe Goods', 11–15.

23 The most common colour of Anna's bodies was incarnadine, carnation or watchet (crimson, pink and blue).

24 Sarah A. Bendall, *Shaping Femininity: Foundation Garments, the Body and Women in Early Modern England* (London: Bloomsbury, 2021), 57–85.

25 CUL: Dd 1.26, fols. 27r, 8r.

26 Susan Vincent, *Dressing the Elite: Clothes in Early Modern England* (Oxford: Berg, 2003), 35; Anna Reynolds, *In Fine Style: The Art of Tudor and Stuart Fashion* (London: Royal Collection, 2013), 42.

27 Bendall, *Shaping Femininity*, 63; Field, *Anna of Denmark*, 129.

28 Field, 'Wardrobe Goods', 18.

29 CUL: Dd 1.26, fol. 22r. State papers reveal that the English court was deeply shaken by the assassination of the French king. James I feared for his own safety after the attack on a fellow sovereign. The Venetian ambassador described the queen and her court as being in 'deep mourning'. Horatio F. Brown, ed., 'Venice: June 1610, 1–15', in *Calendar of State Papers Relating To English Affairs in the Archives of Venice*, Volume 11, 1607–10 (London: n.p., 1904), *British History Online*, https://www.british-history.ac.uk/cal-state-papers/venice/vol11/pp498-506.

30 Other embroidery depicted 'stars, suns, clouds, flies, birds, half-moons and feathers, fountains, flowers and butterflies', as well as scenes of ships and monsters, to name a few. Field, 'Wardrobe Goods', 11.

31 This could also have referred to Anna's mother, Sofie. CUL: Dd 1.26, fol. 7v.

32 CUL: Dd 1.26, fol. 23v.

33 Field, 'Anna of Denmark's Jewellery', 145–55.

34 Field, *Anna of Denmark*, 125; Field, 'Wardrobe Goods', 4; Field, 'Anna of Denmark's Jewellery', 139–59.

35 Mark A. Kishlansky and John Morrill, 'Charles I (1600–1649), King of England, Scotland, and Ireland', *Oxford Dictionary of National Biography*, 23 September 2004, https://doi.org/10.1093/ref:odnb/5143.

36 Malcolm Smuts, 'Religion, European Politics and Henrietta Maria's Circle, 1625–41', in *Henrietta Maria: Piety, Politics and Patronage*, ed. Erin Griffey (Farnham: Ashgate: 2008), 13.

37 Erin Griffey, 'Introduction', in *Henrietta Maria: Piety, Politics and Patronage*, ed. Erin Griffey (London: Routledge, 2016), 1–11; Susan Dunn-Hensley, *Anna of Denmark and Henrietta Maria: Virgins, Witches, and Catholic Queens* (London: Palgrave Macmillan, 2017), 4.

38 Erin Griffey, 'Home Comforts: Stuart Queens Consort and Negotiating Foreignness at Court', in *Rank Matters: New Research on Female Rulers in the Early Modern Era*, eds Christina Strunck and Lukas Maier (Erlangen: FAU University Press, 2022), 125.

39 Griffey, 'Home Comforts', 6.

40 Griffey, *On Display*, 6; Caroline M. Hibbard, 'Henrietta Maria [Princess Henrietta Maria of France] (1609–1669), queen of England, Scotland, and Ireland, consort of Charles I', *Oxford Dictionary of National Biography*, 23 September 2004, https://doi.org/10.1093/ref:odnb/12947.

41 G. E. Seel and David L. Smith, *The Early Stuart Kings, 1603–1642* (London: Routledge, 2001), 62; Dunn-Hensley, *Anna of Denmark and Henrietta Maria*, 1.

42 The contents of her trousseau were valued at £30,000. Griffey, *On Display*, 43–51. For a full analysis of the trousseau, see Suzanne Lussier, '"Habillement De La Dite Dame Reine": An Analysis of the Gowns and Accessories in Queen Henrietta Maria's Trousseau', *Costume* 52, no. 1 (2018): 26–47.

43 Fabrics were sourced from Flanders, France, Genoa, Naples, Piedmont, Spain and Turkey. Griffey, 'Re-Dressing the Evidence', 7, 14; Griffey, *On Display*, 26, 97.

44 Hibbard, 'The Queen's Patronage', 127.

45 Griffey, 'Re-Dressing the Evidence', 5–6; Hibbard, 'The Queen's Patronage', 118–20. This is equivalent to nearly £4 million in today's money. https://www.nationalarchives.gov.uk/currency-converter/#currency-result.

46 Lussier, 'Analysis of the Gowns and Accessories', 32; Griffey, 'Home Comforts', 137.

47 TNA: LR 5/64, George Gelin, October–December 1630; Lussier, 'Analysis of the Gowns and Accessories', 31–41.

48 Huguitt was later replaced by an English farthingale-maker. Griffey, *On Display*, 41; Hibbard, 'The Queen's Patronage', 122; Bendall, *Shaping Femininity*, 83.

49 TNA: LR 5/64. George Gelin, October–December 1630.

50 Griffey, 'Re-Dressing the Evidence', 22; TNA: LR 5/65. These garments were known as 'hongreline's' in French.

51 Bendall, *Shaping Femininity*, 257; TNA: LR 5/66. John Ager, October–March 1638/9.

52 TNA: LR 5/64, October–December 1630; LR 5/64, April–June 1631; TNA: LR 5/65, April–June, 1632.

53 Lussier, 'Analysis of the Gowns and Accessories', 32; Griffey, 'Re-Dressing the Evidence', 25.

54 For an overview of Italian styles in the queen's accounts, see Griffey, 'Re-Dressing the Evidence', 19–21.

55 André Mareschal, *Le Railleur, ou La satyre du temps, comédie* (Paris : n.p., 1638), 90.

56 Griffey, 'Home Comforts', 135.

57 Griffey, *On Display*, 26; Ribeiro, *Fashion and Fiction*, 119–22.

58 Brathwaite, *English gentlewoman*, 21.

59 *Several petitions presented to the Honourable Houses of Parliament now assembled*, A1–A2.

60 Catherine's father, while Duke of Braganza, had led a revolt against the Spanish (who had sought to subsume Portugal into the kingdom of Spain and lessen the power of the Portuguese nobles) when Catherine was just two years old.

61 Susana Varela Flor, 'Que Las Riquezas Del Mundo Parecian Estar Alli Cifradas: Los Festejos De Boda De Catalina De Braganza En El Contexto De La Restauración Portuguesa (1661–1662)', *Archivo Español De Arte* 88, no. 350 (2015): 142–6.

62 João Vicente Melo, 'Catherine of Braganza (1638–1705)', in *Lives in Transit in Early Modern England: Identity and Belonging*, ed. Nandini Das (Amsterdam: Amsterdam University Press, 2022), 61; Tim Harris, '"There is none that love him but Drunk Whores and Whoremongers": Popular Criticisms of the Restoration Court', in *Politics, Transgression, and Representation at the Court of Charles II*, eds Julia Marciari Alexander and Catharine MacLeod (New Haven, CT: Yale University Press, 2007), 41–2; Melo, 'Catherine of Braganza', 62.

63 S. M. Wynne, 'Catherine [Catherine of Braganza, Catarina Henriqueta De Bragança] (1638–1705), Queen of England, Scotland, and Ireland, Consort of Charles II', *Oxford Dictionary of National Biography*, 23 September 2004, https://doi.org/10.1093/ref:odnb/4894.

64 Harris, 'Popular Criticisms', 54; Sharpe, 'Restoration and Reconstitution', 18.

65 Jeremy W. Webster, *Performing Libertinism in Charles II's Court: Politics, Drama, Sexuality* (London: Palgrave Macmillan, 2005), 2; Ribeiro, *Fashion and Fiction*, 216–17.

66 Kevin Sharpe, '"They Longing Country's Darling and Desire": Aesthetics, Sex, and Politics in the England of Charles II', in *Politics, Transgression, and Representation at the Court of Charles II*, eds Julia Marciari Alexander and Catharine MacLeod (New Haven, CT: Yale University Press, 2007), 2; Ribeiro, *Fashion and Fiction*, 216–17.

67 Sharpe, 'Restoration and Reconstitution', 18; Wynne, 'Women at the Court of Charles II', 44; Hayward, 'Fashioning a Place for Catherine of Braganza', 230.

68 Hayward, 'Fashioning a Place for Catherine of Braganza', 228.

69 Catherine is barely discussed in the edited collections. Catharine MacLeod and Julia Marciari Alexander, eds, *Painted Ladies: Women at the Court of Charles II* (London: National Portrait Gallery, 2001) and Julia Marciari Alexander and Catharine MacLeod, eds, *Politics, Transgression, and Representation at the Court of Charles II* (New Haven, CT: Yale University Press, 2007).

70 Contemporaries such as John Evelyn commented on her protruding teeth and short stature. Wynne, 'Catherine'.

71 John Evelyn, *Memoirs, Illustrative of the Life and Writings of John Evelyn*, 2nd edn, ed. William Bray, Vol. 1 (London: H. Colburn, 1901), 358.

72 Samuel Pepys, *Diary and Correspondence of Samuel Pepys, Esq., F.R.S. from his Ms. Cypher in the Pepysian Library*, vol. 3, eds Richard Griffin Braybrooke and Mynors Bright (New York: Dodd, Mead and Company, 1885), 264.

73 Jacob Huysmans, Catherine of Braganza, *c.* 1662–96, oil on canvas, Government Art Collection, 16366. Dirk stoop also depicts Catherine in this style of gown once she is at the English court. Rijksmuseum, RP-P-1879-A-3178.

74 LA: 1-Worsley/8, fol. 11v.

75 'Entry Book: November 1675', in *Calendar of Treasury Books, Volume 4, 1672–1675*, ed. William A Shaw (London: n.p., 1909), *British History Online*, http://www.british-history.ac.uk/cal-treasury-books/vol4/pp841-857.

76 Melo, 'Catherine of Braganza', 61.

77 Hayward, *Stuart Style*, 118.

78 Styles, 'Fashion and Innovation', 40–53.

79 The English terms 'manto' and 'mantua' likely comes from the French 'manteau', meaning loose coat. The queen's dressmakers and tailors (see Chapter 4) all use this French term at various times in their bills. I use 'manto' and 'mantua gown' interchangeably in this book.

80 '*Manteaux*' were not appropriate for court or other ceremonial visits. *Extraordinaire du Mercure galant* (Paris: n.p., 1678), 508–9. Crowston, *Fabricating Women*, 36–7.

81 Henri Forneron, *Louise de Keroualle, Duchess of Portsmouth, 1649–1734: Society in the Court of Charles II* (London: S. Sonnenchein, Lowrey & Co., 1888), 26.

82 Pepys, *Diary and Correspondence of Samuel Pepys*, vol. 9, 264.

83 Griffey has noted that generally the Stuarts avoided the 'rigid court fashions of Spain and France', which 'helped to distinguish the fashion as English'. Griffey, 'Home Comforts', 136.

84 LA: 1-Worsley/7, fol. 31r.

85 'Entry Book: December 1674, 16-31', in *Calendar of Treasury Books, Volume 4, 1672–1675*, ed. William A. Shaw (London: His Majesty's Stationery Office, 1909), British History Online, http://www.british-history.ac.uk/cal-treasury-books/vol4/pp632-642; 'Entry Book: January 1677, 1-10', in *Calendar of Treasury Books, Volume 5, 1676–1679*, ed. William A. Shaw (London: His Majesty's Stationery Office, 1911), 498–504, *British History Online*, http://www.british-history.ac.uk/cal-treasury-books/vol5/pp498-504.

86 Unless otherwise stated, all references to the queen's clothing during the 1680s come from loose bills in TNA: LR 5/76–90.

87 Elizabeth Randall, 'A special case? London's French Protestants', in *A History of the French in London: Liberty, Equality, Opportunity*, eds Debra Kelly and Martyn Cornick (London: University of London Press, 2013), 13–18; Valerie Steele, *Paris Fashion: A Cultural History* (London: Bloomsbury, 2017), 26.

88 All mentions of French lawn and cambric occur in Catherine's records between 1685 and 1688, when there was a brief reprieve on the ban.

89 KKCA: AR33/9/117 (1682); TNA: LR 5/83. Solomon de Medina, April 1687.

90 Susan North, 'Indian Gowns and Banyans – New Evidence and Perspectives', *Costume* 54, no. 1 (2020): 32; Ariane Fennetaux, 'Behind the Seams: Global Circulations in a Group of Japanese-Inspired Cotton Nightgowns C. 1700', *Textile History* 52, no. 1–2 (2021): 56–77; Angelina Illes, 'The Fascination with Japanese-Styled Gowns: A Quantitative Perspective on Ready-Made Garments at the Beginning of the Eighteenth Century', *Journal of Historians of Netherlandish Art* 15, no. 1 (2023), DOI: 10.5092/jhna.2023.15.1.5.

91 Pepys, *Diary and Correspondence of Samuel Pepys*, vol. 2, 75; Pepys, *Diary and Correspondence of Samuel Pepys*, vol. 4, 24, 63; Pepys, *Diary and Correspondence of Samuel Pepys*, vol. 5, 346; Hayward, *Stuart Style*, 239.

92 North notes that the construction of the manto worn by the doll named Lady Clapham is very similar to her Indian gown. North, 'Indian Gowns and Banyans', 46.

93 Evelyn, *The Diary of John Evelyn*, vol. 1., 359.

94 Giorgio Riello, *Cotton: The Fabric that Made the Modern World* (Cambridge: Cambridge University Press, 2013), 90; Leanna Lee-Whitman, 'The Silk Trade: Chinese Silks and the British East India Company', *Winterthur Portfolio* 17, no. 1 (1982), 27; Maxine Berg, *Luxury and Pleasure in Eighteenth-Century Britain* (Oxford: Oxford University Press, 2007), 69.

95 A 'special direction for divers trades of merchandize' in 1595 recorded that 'callicoe cloth', 'Indes cobbard clothes' and other 'Indies wares' were imported into England from Lisbon. TNA: SP 12/255, fol. 81v.

96 In this context, 'brave' means splendid or well-dressed. TNA: LR 5/78, Charles Drift, 1684; Evelyn, *Memoirs*, vol. 2, 201.

97 Evelyn, *The Diary of John Evelyn*, vol. 2., 212.

98 Hayward, 'Fashioning a Place for Catherine of Braganza', 237.

99 Lillias Campbell Davidson, *Catherine of Bragança, Infanta of Portugal, & Queen-Consort of England* (London: John Murray, 1908), 478.

100 Mary of Modena was born Maria Beatrice Anna Margherita Isabella d'Este, the daughter of Alfonso IV d'Este, duke of Modena and Reggio, and his wife Laura.

101 Marschner, 'Mary II', 44.

102 Andrew Barclay, 'Mary [Mary of Modena] (1658–1718), queen of England, Scotland, and Ireland, consort of James II and VII', *Oxford Dictionary of National Biography*, 23 September 2004, https://doi.org/10.1093/ref:odnb/18247.

103 Evelyn, *The Diary of John Evelyn*, vol. 2., 26. For more on hunting attire, see Mark de Vitis, 'Sartorial Transgression as Socio-political Collaboration: Madame and the Hunt', *Konsthistorisk tidskrift / Journal of Art History* 82, no. 3 (2013): 205–18.

104 Cited in James Anderson Winn, *Queen Anne: Patroness of Arts* (Oxford: Oxford University Press, 2014), 654, n. 12.

105 Silks include brocades, lutestrings, mantuas, poudesoy, sarsenets, tabbys, taffetas, tissues. Colours are described as things like 'rich gold', 'crimson moretto' and 'black hair coloured'. BLO: MS. Rawl. C. 987, fol. 93r.

106 William was the son of Charles II and James II's sister Mary, Princess Royal, who had married William II in 1641.

107 Farguson, *Visualising Protestant Monarchy*, 1.

108 Mary had married her cousin William of Orange at St James's Palace on 4 November 1677.

109 Deftware is referred to as 'Dutch china or ware'. BL: Add. MS 5751 A, fols. 99–100.

110 Solomon de Medina helped to finance many of William III's campaigns and was later knighted by the king. BL: Add. MS 5751 A, fol. 129; Anthony Greenstreet, 'Sir Solomon de Medina of Richmond', *Richmond History: Journal of the Richmond Local History Society* 19 (1998): 32.

111 BL: Add. MS 5751 A, fol. 131.

112 Lim, 'World of Interiors', 191.

113 Marschner, 'Mary II', 49; Ribeiro, *Fashion and Fiction*, 288.

114 Farguson, *Visualising Protestant Monarchy*, 55, 106.

115 Barry Coward and Peter Gaunt, *The Stuart Age: England, 1603–1714* (London: Routledge, 2017), 392, 422; Farguson, *Visualising Protestant Monarchy*, 39; Ribeiro, *Fashion and Fiction*, 288.

116 French influence on the Orange-Nassau court increased in the third quarter of the seventeenth century. Jonathan Israel, 'The Courts of the House of Orange, c. 1580–1795', in *The Princely Courts of Europe 1500–1750*, ed. John Adamson (London: Weidenfeld and Nicolson, 1999), 125–9.

117 All the bills referenced in this chapter that relate to Mary's wardrobe are found in BL: Add. MS 5751 A.

118 Marschner, 'Mary II', 46; Ribeiro, *Fashion and Fiction*, 288.

119 Add. MS 61420, fol. 112.

120 Mary Evelyn, *Mundus muliebris: or, The ladies dressing-room unlock'd, And her Toilette spread in Burlesque*, ed. John Evelyn (London: R. Bentley, 1690), 1.

121 Tita Chico, *Designing Women: The Dressing Room in Eighteenth-Century English Literature and Culture* (Lewisburg, PA: Bucknell University Press, 2005), 87; Emilie M. Brinkman, 'Sex, Culture, and the Politics of Fashion in Stuart England' (PhD diss., Purdue University, 2018), 26–7.

122 There are several fashion prints that feature Anne when she was Princess of Denmark. *Madame la Princesse de Dannemark*, c. 1683–1702, engraving. National Portrait Gallery, NPG D11050.

123 The mantua-makers Jane Heath and Mary Needham made 'sultane[s]' and 'halfe sultane[s]' for the Duchess of Somerset in 1688. WSA: PHA 265.

124 Farguson notes that Mary and William 'controlled their image through ceremonial performance, but prompted by the royal couple the commercial sector enacted it in art', hence why most portraits depict them in ceremonial dress of some sort. Farguson, *Visualising Protestant Monarchy*, 80, 90.

125 Ribeiro claims that orange was a favourite colour of Mary II. However, the queen's bills do not indicate this. Ribeiro, *Fashion and Fiction*, 244.

126 Ribeiro, *Fashion and Fiction*, 286.

127 Farguson, *Visualising Protestant Monarchy*, 53–5.

128 Farguson, *Visualising Protestant Monarchy*, 3. After her marriage from 1683 until 1702, Anne was styled 'Princess Anne of Denmark' in many documents and accounts.

129 For a biography of Queen Anne's life, see Anne Somerset, *Queen Anne: The Politics of Passion* (London: Harper Press, 2012).

130 Bucholz, *Augustan Court*, 202, 240–1.

131 Kevin Sharpe, *Rebranding Rule: The Restoration and Revolution Monarchy, 1660–1714* (New Haven, CT: Yale University Press, 2013), 589.

132 Farguson, *Visualising Protestant Monarchy*, 20.

133 Cited in Farguson, *Visualising Protestant Monarchy*, 238–9; BL: Add. MS 61407, fols. 14v, 19r, 22r.

134 Farguson, *Visualising Protestant Monarchy*, 238–9, 249–53; Bucholz, *Augustan Court*, 127, 205.

135 Unless otherwise indicated, all references to Anne's clothing and household accounts refer to BL: Add. MS 61407.

136 Bucholz, *Augustan Court*, 202; Ribeiro, *Fashion and Fiction*, 285.

137 BL: Add. MS 61407, fol. 29v.

138 Bodies worn by Henrietta Maria and Catherine of Braganza, and stays worn by Mary II, were all made by their tailors.

139 BL: Add. MS 61407, fol. 88v; Erin Mackie, 'Lady Credit and the Strange Case of the Hoop-Petticoat', *College Literature* 20, no. 2 (1993): 41–2; Kimberly Chrisman, 'Unhoop the Fair Sex: The Campaign Against the Hoop Petticoat in Eighteenth-Century England', *Eighteenth-Century Studies* 30, no. 1 (1996): 8.

140 BL: Add. MS 61407, 113v–114r. Mrs Hawker, 1710–11.

141 Ribeiro has noted that Anne 'was not able to set styles' but does not give an explanation as to why. Ribeiro, *Fashion and Fiction*, 294.

142 Mackie, 'Lady Credit', 41–2; Reed Benhamou, 'Who Controls This Private Space? The Offense and Defense of the Hoop in Early Eighteenth-Century France and England', *Dress* 28, no. 1 (2001): 14.

143 Bucholz, *Augustan Court*, 206.

144 Farguson, *Visualising Protestant Monarchy*, 185–6.

145 The Popish Plot (1678–81) was a fabricated conspiracy that falsely alleged that Catholics planned to assassinate Charles II and replace him with his Catholic brother James. It led to widespread anti-Catholic hysteria and

prompted a series of Exclusion Bills that sought to exclude James, Duke of York, from inheriting his brother's throne due to his Catholicism.

146 Coward and Gaunt, *The Stuart Age*, 392–7, 408; Farguson, *Visualising Protestant Monarchy*, 181; Ribeiro, *Fashion and Fiction*, 296.

147 Their names appear in registers for the French Church in Threadneedle Street, Westminster Savoy Church and non-conformist registers in Spitalfields.

148 BL: Add. MS 61420, fol. 74v.

149 BL: Add. MS 61407. 20v. Mrs Clifton, 1701–2.

150 BL: Add. MS 61407. 19r. Mr Alexander, 1701–2.

151 *An Historical and Chronological Deduction of the Origin of Commerce, from the Earliest Accounts*, ed. Adam Anderson, vol. 2 (n.p.p.: Logographic Press, 1787), 646. Plain white cotton cloth was still allowed to be imported until the second Calico Act of 1721.

152 Jonathan P. Eacott, 'Making an Imperial Compromise: The Calico Acts, the Atlantic Colonies, and the Structure of the British Empire', *William and Mary Quarterly* 69, no. 4 (2012): 731–2; William Farrell, 'Smuggling Silks into Eighteenth-Century Britain: Geography, Perpetrators, and Consumers', *Journal of British Studies* 55, no. 2 (2016): 268–9.

153 There are sporadic references to these banned items in bills from mercers and milliners, most often 'Persian'. These may have already been imported before these laws were proclaimed.

154 BL: Add. MS 61407, 76v–77v. Mrs Clifton, 1707.

155 All these references come from BL: Add. MS 61407.

156 Peter Thornton, 'The "Bizarre" Silks', *Burlington Magazine* 100, no. 665 (1958): 265–6; Ribeiro, *Fashion and Fiction*, 297.

157 Styles, 'Fashion and Innovation', 37.

158 Cited in Bucholz, *Augustan Court*, 220.

159 Cited in Bucholz, *Augustan Court*, 239.

160 Edward Gregg, *Queen Anne* (London: Routledge & Kegan Paul, 1980), 67.

2 Managing: The Office of the Robes and the work of the Mistress of the Robes

1 The Stuart king's Office of the Robes and attendants has been explored by Hayward, *Stuart Style*.

2 Bucholz, *Augustan Court*, 115.

3 Cathleen Sarti, 'Introduction: Women and Economic Power in Premodern Royal Courts', in *Women and Economic Power in Premodern Royal Courts*, ed. Sarti Cathleen (York: ARC Humanities Press, 2020), 1.

4 Clothing and jewellery were frequently given as gifts to those who held positions in the royal household. Bucholz, *Augustan Court*, 117; Bucholz, 'Going to Court', 188; Field, *Anna of Denmark*, 121.

5 R. Malcolm Smuts, 'The Structure of the Court and the Roles of the Artist and Poet under Charles I', *The Court Historian* 9, no. 2 (2004): 109; Sarti, 'Introduction', 3.

6 TNA: SP 15/35, fol. 61. Persson has argued that the office of Court Mistress at the Swedish court was no sinecure. Fabian Persson, *Women at the Early Modern Swedish Court: Power, Risk, and Opportunity* (Amsterdam: Amsterdam University Press, 2021), 349.

7 BL: Add. MS 61424, fol. 13r.

8 The Bedchamber was named the Privy Chamber in Anna of Denmark's household, which retained the terminology of her Tudor predecessors. Helen Margaret Payne, 'Aristocratic Women and the Jacobean Court, 1603–1625' (PhD diss., University of London, 2001), 51–3.

9 Arnold, *Queen Elizabeth's Wardrobe*, 163–4.

10 Charlotte Merton, 'The Women who served Queen Mary and Queen Elizabeth: Ladies, Gentlewomen and Maids of the Privy Chamber, 1553–1603' (PhD diss., University of Cambridge, 1992), 68–9.

11 The Stuart kings had a Master of the Robes in their Scottish and English households. Pearce, 'Fashioning a Danish Court', 141–2.

12 Bucholz, 'Independent Sub-departments: Robes 1660–1837', https://www.british-history.ac.uk/office-holders/vol11/pp135-141.

13 The Groom of the Stole was first named as a position in the queen's household in 1617. Payne, 'Aristocratic Women', 57; Bucholz, *Augustan Court*, 82

14 Fabian Persson, 'Living in the House of Power: Women at the Early Modern Swedish Court', in *The Politics of Female Households: Ladies-in-Waiting across Early Modern Europe*, eds Nadine Akkerman and Birgit Houben (Leiden: Brill, 2013), 346–9; Katrin Keller, 'Ladies-in-Waiting at the Imperial Court of Vienna from 1550 to 1700: Structures, Responsibilities and Career Patterns', in *The Politics of Female Households: Ladies-in-Waiting across Early Modern Europe*, eds Nadine Akkerman and Birgit Houben (Leiden: Brill, 2013), 82.

15 This position seems to have combined the duties of the Mistress of the Robes, dressers and bedchamber women. Oliver Mallick, 'Clients and Friends: The Ladies-in-Waiting at the Court of Anne of Austria (1615–66)', in *The Politics of Female Households: Ladies-in-Waiting across Early Modern Europe*, eds Nadine Akkerman and Birgit Houben (Leiden: Brill, 2013), 234–5.

16 Sir Thomas Walsingham's cousin was Sir Francis Walsingham, secretary to Elizabeth I. Lady Walsingham was also reportedly a favourite of Sir Robert Cecil, the Lord High Treasurer. Payne, 'Aristocratic Women', 63; Anne Clifford, *The Diaries of Lady Anne Clifford*, ed. D. J. H. Clifford (Stroud: Alan Sutton, 1991), 23.

17 For an overview of the structure of Anna's Bedchamber and Privy chamber, see Barroll, *Anna of Denmark*, 49; Payne, 'Aristocratic Women', 280–4.

18 Barroll notes that, given Lady Walsingham's lower status, she 'must have been chosen for her trustworthiness'. Barroll, *Anna of Denmark*, 183, n. 8.

19 'Entry Book: May 1689, 1–10', in *Calendar of Treasury Books, Volume 9, 1689–1692*, ed. William A Shaw (London: His Majesty's Stationery Office, 1931), *British History Online*, https://www.british-history.ac.uk/cal-treasury-books/vol9/pp101-115.

20 The Duke of Buckingham's brothers John and Christopher Villiers were also made Groom of the Bedchamber and Master of the Robes, respectively, to James I. His brother-in-law William Feilding, Earl of Denbigh, was made Master of the Great Wardrobe in 1622. Roger Lockyer, 'Villiers, George, first duke of Buckingham (1592–1628), royal favourite', *Oxford Dictionary of National Biography*, 23 September 2004, https://doi.org/10.1093/ref:odnb/28293.

21 'Venice: July 1625, 16–31', in *Calendar of State Papers Relating to English Affairs in the Archives of Venice, Volume 19, 1625–1626*, ed. Allen B. Hinds (London: His Majesty's Stationery Office, 1913), *British History Online*, https://www.british-history.ac.uk/cal-state-papers/venice/vol19/pp111-131.

22 'Venice: July 1626, 21–31', in *Calendar of State Papers Relating To English Affairs in the Archives of Venice, Volume 19, 1625–1626*, ed. Allen B. Hinds (London: His Majesty's Stationery Office, 1913), *British History Online*, https://www.british-history.ac.uk/cal-state-papers/venice/vol19/pp483-495.

23 When this administrative reorganization of the queen's household took place, earlier accounts appear to have been stored separately and lost. Henrietta's Mistress of the Robes before 1626 – if such a role existed – was almost certainly someone from the queen's French retinue. Hibbard, 'The Queen's Patronage', 118.

24 WRO: CR2017/C1/7.

25 'Charles I – volume 413: February 16–28, 1639', in *Calendar of State Papers Domestic: Charles I, 1638–9*, eds John Bruce and William Douglas Hamilton (London: Her Majesty's Stationery Office, 1871), *British History Online*, https://www.british-history.ac.uk/cal-state-papers/domestic/chas1/1638-9/pp470-522.

26 Erin Griffey, 'Restoring Henrietta Maria's English Household in the 1660s: Continuity, Kinship and Clientage', *The Court Historian* 26, no. 3 (2021): 196.

27 Barbara's father was Edward Villiers, a half-brother to George Villiers, Duke of Buckingham, and Susan Fielding (née Villiers), Countess of Denbigh. Edward served as Master and then Warden of the Mint from 1619 to 1626. Hayward, *Material World of a Restoration Queen Consort*, 14–20.

28 'Venice: November 1668', in *Calendar of State Papers Relating To English Affairs in the Archives of Venice, Volume 35, 1666–1668*, ed. Allen B. Hinds (London: His Majesty's Stationery Office, 1935), *British History Online*, https://www.british-history.ac.uk/cal-state-papers/venice/vol35/pp306-323.

29 BLO: MS. Rawl. C. 987, fol. 22r. The Countess of Peterborough's husband, Henry Mordaunt, Earl of Peterborough, was Groom of the Stole to James II. He had also helped to arrange the marriage of James to Mary of Modena in 1673.

30 Emilia van Nassau-Beverweert married Thomas Butler, Earl of Ossory in 1659.

31 Elizabeth married William Richard George Stanley, 9th Earl of Derby, in 1673. William died in 1680.

32 John Churchill, Duke of Marlborough, was also appointed 'Knight of the Garter' and 'Captain-General of her majesty's land forces and commander-in-chief of forces'. John B. Hattendorf, 'Churchill, John, first duke of Marlborough (1650–1722), army officer and politician', *Oxford Dictionary of National Biography*, 23 September 2004, https://doi.org/10.1093/ref:odnb/5401.

33 Elizabeth's husband was Charles Seymour, Duke of Somerset. Charles was Master of the Queen's Horse. Amy Lim, 'The Furniture Patronage of Elizabeth Seymour (nee Percy), Duchess of Somerset, 1667–1722', *Furniture History* LVII (2021): 2.

34 Griffey, 'Restoring Henrietta Maria's English Household', 195.

35 John also served as Lord of the Bedchamber to William III. Bucholz, *Augustan Court*, 111.

36 The Countess of Suffolk was Keeper of the Jewels between 1605 and 1608. After this, Bridget Marrow became Keeper. Anna's household also had many female attendants who ordered and received jewels from the queen's principal jeweller, George Heriot. Payne, 'Aristocratic Women', 61–2; Field, 'Anna of Denmark's Jewellery', 143.

37 TNA: SC 6/CHASI/1693; TNA: SC 6/CHASI/1699.

38 BL: Add. MS 61420, fol. 112r–v, 116r–17v.

39 The Countess of Suffolk received court lodgings and board wages of £547 per annum and wages of approximately £300 per annum. The Countess of Derby was paid £1200 per annum, £400 of which was for her position as Mistress of the Robes. Wynne, 'Women at the Court of Charles II', 38; BL: Add. MSS. 78269, fols 66–9. While it is hard to give modern-day equivalents due to the different nature of modern wages and low price of retail goods, £300–£400 is the equivalent of £37,000–£41,000 and £55,000–£64,000 in today's currency. In 1660, £300 was the equivalent of 4,285 days' wages for a skilled tradesman. 'Currency Converter: 1270–2017', The National Archives, UK, https://www.nationalarchives.gov.uk/currency-converter/; 'Inflation Calculator', Bank of England, https://www.bankofengland.co.uk/monetary-policy/inflation/inflation-calculator.

40 Field, 'Wardrobe Goods of Anna of Denmark', 20; TNA: LR 5/65 Antoine Duvall, Christmas Quarter 1632; Griffey, 'Re-Dressing the Evidence', 12.

41 Bucholz, *Augustan Court*, 129.

42 Documents show that Arlington was paid £150 per quarter for her role as Mistress of the Robes and £150 per quarter for Groom of the Stole in 1686–7, giving a combined wage £1,200 per annum. Marlborough's combined annual income from all her offices was £5,600, with £600 for the office of Mistress of the Robes. Somerset's annual salary was £2,600, with £600 for the office of Mistress of the Robes. TNA: LR 5/80; Wynne, 'Women at the Court of Charles II', 38; Somerset, *Queen Anne*, 240; Bucholz, 'Independent Sub-departments: Robes 1660–1837', https://www.british-history.ac.uk/office-holders/vol11/pp135-141; 'Warrant Book: February 1711, 26–28', in *Calendar of Treasury Books, Volume 25, 1711*, ed. William A. Shaw (London: Her Majesty's Stationery Office, 1952), *British History Online*, https://www.british-history.ac.uk/cal-treasury-books/vol25/pp186-197. The figure of £600 is the equivalent of £84,000–£89,000 in today's currency. 'Currency Converter: 1270–2017'; 'Inflation Calculator'.

43 BL: Add. MS 15897, fol. 54v.

44 Hayward, *Stuart Style*, 191. A similar change also occurred in France where the status of the *dame d'atours* (Mistress) and *grand maître de la Garde-robe* (Master) of the Robes was elevated. Styles, 'Fashion and Innovation', 46.

45 Pepys, *Diary and Correspondence of Samuel Pepys*, vol. 9, 35.

46 Amy M. Froide, *Silent Partners: Women as Public Investors during Britain's Financial Revolution, 1690–1750* (Oxford: Oxford University Press, 2017), 68–9.

47 Froide, *Silent Partners*, 70.

48 This is the equivalent of nearly £650,000 today. Griffey, 'Re-Dressing the Evidence', 5–6; 'Currency Converter: 1270–2017'; 'Inflation Calculator'.

49 Modern conversions for these sums are roughly: £2.3 million, £980,000 and £1.2 million, respectively. Field, 'Clothing the Royal Family', 251; BL: Add. MS 15897, fol. 37; 'Currency Converter: 1270–2017'.

50 Modern conversions for these sums are roughly: £375,000 and £4.5 million. BL: Add. MS 15897, fol. 6; A. T. Thompson, *Memoirs of Sarah, Duchess of Marlborough, and of the Court of Queen Anne*, vol. 1 (London: Henry Colburn, 1839), 78; 'Currency Converter: 1270–2017'; 'Inflation Calculator'.

51 These sums are equivalent to £1.9 million, £1.6 million and £1.2 million in today's currency. Sarah Churchill, *An Account of the Conduct of the Dowager Duchess of Marlborough: From Her First Coming to Court, to the Year 1710* (London: James Bettenham, 1742), 276; BL: Add. MS 61424, fol. 14r; 'Currency Converter: 1270–2017'; 'Inflation Calculator'.

52 Whittle and Griffiths, *Consumption and Gender*, 8.

53 TNA: SC 6/JASI/1646. Livia White, 1603.

54 TNA: SC 6/JASI/1646. Francis Britaine, 1604.

55 TNA: LR 6/154/9. Hester Le Telier, 1603.

56 Markham was the niece of Lucy, Countess of Bedford, a member of the queen's Bedchamber and an extremely influential courtier.

57 TNA: SC 6/JASI/1646. Marie Cooke, 1603.

58 It is possible that some bills were written up and delivered by the tradespeople themselves, but they were probably drawn up when goods were delivered.

59 Churchill, *Account of the Conduct*, 280–1.

60 Bucholz, *Augustan Court*, 118.

61 BL: Add. MS 61420, fol. 11.

62 BL: Add. MS 61420, fol. 44.

63 TNA: LR 5/83. Mrs Heath, December 1687.

64 In 1713 the Steward of the Wardrobe, John Elrington, was paid 'for his care in weighing materials purchased for the Wardrobe'. 'Declared Accounts: Civil List', in *Calendar of Treasury Books, Volume 27, 1713*, ed. William A. Shaw and F. H. Slingsby (London: Her Majesty's Stationery Office, 1955), *British History Online*, https://www.british-history.ac.uk/cal-treasury-books/vol27/clxxxix-ccxlii.

65 TNA: SC 6/JASI/1646. James Duncane, 1604; Griffey, 'Re-Dressing the Evidence', 10.

66 TNA: LR 5/65. Hugh Ashton, Christmas quarter 1632; BL: Add. MS 5751 A, fol. 179.

67 TNA: LR: 5/65. Hugh Ashton, May–June 1632.

68 Churchill, *Account of the Conduct*, 281; BL: Add. MS 61407, fol. 9v.

69 Churchill, *Account of the Conduct*, 281; Bucholz, *Augustan Court*, 83, 300, n. 85.

70 Gowing, *Ingenious Trade*, 3; Beverly Lemire, *The Business of Everyday Life: Gender, Practice and Social Politics in England, c.1600–1900* (Manchester: Manchester University Press, 2005), 193.

71 Catherine of Braganza's Yeoman of the Robes was paid £219 in 1663, but he was also a Groom of the Robes too. LS 13–32, fol. 18.
In three years, Queen Anne's Office of the Robes received £10,105 14s. 6d. from the Exchequer and £2,866 18s 1½d. was spent on 'salaries to the Officers of the Robes'. Churchill, *Account of the Conduct*, 281; BL: Add. MS 61407, fols 9v, 58v, 72r; BL: Add. MS 61420, 110r.

72 Bucholz, *Augustan Court*, 83.

73 The women who appear to have kept the household accounts are Mrs Stanhope and Mrs Felton. WSRO: PHA 652; PHA 267; Lim, 'Furniture Patronage of Elizabeth Seymour', 2.

74 Griffey notes that after the Restoration of the monarchy 'there were still a number of suppliers who sought arrears in payments from the 1630s'. Griffey, 'Re-Dressing the Evidence', 5–6; Bucholz, 'Going to Court', 188.

75 This does not include the unpaid bills from tradespeople such as glassmen, saddlers, woodmongers, vintners, gardeners, joiners, silver smiths, wax candlers and picture frame makers, to name a few. BLO: MS. Rawl. C. 987, fol. 138v.

76 BL: Add. MS 5751 A, fol. 136.

77 John Bruce, ed., *Calendar of State Papers Domestic: Charles I, 1625–26* (London: Her Majesty's Public Record office, 1858), 538.

78 TNA: LR 5/80.

79 BL: Add. MS 61407, fols 64v –65v, 76v–77v, 101v.

80 James Falkner, 'Churchill [née Jenyns], Sarah, Duchess of Marlborough (1660–1744), politician and courtier', *Oxford Dictionary of National Biography*, 23 September 2004, https://doi.org/10.1093/ref:odnb/5405.

81 Bucholz, 'Independent Sub-departments: Robes 1660–1837', https://www.british-history.ac.uk/office-holders/vol11/pp135-141.

82 Griffey, 'Re-Dressing the Evidence', 9. Hibbard also notes that English royal households did not provide 'regular subvention, lodging and workshops that artists and craftsmen enjoyed in France or Spain'. Hibbard, 'The Queen's Patronage', 122.

83 TNA: SC 6/JASI/1646, James Duncane, 1605.

84 Catherine of Braganza's privy purse records show that seamstresses could also provide 'work done Extraordinary' and this was billed for separately. LA: 1-Worsley 8, fol. 37r.

85 In cases where there is too little data to make a definite determination between 'making' and 'selling', I have excluded the tradesperson from this graph and the graphs in Figs 0.3 and 3.4.

86 Churchill, *Account of the Conduct*, 279–80.

87 In her own personal papers, the Duchess of Marlborough wrote that 'no tradesmen, or any body bought a place, which had ever been the custom in other courts & therefore were not allowed to cheat to reimburse themselves, nor no poundage was taken, in either of my offices, which was quite a new practice in the court'. BL: Add. MS 61424, 15v.

88 John Styles and Amanda Vickery, 'Introduction', in *Gender, Taste, and Material Culture in Britain and North America, 1700–1830*, eds John Styles and Amanda Vickery (New Haven, CT: Yale University Press, 2006), 2.

89 Bellavitis, *Women's Work and Rights*, 57; Styles and Vickery, 'Introduction', 2; Bendall, *Shaping Femininity*, 75–6.

90 Ala Rekrut, 'Material Literacy: Reading Records as Material Culture', *Archivaria* 60 (2006): 11.

91 Kate Smith, 'Sensing Design and Workmanship: The Haptic Skills of Shoppers in Eighteenth-Century London', *Journal of Design History* 25 (2012): 1–10; Serena Dyer, *Material Lives: Women Makers and Consumer Culture in the 18th Century* (London: Bloomsbury, 2021), 9–14.

92 Dyer, *Material Lives*, 3.

93 Akkerman and Houben, 'Introduction', 22.

94 TNA: LR 6/154/9; TNA: SC 6/JASI/1646.

95 Arabella Stuart, *The Letters of Lady Arbella Stuart*, ed. Sara Jayne Steen (Oxford: Oxford University Press, 1994), 197.

96 Griffey, 'Re-Dressing the Evidence', 13.

97 BL: Add. MS 61407, fol. 25r.

98 KKCA: AR33/9/38; KKCA: AR33/9/98; AR33/9/116-7.

99 For an overview of childbed textiles, see Linda A. Pollock, 'Childbearing and Female Bonding in Early Modern England', *Social History* 22, no. 3 (1997): 289–90.

100 TNA: AO 1/2067/100; 'James I: Volume 12, January–February, 1605', in *Calendar of State Papers Domestic: James I, 1603–1610*, ed. Mary Anne Everett Green (London: Her Majesty's Stationery Office, 1857), *British History Online*, https://www.british-history.ac.uk/cal-state-papers/domestic/jas1/1603-10/pp185-200.

101 TNA: AO 1/2067/100.

102 Griffey, *On Display*, 95–115.

103 'Charles I – volume 145: June 17–30, 1629', in *Calendar of State Papers Domestic: Charles I, 1628–29*, ed. John Bruce (London: Her Majesty's Stationery Office, 1859), *British History Online*, https://www.british-history.ac.uk/cal-state-papers/domestic/chas1/1628-9/pp580-598.

104 'Charles I – volume 152: November 17–30, 1629', in *Calendar of State Papers Domestic: Charles I, 1629–31*, ed. John Bruce (London: Her Majesty's Stationery Office, 1860), *British History Online*, https://www.british-history.ac.uk/cal-state-papers/domestic/chas1/1629-31/pp98-111; TNA: LR5/64.

105 WRO: CR2017/C1/16.

106 Griffey, *On Display*, 95.

107 Griffey, *On Display*, 17–18, 20, 97.

108 Griffey, 'Re-Dressing the Evidence', 13.

109 TNA: LR 5/76, Ann Morgan, Christmas quarter, 1684; BL: Add. MS 61407, fols 21r, 29v, 44v, 76v–77r.

110 TNA: LR 5/81–84.

111 Field, 'Clothing the Royal Family', 252.

112 Cited in Ann Saunders, *The Royal Exchange* (London: London Topographical Society, 1997), 89.

113 Gowing, *Ingenious Trade*, 18–19.

114 Hayward, *Stuart Style*, 181, 190.

115 LA: 1-Worsley/6, fol. 39r; J. C. Sainty, Lydia Wassmann and R. O. Bucholz, 'Household of Queen (from 1685 Queen Dowager) Catherine 1660–1705', *The Database of Court Officers: 1660–1837*, http://courtofficers.ctsdh.luc.edu/indices/Index%2002%20Household%20of%20Queen%20Catherine%201662b.pdf.

116 TNA: C 8/298/61. The Countess of Arlington's daughter was Isabella FitzRoy (née Bennet), Duchess of Grafton. She married the son of Charles II and his mistress Barbara Villiers, Henry FitzRoy, 1st Duke of Grafton, in 1672.

117 WSRO: PHA 272–88; 'Declared Accounts: Civil List', in *Calendar of Treasury Books, Volume 26, 1712*, ed. William A. Shaw (London: Her Majesty's Stationery Office, 1954), *British History Online*, https://www.british-history.ac.uk/cal-treasury-books/vol26/ccvii-cclvii; 'Warrant Books: September 1714, 21–30', in *Calendar of Treasury Books, Volume 29, 1714–1715*, eds William A Shaw and F. H. Slingsby (London: Her Majesty's Stationery Office, 1957), *British History Online*, https://www.british-history.ac.uk/cal-treasury-books/vol29/pp89-106.

118 WSRO: PHA 274, fol. 18; PHA 277, fols 11, 23; PHA 278, fol. 46; 'Declared Accounts: Civil List', in *Calendar of Treasury Books, Volume 26, 1712*.

119 Davidson, *Catherine of Bragança*, 90.

120 Greig, *Beau Monde*, 3, 44–5, 62

121 Cited in Somerset, *Queen Anne*, 244.

122 BL: Add. MS 61455, fol. 41.

123 BL: Add. MS 61455, fol. 171.

124 These letters were from Jane Martha Temple, Countess of Portland, and Barbara Herbert, Countess of Pembroke. BL: Add. MS 61456, fols 157, 180.

125 BL: Add. MS. 61455, fol. 39.

126 BL: Add. MS 61417, fols 162v–63; Somerset, *Queen Anne*, 366–7.

127 Mark Hailwood and Brodie Waddell, 'Work and Identity in Early Modern England', *Transactions of the Royal Historical Society* 1 (2023): 151–3.

128 Barbara J. Harris, *English Aristocratic Women, 1450–1550: Marriage and Family, Property and Careers* (Oxford: Oxford University Press, 2002), 6, 28,

129 Barroll, *Anna of Denmark*, 39.

130 Davidson, *Catherine of Bragança*, 64.

131 Bucholz, 'Independent Sub-departments: Robes 1660–1837', https://www.british-history.ac.uk/office-holders/vol11/pp135-141.

132 These include letters from Lord De La Warr and the Countess of Portland. BL: Add. MS 61474, fol. 159r; BL: Add. MS 61456, fol. 172.

133 'Cecil Papers: 1612', in *Calendar of the Cecil Papers in Hatfield House: Volume 24, Addenda, 1605–1668*, ed. G Dyfnallt Owen (London: Her Majesty's Stationery Office, 1976), *British History Online*, https://www.british-history.ac.uk/cal-cecil-papers/vol24/pp210-229.

134 'Charles I – volume 370: October 19–31, 1637', in *Calendar of State Papers Domestic: Charles I, 1637*, ed. John Bruce (London: Her Majesty's Stationery Office, 1868), *British History Online*, https://www.british-history.ac.uk/cal-state-papers/domestic/chas1/1637/pp481-509.

135 Evelyn, *The Diary of John Evelyn*, vol. 2, 88.

136 Falkner, 'Churchill [née Jenyns], Sarah, Duchess of Marlborough'.

137 Ophelia Field, *The Favourite: Sarah, Duchess of Marlborough* (London: Weidenfeld & Nicolson, 2018), 297.

138 For an overview of these smears, see Frances Harris, 'Accounts of the Conduct of Sarah Duchess of Marlborough, 1704–1742', *British Library Journal* 8 (1982): 12–13; Churchill, *Account of the Conduct*, 272–3.

139 Arthur Maynwaring was a Whig politician and journalist. Harris, 'Accounts of the Conduct', 7–8, 14–16.

140 Sarah also claimed that Edward Harley, the Auditor of Imprests in the Exchequer, had praised her conduct and her accounts from the Robes after comparing them with those who had come before her. Churchill, *Account of the Conduct*, 273–5; BL: Add. MS 61424, fol. 13r.

141 BL: Add. MS 61425, fols 86r–v.

142 Churchill, *Account of the Conduct*, 278–9; BL: Add. MS 61424, fol. 14r; Harris, 'Accounts of the Conduct', 11; Field, *The Favourite*, 295.

143 BL: Add. MS 61424, fol. 15v.

144 Jonathan Swift, *The Works of the Rev. Jonathan Swift*, vol. 3, eds Thomas Sheridan and John Nichols (London: J. Johnson, John Nichols and Son et al., 1801), 33–4; Harris, 'Accounts of the Conduct', 13.

145 Queen Anne and Sarah Churchill had pen names that they used in their correspondence with each other. Anne was Mrs Morley and Sarah was Mrs Freeman. BL: Add. MS 61423, fols 21v–22r.

3 Selling: Fashion retailers, milliners and their social networks

1 BL: Add. MS. 61455, fol. 31.

2 Birt, 'A Fashionable Business', 15; Erickson, 'Eleanor Moseley', 167

3 R. Campbell, *The London Tradesman: Being a Compendious View of All the Trades, Professions, Arts, Both Liberal and Mechanic, Now Practised in the Cities of London and Westminster . . .* (London: T. Gardner, 1747), 206; *A General Description of All Trades: Digested in Alphabetical Order: by which Parents, Guardians, and Trustees, May, with Greater Ease and Certainty, Make Choice of Trades Agreeable to the Capacity, Education, Inclination, Strength, and Fortune of the Youth Under Their Care* (London: T. Waller, 1747), 149; Wendy Gamber, *The Female Economy: The Millinery and Dressmaking Trades, 1860–1930* (Champaign: University of Illinois Press, 1997).

4 Simonton, 'Milliners and Marchandes de modes', 19–38; Erickson, 'Eleanor Mosley',154–67.

5 I build on recent work by Sarah Birt, Amy Lim, Juliet Claxton and Evelyn Welch who have identified that the foreign goods that flowed into England during the seventeenth century were not only drivers of 'economic, social, and cultural change' but also encouraged new forms of merchandising. Birt, 'A Fashionable Business', 289–93; Birt, 'Women, Guilds and the Tailoring Trades', 148–9; Amy Lim, 'John van Collema: a Dutch India Goods Merchant in London', in *Close Encounters: Cross-Cultural Exchange between the Low Countries and Britain, 1600–1830*, eds Karen Hearn, Angela Jager, Sander Karst, Rieke van Leeuwen, David Taylor and Joanna Woodall (The Hague: RKD Studies, 2024), https://close-encounters.rkdstudies.nl/9-john-van-collema-a-dutch-india-goods-merchant-in-london/; Juliet Claxton and Evelyn Welch, 'Chintz, China, and Chocolate: The Politics of Fashion at Charles II's Court', in *Sartorial Politics in Early Modern Europe: Fashioning Women*, ed. Erin Griffey (Amsterdam: Amsterdam University Press, 2019), 258; Lim, 'World of Interiors'.

6 Gowing, *Ingenious Trade*, 86.

7 Lord Sidney was paid £100 in wages and livery in 1617. TNA: SC 6/JASI/1653.

8 Hibbard, 'The Queen's Patronage', 129–30; Griffey, 'Re-Dressing the Evidence', 10.

9 Henrietta Maria's silk mercers often waited three years for payment. Griffey, 'Re-Dressing the Evidence', 12; Claxton and Welch, 'Chintz, China, and Chocolate', 261.

10 Griffey, 'Re-Dressing the Evidence', 10.

11 Hibbard, 'The Queen's Patronage', 129–30.

12 Hicks was a member of the Mercers Company. Arnold, *Queen Elizabeth's Wardrobe*, 12; Field, 'Clothing the Royal Family', 259.

13 Paul Griffiths, 'Politics Made Visible: Order, Residence and Uniformity in Cheapside, 1600–45', in *Londinopolis: Essays in the Cultural and Social history of Early Modern London*, eds Paul Griffiths and Mark S. R. Jenner (Manchester: Manchester University Press, 2000), 176, 181; Vanessa Harding, 'Shops, Markets and Retailers in

London's Cheapside, c. 1500–1700', in *Buyers and Sellers: Retail Circuits and Practices in Medieval and Early Modern Europe*, eds Bruno Blondé, Peter Stabel, Jon Stobart and Ilja Van Damme (Turnhout: Brepols, 2006), 59–60.

14 J. R. Kellett, 'The Breakdown of Gild and Corporation Control over the Handicraft and Retail Trade in London', *Economic History Review* 10 (1957): 94.

15 This is equivalent to £7.9 million in modern currency. Smuts, 'Art and Material Culture of Majesty', 112; Bruce, *Calendar of State Papers Domestic: Charles I, 1625–26*, 538; 'Currency Converter: 1270–2017'; 'Inflation Calculator'.

16 Griffey, 'Re-Dressing the Evidence', 10; Walter Thornbury, *Old and New London: Volume 1* (London: Cassell, Petter & Galpin, 1878), *British History Online*, https://www.british-history.ac.uk/old-new-london/vol1/pp374-383.

17 Alfred P. Beaven, 'Chronological list of aldermen: 1601–1650', in *The Aldermen of the City of London Temp. Henry III – 1912* (London: Corporation of the City of London, 1908), *British History Online*, https://www.british-history.ac.uk/no-series/london-aldermen/hen3-1912/pp47-75; Alfred P. Beaven, 'Aldermen of the City of London: Vintry ward', in *The Aldermen of the City of London Temp. Henry III – 1912* (London: Corporation of the City of London, 1908), *British History Online*, https://www.british-history.ac.uk/no-series/london-aldermen/hen3-1912/pp205-215.

18 Nigel Victor Sleigh-Johnson, 'The Merchant-Taylors Company of London, 1580–1645, with Special Reference to Politics and Government' (PhD diss., University College London, 1989), 387.

19 Sarah Birt has found some examples of women apprenticed or made free of the Merchant Taylors Company in the early seventeenth century. Birt, 'A Fashionable Business', 84.

20 Gowing, 'Girls on Forms', 460; Clare Crowston, 'Women, Gender, and Guilds in Early Modern Europe: An Overview of Recent Research', *International Review of Social History* 53, no. S16 (2008): 19.

21 TNA: JASI/1653, Hester Onslowe, 1617.

22 TNAL: LR 5/64, Gilbert Ward, July–September 1631. Signed by Margaret Ward; Hibbard, 'The Queen's Patronage', 130–1.

23 TNA: LR 5/64, Mr Aldworth, Lady Day Quarter 1627.

24 Amy Louise Erickson, 'Mistresses and Marriage: or, a Short History of the Mrs', *History Workshop Journal* 78 (2014): 39–40; Gowing, *Ingenious Trade*, 99.

25 Richard Aldworth married Margaret Maihew in London All Hallows the Less in 1611. TNA: LR 5/64, Richard Aldworth, Christmas Quarter 1630. 'England, Boyd's Marriage Indexes, 1538–1850', *Findmypast*.

26 TNA: LR 5/64; LR 5/65.

27 In 1653 a petition was submitted to the House of Commons from 'Anne Henshawe Widow, late Wife and Exectrix of Benjamin Henshawe, and her Eight fatherless Children', who was awarded £8,000. 'House of Commons Journal Volume 7: 22 November 1653', in *Journal of the House of Commons: Volume 7, 1651–1660* (London: His Majesty's Stationery Office, 1802), *British History Online*, https://www.british-history.ac.uk/commons-jrnl/vol7/pp354-355; Peter Barber, 'Gambling in wartime: the rise and fall of William Geere', *Camden History Review* 19 (1995): 17–20.

28 Lim, 'John van Collema'; Ribeiro, *Fashion and Fiction*, 252; Greig, *Beau Monde*, 8–11.

29 Janette Dillon, *Theatre, Court and City, 1595–1610: Drama and Social Space in London* (Cambridge: Cambridge University Press, 2000), 109–10.

30 Field, *London, Londoners and the Great Fire*, 119.

31 For example, tailors, shoemakers, farthingale-makers, silkwomen and seamstresses, glovers, feather-dressers, pin-makers, embroiderers, goldsmiths and girdlers.

32 Birt, 'A Fashionable Business', 296–7.

33 Although milliners also made things, in these graphs I have classified them as suppliers as their retailing of ready-made goods set them apart from seamstresses and mantua-makers.

34 TNA: LR 6/154/9, Richard French 1604; TNA: LR 5/64, Arthur Knight, Lady Day Quarter 1628, Christmas Quarters 1630 and 1631.

35 Other goods included scissors, paper and some linen and silk fabrics. LR 5/84, Mathew Bowman, 1688 and 1688/9.

36 Erickson, 'Eleanor Mosley', 156.

37 'milliner (n.), sense 2', *Oxford English Dictionary*, last modified September 2024, https://doi.org/10.1093/OED/6754304927.

38 TNA: LR 6/154/9, Thomas Cooke, 1603.

39 TNA: LR 5/64, Joseph Atkinson, Lady Day Quarter and Christmas Quarter 1631. Humphrey Bradbourne, Lady Day Quarter 1631; LR 5/65, Joseph Atkinson, Michaelmas Quarter and Christmas Quarter 1632.

40 These included things such as silk ribbons, buttons, spices, home furnishings and small accessories. Bellavitis, *Women's Work and Rights*, 227–8.

41 Bellavitis, *Women's Work and Rights*, 227.

42 Crowston, *Credit, Fashion, Sex*, 148.

43 Zara Kesterton, 'The Rise of France's First "Minister of Fashion", Marie-Jeanne Bertin, 1760–1789' (MPhil diss., University of Cambridge, 2020), 25–6. The *rubanièr(e)* was noted to be a type of mercier. The *merciers* trade had several sub-specializations, including those merchants who just dealt in expensive cloth and were akin to the English 'mercer'. Académie Française, *Le Grand Dictionnaire de l'Académie françoise* (Amsterdam : Jean Baptiste Coignard, 1695), 16.

44 On the rise of the *marchande de modes* in France, see Crowston, *Credit, Fashion, Sex*, 139–51

45 Jane Ashelford, *The Art of Dress: Clothes and Society, 1500–1914* (Swindon: National Trust, 1996), 101.

46 These total £240,000 and £207,000 in today's currency. BL: Add. MS. 5751 A, fols 118r, 150r. 'Currency Converter: 1270–2017'; 'Inflation Calculator'.

47 TNA: LR 5/84, Peter Lombard, Lady Quarter 1687; BL: Add. MS 5751 A, fols 118r–121v.

48 Somerset, *Queen Anne*, 244.

49 Sarah Birt has found that out of all the livery companies in London, the haberdashers saw the largest increase in female apprentices between the years 1670 and 1699. This suggests women's increased involvement with the guild's associated small-wares trades, including lace-selling, which petitions from the time signed by women confirm. Birt, 'A Fashionable Business', 145, 293.

50 Simonton, 'Milliners and marchandes de modes', 35; Crowston, *Credit, Fashion, Sex*, 140.

51 The Stuart kings mostly preferred to rely on male suppliers, including milliners, for ribbons and buttons. However, their accounts also contain several women who sold decorative trims. References to women such as a 'Mrs Mary May' for 'gold and silver ribbon' also appear in Charles II's accounts. BLO: MS Eng. Misc. b. 31, fol. 164; TNA: AO 3/926, fols 38, 43.

52 *Advice to the Maidens of LONDON: To Forsake Their Fantastical TOP-KNOTS* (London: J. Blare, 1685–8), cited by Angela McShane and Clare Backhouse, 'Top Knots and Lower Sorts: Print and Promiscuous Consumption in the 1690s', in *Printed Images in Early Modern Britain: Essays in Interpretation*, ed. Michael Hunter (London: Routledge, 2010), 343.

53 Ruth Battersby Tooke, Claire Jowitt, Benjamin W. D. Redding and Francesca Vanke, *The Last Voyage of the Gloucester: Norfolk's Royal Shipwreck, 1682* (Aylsham, Norfolk: Barnwell Print Ltd, 2023), 38–47.

54 Who these goods belonged to is unknown. There is no confirmed presence of a woman being on board the *Gloucester* when it sank. Other objects found in this chest, including a pouch with three crown stamps, men's shoes, fabric weights and mending supplies, suggests its owner could have been a member of James or Mary's household. Or maybe they belonged to someone regularly engaged in the maintenance of clothing within the royal household? This remains unclear. Tooke et. al., *The Last Voyage of the* Gloucester, 62–9.

55 Randle Holme, *The Academy of Armory, or, A Storehouse of Armory and Blazon* (Chester: printed for author, 1688), 12; Tooke et. al., *The Last Voyage of the* Gloucester, 65.

56 BL: Add. MS 61407. fol. 41r.

57 Ribeiro, *Fashion and Fiction*, 263.

58 William Carter, *Englands intrest in securing the woollen-manufacture, of this realm Against the artiffices, and designs of France . . .* (London: Joseph Streater, 1689), 31.

59 Steele, *Paris Fashion*, 2; Avidon, 'Assessing French Fashion Prints', 1–32.

60 These remarks came after Catherine examined a carved piece from an artist, Mr Gibbon, who had been recommended by Evelyn but was dismissed by the queen due to advice from Madame de Bord, who 'found fault with several things in the work'. Evelyn, *The Diary of John Evelyn*, vol. 2., 62–3.

61 LA: 1-Worsley/7, fols 19v, 27r, 32v; LA: 1-Worsley/8, fol. 22r.

62 LA: 1-Worsley/8, fols 20r, 25r, 31v; TNA: LR 5/80; BLO: MS. Rawl. C. 987, fol. 50r; WSRO: PHA 264, fol. 8.

63 Randall, 'London's French Protestants', 26.

64 Bill from Marie Cheret of 'the French shop' reproduced in Diana de Marly, 'Fashionable Suppliers 1660–1700: Leading Tailors and Clothing Tradesmen of the Restoration Period', *Antiquaries Journal* 58, no. 2 (1978): 348.

65 Pepys, *Diary and Correspondence of Samuel Pepys*, vol. 4, 76.

66 LA: 1-Worsley/6, 8, 9; BA: 91/30; TNA: AO3/919; de Marly, 'Fashionable Suppliers', 345.

67 Marie Cheret's husband was also named Thomas. In 1677 George Cheret married Susana Hopkins in St Marylebone church, Westminster. Baptism records of their children (Jane, John and Frances), survive from 1680, 1685 and 1686. 'London, England, Church of England Baptisms, Marriages and Burials, 1538–1812', *Ancestry.com*; 'Westminster, London, England, Church of England Baptisms, Marriages and Burials, 1558–1812', *Ancestry.com*; William H. Hunt, ed., *The Registers of St. Paul's Church, Convent Garden, London, volume 4, Burials, 1653–1752* (London: Publications of the Harleian Society, 1906), 69, 72.

68 Marie Cheret, George and Susana are all recorded as living in the Piazza in Covent Garden. George Cheret is later mentioned at 'the Golden Ball in James Street Covent Garden'. Thomas Cheret is also listed in James Street in 1708. Pepys, *Diary and Correspondence of Samuel Pepys*, vol. 4, 76, n. 1; *London Gazette*, issue 4027, June 12, 1704; 'Westminster Rate Books 1634–1900', *Findmypast*.

69 TNA: LR 5/77, George Cheret, Lady Day, Michaelmas and Christmas Quarters 1685; TNA: LR 5/80, Payments made to artisans by the Mistress of the Robes, 1687; BL: Add. MS 61424, fol. 46r; WSRO: PHA 261, fol. 17, PHA 262, fol. 23, PHA 278, fol. 22.

70 TNA: LC 9/280, fol. 255v.

71 BL: Add. MS 5751 A, fol. 142.

72 BL: Add. MS 5751 A, fol. 142; Elizabeth Graydon also supplied many of these flowered French hoods in the period 1680–1710. TNA: LR 5/84; Elizabeth Graydon, 1687; BL: Add. MS 61407, fol. 32v.

73 James Howard, *The English Mounsieur a Comedy, as It Is Acted, at the Theater-Royal by His Majesty's Servants* (London: H. Bruges for J. Magnus, 1674), 11.

74 de Marly, 'Fashionable Suppliers', 341.

75 William Petyt, *Britannia Languens: Or, a Discourse of Trade Shewing, That the Present Management of Trade in England* (London: Richard Baldwin, 1689), 205.

76 Born Pierre Antoine Motteux in Rouen, Motteux came to England in 1685. WSRO: PHA 274, fol. 18, PHA 277, fols 11, 23, PHA 278, fol. 46; 'Declared Accounts: Civil List', in *Calendar of Treasury Books, Volume 26, 1712*.

77 The Restoration actor William Mountfort and his wife Susanna also ran an India shop in Norfolk Street in the parish of St Clement Danes, selling goods to elites as well as to fellow actors. Christine Ferdinand, 'Commodities and the Acting Profession: A Newly Discovered Inventory for William and Susanna Mountfort's "India Shop" (1692)', *Huntington Library Quarterly* 86, no. 1 (2023): 73–109.

78 Riello, *Cotton*, 93–4; Berg, *Luxury*, 49–50; Lim, 'John van Collema'.

79 Beverly Lemire, 'Fashioning Cottons: Asian trade, domestic industry and consumer demand, 1660 1780', in *The Fashion History Reader: Global Perspectives*, eds Giorgio Riello and Peter McNeil (London: Routledge, 2010), 194–5; Riello, *Cotton*, 113–14.

80 Lee-Whitman, 'The Silk Trade', 25–38; K. N. Chaudhuri, *The Trading World of Asia and the English East India Company, 1660–1760* (Cambridge: Cambridge University Press, 2006), 46–52.

81 J. F., *The merchant's ware-house laid open: or, the plain dealing linnen-draper* (London: John Sprint, 1696), 14.

82 Thomas Southerne, *The Maid's Last Prayer* (London: R. Bentley, 1693), 14.

83 Mary Pix, *The Innocent Mistress a Comedy* (London: J. Orme, for R. Basset and F. Cogan, 1697), 15–16; Colley Cibber, *Woman's wit, or, The lady in fashion* (London: John Sturton, 1697), 35, 63; *Dialogues of the dead in imitation of Lucian, and the French* (London: R.C., 1699), 25.

84 TNA: PROB 4/25866; Claxton and Welch, 'Chintz, China, and Chocolate', 261.

85 Craddock is named as Mary Devet's daughter, and Tombs as her granddaughter, in her will. TNA: PROB 11/561/208.

86 Churchill, *Account of the Conduct*, 281; *London Gazette*, issue 2470, July 15, 1689.

87 BL: Add. MS. 61456, fol. 50.

88 TNA: LR 5/83, Mrs Devet, August 1687 and March 1688; BL: Add. MS 5751 A, fol. 133r; BL: Add. MS 61407; WSRO: PHA 261, PHA 264, PHA 267, PHA 280, PHA 285.

89 Many thanks to Kerry-Louise Apps for these references to Mrs Taylor from BA: MS 413. Apps discusses East Indies furnishings in her forthcoming PhD thesis, 'Imagining Asia at Ham House, c.1672–1698' (PhD diss., Open University, forthcoming). For Pyke, see Gowing, *Ingenious Trade*, 45; Birt, 'A Fashionable Business', 292–8.

90 HL/PO/JO/10/1/484/1051 in 'Petitions to the House of Lords: 1696', in *Petitions to the House of Lords, 1597–1696*, ed. Jason Peacey, *British History Online*, http://www.british-history.ac.uk/petitions/house-of-lords/1696; Eacott, 'Making an Imperial Compromise', 731–2.

91 TNA, LR5/79, Mary Mandoue and Peter Lombard, 1687; BL, Add. MS 5751 A, fols 104r, 106r.

92 TNA, LR 5/83, Matthias Cupper, August 1688.

93 Danielle van den Heuvel, 'New Products, New Sellers? Changes in the Dutch Textile Trades, c.1650–1750', in *Selling Textiles in the Long Eighteenth Century: Comparative Perspectives from Western Europe*, eds John Stobart and Bruno Blondé (London: Palgrave, 2014), 132.

94 The mercer Nicholas Fownes apprenticed another royal mercer, James Alexander, in 1686. After his death, Fownes' son Benjamin Fownes apprenticed under the royal woollen draper John Deacle in 1692. '1686, James Alexander, Mercers' Company', ROLLCO; '1692, Benjamin Fownes, Draper' Company', ROLLCO.

95 Gowing, *Ingenious Trade*, 89.

96 Between 1672 and 1676 Burton was at 'the Exchange' and then in the Strand in 1685. Robert Paston Yarmouth, *The Whirlpool of Misadventures: Letters of Robert Paston, First Earl of Yarmouth, 1663–1679*, ed. Jean Agnew. Volume LXXVI (Norwich: Norfolk Record Society, 2012), 138; WSRO: PHA 652, Deborah Burton, 1685.

97 'England Marriages 1538–1973', *Findmypast.com*; WSA: PHA 264, fol. 24; PHA 267, fol. 4; PHA 268, fol. 15.

98 Judith Burton and Barrell Langrish were married in 1674 at St Paul's church in Covent Garden. 'Westminster Marriages', *Findmypast*.

99 Deborah Burton's will mentions the Vitners Company and it is possible that her deceased husband was a member. Thomas Langrish, father of Barrell, may have been part of the Drapers Company. TNA: PROB 11/523/10; '1656, Thomas Langrishe, Draper' Company', ROLLCO; TNA: E 133/78/54; TNA: C 10/404/36.

100 Deborah was buried at St Bride's church, Fleet Street. TNA: PROB 11/523/10; 'London, England, Church of England Baptisms, Marriages and Burials, 1538–1812', *Ancestry.com*.

101 Gowing, *Ingenious Trade*, 139; Erickson, 'Eleanor Moseley', 151–2; Jennie Batchelor, *Dress, Distress and Desire: Clothing and the Female Body in Eighteenth-Century Literature* (London: Palgrave Macmillan, 2005), 59–78.

102 Gowing, *Ingenious Trade*, 194.

103 This is equal to £150,000 in today's currency. The only other suppliers commanding these types of bills were lacemen and mercers. BL: Add. MS 61424, fols 46r–47r; Add. MS 61425, fols 86v–88r. 'Currency Converter: 1270–2017'; 'Inflation Calculator'.

104 Kesterton, 'The Rise of France's First "Minister of Fashion"', 42.

105 BL: Add. MS 34195, fol. 101.

106 Farguson, *Visualising Protestant Monarchy*, 139.

107 BL: Add. MS 34195, fol. 101.

108 In June 1681 'Daniel Skinner and Robert Graydon' were given extraordinary allowances for doing the work of a third jerquer at the London port. 'Entry Book: June 1681, 13–20', in *Calendar of Treasury Books, Volume 7,*

1681–1685, ed. William A Shaw (London: His Majesty's Stationery Office, 1916), *British History Online*, https://www.british-history.ac.uk/cal-treasury-books/vol7/pp172-185.

109 Robert Graydon lodged a petition dated 4 July 1690 'in right of his Whitehall, brother, Captain John Graydon, commander of the *Defiance*'. TNA: SP 44/235 fol. 89.

110 J. K. Laughton and J. D. Davies, 'Graydon, John (d. 1726), naval officer', *Oxford Dictionary of National Biography*, 23 September 2004, https://doi.org/10.1093/ref:odnb/11359; John Harris, *The History of Kent. In Five Parts, vol. 1* (London: D. Midwinter, 1719), 27.

111 Godfrey Kneller, Vice-Admiral John Graydon, *c.* 1703, National Maritime Museum, Greenwich, London, Greenwich Hospital Collection: BHC2723.

112 'Mr. Graydon's House in the Pell-mell' is mentioned in Thomas Hale, *An account of several new inventions and improvements now necessary for England, in a discourse by way of letter to the Earl of Marlborough . . .* (London: James Astwood, 1691), 96. A later court case describes Graydon as residing in the Parish of St Martin-in-the-Fields, whose border started at the eastern end of this street. TNA: C 8/427/86.

113 TNA: LR 5/84, Elizabeth Graydon, 1687.

114 Muldrew, 'Women, Debt, Litigation and Contract', 48.

115 Muldrew, 'Women, Debt, Litigation and Contract', 48; Dyer, *Material Lives*, 35–6; Margot C. Finn, *The Character of Credit: Personal Debt in English Culture, 1740–1914* (Cambridge: Cambridge University Press, 2003), 21.

116 TNA: C 8/427/86.

117 All references to this 1701 case come from TNA: C 10/364/32.

118 McIntosh, 'The Benefits and Drawbacks of Femme Sole Status', 412, 430.

119 Bellavitis, *Women's Work and Rights*, 74.

120 This is equal to roughly half a million pounds in today's currency. 'Currency Converter: 1270–2017'; 'Inflation Calculator'.

121 'Entry book: May 1695, 16–25', in *Calendar of Treasury Books, Volume 10, 1693–1696*, ed. William A. Shaw (London: His Majesty's Stationery Office, 1935), *British History Online*, https://www.british-history.ac.uk/cal-treasury-books/vol10/pp1073-1087.

122 Simonton, 'Milliners and Marchandes de modes', 32.

123 BL: Add. MS 34195, fol. 101

124 BL: Add. MS 61346. The bill from Graydon was signed for by 'Margaret Watkin', likely an apprentice or journeywoman.

125 BL: MS 61432, fol. 16.

126 Later eighteenth-century women such as Sabine Winn had extensive correspondence with tradespeople such as her London milliner Ann Charlton. Dyer, *Material Lives*, 152, 219, n. 109.

127 BL: Add. MS 61474, fol. 19.

128 BL: Add. MS. 61456.

129 Elizabeth Graydon went from being the highest paid milliner, commanding bills worth £194 in 1702 to bills worth just £13 8s. in 1704, which is the year that the Duchess of Marlborough's relationship with Queen Anne

first began to sour. Mary Wilkins, on the other hand, went from having a bill worth £8 19s. 9d. in 1702 to bills worth £208 in 1704 and £404 13s. in 1710. BL: Add. MS 61407, fols 9r, 38v, 105r.

130 *The Flying Post, or the Post-Master*, issue 3509 (London, July 1, 1714).

131 In 1682 George and Jane Potter pursued the widower Sir Gilbert Gerard for outstanding debts dating back to the late 1670s relating to millinery goods that Jane had sold to Dame Mary Gerard. TNA: C 8/262/23; TNA: C 5/167/44.

132 Jon Stobart, 'Who Were the Urban Gentry? Social Elites in an English Provincial Town, c. 1680–1760', *Continuity and Change* 26, no. 1 (2011): 90, 107.

133 R. O. Bucholz, 'Seymour [née Percy], Elizabeth, duchess of Somerset (1667–1722), courtier and politician', *Oxford Dictionary of National Biography*, 23 September 2004, https://doi.org/10.1093/ref:odnb/21925.

134 Raffling could either refer to a gambling game of chance involving three dice or buying tickets or subscriptions in a draw to win East Indies goods from these shops. TNA: C 5/167/44

135 Potter sold teaspoons, tea pots, 'china cups', a 'Japan Dish', 'yellow & silver Indian stuff' and 'rich purple Atas' and 'rich striped Atlas' to the countess. WSRO: PHA 258, fol. 36, PHA 259, fols 29, 44; TNA: C 10/512/82.

136 WSRO: PHA 259, fol. 44; Lim, 'Furniture Patronage of Elizabeth Seymour', 2.

137 TNA: C 5/167/44.

138 *The player's tragedy. Or, Fatal Love a new novel* (London: Randal Taylor, 1693), 55.

139 Mary Wortley Montagu, *The Selected Letters of Lady Mary Wortley Montagu*, ed. Robert Halsband (London: Longman Group, 1970), 39.

140 TNA: C 10/512/82.

141 'House of Lords Journal Volume 15: 11 January 1696', in *Journal of the House of Lords: Volume 15, 1691–1696* (London: His Majesty's Stationery Office, London, 1767–1830), 638, *British History Online*, https://www. british-history.ac.uk/lords-jrnl/vol15/p638.

142 Thomas Vickers, ed., *The Reports of Sir Creswell Levinz, Knt. Late one of the judges of the Court of Common Pleas at Westminster . . . vol. 3* (n.p.p.: W. Clarke and Sons, 1802), 412–13.

143 BL: Add. MS 34195, fol. 101.

144 Brian Cowan, *The Social Life of Coffee: The Emergence of the British Coffeehouse* (New Haven, CT: Yale University Press, 2005), 79.

145 *The Spectator*, Vol. V, no. 336 (London: 1718): 64–6.

146 Pix, *The innocent mistress*, 3.

147 TNA: PROB 4/25866.

148 The Levellers were known to meet frequently in the Whalebone tavern in Lothbury and the Windmill Tavern, where they organized campaigns and drafted documents during the English Civil Wars

149 BL: Add. MS 34195, fol. 101.

150 Potter's executors were Anthony Lord Ashely, Sir John Cropley, Aaron Kenton and John Rainpayne. TNA: PROB 11/445/146.

4 Making: Seamstresses, silkwomen and the rise of the mantua-maker

1 Other common makers in the queens' accounts include farthingale-makers, stay-makers, shoemakers, glovers, hatters, girdlers, hosiers, feather-dressers, pin-makers, fan-makers, goldsmiths, watchmakers, perfumers and auxiliary trades such as embroiders and weavers.

2 Ellen Jordan, *The Women's Movement and Women's Employment in Nineteenth Century Britain* (London: Routledge, 1999), 1–19; Barbara Burman and Nigel Rapport, eds, *The Culture of Sewing: Gender, Consumption and Home Dressmaking* (Oxford: Berg, 1999).

3 Crowston, *Fabricating Women.*

4 Styles, *Dress of the People*, 155.

5 Inder, *Busks, Basques and Brush-Braid*, 16–20.

6 For a discussion of household linen production and sewing, see Susan North, *Sweet and Clean? Bodies and Clothes in Early Modern England* (Oxford: Oxford University Press, 2020), 179–80.

7 Beverly Lemire, '"In the Hands of Work Women": English Markets, Cheap Clothing and Female Labour, 1650–1800', *Costume* 33, no. 1 (1999): 29–33; Birt, 'Women, Guilds and the Tailoring Trades', 148–9.

8 Anne Sutton, 'Two Dozen and More Silkwomen of Fifteenth-Century London', *Ricardian* 16 (2006): 1–2.

9 Stephanie Trigg, '"Ye Louely Ladyes with Youre Longe Fyngres": The Silkwomen of Medieval London', *Studia Anglica Posnaniensia: International Review of English Studies* 38 (2002): 472; Gowing, *Ingenious Trade*, 72.

10 North, *Sweet and Clean*, 185–7.

11 Susan North and Jenny Tiramani, eds, *Seventeenth-Century Women's Dress Patterns: Book One* (London: V&A Publishing, 2011), 5–12.

12 North, *Sweet and Clean*, 178.

13 TNA: SC 6/JASI/1646; TNA: AO 1/2067/100.

14 Arnold, *Queen Elizabeth's Wardrobe*, 226.

15 TNA: AO 1/2067/100.

16 Fiebranz, Lindberg, Lindström and Ågren, 'Making Verbs Count', 278; Sutton, 'Two Dozen and More Silkwomen', 2.

17 TNA: LR 6/154/9, Hester le Telier, 1603.

18 TNA: SC 6/JASI/1646, Livia White, 1605.

19 Silkwomen in Elizabeth's wardrobe accounts are recorded as doing similar types of work.

20 The silk trade was well out of women's hands by the end of the sixteenth century. Gowing, *Ingenious Trade*, 62; Anne F. Sutton, *The Mercery of London: Trade, Goods and People, 1130–1578* (Farnham: Ashgate Publishing, 2005), 443–7.

21 A Nicholas Du Val is listed as the Queen's Page of the Backstairs and received a payment in 1627 for services to the Great Wardrobe. It is likely that Antonia and Nicholas were related, possibly married. TNA: LR 5/65, Antonia Du Val, July and Christmas Quarters, 1632; TNA: SO 3/9, Nicholas Du Val, 1627.

22 BL: Add MS 61425, fol. 86v; TNA: AO 3/935; WSRO: PHA 264, fol. 6.

23 Catherine of Braganza's tailor outsourced most of the embroidery for her clothing. BL: Add. MS 5751 A, fol. 115.

24 *To the Right Honourable the Lords Spiritual and Temporal, in Parliament Assembled, the Petition and Case of the Embroiderers Flourishers, Raisers and Stitchers of East-India Silks, and Other Goods, and Stainers . . .* (London: anon., 1696), 6.

25 Gowing, *Ingenious Trade*, 62.

26 Arnold, *Queen Elizabeth's Wardrobe*, 224–5.

27 TNA: SC 6/JASI/1646, Francis Britaine, 1604.

28 Henrietta's seamstresses both made and washed shirts, ruffs, falling bands, handkerchiefs, boothose and socks for the queen's music boys. TNA: LR 5/65, Alice Waggit, Midsummer Quarter, 1632; TNA: LR 5/65, Ann Davenport, April–June, 1633.

29 LA: 1-Worsley/7–8.

30 TNA: LR 5/81, Mrs Calvaert, 1687; LR 5/88, Mrs Calvaert, February–November 1688; LR 5/84, Mrs Calvaert, June 1689.

31 TNA: LR 5/84, Mr Matthias Cupper, 1688.

32 TNA: LR 5/85, William Rutland Laceman, January 1688.

33 Seamstresses in the accounts of the Duchess of Richmond and Lennox made only linen goods such as coifs, handkerchiefs and napkins. TNA: C 104/46, Mary Blow, 1694; Mrs Elizabeth Anderson, 1701.

34 BL: Add. MS 61407, fol. 32r.

35 Holme, *Academy of Armory*, 97.

36 Erickson, 'Mistresses and Marriage', 39–40.

37 Campbell, *London Tradesman*, 227.

38 It was also common for both male and female retailers not to be given occupational titles due to the changing nature of the types of goods they sold. However, male makers were much more likely to be given trade identities compared to female makers.

39 TNA: LR 5/79, Mary Mandove Lady Day Quarter, 1685/6.

40 TNA: LR 5/95.

41 Hayward, *Stuart Style*, 239; Birt, 'A Fashionable Business', 66–7; North, 'Indian Gowns and Banyans', 40, 46.

42 The wooden doll known as 'Lady Clapham' belonged to the Cockerell family who had a home in Clapham, London. There is also a partner doll from the same family collection known as Lord Clapham. Both are dressed in the latest fashions of the 1690s. For more, see North, 'Indian Gowns and Banyans', 46.

43 Sarah Birt has also noted that in the Merchant Taylors' Guild no mistress was given the occupation title of 'mantuamaker' during this time. Birt, 'Women, Guilds and the Tailoring Trades', 10.

44 TNA: LR 5/80, Mrs Alexander, 1686; TNA: LR 5/83, Mrs Alexander, 1688.

45 TNA: LR 5/76, Ann Morgan, 1684; TNA: LR 5/81, Mrs Anne Morgan, 1685–6; TNA: LR 5/95.

46 It is possible that Becker had also made clothing for Princess Anne of Denmark. In 1682 an 'Elinor Becker' was listed in an 'Abstract of bills paid to several tradesmen'. Another woman named 'Anne Becker' was also labelled a

'Petty Coatmaker' in Anne's household accounts. Ellen and Anne were likely relatives, perhaps sisters working in business together. BL: Add. MS 61424, fols 46–50; BL: Add. MS 61425, fol. 86v.

47 BL: Add. MS 5751 A, fols 140–1.

48 Campbell, *London Tradesman*, 227; Inder, *Busks, Basques and Brush-Braid*, 18–20.

49 Sarah A. Bendall, 'The Queens' Dressmakers: Women's Work and the Clothing Trades in Late Seventeenth-Century London', *Women's History Review* 32, no. 3 (2023): 411, n. 45.

50 Anthony Harvey and Richard Mortimer, eds, *The Funeral Effigies of Westminster Abbey* (Woodbridge: Boydell Press, 2003), 98–100.

51 Fringe, tassels, 'foot' (ribbon for the bottom of the skirt) were delivered to the Robes to be used 'by Ms Becker' who made Mary II's petticoats. BL: Add. MS 5751 A, fol. 119.

52 LA: 1-Worsley/8, fols 11r, 34v.

53 TNA: C 10/485/2.

54 *A General descriptions of all Trades*, 117.

55 The Huguenot embroiderer Mary Ganeron is also listed in 1714 treasury payment lists as 'making manteaus and petticoats', but it is unclear if this refers to embroidering or constructing the garment. 'Declared Accounts: Civil List', in *Calendar of Treasury Books, Volume 28, 1714*, eds William A. Shaw and F. H. Slingsby (London: Her Majesty's Stationery Office, 1955), *British History Online*, https://www.british-history.ac.uk/cal-treasury-books/vol28/cc-cclxii.

56 BL: Add. MS 61407, fol. 66v.

57 Susannah also made matching pockets for the petticoats. BL: Add. MS 61424, fol. 113v.

58 'Westminster Marriages', *Findmypast*; 'England Births & Baptisms 1538–1975', *Findmypast*.

59 'Declared Accounts: Civil List', in *Calendar of Treasury Books, Volume 28, 1714*, ed. William A. Shaw and F. H. Slingsby (London: Her Majesty's Stationery Office, 1955), cc–cclxii, *British History Online*, http://www.british-history.ac.uk/cal-treasury-books/vol28/cc-cclxii.

60 LMA: P76/JS1/003 via 'London, England, Church of England Baptisms, Marriages and Burials, 1538–1812', *Ancestry.com*.

61 TNA: AO 1/2067/103; PROB 11/517/287; PROB 11/616/223.

62 Bellavitis, *Women's Work and Rights*, 32.

63 K. Tawny Paul, 'Accounting for men's work: multiple employments and occupational identities in early modern England', *History Workshop Journal* 85 (2018): 26–8.

64 Susan North has found the same in court testimonies where women described earning their living by 'making and mending clothes', 'plainwork', 'sewing' or 'at their needle'. North, *Sweet and Clean*, 180–1.

65 Gowing, *Ingenious Trade*, 1–2, 60–1.

66 TNA: LR 5/76, Ann Morgan Christmas Quarter, 1684; BL: Add. MS 61407, fols 20v, 36r.

67 TNA: LR 5/64, Yeoman of the Males bill, 1631.

68 LA: 1-Worsley/6. BL: Add. MS 15897, fol. 34. Catherine of Braganza's household establishment, 1678.

69 Cited in Birt, 'Women, Guilds and the Tailoring Trade', 5–6.

70 Lien Bich Luu, *Immigrants and the Industries of London, 1500–1700* (Farnham: Ashgate, 2005), 19, 118–19.

71 Gowing, *Ingenious Trade*, 1–2, 60–1, 244.

72 It is unclear if Barne made these himself, or if he was selling ready-made garments. LR 5/83: John Barne, 1688.

73 TNA: LR 5/76, Ann Morgan Christmas Quarter, 1684.

74 The gender of La Hay is unknown. The hosier Francis Kynnesman also provided knitted cotton petticoats and sleeves for Mary II in addition to hose of all types, which reflects his skills in producing knitted goods. BL: Add. MS 5751 A, fol. 163v.

75 Anne Howe also billed the Duchess of Somerset for making body linens and mantua gowns in 1701. WSRO: PHA 275, fol. 78.

76 Labour costs were also listed separately from the cost of materials on bills. In most cases, tailors, dressmakers and seamstresses were supplied with fabrics by the Office of the Robes. I have not included an analysis of petticoats here because cost splits between labour and material are not as obvious in all bills.

77 TNA: LR 5/83, Jane Heath, August 1687; TNA: LR 5/84, Peter Lombard Lady Quarter, 1687.

78 BL: Add. MS 5751 A, fols 135, 139.

79 Janet Arnold et al., *Patterns of Fashion 6: The Content, Cut, Construction and Context of European Women's Dress c. 1695–1795* (London: School of Historical Dress, 2021), 56–7.

80 BL: Add. MS 61420, fol. 112.

81 BL: Add. MS 61407, fol. 20v. The national Archives Currency Convertor for purchasing power calculates £1 in 1680 to be roughly the same as £1 in 1710. 'Currency Converter: 1270–2017'.

82 BL: Add. MS 61407, fol. 112v.

83 Rebecca Morrison, 'Unpicking Process: experiments in recreating and reimagining the methods of making', Keynote lecture at Workshop Three. Learning from Making: Methods and Processes, *Making Historical Dress Network*, 18 March 2023, https://makinghistoricaldress.dmu.ac.uk/Workshop-Three.html.

84 The first mention of 'robings' in Queen Anne's accounts comes from the embroiderer Mrs Collins, who embroidered some robings in 1702. BL: Add. MS 61407, fols 15v, 77r.

85 TNA: LR 5/76, Peter Lombard Midsummer Quarter, Mary Mandove Midsummer Quarter, 1685.

86 BL: Add. MS 5751 A, fol. 139.

87 BL: Add. MS 61407, fols 20v–21r, 76v–77r.

88 BL: Add. MS 5751 A, fol. 140; BL: Add. MS 61407, fols 14v–15r, 66r –v.

89 Bellavitis, *Women's Work and Rights*, viii, 3–13; Eleanor Hubbard, *City Women: Money, Sex, and the Social Order in Early Modern London* (Oxford: Oxford University Press, 2012), 198; Lemire, 'English Markets, Cheap Clothing and Female labour', 29–33.

90 Judith M. Bennett, '"History that stands still": Women's Work in the European Past', *Feminist Studies* 14, no. 2 (1988): 278.

91 de Marly, 'Fashionable Suppliers', 346.

92 Crowston, *Fabricating Women*, 136.

93 'Ceux qui en voudront faire faire comme on les fait à la Cour, n'ont qu'à s'adresser à Madame du Creux, Rue Traversine, qui habille la plus grande partie des Personnes de la premiere qualité', *Extraordinaire du Secretaire Galant* (1690), 405.

94 TNA: C 8/298/61.

95 BL: Add. MS. 61456, fol. 59.

96 *Dialogues of the dead*, 25.

97 The following information comes from transcriptions of this journal in TNA: C 8/298/61.

98 Somerset, *Queen Anne*, 245.

99 Crowston, *Credit, Fashion, Sex*, 176–9.

100 The Duchess of Lauderdale's tailor John Ferguson also charged different prices for mantua gowns he made for the duchess. One mantua cost 16s. and another £1. This suggests that 'manto' could designate a variety of styles of varying complexity. BA: 911-1, 911-36.

101 Diana de Marly has noted that Parisian tailors always outclassed competent English ones. While she does suggest that luxury French goods bought from French and Parisian artisans cost more, she has not done a comparative study. de Marly, 'Fashionable Suppliers', 339–40.

102 To put this in perspective, 8s. is the equivalent of approximately £60 in today's currency, or four days' wages for a skilled tradesman in 1680. English dressmakers named in Elizabeth Seymour's accounts were Mary Grove, Mary Lambert and Mary Nedham. The only time they commanded more than £1 for their labour was when they made sultanes for the Duchess of Somerset, indicating that this Turkish inspired dress (see Fig. 1.15) was far more complex to make than a regular manto. WSRO: PHA 259, 264, 265; 'Currency Converter: 1270–2017'; 'Inflation Calculator'.

103 WSRO: PHA 258, fol. 20.

104 *The Ladies Catechism useful for all Eminent Females, and necessary to be Learnt by all Young Gentlewomen, that would attain to the Dignity of the Mode* (n.p.p.: n.p., 1703), 3.

105 Buck, 'Mantuamakers and Milliners', 145; Janet Arnold, 'The Dressmaker's Craft', *Costume* 7, sup. 1 (1973): 29; Norah Waugh, *The Cut of Women's Clothes, 1600–1930* (London: Faber, 1973), 101.

106 Hart, 'The Mantua', 100.

107 Rebecca Morrison, '(Re)Making Mantuas: From Seamstresses to Mantuamakers', online lecture, *Sartorial Society Series*, 10 December 2020; Arnold et al., *Patterns of Fashion 6*, 11.

108 Hart, 'The Mantua', 93–100.

109 Quoted in W. Trueman, 'The First Mantua-Makers in Durham', *Archaeologia Aeliana* 2 (1858): 168.

110 KKC: AR33/9/117.

111 BA: 911-36.

112 Trueman, 'First Mantua-Makers', 168–9.

113 Many thanks to Michelle Barker and Rebecca Morrison for their insights on this gown. Michelle Barker and Rebecca Morrison, private email correspondence, 12 November 2023, 16 November 2023. Rebecca Morrison,

'The Rise of the English Mantua-Maker in the Long Eighteenth Century' (PhD diss., Queen Mary University of London, 2024), 136–7.

114 Birt, 'Women, Guilds and the Tailoring Trade', 9; Gowing, *Ingenious Trade*, 147.

115 These examples are cited in Birt, 'Women, Guilds and the Tailoring Trade', 13; Lemire, 'English Markets, Cheap Clothing and Female labour', 32.

116 Cited in Gowing, *Ingenious Trade*, 223.

117 The accounts of the Oxford Tailors Guild show that many widows trained apprentices, hired journeymen and were fined for disobeying orders, just as male members of the guild were. BLO: MS Morrell 6, fols 90r, 93v, 170v.

118 Birt, 'Women, Guilds and the Tailoring Trade', 11.

119 TNA: LR 5/64–65.

120 Inder, *Busks, Basques and Brush-Braid*, 16; Sanderson, 'A Look at how Mantuamaking Became Established in Scotland', 18.

121 Sufford and Mee, *Clothing of the Common Sort*, 216.

122 Cited in E. Hubbard, *City Women: Money, Sex, and the Social Order in Early Modern London* (Oxford: Oxford University Press, 2012), 198.

123 John Styles, 'Transformations in Textiles, 1400–1760', in *Refashioning the Renaissance: Everyday Dress and the Reconstruction of Early Modern Material Culture, 1550–1650*, ed. Paula Hohti (Manchester: Manchester University Press, 2025), 40–1.

124 Bendall, 'Queens' Dressmakers', 395, 406; BL, Add. MS 61407, fol. 20v.

125 TNA: C 8/298/61.

126 TNA: LR 5/76-83. The dressmaker Mary Lambert made mantuas and petticoats for the Countess of Ogle (later Duchess of Somerset) from a mixture of satins, persians, calico, crape, 'cloth' fabrics. WSRO: PHA 259, fol. 15.

127 The pattern for this gown was taken by Rebecca Morrison. Morrison, 'The Rise of the English Mantua-Maker'. Funding to recreate this project was generously provided by the Making Historical Dress Network (Arts and Humanities Council UK Research Grant – Making Historical Dress: hands, bodies and methods. AH/X007790/1) and De Montfort University. Many thanks to Polly Putnam at Historic Royal Palaces for allowing it to be photographed at Hampton Court Palace.

128 TNA: LR 5/83, Jane Heath, December 1687.

129 BL: Add. MS 61407, fol. 21v.

130 Janet Arnold, 'Decorative Features: Pinking, Snipping and Slashing', *Costume* 9, no. 1 (1975): 22–5.

131 TNA: LR 5/64, Charles Genty Christmas Quarter, 1630.

132 He is listed in the king's accounts between 1662 and 1682. Hayward, *Stuart Style*, 120.

133 Linings are described as as 'piqué & moucheté', meaning to make small cuts or marks, in essence, pinking. *Extraordinaire du Mercure galant* (1678), 541.

134 TNA: C 8/298/61.

135 Racing in this context refers to cutting or slashing fabric. BL: Add. MS 61407, fol. 111v.

136 Bills in the Duchess of Somerset's accounts show that Alexander could make mantuas, nightgowns and petticoats. However, Catherine of Braganza's Robes employed her solely to make waistcoats. WSRO: PHA 258, fol. 20.

137 Waistcoats accounts for 48 per cent of the garments made and altered for Catherine of Braganza by Mary Mandove.

138 'Robbes de Chambre, Jupes, Justacorps, Manteaux, Hongrelines, Camisoles, Corps de Jupes, & toutes autres Ouvrages de toutes sortes d'étoffes pour habiller les Femmes & Filles'. *Statuts, ordonnances et déclaration du roy, confirmative d'iceux, pour la communauté des couturieres de la ville, fauxbourgs & banlieue de Paris. Vérifié en Parlement le 7 octobre 1675* (Paris: Veuve de Ph. N. LOTTIN, 1734), 3–4

139 John Florio, *Queen Anna's New World of Words, Or Dictionarie of the Italian and English tongues* (London: Melch. Bradwood, 1611), 464; Adelina Modesti, *Women's Patronage and Gendered Cultural Networks in Early Modern Europe: Vittoria della Rovere, Grand Duchess of Tuscany* (London: Routledge, 2019), 116.

140 David Garrioch has noted that 'Craftswomen are usually discussed in the context of guild regulation or of the urban family economy, while work on migration rarely has much to say about female artisans'. David Garrioch, 'Introduction: Artisan Mobility and Innovation in Pre-Industrial Europe', in *The Republic of Skill: Artisan Mobility, Innovation, and the Circulation of Knowledge in Premodern Europe,* ed. David Garrioch (Leiden: Brill, 2022), 4.

141 I use their anglicized names, Jane Heath and Francis Heath, in this chapter for clarity. However, they were also referred to in these court documents as Jeanne Haite and François Haite d'Este. TNA: C 8/298/61; TNA: C 10/485/2.

142 Maria Hayward has suggested that Mary was the wife of Francis Alexander, a Gentleman Usher in Catherine of Braganza's household during the 1670s. Hayward, *Material World of a Restoration Queen Consort*, 335.

143 LA: 1-Worsley/8, fols 11r, 34v.

144 These bills are in French: 'Une manto de tissu, une manto noir, une Jupe noir, un manto violet, une robe de cambre, une camisole'. WSRO: PHA 258.

145 As a historian-maker who has primarily used recreative practice to make seventeenth-century garments constructed by tailors, as well as those linen goods of seamstresses, the complex draping and pleating of mantua-making is a technique not easily adapted from other earlier forms of making knowledge. Like Mary Alexander, I have had to receive instruction in the 'Art' of mantua-making from others with much more expertise, such as Rebecca Morrison, Michelle Barker, Brooke Welborn and Serena Dyer.

146 Crowston, *Fabricating Women*, 40.

147 TNA: C 8/298/61; Annalisa Nicholson, 'Like Mother, like Daughter: Hortense Mancini, Duchesse de Mazarin, and Marie-Charlotte de La Porte-Mazarin, Marquise de Richelieu', *Early Modern Women* 16, no. 1 (2021): 14–35.

148 Nicholson, 'Hortense Mancini, Duchesse de Mazarin', 22; 'Entry Book: April 1684, 21–30', in *Calendar of Treasury Books, Volume 7, 1681–1685*, https://www.british-history.ac.uk/cal-treasury-books/vol7/pp1100-1114.

149 Trueman, 'First Mantua-Makers', 168.

150 TNA C 10/485/2.

151 £79 16s. 6d. is the equivalent of approximately £12,000 in today's currency, or 886 days' wages for a skilled tradesman in 1680. This was therefore a very profitable partnership. TNA: C 8/298/61; 'Currency Converter: 1270–2017'; 'Inflation Calculator'.

152 Embroiders were 'Mrs Ginleson' and 'Mrs Morice'. The Pinkers were located in 'Newport St' and 'Henrietta St'.

153 The workwomen mentioned included a 'Mrs Edwards', a 'Mrs Marya' and 'Anne'.

154 TNA: C 8/298/61.

155 TNA: LR 5/83, Jane Heath, August 1687.

156 Mary Blurton 1690 in 'Westminster Marriages', *Findmypast*; John Laforce and Mary Laforce 1691–1737 in 'Westminster Rate Books 1634–1900', *Findmypast*; Mary Laforce 1720 in 'Britain, Country Apprentices 1710–1808', *Findmypast*.

5 Caring: Maintaining clothing and appearances in the care economy of the royal household

1 Alexandra Shepard, 'Care', in *The Whole Economy: Work and Gender in Early Modern Europe*, eds Catriona Macleod, Alexandra Shepard and Maria Ågren (Cambridge: Cambridge University Press, 2023), 58.

2 It was not until the eighteenth century that having domestic servants 'became a marker of status'. Mansell, *Female Servants*, 2, 5.

3 Whittle and Hailwood, 'Gender Division of Labour', 20–2.

4 Mansell, *Female Servants*, 5.

5 M. T. W. Payne, 'An Inventory of Queen Anne of Denmark's "Ornaments, Furniture, Householde Stuffe, and Other Parcells" at Denmark House, 1619', *Journal of the History of Collections* 13, no. 1 (2001): 23; Manolo Guerci, *London's 'Golden Mile': The Great Houses of the Strand, 1550–1650* (New Haven, CT: Yale University Press, 2021), 61.

6 Griffey, *On Display*, 63–9; Guerci, *London's 'Golden Mile'*, 55–74.

7 Payments were made to seamstresses and wardrobe men at Somerset House from her privy purse during the 1670s. LA: 1-Worsley/8.

8 Payne, 'An Inventory', 27–41.

9 TNA: AO 1/2067/103.

10 The bills of these housekeepers and wardrobe keepers have survived and describe these daily tasks. In 1691, the Wardrobe Keeper's man at Somerset House, Paul Bridge, billed the Robes for 'For things to destroy the Moths in ye Wardrobe'. TNA: LR 5/88, Paul Bridges, 1691.

11 By the early eighteenth century, Somerset House was somewhat dilapidated and in need of repair. Guerci, *London's 'Golden Mile'*, 74

12 CUL: Dd 1.26.

13 Griffey, *On Display*, 108.

14 BL: Add. MS 5751 A, fol. 181.

15 BL: Add. MS 61407, fol. 37r.

16 TNA: LC 5/184, fol. 130v.

17 *Catholic Record Society Registers of the Catholic Chapels Royal and of the Portuguese Embassy Chapel, 1662–1829*, vol. 1, *Marriages*, ed. J. Cyril M. Weale (Leeds: John Whitehead & Son, 1941), xxx; TNA: LC 5/184, fol. 130v.

18 Henrietta Maria's Mistress of the Sweet Coffers was listed alongside tradespeople in a document outlining 'Debts owing by her Majesty to divers Creditors and Artificers of London' by the Office of the Robes in 1630. TNA: LR 5/63; Payne, 'Aristocratic Women', 65.

19 Wynne, 'Women at the Court of Charles II', 40.

20 TNA: LR 5/84, Dame Charlotte Killigrew, Lady of the Sweet Coffers, 1684.

21 TNA: LR 5/65, Thomazine Carew, Mistress of the Sweet Coffers, Michaelmas Quarter 1631.

22 Holly Dugan, 'Scent', in *Early Modern Court Culture*, ed. Erin Griffey (London: Routledge, 2022), 429.

23 Grooms of the Robes supervised and perfumed chests in Charles II's household. Hayward, *Stuart Style*, 199.

24 Miasma theory dictated that foul smelling air was thought to carry disease, thus sweet smells indicated cleanliness and health. Dugan, 'Scent', 431.

25 TNA: LR 5/64, Henry Lenger, Midsummer to Michaelmas 1628.

26 BLO: MS. Eng. misc. b. 31, fol. 238. One of Mary of Modena's trunks has survived and is in the National Trust Northern Ireland collection, NT 114126. Charles II's trunks are similarly described. Hayward, *Stuart Style*, 195–6. For more on chests and trunks, see Olivia Fryman, 'Coffer-Makers to the Late Stuart Court, 1660–1714', *Furniture History* 52 (2016): 1–16.

27 Simon Barbe, *The French Perfumer teaching the several ways of extracting the odours of drugs and flowers . . .* (London: Sam. Buckley, 1696), 88–90.

28 Barbe, *French Perfumer*, 87. In 1694 Godfrey Poole provided sweet bags and perfumed quilts of several baskets in Mary II's Robes. BL: Add. MS 5751 A, fol. 160.

29 Payne, 'An Inventory', 42; BL: Add. MS 61407, fol. 100r.

30 TNA: LR 5/84, Mrs Calvaert, June 1689; TNA: LR 5/64, George Gelin, July–September 1631; TNA: LR 5/76, Peter Lombard, Christmas Quarter 1684.

31 BL: Add. MS 61407, fol. 88v.

32 TNA: LR 5/64, Daniel Tomson, Lady Quarter 1631.

33 Hayward, *Stuart Style*, 240–1.

34 Payne, 'An Inventory', 27.

35 Barbe, *French Perfumer*; John Partridge, *The Treasurie of Commodious Conceits* (London: Richard Jones, 1591); Johann Jacob Wecker, *Cosmeticks or, the beautifying part of physick* (London: Tho. Johnson, 1660)

36 Wecker, *Cosmeticks*, 129–37; Partridge, *The Treasurie of Commodious Conceits*.

37 Payne, 'An Inventory', 40; Griffey, *On Display*, 101.

38 Chico, *Designing Women*, 46, 55; Anna Keay, 'The Ceremonies of Charles II's Court' (PhD diss., Queen Mary University of London, 2004), 34–5.

39 Pepys, *Diary and Correspondence of Samuel Pepys*, vol. 5, 285, 341.

40 Chico, *Designing Women*, 72.

41 Chico, *Designing Women*, 60.

42 Evelyn, *The Diary of John Evelyn*, vol. 2, 88.

43 Evelyn, *The Diary of John Evelyn*, vol. 2, 188.

44 Payne, 'An Inventory', 40–1.

45 Lim, 'Furniture Patronage of Elizabeth Seymour', 5, 10.

46 Lim, 'Furniture Patronage of Elizabeth Seymour', 11.

47 Elizabeth Oxley was regularly paid for making quilted toilets for Queen Anne's 'dressing table'. BL: Add. MS 61407, fol. 115r.

48 Evelyn, *The Diary of John Evelyn*, vol. 2, 88.

49 Ribeiro, *Fashion and Fiction*, 263.

50 BL: Add. MS 5751 A, fol. 125.

51 Erin Griffey, '"The Rose and Lily Queen": Henrietta Maria's Fair Face and the Power of Beauty at the Stuart Court', *Renaissance Studies* 35, no. 5 (2021): 829.

52 Griffey, 'Henrietta Maria's Fair Face', 830; Jill Burke, *How to be a Renaissance Woman: The Untold History of Beauty and Female Creativity* (London: Profile Books, 2023); Erin Griffey, *Facing Decay: Beauty, Aging, and Cosmetics in Early Modern Europe* (University Park, PA: Penn State University Press, 2025).

53 These women who waited on the Countess at Brougham Castle were Frances Pate and Susan Machell and they were paid £10 per year. RBSC: RB Supp. MS. 74: Household Accounts book of Anne Clifton, 1675–76. The servants Jane and Deborah are mentioned helping Samuel and Elisabeth Pepys. Pepys, *Diary and Correspondence of Samuel Pepys*, vol. 9, 198.

54 I have learned this through numerous experiences wearing reconstructed seventeenth-century gowns. While some of these things can be pinned, looped and buttoned before placing the garment on the body, it is always preferable to have someone there to assist you.

55 In 1713, Mrs Alice Haberly was described as a 'necessary woman to the Bedchamberwomen'. 'The bedchamber: Women of the Bedchamber 1702–14', in *Office-Holders in Modern Britain: Volume 11 (Revised), Court Officers, 1660–1837*, https://www.british-history.ac.uk/office-holders/vol11/pp24-25; 'Declared Accounts: Civil List', in *Calendar of Treasury Books, Volume 27, 1713*, https://www.british-history.ac.uk/cal-treasury-books/vol27/clxxxix-ccxlii.

56 BL: MS 78269, fol. 67r. Catherine of Braganza's records make no distinction between Ladies and Women of the bedchamber, but pay discrepancies did exist as these women were paid between £50 to £200 per year. Thus, it appears that these women were paid more for serving queens regnant compared to queens consort. TNA: LR 5/84, Queen Catherine's Household Establishment, 1689. BL: Add MS 15897, fol. 34v.

57 BLO: MS. Eng. misc. b. 31, fol. 238.

58 Hayward, 'Fashioning a Place for Catherine of Braganza', 233.

59 LS 13/32, fol. 17; 'Entry Book: May 1663', in *Calendar of Treasury Books, Volume 1, 1660–1667*, ed. William A. Shaw (London: His Majesty's Stationery Office, 1904), *British History Online*, https://www.british-history.ac.uk/cal-treasury-books/vol1/pp520-527.

60 BL: MS 78269, fols 66r–67v; Anna Hackett, 'Household of Mary II, 1689–1694', *The Database of Court Officers: 1660–1837*, Loyola University of Chicago, https://courtofficers.ctsdh.luc.edu/MaryII.list.pdf.

61 Campbell, *London Tradesman*, 209–10.

62 Natasha Korda, *Labors Lost: Women's Work and the Early Modern English Stage* (Philadelphia: University of Pennsylvania Press, 2011), 31.

63 B. E., *A new dictionary of the canting crew in its several tribes of gypsies, beggers, thieves, cheats . . .* (London: W. Hawes, P. Gilbourne and W. Davis, 1699), TI.

64 Christopher Mountjoy was taxed as 'stranger' (foreigner) and his application for denizen status mentions that he was originally from Cressey in France. The Mountjoys were connected to the French Church in London, indicating that they were Huguenots. It is likely that they fled to London during the French Wars of Religion that were fought throughout the country between 1562 and 1598. Charles William Wallace, 'Shakespeare and His London Associates as Revealed in Recently Discovered Documents', *University Studies* 10, no. 4 (1910): 267.

65 TNA: LR 6/154/9, Marie Mountjoy, 1603. This masque was Samuel Daniel's *The Vision of the Twelve Goddesses,* in which Anna played the part of Pallas Athena, costumed in a helmet, spear and tunic. John Pitcher, 'Samuel Daniel's Masque "The Vision of the Twelve Goddesses": Texts and Payments', *Medieval & Renaissance Drama in England* 26 (2013): 33, 38.

66 TNA: LR 5/64, Blanche Browne, June 1630 to March 1631; TNA: LR 5/65, Blanche Brown, April–June 1632.

67 Natasha Korda, 'Insubstantial Pageants: Women's Work and the (Im)Material Culture of the Early Modern Stage', *Shakespeare* 7, no. 4 (2011): 420.

68 This court document is transcribed in Wallace, 'Shakespeare and His London Associates', 268–9.

69 Campbell, *London Tradesman*, 209–10.

70 Payne, 'An Inventory', 41.

71 The petition mentions Princess Elizabeth as well. TNA: SP 14/107, fol. 121.

72 Field, 'Dressing a Queen', 159.

73 Phillip Stubbes, *The Anatomy of Abuses* (London: John Kingston for Richard Jones, 1583).

74 Entries in the original Scots are: 'Item, for ane tyer of prell to ver on my head', 'ane sillk tyre to ver on my heade', 'ane vyer to my haed vith nyne pykis'. William Fraser, ed., *Memorials of the Montgomeries, Earls of Eglinton*, vol. 2 (Edinburgh: William Fraser, 1859), 245–9. A later court case involving the Mountjoys described 'Comodities Concerning their trade' of tiremaking that they had purchased, including 'silvered wyer'. Wallace, 'Shakespeare and His London Associates', 272.

75 TNA: SP 14/107, fol. 121.

76 BL: Add. MS 61407, 80v–81r.

77 BL: Add. MS 61407, fols 18r, 32v, 48v, 59v, 80v–81r, 92r. This amounts to roughly £300 for cutting and styling in today's currency. 'Currency Converter: 1270–2017'; 'Inflation Calculator'.

78 WSRO: PHA 261, fol. 2; TNA: LR 5/80, Payments made to the Countess of Arlington to clear arrears from Privy purse, 1687.

79 BL: Add. MS 61407, 18r.

80 Fiennes, *Through England on a Side Saddle*, 255.

81 The real gemstones were probably replaced by paste glass for the effigy. Harvey and Mortimer, eds, *Funeral Effigies of Westminster Abbey*, 105–7.

82 Although this was a translation of the Latin author Juvenal's satires, the language was updated by Dryden for a contemporary English audience. Juvenal, *The Satires of Decimus Junius Juvenalis. Translated into English Verse*, trans. John Dryden (London: Jacob Tonson, 1693), 114.

83 'Curl papers' are also mentioned in the letters of French courtier Madame de Sévigné. Harvey and Mortimer, eds, *Funeral Effigies of Westminster Abbey*, 92, 102; Ribeiro, *Fashion and Fiction*, 249

84 BL: Add. MS 61407, 59v.

85 BL: Add. MS 61407, fol. 108v.

86 Harvey and Mortimer, eds, *Funeral Effigies of Westminster Abbey*, 92, 102.

87 Barbe, *French Perfumer*, 9; TNA: LR 5/78, Dr Lightfoot, Christmas Quarter 1685.

88 BL: Add. MS 5751 A, fol. 152.

89 Cited in Somerset, *Queen Anne*, 241.

90 In 1669 Samuel Pepys referred to Catherine of Braganza's tirewoman Mrs Gotier as 'an oldish French woman' whom he visited to buy 'a pair of locks for my wife'. Pepys, *Diary and Correspondence of Samuel Pepys*, vol. 9, 163–4.

91 WSRO: PHA 261, fol. 64.

92 BL: Add. MS 61407, fol. 92r. Mary's burial record also mentions that 'Mary Ducaila alias Gazai' was the 'widow of Francis Ducaila'. Francis was buried in 1697 at the same church. The Ducailas and Gazains appear to have been French Catholic migrants, as Gazain's widow later registered their property under the direction of the Papist Act issued by Parliament. 'London, England, Church of England Baptisms, Marriages and Burials, 1538–1812', *Ancestry.com*; Middlesex Sessions: Sessions Papers – Justices' Working Documents, April 1717, London Lives, 1690–1800 (www.londonlives.org, version 1.1, 17 June 2012), https://www.londonlives.org/browse.jsp?div=LMSMPS501610124.

93 BL: Add. MS 5751 A, fol. 142.

94 KKCA: AR33/9/120.

95 BL: Add. MS 61407, 1704–5, fol. 48v.

96 BL: Add. MS 61407, fol. 18r.

97 Campbell, *London Tradesman*, 209–10.

98 'Une bouteille Sirop de Capillaire' and 'poudre de Cipree'. PHA: 261, fol. 64. *The Compleat Doctoress: or, A choice Treatise of all Diseases insident to Women . . .* (London: Edward Farnham, 1656).

99 BL: Add. MS 5751 A, fol. 149v; BL: Add. MS 61407, fol. 54r.

100 Erin Griffey with Michél Nieuwoudt, 'Beautiful Experiments: Reading and Reconstructing Early Modern European Cosmetic Recipes', in *Embodied Experiences of Making in Early Modern Europe: Bodies, Gender, and Material Culture*, eds Sarah A. Bendall and Serena Dyer (Amsterdam: Amsterdam University Press, 2024), 147.

101 Griffey, 'Henrietta Maria's Fair Face', 811–12, 826–35.

102 Michele Nicole Robinson, 'Dirty Laundry: Caring for Clothing in Early Modern Italy', *Costume* 55, no. 1 (2021): 3; North, *Sweet and Clean*, 18, 53–82; Carole Rawcliffe, 'A Marginal Occupation? The Medieval Laundress and Her Work', *Gender & History* 21, no. 1 (2009): 149.

103 North, *Sweet and Clean*, 1–28; Hayward, *Stuart Style*, 191–2; LR 5/88, Paul Bridges, May 1691.

104 North, *Sweet and Clean*, 209–10.

105 BLO: MS. Rawl. C. 987, fol. 45r.

106 BL: Add. MS 61407, fol. 54r.

107 North, *Sweet and Clean*, 209–10.

108 Griffey, 'Re-Dressing the Evidence', 14.

109 The Pages and Grooms of the Robes sometimes sought payment for washing petticoats and other textiles in the Robes. However, it is unclear if they washed these things themselves or paid someone else to do it.

110 North, *Sweet and Clean*, 37, 231.

111 Mansell, *Female Servants*, 191.

112 Holme, *Academy of Armory*, 98; Robinson, 'Dirty Laundry', 8. The treating of linens with sweet waters before being stored in chests with sweet bags has been common in Western Europe since the medieval period. Barbe, *French Perfumer*, 68–73; North, *Sweet and Clean*, 104, 267; Rawcliffe, 'The Medieval Laundress', 149–50.

113 TNA: LR 5/94, Robert Paxton, Midsummer 1689.

114 North, *Sweet and Clean*, 230; Rawcliffe, 'The Medieval Laundress', 147.

115 Rawcliffe, 'The Medieval Laundress', 147, 156–8; North, *Sweet and Clean*, 231–7.

116 North, *Sweet and Clean*, 237.

117 Robinson, 'Dirty Laundry', 6.

118 'Charles II – volume 40: August 1661', in *Calendar of State Papers Domestic: Charles II, 1661–2*, ed. Mary Anne Everett Green (London: Her Majesty's Stationery Office, 1861), *British History Online*, https://www.british-history.ac.uk/cal-state-papers/domestic/chas2/1661-2/pp54-79.

119 BL: Add. MS 15897, fol. 34v.

120 BLO: MS. Rawl. C. 987, fol. 30r.

121 Hayward, *Stuart Style*, 195; BL: MS 78269, fol. 67r. The Countess Anne Clifford had four 'laundry maids' on her household books. RBSC: RB Supp. MS. 74.

122 TNA: LS 13/32, fol. 14.

123 North, *Sweet and Clean*, 215–17; Robinson, 'Dirty Laundry', 8.

124 BLO: MS. Rawl. C. 987, f. 30r.

125 Olivia Fryman, 'Making the Bed: The Practice, Role and Significance of Housekeeping in the Royal Bedchambers at Hampton Court Palace 1689–1737' (PhD diss., Kingston University, 2011), 150–2; Rawcliffe, 'The Medieval Laundress', 153; Robinson, 'Dirty Laundry', 9.

126 Fryman, 'Making the Bed', 150.

127 North, *Sweet and Clean*, 225.

128 Robinson, 'Dirty Laundry', 5.

129 Korda, *Labors Lost*, 93–7, 127.

130 Jenny Tiramani, 'Janet Arnold and the Globe Wardrobe: Handmade Clothes for Shakespeare's Actors', *Costume* 34, no. 1 (2000): 121; Korda, *Labors Lost*, 96–7, 127.

131 Korda, *Labors Lost*, 125.

132 TNA: LS 13/32, fol. 14; TNA: LR 5/80, Mr Rutland, January 1686.

133 Fryman, 'Making the Bed', 153.

134 Gowing, *Ingenious Trade*, 163.

135 Woolley, *Guide to Ladies*, 37.

136 TNA: SC 6/JASI/.1646, Susanna Greene, 1605.

137 TNA: LS 13/32, fol. 19; Campbell, *Catherine of Bragança*, 311.

138 The ways that the care economy could lead to social mobility for domestic servants has been discussed by Mansell, *Female Servants*, 290.

139 This term has been discussed in 'Restoring Henrietta Maria's English Household', 192.

140 Hayward, *Dress at the Court of King Henry VIII*, 112.

141 Charles I's seamstress was paid £52 annually and Catherine of Braganza's seamstress Elizabeth Elliot was paid an annual salary of £60 in 1678. North, *Sweet and Clean*, 180; BL: Add. MS 15897, fol. 34v.

142 Catherine of Braganza's privy purse accounts from the 1670s contain several references to a 'Mrs Hemden' for the mending of linen and for 'journeys to and from London'. BL: Add. MS 61407, fol. 10r.

143 Arnold, *Queen Elizabeth's Wardrobe*, 226; TNA: AO 1/2067/100; SC 6/JASI/1646, Abraham and Dorothy Speckard, 1604; Patricia Wardle, '"Divers Necessaries for His Majesty's Use and Service": Seamstresses to the Stuart Kings', *Costume* 31, no. 1 (1997): 16.

144 TNA: SC 6/JASI/1646, Abraham and Dorothy Speckard, 1604. Abraham Speckard is listed as an original adventurer (investor) in the Somers Isles Company which operated in and colonized what is now Bermuda. J. H. Lefroy, *Memorials of the Discovery and Early Settlement of the Bermudas or Somers Islands, 1515–1685*, vol. 1 (London: Longmans, Green, and co., 1877), 100.

145 Dorothy is listed as a 'gentlewoman' and Abraham a 'gentleman' in a list of people who gave New Year's gifts to Elizabeth I in 1599–1600. Wardle, 'Seamstresses to the Stuart Kings', 25, n. 2; John Nichols, *The Progresses and Public Processions of Queen Elizabeth*, Vol. 3 (London: AMS Press, 1823), 456–7, 464–5.

146 Payne, 'Aristocratic Women', 280. In 1605 Hester le Telier was recorded as receiving 'wages for one whole year', indicating that she had replaced Speckard as the salaried silkwoman in the Robes. TNA: SC 6/JASI/1646.

147 Merton, 'The Women who served Queen Mary and Queen Elizabeth', 78–9.

148 Payne, 'An Inventory', 40.

149 CUL: Dd 1.26, fol. 21v.

150 Payne, 'An Inventory', 44, n. 75.

151 Wardle, 'Seamstresses to the Stuart Kings', 16–20; Hayward, *Stuart Style*, 195.

152 Gilbert Abrahall Esq was also a Page of the Back Stairs and also submitted bills as a starcher. A plaque for Elizabeth is on the wall of the east cloister of Westminster Abbey. BL: Add. MS 61407, fols 22v, 75v; Bucholz, *Augustan Court*, 300, n. 85; 'Elizabeth Abrahall', Westminster Abbey, https://www.westminster-abbey.org/abbey-commemorations/commemorations/elizabeth-abrahall/.

153 As there was no formal training available in the form of apprenticeships for seamstresses, it is reasonable to assume that Elizabeth was trained by her mother and had likely worked for her. Wardle, 'Seamstresses to the Stuart Kings', 19–20; BL: Add. MS 15897, fol. 33.

154 Claxton and Welch, 'Chintz, China, and Chocolate', 266–7; Ewan Fernie, 'Chiffinch [Cheffin], Thomas (1600–1666), courtier and royal official', *Oxford Dictionary of National Biography*, 23 September 2004, https://doi.org/10.1093/ref:odnb/5280.

155 Hayward, *Stuart Style*, 195.

156 Dorothy is recorded as washing the king's linens and making items such as shirts. Hayward, *Stuart Style*, 195; Wardle, 'Seamstresses to the Stuart Kings', 20.

157 Willliam Chiffinch's wife was Barbara Nun. TNA: SP 44/15 fol. 29.

158 Privy Council, *At the Council-chamber in Whitehall, Monday the 22th of October, 1688* . . . (London: Charles Bill, H. Hills, and Th. Newcomb, 1688), 2.

159 Cited in Bucholz, *Augustan Court*, 78.

160 Pepys, *Diary and Correspondence of Samuel Pepys*, vol. 9, 272.

161 Thomas Chiffinch died in 1666, and his wife Dorothy died in 1680. William Chiffinch took over many of his brother's offices after his death. Claxton and Welch, 'Chintz, China, and Chocolate', 266.

162 Several individuals with the surname Sayer worked in the household of Catherine of Braganza. Sainty, Wassmann and Bucholz, 'Household of Queen (from 1685 Queen Dowager) Catherine 1660–1705', *The Database of Court Officers: 1660–1837*, http://courtofficers.ctsdh.luc.edu/indices/Index%2002%20Household%20of%20Queen%20Catherine%201662b.pdf. BL: Add. MS 10613, fol. 18v; Queen Catherine's Household Establishment, 1689. TNA: LR 5/84, Catherine Braganza Household Establishment, 1689–90.

163 Patricia Wardle has posed this question in her discussion. Wardle, 'Seamstresses to the Stuart Kings', 23.

164 Woolley, *Guide to Ladies*, 37.

165 The Ireland family appear to have been well known at court and was likely another low-ranking 'dynasty of service' family. Fryman, 'Making the Bed', 143–4.

166 BL: Add. MS 5751 A, fol. 44v; BL: Add. MS 61407, fol. 109r.

167 North, *Sweet and Clean*, 210, 232–4.

168 For a discussion of sinecures by the time of George I, see Fryman, 'Making the Bed', 147–9.

169 Several members of the Chiffinch family, as well Queen Anne's starcher Elizabeth Abrahall and her laundress Elizabeth Atkinson, are buried in Westminster Abbey. William Chiffinch's daughter Barbara married into the Villiers family.

Conclusion: Women's patronage and women's work

1 Elizabeth Gates died in 1737. She was the wife of Bernard Gates, Master of the Choristers at Westminster Abbey. Her inscription implies that Elizabeth Atkinson had helped to raise her, and Atkinson left all her personal estate to Gates in 1726. TNA: PROB 11/607/421.

2 'Bernard & Elizabeth Gates', Westminster Abbey, https://www.westminster-abbey.org/abbey-commemorations/commemorations/bernard-elizabeth-gates/.

3 Atkinson appears to have come from a Welsh family. Her aunt, Mrs Eleanor Bust, was also a bedchamber woman to Princess Anne. Margaret R. Toynbee, 'William Duke of Gloucester and Camden House Kensington', *Notes and Queries* (1947): 244–5.

4 TNA: PROB 11/607/421.

5 Bucholz has suggested that Queen Anne's court was dominated by women due to her 'constitution, heavy personality, and sense of propriety', which limited her contact with male courtiers. Bucholz, *Augustan Court*, 149.

Appendix I: Makers and suppliers to the Stuart queens

1 This only includes those directly connected to the queen, either making her clothing or supplying accessories for her clothing. There are others who appear in the accounts that clothed the queen's servants with livery, made costumes for those participating in her masques, or provided goods for furnishings in her household. I have not included them here.

2 Son of Thomas Henshawe.

3 In partnership with William Honywood, 1637.

4 In partnership with Robert Austin.

5 Richard Miller was in partnerships with William Ward (1627–30) and Rice Williams (1631–9).

6 Mostly recorded as a tailor to the dwarfs and music boys. However, sometimes he appears to have made clothing for the queen.

7 In partnership with Richard Miller.

8 In partnership with Richard Miller.

9 Later Queen Anne.

10 Countess of Ogle (1679–80), later the Duchess of Somerset (1682–1722).

11 Lady Churchill (1677–89), Countess of Marlborough (1689–1702), later Duchess of Marlborough (1702–44). I have chosen to use her forename and surname rather than her titles in these tables, as she was known by all these titles during various periods covered by Tables 3–6.

12 These names come from bills dating from 1687–8. Some tradespeople supplied goods for liveries but it is unclear if they regularly supplied goods for the queen's clothing too.

13 Likely the skinner Daniel Brown who appears in the accounts of Catherine of Braganza, Mary II and William III.

14 Probably related to the mercer William Sherrard.

15 In partnership with Jeremy Percie.

16 In partnership with Windsor Sandys.

17 Possibly William Garway MP. He was the son of Sir Henry Garway, an English merchant and member of the East India Company.

18 A John Hay appears in the accounts of Charles II, James II and Mary of Modena. It is unclear if Hay and La Hay are the same person.

19 The Haraches were a famous Huguenot silversmithing family in London.

20 Lombard's daughter married Horatio Walpole MP.

21 Brother of the famous Huguenot designer Daniel Marot.

22 In partnership with Thomas Sutton.

23 In partnership with John Bishop.

24 In partnership with George Caldecott.

25 In partnership with George Noble.

26 Tompion is often referred to as the father of English clockmaking.

27 William Tuer married Deborah Burton in St Marylebone London on 5 May 1684. Deborah was the daughter of Deborah Burton, milliner to Catherine of Braganza.

28 Daughter of the pinman Thomas Smith.

29 In addition to owning an Indian shop, Motteux was a famous Huguenot writer, playwright and translator.

30 Musard's daughter Mary married Christopher Wren the Younger.

31 Probably related to the mercer Richard Sherrard.

Appendix II: Clothing and accessories of the Stuart queens

1 BL: Add. MS 5751 A; BL: Add. MS 61407; CUL: Dd 1.26; KKCA: AR/33/9/63–151; LA: 1 WORSLEY 6–9; TNA: AO 1/2067/100–1; TNA: LR 5/63–7; TNA: LR 5/76–94; TNA: LR 6/154/9; TNA: SC 6/JASI/1639–55; Griffey, 'Re-Dressing the Evidence', 8–9, 15–19; Field, 'Wardrobe Goods'; Payne, 'An Inventory', 27–41.

2 This is not an exhaustive table but representative of the most common garments, fabrics and trims in the surviving accounts of each queen. The table does not include royal robes or masque costumes. Items might also be missing due to incomplete accounts; for example, bills from Henrietta Maria and Mary II's seamstress who made their linen undergarments and accessories have not survived.

Appendix III: A list of Queen Mary II's jewels, 1695

1 Also known as the 'beau sancy'. Originating in India, this diamond was owned by other queens such as Marie de' Medici, before it was sold to the House of Orange. It was a wedding gift from William to Mary.

Appendix IV: Debts owed to Robert and Elizabeth Graydon, 1701

1 Brackets indicate parts of the document that are illegible due to damage or faded ink.

Glossary of clothing, textile and sewing terms

1 *Oxford English Dictionary*, https://www.oed.com/; Appleby, 'Trade, Consumption and Industry', 205, 221; Bendall, *Shaping Femininity*, 255–9; Claxton and Welch, 'Chintz, China, and Chocolate', 265; Cumming, Cunnington and Cunnington, *The Dictionary of Fashion History*; Evelyn, *Mundus muliebris*, 15–23; Hayward, *Stuart Style*, 324–5; Hayward, *Material World of a Restoration Queen Consort*, 332–485; Holme, *The Academy of Armory*; Lemire, *The British Cotton Trade*, xxxiii–xlv; North, 'Indian Gowns and Banyans', 32.

Bibliography

Manuscript sources

Buckminster Archives, Buckminster (BA)

911-1 to 911-52: Accounts of Personal and Household Expenditure of the Duke and Duchess of Lauderdale, 1672–1729.

Bodleian Libraries, Oxford (BLO)

MS Morrell 6: Oxford Tailors' Guild Election and Order book, 1570–1710.
MS. Eng. misc. b. 31: Charles II and James II. Contemporary copies of royal warrants, 1667–87.
MS. Rawl. C. 987: Papers relating to the Household of Mary of Modena, 1685–1717.

The British Library, London (BL)

Add. MS 15897: Papers relating to Pensions, Establishments of the Court, 1677–1702.
Add. MS 34195: Official Papers, etc. 1576–1763.
Add. MS 45122: Account books of Francis Kynnesman, hosier of London, 1690–1703.
Add. MS 5751 A: Mary II. Tradespeople's bills due at the time of her death, 1691–4.
Add. MS 61346: Blenheim Papers. Receipt-book for domestic expenses, kept by Sarah and John Churchill, 1677–90.
Add. MS 61407: Blenheim Papers. Sarah Duchess Accounts as Mistress of the Robes (Office of the Robes accounts of Queen Anne), 1702–11.
Add. MS 61417: Blenheim Papers. Correspondence and papers of Sarah, Duchess of Marlborough.
Add. MS 61420–4: Blenheim Papers. Papers of Duchess of Marlborough as Mistress of the Robes and Keeper of the Privy Purse, 1702–17.
Add. MS 61425: Blenheim Papers. Correspondence and papers of Sarah, Duchess of Marlborough.
Add. MS 61432: Blenheim Papers. Correspondence and papers of Sarah, Duchess of Marlborough: Family correspondence.
Add. MS 61455–6: Blenheim Papers. Correspondence and papers of Sarah, Duchess of Marlborough: Personal correspondence.
Add. MS 61472: Blenheim Papers. Correspondence and papers of Sarah, Duchess of Marlborough: Bills and Financial, 1684–1744.
Add. MS 61474. Blenheim Papers. Correspondence and papers of Sarah, Duchess of Marlborough, 1677–1709.
Add. MS 75388. James, Duke of York Household Establishment, includes Princess Anne, 1682.
Add. MS 78269: Documents partly relating to the household establishments of Mary II and Queen Anne, 1689–1706.

Cambridge University Library, Cambridge (CUL)

Dd 1.26: Inventory of Queen Anne of Denmark's wardrobe, 1607–11.

Devonshire Collections, Chatsworth House (DCCH)

CH37/1: Papers of William Cavendish, 1st Duke of Devonshire.

Kresen Kernow Cornish Archives, Redruth (KKCA)

AR/33/9/63–151: Papers relating to Queen Catherine of Braganza. Correspondence and accounts of Sir Richard
    Bellings, 1672–1708.

Lincolnshire Archives, Lincoln (LA)

1 WORSLEY 6–9: Catherine of Braganza. Accounts of the Queen's privy purse, 1665–81. Account set.

London Metropolitan Archives (LMA)

P76/JS1/003: Marriages and Burials, Saint James, Clerkenwell, 1561–1670.

National Art Library, Victoria and Albert Museum (NAL)

RC.U.21: Bills for haberdashery, drapery, tailoring, etc., supplied to members of the Russell family, 1666–93.
RC.K.3–4: Bills for haberdashery, drapery, tailoring, etc., supplied to members of the Russell family, 1665–99.

NatWest archives, Edinburgh (NWA)

CH 194/7: Child's bank ledgers of John Cecil, 5th Earl of Exeter, 1680s.

Rare Books and Special Collections, University of Sydney (RBSC)

Supplementary Ms. 074: Account book for household expenses and private purse of Anne Clifford, Countess of
    Dorset, Pembroke and Montgomerey, 1675–6.

Royal Archives Online (RAO)

GEO/ADD/17/75: Wardrobe and Nursery Accounts of Caroline, Queen Consort to George II, 1730–4.

The National Archives, Kew (TNA)

AO 1/2067/100–1: Anna of Denmark. Auditors of the Imprest and Commissioners of Audit: Declared Accounts of
    the Mistress of the Robes, Lady A. Walsingham, 1606. Account set.
AO 1/2067/103: Declared Accounts. Queen Anne's Accounts. Roll 103 C. Hodges, by order of the Duchess of
    Marlborough, 1702–6.

AO 3/919–929: Robes, Accounts. Charles II, 1669–82

AO 3/935–936: Robes, Accounts. William III, 1689–91.

C 104/46: Chancery, Master Tinney's Exhibits. An account of money received and paid by Sir James Gray Bar. out of the Trust Estate of Frances late Duchess Dowager of Richmond and Lennox, 1715–16.

C 5/167/44: Hall v Potter. Court of Chancery, 1688.

C 8/262/23: Gerard v Potter. Court of Chancery, 1682.

C 8/298/61: Alexander v Hette (Haite). Court of Chancery, 1684.

C 8/427/86: Francklyn v Tillie. Court of Chancery, 1692.

C 10/364/32: Sherard v Graydon. Court of Chancery, 1701.

C 10/404/36: Langrish v Burton. Court of Chancery, 1698.

C 10/485/2: Alexander v Harte (Haite). Court of Chancery, 1684.

C 10/512/82: Keene v Potter. Court of Chancery, 1693.

E 133/78/54: Langrish v Burton. Exchequer, King's Remembrancer, Barons' Depositions, 1687.

LC 2/4/5: Progress of James I through the city of London, March 15, 1604.

LC 5/184: Lord Chamberlain's Department. Miscellaneous Records, petitions, 1660–62.

LC 9/280: Great Wardrobe bills. Lord Chamberlain's Department – Great Wardrobe bill books, 1690–6.

LR 5/63: Henrietta Maria. Documents subsidiary to the accounts of the Treasurer and Receiver General, 1629–39.

LR 5/64–7: Henrietta Maria. Office of the Auditors of Land Revenue and predecessors and successors, Household Vouchers, 1627–67. Account set.

LR 5/76–94: Catherine of Braganza. Office of the Auditors of Land Revenue and predecessors and successors: Vouchers and Accounts, 1672–94. Account set.

LR 6/154/9: Anna of Denmark. Declaration of account of Sir George Carew, Vice-Chamberlain and Receiver General, 1603–5.

LS 13/32–6: Catherine of Braganza. Lord Steward's Department: Establishment Books, 1663–74. Account Set.

LS 13/168: Lord Steward's Department: Miscellaneous Books, 1598–1630.

LS 13/280: Lord Steward's Department: Miscellaneous Books, 1603–25.

PROB 4/25866: Will of Unnamed Testatrix, August 11, 1682.

PROB 11/445/146: Will of Jane Potter, Widow of Saint James Westminster, Middlesex, April 15, 1698.

PROB 11/517/287: Will of Thomas Clifton, Bowyer of London, October 10, 1710.

PROB 11/523/10: Will of Deborah Burton, Widow of Saint Bride, City of London, September 4, 1711.

PROB 11/561/208: Will of Mary Devett, Widow of Saint Andrew Undershaft, City of London, December 9, 1717.

PROB 11/607/421: Will of Elizabeth Atkinson, Widow of Saint Margaret Westminster, Middlesex, March 18, 1726.

PROB 11/616/223: Will of Ann Clifton, Widow of Saint Martin in the Fields, Middlesex, July 12, 1727.

SC 6/JASI/1639–55: Anna of Denmark. Declaration of receiver-general's accounts, 1603–20. Account set.

SC 6/CHASI/1692–1705: Henrietta Maria. Accounts of the Treasurer, 1626–49. Account set.

SO 3/9: Signet Office and Home Office – Docquet Books and Letters Recommendatory. Henrietta Maria, 1627–30.

SP 12/255: State Papers Domestic, Elizabeth I, 1595.

SP 14/107: State Papers Domestic, James I, 1619–23.

SP 15/35: State Papers Domestic, Edward VI to Charles I, 1603.

SP 44/15: Secretaries of State: State Papers: Entry Books, 1633.

SP 44/235: State Papers Domestic Petition Entry Book: 1, 1688–93.

Warwickshire Record Office, Warwick (WRO)

CR2017/C1/5–29: Volume of family letters entitled 'Letters written by, or occasionally addressed to, members of the Feilding family during the times of William and Basil, the two first Earls of Denbigh in two volumes'.

West Sussex Record Office, Chichester (WSRO)

PHA: 252–90: Receipted accounts of the Countess of Ogle (afterwards Duchess of Somerset), 1679–1715.

Online databases and online archives

Ancestry.com. 'England, Select Births and Christenings, 1538–1975'. https://www.ancestry.com/search/collections/9841/.

Ancestry.com. 'London, England, Church of England Baptisms, Marriages and Burials, 1538–1812'. From *Church of England Parish Registers, 1538–1812*, London, England: London Metropolitan Archives. https://www.ancestry.com.au/search/collections/1624/.

Ancestry.com. 'Westminster, London, England, Church of England Baptisms, Marriages and Burials, 1558–1812'. From *Westminster, Anglican Parish Registers, City of Westminster Archives*, Westminster, London, England. https://www.ancestry.com.au/search/collections/61865/.

Bank of England. 'Inflation Calculator'. https://www.bankofengland.co.uk/monetary-policy/inflation/inflation-calculator.

British History Online. https://www.british-history.ac.uk/.

Bucholz, R. O. *The Database of Court Officers: 1660–1837*. Loyola University of Chicago. https://courtofficers.ctsdh.luc.edu/.

Findmypast. 'Boyd's Inhabitants of London and Boyd's Family Units, 1200–1946'. https://www.findmypast.com.au/discover/census-land-and-surveys/surveys/boyds-inhabitants-of-london-and-family-units-1200-1946.

Findmypast. 'Britain, Country Apprentices 1710–1808'. https://search.findmypast.com.au/search-world-records/britain-country-apprentices-1710-1808.

Findmypast. 'City of London, Haberdashers, apprentices and freemen 1526–1933'. https://www.findmypast.com.au/discover/education-and-work/apprentices/city-of-london-haberdashers-apprentices-and-freemen-1526-1933.

Findmypast. 'England Births & Baptisms 1538–1975'. https://search.findmypast.com.au/search-world-records/england-births-and-baptisms-1538-1975.

Findmypast. 'England, Boyd's Marriage Indexes, 1538–1850'. https://search.findmypast.com.au/search-world-records/england-boyds-marriage-indexes-1538-1850.

Findmypast. 'England Marriages 1538–1973'. https://search.findmypast.co.uk/search-world-records/england-marriages-1538-1973.

Findmypast. 'Westminster Baptisms'. https://www.findmypast.com.au/articles/world-records/full-list-of-united-kingdom-records/life-events-bmds/westminster-baptisms.

Findmypast. 'Westminster Marriages'. https://www.findmypast.com.au/articles/world-records/full-list-of-united-kingdom-records/life-events-bmds/westminster-marriages.

Findmypast. 'Westminster Rate Books 1634–1900'. https://search.findmypast.com.au/search-world-records/westminster-rate-books-1634-1900.

Hitchcock, Tim, Robert Shoemaker, Sharon Howard and Jamie McLaughlin, et al. *London Lives, 1690–1800*, Version 1.1. 24 April 2012. www.londonlives.org.

National Archives, UK. 'Currency Converter: 1270–2017'. https://www.nationalarchives.gov.uk/currency-converter/.

Oxford English Dictionary. https://www.oed.com/.

Peacey, Jason, ed. *Petitions to the House of Lords, 1597–1696. British History Online.* https://www.british-history.ac.uk/petitions/house-of-lords/1696.

Proceedings of the Old Bailey (OBP). https://www.oldbaileyonline.org.

ROLLCO. 'Records of London's Livery Companies Online'. http://londonroll.org.

Royal Archives Online. https://ra.rct.uk/Record.aspx?src=CalmView.Catalog&id=ADD17%2f4&pos=1, March 2025.

Uppsala Universitet. 'Gender and Work'. https://www.uu.se/en/research/gender-and-work.

Westminster Abbey. https://www.westminster-abbey.org/abbey-commemorations/commemorations/.

Printed primary sources

Advice to the Maidens of LONDON: To Forsake Their Fantastical TOP-KNOTS. London: J. Blare, 1685–8.

A General Description of All Trades: Digested in Alphabetical Order: by which Parents, Guardians, and Trustees, May, with Greater Ease and Certainty, Make Choice of Trades Agreeable to the Capacity, Education, Inclination, Strength, and Fortune of the Youth Under Their Care. London: T. Waller, 1747.

An Historical and Chronological Deduction of the Origin of Commerce, from the Earliest Accounts. Volume 2. Edited by Adam Anderson. London: Logographic Press, 1787.

At the Council-chamber in Whitehall, Monday the 22th of October, 1688: This day an extraordinary council met, where were likewise present, by His Majesties desire and appointment, Her Majesty the Queen Dowager, and such of the peers of this kingdom, both spiritual and temporal, as were in town. London: Charles Bill, H. Hills and Th. Newcomb, 1688.

Barbe, Simon. *The French Perfumer teaching the several ways of extracting the odours of drugs and flowers and making all the compositions of perfumes for powder, wash-balls, essences, oyls, wax, pomatum, paste, Queen of Hungary's Rosa Solis, and other sweet waters.* London: Sam. Buckley, 1696.

Brathwaite, Richard. *The English Gentlewoman.* London: B. Alsop and T. Favvcet, for Michaell Sparke, 1631.

Brown, Horatio F., ed. *Calendar of State Papers Relating To English Affairs in the Archives of Venice, Volume 11, 1607–1610.* London: His Majesty's Stationery Office, 1904.

Bruce, John. *Calendar of State Papers Domestic: Charles I, 1625–26.* London: Her Majesty's Stationery Office, 1858.

Bruce, John. *Calendar of State Papers Domestic: Charles I, 1628–29.* London: Her Majesty's Stationery Office, 1859.

Bruce, John. *Calendar of State Papers Domestic: Charles I, 1629–31.* London: Her Majesty's Stationery Office, 1860.

Bruce, John. *Calendar of State Papers Domestic: Charles I, 1635–6.* London: Her Majesty's Stationery Office, 1866.

Bruce, John. *Calendar of State Papers Domestic: Charles I, 1637.* London: Her Majesty's Stationery Office, 1868.

Bruce, John and William Douglas Hamilton, eds. *Calendar of State Papers Domestic: Charles I, 1638–9.* London: Her Majesty's Stationery Office, 1871.

Campbell, R. *The London Tradesman: Being a Compendious View of All the Trades, Professions, Arts, Both Liberal and Mechanic, Now Practised in the Cities of London and Westminster. Calculated for the Information of Parents, and Instruction of Youth in Their Choice of Business.* London: T. Gardner, 1747.

Carter, William. *Englands intrest in securing the woollen-manufacture, of this realm Against the artiffices, and designs of France, asserted and made evident to all true lovers of their country. To which is added a reply to some objections formerly made to the same subject.* London: Joseph Streater, 1689.

Catholic Record Society Registers of the Catholic Chapels Royal and of the Portuguese Embassy Chapel, 1662–1829. Volume 1. Marriages. Edited by J. Cyril M. Weale. London: John Whitehead & Son, 1941.

Churchill, Sarah. *An Account of the Conduct of the Dowager Duchess of Marlborough: From Her First Coming to Court, to the Year 1710.* London: James Bettenham, 1742.

Cibber, Colley. *Woman's wit, or, The lady in fashion a comedy acted at the Theatre Royal by His Majesties servants.* London: John Sturton, 1697.

Clifford, Anne. *The Diaries of Lady Anne Clifford.* Edited by D. J. H. Clifford. Stroud: Alan Sutton, 1991.

The Compleat Doctoress: or, A choice Treatise of all Diseases insident to Women. With experimentall remedies against the same. Being safe in the composition. Pleasant in the use. Effectuall in the operation. Faithfully translated out of Latine into English for a common good. London: Edward Farnham, 1656.

Dialogues of the dead in imitation of Lucian, and the French. London: R.C., 1699.

E., B. *A new dictionary of the canting crew in its several tribes of gypsies, beggers, thieves, cheats . . .* London: W. Hawes, P. Gilbourne and W. Davis, 1699.

Evelyn, John. *The Diary of John Evelyn.* Edited by William Bray. Vols 1–2. London and Washington: M. Walter Dunne, 1901.

Evelyn, Mary. *Mundus muliebris: or, The ladies dressing-room unlock'd, And her Toilette spread in Burlesque.* Edited by John Evelyn. London: R. Bentley, 1690.

Extraordinaire du Mercure galant. Paris: n.p., 1678.

Extraordinaire du Secretaire Galant. Paris: n.p., 1690.

F., J. *The Merchant's Ware-House Laid Open: Or, the Plain Dealing Linnen-Draper: Shewing How to Buy All Sorts of Linnen and In dian Goods . . .* London: John Sprint, 1696.

Fiennes, Celia. *Through England on a Side Saddle: In the Time of William and Mary.* London: Field and Tuer, 1888.

Florio, John. *Queen Anna's New World of Words, Or Dictionarie of the Italian and English Tongues.* London: Melch. Bradwood, 1611.

The Flying Post, or the Post-Master, Issue 3509. London, July 1, 1714.

Française, Académie. *Le Grand Dictionnaire de l'Académie françoise, dédié au Roy. Seconde édition, reveüe et corrigée de plusieurs fautes, et où l'on a mis dans l'ordre alphabétique les additions qui estoient à la fin de l'édition précédente.* Paris : Jean Baptiste Coignard, 1695.

Fraser, William, ed. *Memorials of the Montgomeries, Earls of Eglinton, Volume 2.* Edinburgh: William Fraser, 1859.

Green, Mary Anne Everett. *Calendar of State Papers Domestic: James I, 1603–1610.* London: Her Majesty's Stationery Office, 1857.

Green, Mary Anne Everett. *Calendar of State Papers Domestic: Charles II, 1661–2.* London: Her Majesty's Stationery Office, 1861.

Hale, Thomas. *An account of several new inventions and improvements now necessary for England, in a discourse by way of letter to the Earl of Marlborough . . .* London: James Astwood, 1691.

Hamilton, Wiliam Douglas. *Calendar of State Papers Domestic: Charles I, 1639–40.* London: Her Majesty's Stationery Office, 1877.

Harris, John. *The History of Kent. In Five Parts. Volume 1.* London: D. Midwinter, 1719.

Hinds, Allen B., ed. 'Venice: July 1625, 16–31'. In *Calendar of State Papers Relating To English Affairs in the Archives of Venice, Volume 19, 1625–1626.* London: His Majesty's Stationery Office, 1913.

Hinds, Allen B., ed. *Calendar of State Papers Relating To English Affairs in the Archives of Venice, Volume 35, 1666–1668.* London: His Majesty's Stationery Office, 1935.

Howard, James. *The English Mounsieur a Comedy, as It Is Acted, at the Theater-Royal by His Majesty's Servants.* London: H. Bruges for J. Magnus, 1674.

Hunt, William H., ed. *The Registers of St. Paul's Church, Covent Garden, London, Volume 4, Burials, 1653–1752.* London: Publications of the Harleian Society, 1906.

Journal of the House of Commons: Volume 7, 1651–1660. London: His Majesty's Stationery Office, 1802.

Journal of the House of Lords: Volume 15, 1691–1696. London: His Majesty's Stationery Office, 1767–1830.

Juvenal. *The Satires of Decimus Junius Juvenalis. Translated into English Verse. By Mr. Dryden, and Several Other Eminent Hands.* Translated by John Dryden. London: Jacob Tonson, 1693.

The Ladies Catechism useful for all Eminent Females, and necessary to be Learnt by all Young Gentlewomen, that would attain to the Dignity of the Mode. London: n.p., 1703.

Lefroy, J. H. *Memorials of the Discovery and Early Settlement of the Bermudas or Somers Islands, 1515–1685, Volume 1.* London: Longmans, Green, and co., 1877.

London Gazette, Issue 2470. July 15, 1689.

London Gazette, Issue 4027. June 12, 1704.

Mareschal, André. *Le Railleur, ou La satyre du temps, comédie.* Paris: chez Toussainct Quinet, 1638.

Montagu, Mary Wortley. *The Selected Letters of Lady Mary Wortley Montagu.* Edited by Robert Halsband. London: Longmans, 1970.

Nichols, John. *The Progresses and Public Processions of Queen Elizabeth: Among Which Are Interspersed Other Solemnities, Public Expenditures, and Remarkable Events during the Reign of That Illustrious Princess*, Volume 3. n.p.p.: AMS Press, 1823.

Owen, G. Dyfnallt. *Calendar of the Cecil Papers in Hatfield House: Volume 24, Addenda, 1605–1668*. London: Her Majesty's Stationery Office, 1976.

Partridge, John. *The Treasurie of Commodious Conceits, and Hidden Secretes Commonlie called The good huswiues closet of prouision, for the health of her household*. London: Richard Jones, 1591.

Pepys, Samuel. *Diary and Correspondence of Samuel Pepys, ESQ., F.R.S., from his Ms. Cypher in the Pepysian Library*. Edited by Richard Griffin Braybrooke and Mynors Bright. Vols 1–9. New York: Dodd, Mead and Company, 1885.

Petyt, William. *Britannia Languens: Or, a Discourse of Trade Shewing, That the Present Management of Trade in England*. London: Richard Baldwin, 1689.

Pix, Mary. *The Innocent Mistress a Comedy*. London: J. Orme, for R. Basset, and F. Cogan, 1697.

The Player's Tragedy. Or, Fatal Love a new novel. London: Randal Taylor, 1693.

Privy Council, England and Wales. *At the Council-chamber in Whitehall, Monday the 22th. of October, 1688: This day an extraordinary council met, where were likewise present, by His Majesties desire and appointment, Her Majesty the Queen Dowager, and such of the peers of this kingdom, both spiritual and temporal, as were in town*. London: Charles Bill, H. Hills, and Th. Newcomb, 1688.

Several petitions presented to the Honourable Houses of Parliament now assembled.: 1 The humble petition of many thousands of courtiers, citizens, gentlemen, and trades-mens wives, inhabiting within the cities of London and Westminster . . . London: Printed by a true copy for John Wright, 1641.

Shaw, William A., ed. *Calendar of Treasury Books, Volume 1, 1660–1667*. London: His Majesty's Stationery Office, 1904.

Shaw, William A., ed. *Calendar of Treasury Books, Volume 4, 1672-1675*. London: His Majesty's Stationery Office, 1909.

Shaw, William A., ed. *Calendar of Treasury Books, Volume 5, 1676–1679*. London: His Majesty's Stationery Office, 1911.

Shaw, William A., ed. *Calendar of Treasury Books, Volume 7, 1681–1685*. London: His Majesty's Stationery Office, 1916.

Shaw, William A., ed. *Calendar of Treasury Books, Volume 9, 1689–1692*. London: His Majesty's Stationery Office, 1931.

Shaw, William A., ed. *Calendar of Treasury Books, Volume 10, 1693–1696*. London: His Majesty's Stationery Office, 1935.

Shaw, William A., ed. *Calendar of Treasury Books, Volume 17, 1702*. London: His Majesty's Stationery Office, 1939.

Shaw, William A., ed. *Calendar of Treasury Books, Volume 25, 1711*. London: Her Majesty's Stationery Office, 1952.

Shaw, William A., ed. *Calendar of Treasury Books, Volume 26, 1712*. London: Her Majesty's Stationery Office, 1954.

Shaw, William A. and F. H. Slingsby, eds. *Calendar of Treasury Books, Volume 27, 1713*. London: Her Majesty's Stationery Office, 1955.

Shaw, William A. and F. H. Slingsby, eds. *Calendar of Treasury Books, Volume 28, 1714*. London: Her Majesty's Stationery Office, 1955.

Shaw, William A. and F. H. Slingsby, eds. *Calendar of Treasury Books, Volume 29, 1714–1715*. London: Her Majesty's Stationery Office, 1957.

Southerne, Thomas. *The maids last prayer, or, Any, rather than fail a comedy, as it is acted at the Theatre Royal by Their Majesties servants*. London: R. Bentley, 1693.

The Spectator, Volume V, no. 336. London, 1718.

Statuts, ordonnances et déclaration du roy, confirmative d'iceux, pour la communauté des couturieres de la ville, fauxbourgs & banlieue de Paris. Vérifié en Parlement le 7 octobre 1675. Paris : Veuve de Ph. N. LOTTIN, 1734.

Stuart, Arabella. *The Letters of Lady Arbella Stuart*. Edited by Sara Jayne Steen. Oxford: Oxford University Press, 1994.

Stubbes, Phillip. *The Anatomy of Abuses*. London: John Kingston for Richard Jones, 1583.

Swift, Johnathan. *The Works of the Rev. Jonathan Swift, Volume 3*. Edited by Thomas Sheridan and John Nichols. London: Nichols and Son, 1801.

To the Right Honourable the Lords Spiritual and Temporal, in Parliament Assembled, the Petition and Case of the Embroiderers Flourishers, Raisers and Stitchers of East-India Silks, and Other Goods, and Stainers . . . London: anon., 1696.

Vickers, Thomas, ed. *The Reports of Sir Creswell Levinz, Knt. Late one of the judges of the Court of Common Pleas at Westminster . . ., Volume 3*. n.p.p.: W. Clarke and Sons, 1802.

Wecker, Johann Jacob. *Cosmeticks or, the beautifying part of physick. By which all deformities of nature in men and women are corrected, age renewed, youth prolonged, and the least impediment, from a hair to a tooth, fairly amended*. London: Tho. Johnson, 1660.

Woolley, Hannah (attributed). *The Gentlewomans Companion; or, A guide to the female sex containing directions of behaviour, in all places, companies, relations, and conditions, from their childhood down to old age*. London: Printed by A. Maxwell for Dorman Newman, 1673.

Yarmouth, Robert Paston. *The Whirlpool of Misadventures: Letters of Robert Paston, First Earl of Yarmouth, 1663–1679, Volume LXXVI*. Edited by Jean Agnew. Norwich: Norfolk Record Society, 2012.

Secondary works

Ågren, Maria. 'Making Her Turn Around: The Verb-Oriented Method, the Two-Supporter Model, and the Focus on Practice'. *Early Modern Women* 13, no. 1 (2018): 144–52.

Akkerman, Nadine and Birgit Houben. 'Introduction'. In *The Politics of Female Households: Ladies-in-Waiting across Early Modern Europe*. Edited by Nadine Akkerman and Birgit Houben, 1–27. Leiden: Brill, 2013.

Appleby, John C. 'Trade, Consumption and Industry: Transatlantic Constraints on the Bay Trade'. In *Fur, Fashion and Transatlantic Trade during the Seventeenth Century: Chesapeake Bay Native Hunters, Colonial Rivalries and London Merchants*, 205–40. Woodbridge: Boydell & Brewer, 2021.

Ashelford, Jane. *The Art of Dress: Clothes and Society, 1500–1914*. Swindon: National Trust, 1996.

Arnold, Janet. 'The Dressmaker's Craft'. *Costume* 7, no. 1 (1973): 29–40.

Arnold, Janet. 'Decorative Features: Pinking, Snipping and Slashing'. *Costume* 9, no. 1 (1975): 22–6.

Arnold, Janet. *Queen Elizabeth's Wardrobe Unlock'd: the inventories of the Wardrobe of Robes prepared in July 1600, edited from Stowe MS 557 in the British Library, MS LR 2/121 in the Public Record Office, London, and MS V.b.72 in the Folger Shakespeare Library, Washington DC*. Leeds: Maney, 1988.

Arnold, Janet, Sébastien Passot, Claire Thornton, Jenny Tiraminai, Melanie Braun, Adrien Chombart de Lauwe, Luca Costigliolo, et al. *Patterns of Fashion. 6, The Content, Cut, Construction and Context of Women's European Dress c. 1695–1795*. London: School of Historical Dress, 2021.

Avidon, Marlo. '"Instructive Types" or Mere "Fancies": Assessing French Fashion Prints in the Library of Samuel Pepys'. *The Seventeenth Century* 39, no. 4 (2024): 663–94.

Barber, Peter. 'Gambling in wartime: the rise and fall of William Geere'. *Camden History Review* 19 (1995): 17–20.

Barclay, Andrew. 'Mary [Mary of Modena] (1658–1718), queen of England, Scotland, and Ireland, consort of James II and VII'. *Oxford Dictionary of National Biography*, 23 September 2004, https://doi.org/10.1093/ref:odnb/18247.

Barroll, J. Leeds. *Anna of Denmark, Queen of England: A Cultural Biography*. Philadelphia: University of Pennsylvania Press, 2001.

Batchelor, Jennie. *Dress, Distress and Desire: Clothing and the Female Body in Eighteenth-Century Literature*. London: Palgrave Macmillan, 2005.

Beaven, Alfred P. *The Aldermen of the City of London Temp. Henry III–1912*. London: Corporation of the City of London, 1908.

Berg, Maxine. *Luxury and Pleasure in Eighteenth-Century Britain*. Oxford: Oxford University Press, 2007.

Bellavitis, Anna. *Women's Work and Rights in Early Modern Urban Europe*. London: Palgrave Macmillan, 2016.

Bendall, Sarah A. *Shaping Femininity: Foundation Garments, the Body and Women in Early Modern England*. London: Bloomsbury, 2021.

Bendall, Sarah A. 'Women's Dress and the Demise of the Tailoring Monopoly: Farthingale-Makers, Body-Makers and the Changing Textile Marketplace of Seventeenth-Century London'. *Textile History* 52, no. 1–2 (2021): 23–55.

Bendall, Sarah A. 'The Queens' Dressmakers: Women's Work and the Clothing Trades in Late Seventeenth-Century London'. *Women's History Review* 32, no. 3 (2023): 389–414.

Benhamou, Reed. 'Who Controls This Private Space? The Offense and Defense of the Hoop in Early Eighteenth-Century France and England'. *Dress* 28, no. 1 (2001): 13–22.

Bennett, Judith M. '"History that stands still": Women's Work in the European Past'. *Feminist Studies* 14, no. 2 (1988): 269–83.

Birt, Sarah. 'Women, Guilds and the Tailoring Trades: The Occupational Training of Merchant Taylors' Company Apprentices in Early Modern London'. *London Journal* 46, no. 2 (2021): 146–64.

Bucholz, R. O. *The Augustan Court: Queen Anne and the Decline of Court Culture*. Stanford, CA: Stanford University Press, 1993.

Bucholz, R. O. 'Going to Court in 1700: A Visitor's Guide'. *Court historian* 5, no. 3 (2000): 181–215.

Bucholz, R. O., 'Seymour [née Percy], Elizabeth, duchess of Somerset (1667–1722), courtier and politician'. *Oxford Dictionary of National Biography*, 23 September 2004, https://doi.org/10.1093/ref:odnb/21925.

Bucholz, R. O., ed. *Office-Holders in Modern Britain: Volume 11 (Revised), Court Officers, 1660–1837*. London: University of London, 2006.

Buck, Anne. 'Mantuamakers and Milliners: Women Making and Selling Clothes in Eighteenth-Century Bedfordshire'. *Bedfordshire Historical Miscellany* 72 (1993): 142–55.

Burke, Jill. *How to be a Renaissance Woman: The Untold History of Beauty and Female Creativity*. London: Profile Books, 2023.

Burke, Peter. *The Fortunes of the Courtier: The European Reception of Castiglione's Cortegiano*. Oxford: Polity Press, 1995.

Burman, Barbara and Nigel Rapport, eds. *The Culture of Sewing: Gender, Consumption and Home Dressmaking*. Oxford: Berg, 1999.

Chaudhuri, K. N. *The Trading World of Asia and the English East India Company, 1660–1760*. Cambridge: Cambridge University Press, 2006.

Chico, Tita. *Designing Women: The Dressing Room in Eighteenth-Century English Literature and Culture*. Lewisburg, PA: Bucknell University Press, 2005.

Chrisman, Kimberly. 'Unhoop the Fair Sex: The Campaign Against the Hoop Petticoat in Eighteenth-Century England'. *Eighteenth-Century Studies* 30, no. 1 (1996): 5–23.

Clark, Alice. *Working Life of Women in the Seventeenth Century*. Edited by Amy Louise Erickson. London: Routledge, 1992.

Claxton Juliet and Evelyn Welch, 'Chintz, China, and Chocolate: The Politics of Fashion at Charles II's Court'. In *Sartorial Politics in Early Modern Europe: Fashioning Women*. Edited by Erin Griffey, 253–76. Amsterdam: Amsterdam University Press, 2019.

Cowan, Brian William. *The Social Life of Coffee: The Emergence of the British Coffeehouse*. New Haven, CT: Yale University Press, 2005.

Coward, Barry. *The Stuart Age: England, 1603–1714*. 2nd edn. London: Longman, 1994.

Coward, Barry and Peter Gaunt. *The Stuart Age: England, 1603–1714*. London: Routledge, 2017.

Cox, Nancy C. and Karin Dannehl. *Perceptions of Retailing in Early Modern England*. London: Routledge, 2016.

Crowston, Clare. 'Women, Gender, and Guilds in Early Modern Europe: An Overview of Recent Research'. *International Review of Social History* 53, no. S16 (2008): 19–44.

Crowston, Clare Haru. *Fabricating Women: The Seamstresses of Old Regime France, 1675–1791*. Durham, NC: Duke University Press, 2001.

Crowston, Clare Haru. *Credit, Fashion, Sex: Economies of Regard in Old Regime France*. Durham, NC: Duke University Press, 2013.

Cumming, Valerie, C. Willett Cunnington and Phillis Cunnington. *The Dictionary of Fashion History*. Oxford: Berg, 2010.

Davidson, Lillias Campbell. *Catherine of Bragança, Infanta of Portugal, & Queen-Consort of England*. London: John Murray, 1908.

Davis, Elizabeth. 'Habit de Qualité: Seventeenth-Century French Fashion Prints as Sources for Dress History'. *Dress* 40 (2014): 117–43.

De Vries, Jan. *The Industrious Revolution: Consumer Behaviour and the Household Economy, 1650 to the Present*. Cambridge: Cambridge University Press, 2008.

Dillon, Janette. *Theatre, Court and City, 1595–1610: Drama and Social Space in London*. Cambridge: Cambridge University Press, 2000.

Dowdell, Carolyn. '"No Small Share of Ingenuity": An object orientated analysis of eighteenth-century English dressmaking'. *Costume* 55, no. 2 (2021): 186–211.

Dugan, Holly. 'Scent'. In *Early Modern Court Culture,*. Edited by Erin Griffey, 428–43. London: Routledge, 2022.

Duindam, Jeroen. 'The Politics of Female Households: Afterthoughts'. In *The Politics of Female Households: Ladies-in-Waiting across Early Modern Europe*. Edited by Nadine Akkerman and Birgit Houben, 365–70. Leiden: Brill, 2013.

Dunn-Hensley, Susan. *Anna of Denmark and Henrietta Maria: Virgins, Witches, and Catholic Queens*. London: Palgrave Macmillan, 2017.

Dyer, Serena. *Material Lives: Women Makers and Consumer Culture in the 18th Century*. London: Bloomsbury, 2021.

Dyer, Serena. *Labour of the Stitch: The Making and Remaking of Fashionable Georgian Dress*. Cambridge: Cambridge University Press, 2024.

Eacott, Jonathan P. 'Making an Imperial Compromise: The Calico Acts, the Atlantic Colonies, and the Structure of the British Empire'. *The William and Mary Quarterly* 69, no. 4 (2012): 731–62.

Earle, Peter. 'The Female Labour Market in London in the Late Seventeenth and Early Eighteenth Centuries'. *Economic History Review* 42, no. 3 (1989): 328–53.

Edwards, Peter. *Horses and the Aristocratic Lifestyle in Early Modern England*. Woodbridge: Boydell, 2018.

Erickson, Amy Louise. 'Coverture and Capitalism'. *History Workshop Journal* 59, no. 1 (2005): 1–16.

Erickson, Amy Louise. 'Married Women's Occupations in Eighteenth-Century London'. *Continuity and Change* 23, no. 2 (2008): 267–307.

Erickson, Amy Louise. 'Eleanor Mosley and Other Milliners in the City of London Companies 1700–1750'. *History Workshop Journal* 71, no. 1 (2011): 147–72.

Erickson, Amy Louise. 'Mistresses and Marriage: Or, a Short History of the Mrs'. *History Workshop Journal* 78 (2014): 39–57.

Falkner, James. 'Churchill [née Jenyns], Sarah, Duchess of Marlborough (1660–1744), politician and courtier'. *Oxford Dictionary of National Biography*, 23 September 2004, https://doi.org/10.1093/ref:odnb/5405.

Farguson, Julie. *Visualising Protestant Monarchy: Ceremony, Art and Politics after the Glorious Revolution (1689–1714)*. Woodbridge: Boydell, 2021.

Farrell, William. 'Smuggling Silks into Eighteenth-Century Britain: Geography, Perpetrators, and Consumers'. *Journal of British Studies* 55, no. 2 (2016): 268–94.

Fennetaux, Ariane. 'Behind the Seams: Global Circulations in a Group of Japanese-Inspired Cotton Nightgowns C. 1700'. *Textile History* 52, no. 1–2 (2021): 56–77.

Ferdinand, Christine. 'Commodities and the Acting Profession: A Newly Discovered Inventory for William and Susanna Mountfort's "India Shop" (1692)'. *Huntington Library Quarterly* 86, no. 1 (2023): 73–109.

Fernie, Ewan. 'Chiffinch [Cheffin], Thomas (1600–1666), courtier and royal official'. *Oxford Dictionary of National Biography*, 23 September 2004, https://doi.org/10.1093/ref:odnb/5280.

Fiebranz, Rosemarie, Erik Lindberg, Jonas Lindström and Maria Ågren. 'Making Verbs Count: The Research Project "Gender and Work" and Its Methodology'. *Scandinavian Economic History Review* 59, no. 3 (2011): 273–93.

Field, Jacob F. *London, Londoners and the Great Fire of 1666: Disaster and Recovery*. London: Routledge, 2017.

Field, Jemma. 'The Wardrobe Goods of Anna of Denmark, Queen Consort of Scotland and England (1574–1619)'. *Costume* 51, no. 1 (2017): 3–27.

Field, Jemma. 'A "Cipher of a and C Set on the One Syde with Diamonds": Anna of Denmark's Jewellery and the Politics of Dynastic Display'. In *Sartorial Politics in Early Modern Europe: Fashioning Women*. Edited by Erin Griffey, 139–59. Amsterdam: Amsterdam University Press, 2019.

Field, Jemma. 'Dressing a Queen: The Wardrobe of Anna of Denmark at the Scottish Court of King James VI, 1590–16031'. *Court Historian* 24, no. 2 (2019): 152–67.

Field, Jemma. *Anna of Denmark: The Material and Visual Culture of the Stuart Courts, 1589–1619*. Manchester: Manchester University Press, 2020.

Field, Jemma. 'Clothing the Royal Family: The Intersection of the Court and City in Early Stuart London'. In *Monarchy, the Court, and the Provincial Elite in Early Modern Europe*. Edited by Peter Edwards, 247–71. Leiden: Brill, 2024.

Field, Ophelia. *The Favourite: Sarah, Duchess of Marlborough*. London: Weidenfeld & Nicolson, 2018.

Finn, Margot C. *The Character of Credit: Personal Debt in English Culture, 1740–1914*. Cambridge: Cambridge University Press, 2003.

Forneron, Henri. *Louise de Keroualle, Duchess of Portsmouth, 1649–1734: Society in the Court of Charles II*. London: Swan Sonnenschein, Lowrey & Co., 1888.

Franits, Wayne. *Godefridus Schalcken: A Dutch Painter in Late Seventeenth-Century London*. Amsterdam: Amsterdam University Press, 2018.

Froide, Amy M. *Silent Partners: Women as Public Investors during Britain's Financial Revolution, 1690–1750*. Oxford: Oxford University Press, 2017.

Fryman, Olivia. 'Coffer-Makers to the Late Stuart Court, 1660–1714'. *Furniture History* 52 (2016): 1–16.

Gamber, Wendy. *The Female Economy: The Millinery and Dressmaking Trades, 1860–1930*. Champaign: University of Illinois Press, 1997.

Garrioch, David. 'Introduction: Artisan Mobility and Innovation in Pre-Industrial Europe'. In *The Republic of Skill: Artisan Mobility, Innovation, and the Circulation of Knowledge in Premodern Europe*. Edited by David Garrioch, 1–34. Leiden: Brill, 2022.

Gowing, Laura. 'Girls on Forms: Apprenticing Young Women in Seventeenth-Century London'. *Journal of British Studies* 55, no. 3 (2016): 447–73.

Gowing, Laura. *Ingenious Trade: Women and Work in Seventeenth-Century London*. Cambridge: Cambridge University Press, 2022.

Greenstreet, Anthony. 'Sir Solomon De Medina of Richmond'. *Richmond History: Journal of the Richmond Local History Society* 19 (1998): 32–5.

Gregg, Edward. *Queen Anne*. London: Routledge & Kegan Paul, 1980.

Gregory, Eilish and Michael C. Questier, eds. *Later Stuart Queens, 1660–1735: Religion, Political Culture, and Patronage*. London: Palgrave Macmillan, 2023.

Greig, Hannah. *The Beau Monde: Fashionable Society in Georgian London*. Oxford: Oxford University Press, 2013.

Griffey, Erin. *On Display: Henrietta Maria and the Materials of Magnificence at the Stuart Court*. New Haven, CT: Yale University Press, 2015.

Griffey, Erin. 'Introduction'. In *Henrietta Maria: Piety, Politics and Patronage*. Edited by Erin Griffey, 1–11. London: Routledge, 2016.

Griffey, Erin. 'Introduction'. In *Sartorial Politics in Early Modern Europe: Fashioning Women*. Edited by Erin Griffey, 15–32. Amsterdam: Amsterdam University Press, 2019.

Griffey, Erin. 'Restoring Henrietta Maria's English Household in the 1660s: Continuity, Kinship and Clientage'. *Court Historian* 26, no. 3 (2021): 189–209.

Griffey, Erin. '"The Rose and Lily Queen": Henrietta Maria's Fair Face and the Power of Beauty at the Stuart Court'. *Renaissance studies* 35, no. 5 (2021): 811–36.

Griffey, Erin. 'Home Comforts: Stuart Queens Consort and Negotiating Foreignness at Court'. In *Rank Matters: New Research on Female Rulers in the Early Modern Era*. Edited by Christina Strunck and Lukas Maier, 121–48. Boca Raton, FL: FAU University Press, 2022.

Griffey, Erin. 'Re-Dressing the Evidence: Henrietta Maria's Wardrobe Accounts, 1627–1639'. *Costume* 57, no. 1 (2023): 3–30.

Griffey, Erin. *Facing Decay: Beauty, Aging, and Cosmetics in Early Modern Europe*. University Park, PA: Penn State University Press, 2025.

Griffey, Erin and Michél Nieuwoudt. 'Beautiful Experiments: Reading and Reconstructing Early Modern European Cosmetic Recipes'. In *Embodied Experiences of Making in Early Modern Europe: Bodies, Gender, and Material Culture*. Edited by Sarah A. Bendall and Serena Dyer, 135–61. Amsterdam: Amsterdam University Press, 2024.

Griffiths, Paul. 'Politics made visible: order, residence and uniformity in Cheapside, 1600–45'. In *Londinopolis: Essays in the Cultural and Social history of Early Modern London*. Edited by Paul Griffiths and Mark S. R. Jenner, 176–96. Manchester: Manchester University Press, 2000.

Guerci, Manolo. *London's 'Golden Mile': The Great Houses of the Strand, 1550–1650*. New Haven, CT: Yale University Press, 2021.

Hackett, Anna. 'Household of Mary II, 1689–1694', *The Database of Court Officers: 1660 –1837*, Loyola University of Chicago, https://courtofficers.ctsdh.luc.edu/MaryII.list.pdf.

Hailwood, Mark and Brodie Waddell. 'Work and Identity in Early Modern England'. *Transactions of the Royal Historical Society* 1 (2023): 145–58.

Hanß, Stefan. 'Gendering the Material Renaissance: Women, Industriousness and the Female Body at the Court of Württemberg'. *German History* 41, no. 3 (2023): 367–99.

Harding, Vanessa. 'Shops, Markets and Retailers in London's Cheapside, c. 1500–1700'. In *Buyers and Sellers: Retail Circuits and Practices in Medieval and Early Modern Europe*. Edited by Bruno Blondé, Peter Stabel, Jon Stobart and Ilja Van Damme, 155–70. Turnhout: Brepols, 2006.

Harding, Vanessa. 'London and Middlesex in the 1660s'. In *London and Middlesex 1666 Hearth Tax*. Edited by Catherine Ferguson, Matthew Davies, Vanessa Harding, Elizabeth Parkinson and Andrew Wareham, 25–57. London: British Record Society, 2014.

Harris, Barbara J. *English Aristocratic Women, 1450–1550: Marriage and Family, Property and Careers*. Oxford: Oxford University Press, 2002.

Harris, Frances. 'Accounts of the Conduct of Sarah, Duchess of Marlborough, 1704–1742'. *British Library Journal* 8 (1982): 7–35.

Harris, Tim. '"There is none that love him but Drunk Whores and Whoremongers": Popular Criticisms of the Restoration Court'. In *Politics, Transgression, and Representation at the Court of Charles II*. Edited by Julia Marciari Alexander and Catharine MacLeod, 35–58. New Haven, CT: Yale University Press, 2007.

Hart, Avril. 'The Mantua: its Evolution and Fashionable Significance in the Seventeenth and Eighteenth Centuries'. In *Defining Dress: Dress as Object, Meaning, and Identity*. Edited by Amy Le Haye, 93–103. Manchester: Manchester University Press, 1999.

Harte, N. B. 'State Control of Dress and Social Change in Pre-Industrial England'. In *Trade, Government and Economy in Pre-Industrial England*. Edited by D. C. Coleman and A. H. John, 132–65. London: Weidenfeld & Nicolson: 1976.

Harvey, Anthony and Richard Mortimer, eds. *The Funeral Effigies of Westminster Abbey*. Woodbridge: Boydell, 1994.

Hattendorf, John B. 'Churchill, John, first duke of Marlborough (1650–1722), army officer and politician'. *Oxford Dictionary of National Biography*, 23 September 2004, https://doi.org/10.1093/ref:odnb/5401.

Hayward, Maria. *Dress at the Court of King Henry VIII*. Leeds: Maney, 2007.

Hayward, Maria. '"The best of Queens, the most obedient wife": Fashioning a Place for Catherine of Braganza as Consort to Charles II'. In *Sartorial Politics in Early Modern Europe: Fashioning Women*. Edited by Erin Griffey, 227–52. Amsterdam: Amsterdam University Press, 2019.

Hayward, Maria. *Stuart Style: Monarchy, Dress and the Scottish Male Elite*. New Haven, CT: Yale University Press, 2020.

Hayward, Maria, ed. *The Material World of a Restoration Queen Consort: The Privy Purse Accounts of Catherine of Braganza*. Publications of the Lincoln Record Society, Vol. 112. Woodbridge: Boydell and Brewer, 2024.

Heuvel, Danielle van den. 'New Products, New Sellers? Changes in the Dutch Textile Trades, c.1650–1750'. In *Selling Textiles in the Long Eighteenth Century: Comparative Perspectives from Western Europe*. Edited by Jon Stobart and Bruno Blondé, 118–37. London: Palgrave Macmillan UK, 2014.

Heuvel, Danielle van den and Sheilagh Ogilvie. 'Retail Development in the Consumer Revolution: The Netherlands, C. 1670–C. 1815'. *Explorations in Economic History* 50, no. 1 (2013): 69–87.

Hibbard, Caroline. '"By Our Directions and for Our Use": The Queen's Patronage of Artists and Artisans'. In *Henrietta Maria: Piety, Politics and Patronage*. Edited by Erin Griffey, 115–37. Farnham: Ashgate, 2008.

Hibbard, Caroline M. 'Henrietta Maria [Princess Henrietta Maria of France] (1609–1669), queen of England, Scotland, and Ireland, consort of Charles I'. *Oxford Dictionary of National Biography*, 23 September 2004, https://doi.org/10.1093/ref:odnb/12947.

Holford, Christopher, ed. *A Chat About the Broderers' Company*. London: George Allen & Sons, 1910.

Holme, Randle. *The Academy of Armory, or, A Storehouse of Armory and Blazon*. Chester: Randle Holme, 1688.

Hubbard, Eleanor. *City Women: Money, Sex, and the Social Order in Early Modern London*. Oxford: Oxford University Press, 2012.

Hunt, Margaret R. and Alexandra Shepard. 'Introduction: Producing Change'. In *The Whole Economy: Work and Gender in Early Modern Europe*. Edited by Catriona Macleod, Alexandra Shepard and Maria Ågren, 1–25. Cambridge: Cambridge University Press, 2023.

Illes, Angelina. 'The Fascination with Japanese-Styled Gowns: A Quantitative Perspective on Ready-Made Garments at the Beginning of the Eighteenth Century'. *Journal of Historians of Netherlandish Art* 15, no. 1 (2023). DOI: 10.5092/jhna.2023.15.1.5.

Inder, Pam. *Busks, Basques and Brush-Braid: British Dressmaking in the 18th and 19th Centuries*. London: Bloomsbury, 2020.

Israel, Jonathan. 'The Courts of the House of Orange, C. 1580–1795'. In *The Princely Courts of Europe 1500–1750*. Edited by John Adamson, 119–39. London: Weidenfeld and Nicolson, 1999.

Jordan, Ellen. *The Women's Movement and Women's Employment in Nineteenth Century Britain*. London: Routledge, 1999.

Keene, D. J. and Vanessa Harding, *Historical Gazetteer of London Before the Great Fire Cheapside; Parishes of All Hallows Honey Lane, St Martin Pomary, St Mary Le Bow, St Mary Colechurch and St Pancras Soper Lane*. London: Centre for Metropolitan History, 1987.

Keller, Katrin. 'Ladies-in-Waiting at the Imperial Court of Vienna from 1550 to 1700: Structures, Responsibilities and Career Patterns'. In *The Politics of Female Households: Ladies-in-Waiting across Early Modern Europe*. Edited by Nadine Akkerman and Birgit Houben, 73–97. Leiden: Brill, 2013.

Kellett, J. R. 'The Breakdown of Gild and Corporation Control over the Handicraft and Retail Trade in London'. *Economic History Review* 10 (1957): 381–94.

Kishlansky, Mark A. and John Morrill. 'Charles I (1600–1649), King of England, Scotland, and Ireland'. *Oxford Dictionary of National Biography*, 23 September 2004, https://doi.org/10.1093/ref:odnb/5143.

Korda, Natasha. 'Insubstantial Pageants: Women's Work and the (Im)Material Culture of the Early Modern Stage'. *Shakespeare* 7, no. 4 (2011): 413–31.

Korda, Natasha. *Labors Lost: Women's Work and the Early Modern English Stage*. Philadelphia: University of Pennsylvania Press, 2011.

Laughton, J. K. and J. D. Davies. 'Graydon, John (d. 1726), naval officer'. *Oxford Dictionary of National Biography*, 23 September 2004, https://doi.org/10.1093/ref:odnb/11359.

Lee-Whitman, Leanna, 'The Silk Trade: Chinese Silks and the British East India Company'. *Winterthur Portfolio* 17, no. 1 (1982): 21–41.

Lemire, Beverly. '"In the Hands of Work Women": English Markets, Cheap Clothing and Female Labour, 1650–1800'. *Costume* 33, no. 1 (1999): 23–35.

Lemire, Beverly. *The Business of Everyday Life: Gender, Practice and Social Politics in England, c.1600–1900*. Manchester: Manchester University Press, 2005.

Lemire, Beverly. *The British Cotton Trade, 1660–1815, Volume 1*. London: Routledge, 2010.

Lemire, Beverly. 'Fashioning Cottons: Asian Trade, Domestic Industry and Consumer Demand, 1660–1780'. In *The Fashion History Reader: Global Perspectives*. Edited by Giorgio Riello and Peter McNeil, 194–213. London: Routledge, 2010.

Lemire, Beverly. *Global Trade and the Transformation of Consumer Cultures: The Material World Remade, C.1500–1820*. Cambridge: Cambridge University Press, 2018.

Lim, Amy. 'The Furniture Patronage of Elizabeth Seymour (née Percy), Duchess of Somerset, 1667–1722', *Furniture History* 57 (2021): 1–23.

Lim, Amy. 'World of Interiors: Mary II, the Decorative Arts, and Cultural Transfer'. In *Later Stuart Queens, 1660–1735: Religion, Political Culture, and Patronage*. Edited by Eilish Gregory and Michael C. Questier, 175–201. London: Palgrave Macmillan, 2023.

Lim, Amy. 'John van Collema: A Dutch India Goods Merchant in London', in *Close Encounters: Cross-Cultural Exchange between the Low Countries and Britain, 1600–1830*. Edited by Karen Hearn, Angela Jager, Sander Karst, Rieke van Leeuwen, David Taylor and Joanna Woodall (RKD Studies, 2024), https://close-encounters.rkdstudies.nl/9-john-van-collema-a-dutch-india-goods-merchant-in-london/.

Ling, Sofia, Karin Hassan Jansson, Marie Lennersand, Christopher Pihl and Maria Ågren. 'Marriage and Work: Intertwined Sources of Agency and Authority'. In *Making a Living, Making a Difference: Gender and Work in Early Modern European Society*. Edited by Maria Ågren, 80–102. Oxford: Oxford University Press, 2017.

Lockyer, Roger. 'Villiers, George, first duke of Buckingham (1592–1628), royal favourite'. *Oxford Dictionary of National Biography*, 23 September 2004, https://doi.org/10.1093/ref:odnb/28293.

Lussier, Suzanne. '"Habillement De La Dite Dame Reine": An Analysis of the Gowns and Accessories in Queen Henrietta Maria's Trousseau'. *Costume* 52, no. 1 (2018): 26–47.

Luu, Lien Bich. *Immigrants and the Industries of London, 1500–1700*. Farnham: Ashgate, 2005.

Lyon-Whaley, Susannah, ed. *Floral Culture and the Tudor and Stuart Courts*. Amsterdam: Amsterdam University Press, 2024.

Mackie, Erin. 'Lady Credit and the Strange Case of the Hoop-Petticoat'. *College Literature* 20, no. 2 (1993): 27–43.

Mallick, Oliver. 'Clients and Friends: The Ladies-in-Waiting at the Court of Anne of Austria (1615–66)'. In *The Politics of Female Households: Ladies-in-Waiting across Early Modern Europe*. Edited by Nadine Akkerman and Birgit Houben, 231–64. Leiden: Brill, 2013.

Mansell, Charmain. *Female Servants in Early Modern England*. Oxford: Oxford University Press, 2024.

Marly, Diana de. 'Fashionable Suppliers 1660–1700: Leading Tailors and Clothing Tradesmen of the Restoration Period'. *Antiquaries Journal* 58, no. 2 (1978): 333–51.

Marschner, Joanna. 'Mary II: Her Clothes and Textiles'. *Costume* 34, no. 1 (2000): 44–50.

McIntosh, Marjorie K. 'The Benefits and Drawbacks of Femme Sole Status in England, 1300–1630'. *Journal of British Studies* 44 (2005): 410–38.

McKendrick, Neil, John Brewer and J. H. Plumb, eds. *The Birth of a Consumer Society: The Commercialization of Eighteenth-Century England*. Bloomington: Indiana University Press, 1982.

McShane, Angela and Clare Backhouse. 'Top Knots and Lower Sorts: Print and Promiscuous Consumption in the 1690s'. In *Printed Images in Early Modern Britain: Essays in Interpretation*. Edited by Michael Hunter, 337–57. London: Routledge, 2010.

Melo, João Vicente. 'Catherine of Braganza (1638–1705)'. In *Lives in Transit in Early Modern England*. Edited by Nandini Das, 61–8. Amsterdam: Amsterdam University Press, 2022.

Modesti, Adelina. *Women's Patronage and Gendered Cultural Networks in Early Modern Europe: Vittoria della Rovere, Grand Duchess of Tuscany*. London: Routledge, 2019.

Morrison, Rebecca. '(Re)Making Mantuas: From Seamstresses to Mantuamakers'. Online lecture. *Sartorial Society Series*, 10 December 2020.

Morrison, Rebecca. 'Unpicking process: experiments in recreating and reimagining the methods of making'. Keynote lecture at Workshop Three. Learning from Making: Methods and Processes, *Making Historical Dress Network*, 18 March 2023, https://makinghistoricaldress.dmu.ac.uk/Workshop-Three.html.

Morton, Adam. 'Introduction: Politics, Culture and Queens Consort'. In *Queens Consort, Cultural Transfer and European Politics, C. 1500–1800*. Edited by Helen Watanabe-O'Kelly and Adam Morton, 1–14. London: Routledge, 2017.

Muldrew, Craig. '"A Mutual Assent of Her Mind?" Women, Debt, Litigation and Contract in Early Modern England'. *History Workshop Journal* 55, no. 1 (2003): 47–71.

Murdoch, Steve. *Britain, Denmark-Norway and the House of Stuart, 1603–1660: A Diplomatic and Military Analysis*. East Linton: Tuckwell Press, 2000.

Nicholson, Annalisa. 'Like Mother, like Daughter: Hortense Mancini, Duchesse de Mazarin, and Marie-Charlotte de La Porte-Mazarin, Marquise de Richelieu'. *Early Modern Women* 16, no. 1 (2021): 14–35.

North, Susan. 'Indian Gowns and Banyans – New Evidence and Perspectives'. *Costume* 54, no. 1 (2020): 30–55.

North, Susan. *Sweet and Clean? Bodies and Clothes in Early Modern England*. Oxford: Oxford University Press, 2020.

North, Susan and Jenny Tiramani, eds. *Seventeenth-Century Women's Dress Patterns: Book One*. London: V&A Publishing, 2011.

Paul, K. Tawny. 'Accounting for Men's Work: Multiple Employments and Occupational Identities in Early Modern England'. *History Workshop Journal* 85 (2018): 26–46.

Payne, M. T. W. 'An Inventory of Queen Anne of Denmark's "Ornaments, Furniture, Householde Stuffe, and Other Parcells" at Denmark House, 1619'. *Journal of the History of Collections* 13, no. 1 (2001): 23–44.

Pearce, Michael. 'Anna of Denmark: Fashioning a Danish Court in Scotland'. *Court Historian* 24, no. 2 (2019): 138–51.

Persson, Fabian. 'Living in the House of Power: Women at the Early Modern Swedish Court'. In *The Politics of Female Households: Ladies-in-Waiting across Early Modern Europe*. Edited by Nadine Akkerman and Birgit Houben, 343–63. Leiden: Brill, 2013.

Persson, Fabian. *Women at the Early Modern Swedish Court: Power, Risk, and Opportunity*. Amsterdam: Amsterdam University Press, 2021.

Pitcher, John. 'Samuel Daniel's Masque "The Vision of the Twelve Goddesses": Texts and Payments'. *Medieval & Renaissance Drama in England* 26 (2013): 17–42.

Pollock, Linda A. 'Childbearing and Female Bonding in Early Modern England'. *Social History* 22, no. 3 (1997): 286–306.

Poska, Allyson M. 'The Case for Agentic Gender Norms for Women in Early Modern Europe'. *Gender & History* 30, no. 2 (2018): 354–65.

Randall, Elizabeth. 'A special case? London's French Protestants'. In *A History of the French in London: Liberty, Equality, Opportunity*. Edited by Debra Kelly and Martyn Cornick, 13–42. London: University of London Press, 2013.

Rawcliffe, Carole. 'A Marginal Occupation? The Medieval Laundress and Her Work'. *Gender & History* 21, no. 1 (2009): 147–69.

Rekrut, Ala. 'Material Literacy: Reading Records as Material Culture'. *Archivaria* 60 (2006): 11–37.

Reynolds, Anna. *In Fine Style: The Art of Tudor and Stuart Fashion*. London: Royal Collection, 2013.

Ribeiro, Aileen. *Fashion and Fiction: Dress in Art and Literature in Stuart England*. New Haven, CT: Yale University Press, 2005.

Riello, Giorgio. *Cotton: The Fabric That Made the Modern World*. Cambridge: Cambridge University Press, 2013.

Riley, W. Edward and Laurence Gomme, eds. *Survey of London: Volume 5, St Giles-in-The-Fields, Pt II*. London: London County Council, 1914.

Robinson, Michele Nicole. 'Dirty Laundry: Caring for Clothing in Early Modern Italy'. *Costume* 55, no. 1 (2021): 3–23.

Sainty, J. C., Lydia Wassmann and R. O. Bucholz. 'Household of Queen (from 1685 Queen Dowager) Catherine 1660–1705'. *Database of Court Officers: 1660–1837*, http://courtofficers.ctsdh.luc.edu/indices/Index%2002%20Household%20of%20Queen%20Catherine%201662b.pdf.

Sanderson, Elizabeth. 'The "New Dresses": A Look at How Mantuamaking Became Established in Scotland'. *Costume* 35, no.1 (2001): 14–23.

Santaliestra, Laura Oliván. 'Isabel of Borbón's Sartorial Politics: From French Princess to Habsburg Regent'. In *Early Modern Habsburg Women*. Edited by Anne J. Cruz and Maria Galli Stampino, 224–42. London: Routledge, 2013.

Sarti, Cathleen. 'Introduction: Women and Economic Power in Premodern Royal Courts'. In *Women and Economic Power in Premodern Royal Courts*. Edited by Cathleen Sarti, 1–8. York: ARC Humanities Press, 2020.

Sarti, Raffaella, Anna Bellavitis and Manuela Martini. 'Introduction'. In *What Is Work? Gender at the Crossroads of Home, Family, and Business from the Early Modern Era to the Present*. Edited by Raffaella Sarti, Anna Bellavitis and Manuela Martini, 1–84. New York: Berghahn Books, 2018.

Saunders, Ann. *The Royal Exchange*. London: London Topographical Society, 1997.

Schwarz, L. D. *London in the Age of Industrialisation: Entrepreneurs, Labour Force and Living Conditions, 1700–1850*. Cambridge: Cambridge University Press, 1992.

Seel, G. E. and David L. Smith. *The Early Stuart Kings, 1603–1642*. London: Routledge, 2001.

Sharpe, Kevin. 'Restoration and Reconstitution: Politics, Society and Culture in the England of Charles II'. In *Painted Ladies: Women at the Court of Charles II*. Edited by Catharine MacLeod and Julia Marciari Alexander, 10–23. London: National Portrait Gallery, 2001.

Sharpe, Kevin. '"Thy Longing Country's Darling and Desire": Aesthetics, Sex, and Politics in the England of Charles II'. In *Politics, Transgression, and Representation at the Court of Charles II*. Edited by Julia Marciari Alexander and Catharine MacLeod, 1–32. New Haven, CT: Yale University Press, 2007.

Sharpe, Kevin. *Rebranding Rule: The Restoration and Revolution Monarchy, 1660–1714*. New Haven, CT: Yale University Press, 2013.

Shepard, Alexandra. *Accounting for Oneself: Worth, Status, and the Social Order in Early Modern England*. Oxford: Oxford University Press, 2015.

Shepard, Alexandra. 'Care'. In *The Whole Economy: Work and Gender in Early Modern Europe*. Edited by Catriona Macleod, Alexandra Shepard and Maria Ågren, 53–83. Cambridge: Cambridge University Press, 2023.

Simonton, Deborah. *A History of European Women's Work: 1700 to the Present*. London: Routledge, 1998.

Simonton, Deborah. 'Milliners and Marchandes De Modes: Gender, Creativity and Skill in the Workplace'. In *Luxury and Gender in European Towns, 1700–1914*. Edited by Deborah Simonton, Marjo Kaartinen and Anne Montenach, 19–38. London: Routledge, 2015.

Smith, Kate. 'Sensing Design and Workmanship: The Haptic Skills of Shoppers in Eighteenth-Century London'. *Journal of Design History* 25, no. 1 (2012): 1–10.

Smith, Woodruff D. *Consumption and the Making of Respectability, 1600–1800*. London: Routledge, 2002.

Smuts, R. Malcolm. 'Art and Material Culture of Majesty'. In *The Stuart Court and Europe: Essays in Politics and Political Culture*. Edited by R. Malcolm Smuts, 86–112. Cambridge: Cambridge University Press, 1996.

Smuts, R. Malcolm. 'The Structure of the Court and the Roles of the Artist and Poet under Charles I'. *Court Historian* 9, no. 2 (2004): 103–17.

Smuts, R. Malcolm. 'Religion, European Politics and Henrietta Maria's Circle, 1625–41'. In *Henrietta Maria: Piety, Politics and Patronage*. Edited by Erin Griffey, 13–38. Farnham: Ashgate: 2008.

Somerset, Anne. *Queen Anne: The Politics of Passion*. London: HarperPress, 2012.

Sorge-English, Lynn. *Stays and Body Image in London: The Staymaking Trade, 1680–1810*. London: Routledge, 2011.

Spufford, Margaret and Susan Mee, *The Clothing of the Common Sort: 1570–1700*. Oxford: Oxford University Press, 2017.

Steele, Valerie. *Paris Fashion: A Cultural History*. [Revised edition.]. New York: Bloomsbury USA, 2017.

Stobart, Jon. 'A History of Shopping: The Missing Link between Retail and Consumer Revolutions'. *Journal of Historical Research in Marketing* 2, no. 3 (2010): 342–9.

Stobart, Jon. 'Who Were the Urban Gentry? Social Elites in an English Provincial Town, c. 1680–1760'. *Continuity and Change* 26, no. 1 (2011): 89–112.

Styles, John. *The Dress of the People: Everyday Fashion in Eighteenth-Century England*. New Haven, CT: Yale University Press, 2007.

Styles, John. 'Fashion and Innovation in Early Modern Europe'. In *Fashioning the Early Modern: Dress, Textiles, and Innovation in Europe, 1500–1800*. Edited by Evelyn Welch, 33–55. Oxford: Oxford University Press, 2017.

Styles, John. 'Transformations in Textiles, 1400–1760'. In *Refashioning the Renaissance: Everyday Dress and the Reconstruction of Early Modern Material Culture, 1550–1650*. Edited by Paula Hohti, 27–63. Manchester: Manchester University Press, 2025.

Styles, John and Amanda Vickery. 'Introduction'. In *Gender, Taste, and Material Culture in Britain and North America, 1700–1830*. Edited by John Styles and Amanda Vickery, 1–36. New Haven, CT: Yale University Press, 2006.

Sutton, Anne. 'Two Dozen and More Silkwomen of Fifteenth-Century London'. *Ricardian* 16 (2006): 1–8.

Sutton, Anne F. *The Mercery of London: Trade, Goods and People, 1130–1578*. Farnham: Ashgate Publishing, 2005.

Tankard, Danae. *Clothing in 17th-Century Provincial England*. London: Bloomsbury, 2019.

Taylor, Emily. 'Gendered making and material knowledge: Tailors and mantua-makers, c. 1760–1820'. In *Material Literacy in Eighteenth-Century Britain: A Nation of Makers*. Edited by Serena Dyer and Chloe Wigston Smith, 151–72. London: Bloomsbury Visual Arts, 2020.

Thompson, A. T. *Memoirs of Sarah, Duchess of Marlborough, and of the Court of Queen Anne, Volume 1*. London: Henry Colburn, 1839.

Thornbury, Walter. *Old and New London, Volume 1*. London: Cassell, Petter & Galpin, 1878.

Thornton, Peter. 'The "Bizarre" Silks'. *Burlington Magazine* 100, no. 665 (1958): 265–70.

Tiramani, Jenny. 'Janet Arnold and the Globe Wardrobe: Handmade Clothes for Shakespeare's Actors'. *Costume* 34, no. 1 (2000): 118–22.

Tooke, Ruth Battersby, Claire Jowitt, Benjamin W. D. Redding and Francesca Vanke. *The Last Voyage of the Gloucester: Norfolk's Royal Shipwreck, 1682*. Norwich: Barnwell Print Ltd, 2023.

Toynbee, Margaret R., 'William Duke of Gloucester and Camden House Kensington'. *Notes and Queries* 192, no. 12 (1947): 244–8.

Trigg, Stephanie. '"Ye Louely Ladyes with Youre Longe Fyngres": The Silkwomen of Medieval London'. *Studia Anglica Posnaniensia: International Review of English Studies* 38 (2002): 469–84.

Trueman, W. 'The First Mantua-Makers in Durham'. *Archaeologia Aeliana* 2 (1858): 165–70.

Varela Flor, Susana. 'Que Las Riquezas Del Mundo Parecian Estar Alli Cifradas: Los Festejos De Boda De Catalina De Braganza En El Contexto De La Restauración Portuguesa (1661–1662)'. *Archivo Español De Arte* 88, no. 350 (2015): 141–56.

Vincent, Susan. *Dressing the Elite: Clothes in Early Modern England*. Oxford: Berg, 2003.

Vitis, Mark de. 'Sartorial Transgression as Socio-Political Collaboration: Madame and the Hunt'. *Konsthistorisk tidskrift / Journal of Art History* 82, no. 3 (2013): 205–18.

Wallace, Charles William. 'Shakespeare and His London Associates as Revealed in Recently Discovered Documents'. *University Studies* 10, no. 4 (1910): 261–356.

Ward, Joseph P. *Metropolitan Communities: Trade Guilds, Identity, and Change in Early Modern London*. Stanford, CA: Stanford University Press, 1997.

Wardle, Patricia. '"Divers Necessaries for His Majesty's Use and Service": Seamstresses to the Stuart Kings'. *Costume* 31, no. 1 (1997): 16–27.

Waugh, Norah. *The Cut of Women's Clothes, 1600–1930*. London: Faber, 1973.

Weatherill, Lorna. 'The Meaning of Consumer Behaviour in Late Seventeenth- and Early Eighteenth-century England'. In *Consumption and the World of Goods*. Edited by John Brewer and Roy Porter, 206–27. London: Routledge, 1994.

Webster, Jeremy W. *Performing Libertinism in Charles II's Court: Politics, Drama, Sexuality*. London: Palgrave Macmillian, 2005.

Westman, Annabel, 'William Elliot "the laceman", 164? –1728'. *Furniture History* 50 (2014): 89–102.

Whittle, Jane and Elizabeth Griffiths. *Consumption and Gender in the Early Seventeenth-Century Household: The World of Alice Le Strange*. Oxford: Oxford University Press, 2012.

Whittle, Jane and Mark Hailwood. 'The Gender Division of Labour in Early Modern England'. *Economic History Review* 73, no. 1 (2020): 3–32.

Wiesner-Hanks, Merry E. 'Gender and Social Structures'. In *Interpreting Early Modern Europe*. Edited by C. Scott Dixon and Beat Kümin, 72–92. London: Routledge, 2020.

Wiesner-Hanks, Merry E. 'Women's Agency: Then and Now'. *Parergon* 40, no. 2 (2023): 9–25.

Winn, James Anderson. *Queen Anne: Patroness of Arts*. Oxford: Oxford University Press, 2014.

Working, Lauren. 'Anna of Denmark (1574–1619)'. In *Lives in Transit in Early Modern England*. Edited by Nandini Das, 47–54. Amsterdam: Amsterdam University Press, 2022.

Wrightson, Keith. 'The Social Order of Early-Modern England: Three Approaches'. In *The World We Have Gained: Histories of Population and Social Structure*. Edited by Lloyd Bonfield, Richard Michael Smith, Keith Wrightson and Peter Laslett, 177–202. Oxford: B. Blackwell, 1986.

Wrightson, Keith. *Earthly Necessities: Economic Lives in Early Modern Britain, 1470–1750*. London: Penguin, 2002.

Wunder, Heide. *He Is the Sun, She Is the Moon: Women in Early Modern Germany*. Translated by Thomas Dunlap. Cambridge, MA: Harvard University Press, 1998.

Wynne, Sonya. '"The Brightest Glories of the British Sphere": Women at the Court of Charles II'. In *Painted Ladies: Women at the Court of Charles II*. Edited by Catharine MacLeod and Julia Marciari Alexander, 37–49. London: National Portrait Gallery, 2001.

Wynne, S. M. 'Catherine [Catherine of Braganza, Catarina Henriqueta De Bragança] (1638–1705), Queen of England, Scotland, and Ireland, Consort of Charles II'. *Oxford Dictionary of National Biography*, 23 September 2004, https://doi.org/10.1093/ref:odnb/4894.

Unpublished MA and PhD theses

Birt, Sarah. 'A Fashionable Business: Seamstresses, Mantua-Makers, and Milliners in Seventeenth and Eighteenth Century London'. PhD diss., Birkbeck, University of London, 2021.

Brinkman, Emilie M. 'Sex, Culture, and the Politics of Fashion in Stuart England'. PhD diss., Purdue University, 2018.

Fryman, Olivia. 'Making the Bed: The Practice, Role and Significance of Housekeeping in the Royal Bedchambers at Hampton Court Palace 1689–1737'. PhD diss., Kingston University, 2011.

Keay, Anna. 'The Ceremonies of Charles II's Court'. PhD diss., Queen Mary University of London, 2004.

Kesterton, Zara. 'The Rise of France's First "Minister of Fashion", Marie-Jeanne Bertin, 1760–1789'. MPhil diss., University of Cambridge, 2020.

Merton, Charlotte. 'The Women Who Served Queen Mary and Queen Elizabeth: Ladies, Gentlewomen and Maids of the Privy Chamber, 1553–1603'. PhD diss., University of Cambridge, 1992.

Morrison, Rebecca. 'The Rise of the English Mantua-Maker in the Long Eighteenth Century'. PhD diss., Queen Mary University of London, 2024.

Payne, Helen Margaret. 'Aristocratic Women and the Jacobean Court, 1603–1625'. PhD diss., University of London, 2001.

Pitman, Sophie Jane. 'The Making of Clothing and the Making of London, 1560–1660'. PhD diss., University of Cambridge, 2017.

Sleigh-Johnson, Nigel Victor. 'The Merchant-Taylors Company of London, 1580–1645, with Special Reference to Politics and Government'. PhD diss., University College London, 1989.

Index

Abrahall, Elizabeth, starcher 79, 207, 209, 238, 310
accessories
    aprons 104, 141, 147, 153, 198, 248
    bands *see* collars
    caps 143, 194–5
    cauls 138
    coifs 125, 139–41, 207, 246–8
    collars 24, 26, 28–9, 31, 84–5, 103, 141, 193, 201, 204,
        246–8, *see also* ruffs
    commode *see* fontange
    cornets 111, 125, 141, 248
    cravats 41, 44
    cuffs 85–6, 114, 116, 140, 143, 193, 204, 246, 248, 250
    engageantes 149–50, 248
    fans 38, 39, 47, 84, 85, 103–4, 108, 111–14, 116, 122,
        126, 129, 181, 191, 193
    fontanges 47, 106–8, 142–3, 249
    garters 103–4, 114, 141, 149, 247, 249–50
    girdles 35, 103–4, 114, 140, 247–50
    gloves 37–8, 84–5, 103–4, 111–12, 113–14, 129, 149,
        169, 181–2, 246–9
    handkerchiefs 119, 138, 141, 210, 246–8, 250
    hats 42, 103–4, 181, 183, 246–8
    headcloth 207
    headdress 71, 123, 140, 193–4, 196–7, 246
    hoods 35, 38, 84, 107, 110, 112, 114, 122, 125, 248–50
    hose 247–50
    jewellery 23, 25–7, 29, 46, 57, 64, 71, 89, 119, 154, 194,
        196–7, 207–8, 251–2
    kerchiefs 84, 104, 119, 138, 141, 210, 246–8, 250
    lappets 111, 143
    masks 85, 104, 110, 114, 126, 181, 247, 250
    muffs 38, 104, 108, 112, 114, 181, 248–50
    neckcloths 84, 248, 250
    palatines 112, 114, 122, 248–9
    paper patches 84, 111, 126, 188–90, 249–50
    rebatos 138
    ruffles 84, 110, 141, 143, 149, 210, 248–50
    ruffs 138, 193, 201, 204–5, 246
    scarves 84, 104, 108, 110, 114, 125, 181, 246–50
    shoes 38, 43, 110, 247–50
    socks 141, 248, 297
    sorties 125, 249
    steinkirks 250
    suits for the head 110–11, 114, 125, 140–1, 207, 209,
        248–50
    surtouts 141
    tippets 112, 114, 248–50
    tires 193–7, 246
    topknots *see* fontange
    tuckers 143, 250
    veils 84, 114, 138, 207, 247–8
agentic gender norms 9–10
Ågren, Maria 9
Akkerman, Nadine 11
alderman 98–9
Aldworth, Margaret, widow 76, 99, 222
Alexander, Mary, milliner and mantua-maker 86,
       147, 149, 152, 157–9, 163, 165–6, 168–74,
       217, 225
Americas
    Brazil 39
    North America 12, 46, 257
    West Indies 123
Anglo-Dutch relations 45, 51, 66, 68, 71
Anna of Denmark, Queen Consort 2, 4, 22–7, 34, 64, 71,
       85, 194
    clothing of 22–7, 74, 83–4, 104, 139, 189, 193, 206,
       246
    household and wardrobe administration 18, 23,
       62–5, 71, 74, 83, 90, 178–9, 181–2, 185–6, 204
    queen consort of Scotland 23, 63

tradespeople to 6, 81–2, 97–100, 103–4, 112, 138, 141, 143, 193, 204, 206–7, 219–21
Anne, Queen of England and Great Britain 1–2, 4, 51–9, 89, 91, 141, 149, 151, 153–4, 181, 188, 200, 208–9, 213
    clothing of 1, 51–9, 71–2, 83–4, 89, 92, 116, 143, 149, 154–5, 188, 195–6, 200, 250
    coronation 51, 149, 195–6
    household and wardrobe administration 18–19, 52, 65, 68–71, 74, 83, 87, 91–3, 179, 181–2, 201, 208–9
    Lady Anne 41–2, 70, 110, 122, 125, 127
    patronage 6, 54–5
    Princess of Denmark 44, 46, 52, 70, 74, 87, 106, 108, 170
    tradespeople to 13–14, 53, 55, 80–2, 85, 103–4, 116, 119, 122, 129, 141, 143, 149, 151–2, 154–6, 165, 194–8, 206–7, 210, 213, 216, 238–43
apothecaries 185, 228
apprenticeship 12, 14, 32, 98–9, 122, 138, 151–2, 161–3, 173–4, 196, 204, 209, 217
Arnold, Janet 160
Arnoult, Nicolas 111, 157–8, 169
Ashelford, Jane 106
Ashton, Hugh, Clerk of the Robes 79, 91
Atkinson, Elizabeth, Laundress of the Body 213, 216, 238
Atkinson, Joseph, milliner 85, 104, 222

Backhouse, Flower, Countess of Clarendon 91, 126
Baillon, Frances, tirewoman 194, 196, 238
Banks, Elizabeth, petticoat-maker 1, 149, 156, 238
Bardou, Jacques, tailor 29, 143, 222
Barne, John, gownman 153, 225
Barroll, Leeds 90
bathing practices 188, 190, 201
Bathurst, Lady Frances 87, 89
beau monde 6, 87, 128, 216
Becker, Ellen, tailor 147–8, 154, 156, 162, 232
Bedchamber 17, 61, 64, 83, 91, 179, 182, 185–6, 191–2, 201, 209, 214–16
    Gentlemen of 64
    Ladies of 63–5, 66, 70, 79, 84, 86, 90, 127, 185, 190–1, 196
    members of 6, 190, 206–7, 209, 226
    Page of 208
    Ushers 17, 181

    Women of 86, 178, 182, 190–1, 196, 200, 209, 214, 226
    see also dressers, Groom of the Stole, necessary women
beds 84, 117, 119, 185–6
Bellavitis, Anna 151
Bellings, Lady Frances, dresser 84, 182
Bellings, Sir Richard, secretary 18, 84, 161
Bennet, Isabella, Countess of Arlington, Mistress of the Robes 65–8, 72, 75, 80, 86, 90–1, 179, 185
Bennett, Judith 156
Birt, Sarah 12, 161
Bonnart, Henri 40, 108
Bord, Madame de, pedlar woman 113, 225
Bosse, Abraham 85–6
Bourbon dynasty 27–8, 31, 54
Boyle, Elizabeth, Countess of Guildford, Mistress of the Robes 65
Braithwaite, Richard 6
brushers 17, 63, 182, 201–2
Bucholz, R. O. 5, 10, 51, 53
Buck, Anne 160
Burton, Deborah, milliner 121–2, 225
business
    families 79, 96, 99, 114, 121–2, 133, 193
    networks 97, 121, 128, 131, 129–33
    opportunities 81, 97, 149
    partnerships 157–8, 168–73, 311–12
    women 9, 14, 99–100, 120–2, 125–6, 134, 136–7, 157, 161, 163, 216–17

Campbell, Robert 143
Carew, Lady Thomazine, Mistress of the Sweet Coffers 182
Carey, Elizabeth, Countess of Monmouth, Mistress of the Sweet Coffers 182
Catherine of Braganza, Queen Consort 32–41, 51, 87, 113, 201
    clothing of 32–42, 84, 86–7, 106, 141, 146, 149, 161, 164, 166, 169–70, 188, 195, 197, 248
    household and wardrobe administration 18, 35, 38–9, 65, 73–5, 80–1, 85, 178–9, 181–3, 187, 191–2, 195, 202–5, 207–9
    influence on fashion 39, 41, 170
    tradespeople to 14, 84–6, 103–4, 113–14, 119, 122, 125, 141, 143, 147, 149, 152–4, 156, 159, 161, 163–4, 166, 169, 172–4, 225–30
Cavendish, William, Duke of Devonshire 133

Chamberlayne, Edward 146
Charles I, King of England and Scotland 18, 27–9, 32–3,
     64, 99, 208
  tradespeople to 207, 221–4
Charles II, King of England and Scotland 28, 33–7, 39,
     41, 51, 64, 73, 91, 100, 114, 161, 178–9, 185, 201,
     203, 208, 222, 226–7
  clothing of 35, 39, 114, 164
  mistresses of 33, 35, 38, 41, 119, 170
  tradespeople to 114, 164, 208, 229–31, 237, 240
Cheret, Marie, of the French Shop 8, 14, 104, 113–14,
     121, 125, 226
Cheret, Thomas, milliner 106, 114, 121, 125, 197, 210–1,
     233
Chico, Tita 185
Chiffinch, Dorothy, Laundress of the Body 208–9, 211
Chiffinch, Mary, Laundress of the Body 203, 208–9,
     211
China 39, 117–18
  Canton 117
  goods from 45, 55, 11–19, 132, 186
Churchill, John, Duke of Marlborough 8, 71, 239
Churchill, Sarah, Duchess of Marlborough 8, 51, 68–71,
     73, 196, 207–9
  influence on fashion 6, 55, 62, 87–9, 95, 119, 217
  Mistress of the Robes 19, 63, 65, 72–3, 75, 79, 80–1,
     83, 89, 216
  work and identity 63, 89, 90, 91–3
  relationship with tradespeople 119, 127–8, 157, 207,
     213
  tradespeople to 156–7, 159, 170
Clark, Alice 7–8
clerks 10, 63, 71, 75, 79, 80, 91, 161, 185
  see also Office of the Robes
Clifton, Anne, mantua-maker 1, 151–2, 154–6, 164, 213,
     216, 238
clothing
  altering 23, 29, 149, 153–5, 173
  cleanliness 84, 201
  delivery of 35, 63, 74–5, 79, 83, 85, 99, 141, 152,
     182–3, 196, 203
  dry cleaning 201–2
  fitting 152, 157
  gifting of 29, 35, 71, 84–85, 182, 207
  laundering 177, 193, 202–10
  mending 138, 141, 161, 202, 204, 206, 208
  remaking 206, 209–10
  storage of 179–86, 198, 202, 207

  transportation of 75, 181
  see also garments, shopping
coiffeuse *see* tirewoman
Colbert, Jean-Baptiste 35, 116, 257
Collema, John van, merchant 45, 233, 239
colonization 3, 39, 46, 119
consumption
  changing 5–6, 81–2, 96, 117, 151, 214
  consumer revolution 3, 13, 32, 96, 216
  gender 11, 82
  producer/consumer binary 82–3
  urban sites of 5, 8, 96, 100–3, 112–21
  women 3, 8, 11, 13, 39, 82–3
Cooke, Marie, milliner 74–5, 104, 219
Cooper, Richard, mercer 125–6, 233
coronation 15, 149, 195–6
  coronation portraits 51
  coronation robes 1–2, 22, 41, 47, 154
  see also Anne, Queen of England and Great Britain
cosmetics 112, 185, 189, 200
courts, royal
  administration 10, 15–19, 80, 152
  anti-court 32
  ceremony 6, 51, 73, 185, 193
  corruption 54
  court-city connections 3, 5–7, 46, 81, 85–6, 90, 96–8,
     100, 123, 159, 214–16
  courtiers 5, 9, 12, 21, 29, 32, 83, 85, 119, 126, 128–9,
     170
  culture 21–3
  Danish 22–3, 25, 27, 63
  decline 6, 532
  dress 6, 25, 31–2, 42, 46, 87, 159, 167, 169, 170, 194
  French 6, 28–30, 35, 42, 157–8, 185
  Georgian 6
  Habsburg 64
  masques 22, 83, 193,
  offices 8, 10–12, 16–17, 61–2, 71, 79–80, 182,
     207–8
  Orange-Nassau 45–7, 66, 188–9
  patronage 3, 5–6, 20, 22–3, 27, 31–2, 87, 96, 136, 206,
     214–18
  Portuguese 33, 41
  Scottish 23, 63–4
  Swedish 63
  Tudor 23, 25, 63–4, 74, 97, 178, 207, 216
  women 3, 9–12, 20, 42, 46, 61–2, 73, 83, 90, 177–8,
     214–18

see also dynasties of service, Mistress of the Robes, Mistress of the Sweet Coffers, Office of the Robes
Cousein, Antoine, staymaker 53, 154, 239
couturières 20, 135–6, 157–8, 160–1, 166–8, 170–5, 217
couverture 14, 170, 193
Craddock, Sarah, milliner and Indian woman 119, 133, 239
credit
 financial credit 12, 97, 103, 121, 125
 litigation over 125–6
 royal creditors 29, 96–7
 social capital 123, 174
Crowston, Clare Haru 99, 135, 159
Cupper, Matthias, linen draper 121, 141, 226

de Calvaert, Barbara Anna, seamstress 141, 226
de Larmessin, Nicolas 104–5, 166–7, 196–9
de Marly, Diana 156
de Vries, Jan 8
Denmark 22–3, 25–7, 51, 63, 155, 207
Devet, Mary, milliner and Indian woman 8, 95, 119–20, 123, 125, 133, 186, 226, 233, 239
drapers 76, 99, 121, 141, 162
dressers 63, 84, 178, 191–2, 196, 200, 207, 209
dressing 63–4, 103, 177–8, 190, 193, 205–7
 dressing room 46, 178, 185–7, 193, 200
 dressing table 186–9
 looking glasses 181, 185
 toilette 184, 186–8, 190, 196, 200, 201
 vanity set 186–90
 see also dressers
Ducaila, Mary, tirewoman 1, 14, 194–8, 200, 227, 239
Dugan, Holly 182
Duncane, James, tailor 79, 81, 143, 220
Dutch East India Company (VOC) 39, 45, 116–17
Dutch Republic 3, 33–4, 39, 45–6, 51
 Amsterdam 132
 Delft 45
 The Hague 35, 45, 47, 79
Dyer, Serena 83, 165
dynasties of service 71, 178, 206–11, 213

Earle, Peter 7, 13
East Indies 39, 55
 fashion for 41, 96, 123, 132
 goods 5, 8, 112–21
 merchants 118

retailers 87, 116, 119–21, 123, 125, 129–33
textiles 55, 117, 119, 146
trade 39, 55, 118, 214
see also Dutch East India Company, English East India Company, Indian
economic
 agents 61–2
 change 3, 57, 152, 215
 policies 35, 39, 55, 116, 118, 120
economies
 care 177, 205–6
 global 7–8
 household 7, 61, 73, 79, 82
 local 7, 11, 22
 women's contribution to 7–10, 12–14, 79, 125, 214
Elizabeth I, Queen of England 23, 25, 63–4, 71, 83, 97, 112, 138, 141, 179, 182, 206–7
Elliot, Elizabeth, laundress and seamstress 181, 207
Elliot, Julian, seamstress 207, 209
embroiderers 23, 29, 55, 62, 84, 117, 139, 141, 154, 164, 220–1, 223–4, 231, 235, 238, 240–2
embroidery 25, 29, 35, 37, 41, 43, 46, 74, 84, 106, 139–40, 162, 173, 184, 201–2, 206–7, 246–50
England
 Bath 181
 Bristol 136
 Chester 136
 Durham 161
 Holywell House, St Albans 8, 128, 215
 Portsmouth 34, 87, 119, 186
 see also London, palaces
English Civil Wars 6, 27–8, 32–3, 99, 178, 207–8
 Wars of the Three Kingdoms 18, 27, 33
English East India Company 39, 99, 116
Erickson, Amy 7, 12
Evelyn, John 39–40, 46, 91, 113, 185–7
Evelyn, Mary 46

fame 68, 87, 95, 96, 122–3, 133, 156, 173
Farguson, Julie 45
farthingale-maker 6, 29, 220
fashion
 advice 83–5, 86–9, 93, 106, 157, 170, 174, 291
 cycle 5, 46, 106, 143
 dissemination 6–7, 11, 19, 28, 30–2, 35–7, 39, 46–7, 53, 85, 95, 113, 166–7, 174, 217
 dolls 38, 113, 146–7, 163–4
 Dutch 34, 39, 45–7, 83–4

French 3, 19, 29–32, 34–5, 37–8, 40–1, 46–8, 51, 53–4, 57–9, 84, 106–7, 112–4, 134, 170–1, 214, 217

Innovation 5–6, 8, 21

Knowledge 11, 15, 41, 62, 81, 89, 136, 161, 173–4, 204

leaders of 6, 31–2, 59, 62, 70, 83, 87, 218

novelty 3, 5–6, 8, 96, 106, 112–21, 133–4, 160, 217

press 5, 35, 38, 47, 53, 59, 113–14, 116, 144, 157, 164–5

prints 19, 30, 35, 38, 40, 46–8, 59, 104–8, 111, 113, 144, 158, 167–9, 188–9, 198–9

trends 5–6, 22, 31–2, 34, 53, 59, 62, 96, 103, 112–21, 160

feather dressers/makers 112, 220, 223

Feilding, Basil 85

Feilding, Susan, Countess of Denbigh, Mistress of the Robes 64–6, 71, 75, 79, 80, 84–5, 91, 181

Feilding, William, Earl of Denbigh 65, 71

feme sole 14, 125, 129, 151

Ferand, Jeanne, milliner 113, 227, 230

Ferguson, Mary 123, 233

Fiebranz, Rosemarie 9

Field, Jemma 22–3, 194

financial

accounting 12, 18–9, 35, 63, 73–80, 91–2, 172–3

disputes 168, 172–4

literacy 12, 73, 83, 93

management 73–4, 79–81, 91–3

revolution 73

Finch, Daniel, Earl of Nottingham 122–3, 125–6, 129, 131, 133

Lady of the Bedchamber *see* bedchamber

Fitzroy, Isabella, Duchess of Grafton 86, 157, 159, 170–1

France

buying from 29, 31, 35, 37–8, 83–4, 113, 152, 197

exile in 18, 33, 35, 45, 126, 208

monarchy 25, 28, 32

Paris 27, 35, 37–8, 57, 65, 84, 105–6, 113–14, 116, 135, 157, 164–5, 167, 170, 208

trade sanctions on 39, 55

Versailles 35, 37, 186

war with 53–4

see also courts, Bourbon dynasty

French

fashion 3, 23, 25, 29–32, 34–8, 40–1, 46–8, 53, 84, 96, 104–8, 112–16, 161, 164–5, 168

shops 8, 85–6, 113–16

tradespeople 29, 53–5, 96, 104–5, 113, 135–6, 140, 143–4, 147, 152, 157–61, 166–70, 173–5, 193, 196–9

see also couturières, Huguenots, migrants

friendships

across classes 123, 126–8, 157

female 51, 68, 70–1, 87–9, 91, 93, 157, 213–4

tradespeople 151, 213–4

Froide, Amy M. 73

garments

bedgowns 57, 250

bodice 23, 25, 29, 35, 37, 153, 154, 160, 167, 168–9, 246

bodies 23–5, 29, 35, 46, 84, 153, 167, 246, 247–9

camisoles 168–9

chamber gowns 146–7, 156, 159, 167–9, 248, 153, 159–60, 167–9, 248

cloaks 153, 184, 247–8, 250

dust gowns 153, 248

farthingales 24–5, 29, 53, 246–7

gowns 25, 29, 30, 35–6, 50–1, 57, 84, 85, 117, 143, 146, 201, 207, 246–7, 251

guardainfante 34

hoop petticoats 53, 59, 88, 149, 250

hungerlines 29–31, 167, 247

hunting attire 41–2, 44

Indian gowns 14, 39–40, 146–7, 248

jerkins 23, 246

justacorps 29, 41, 138

kirtles 24, 246

loose gowns 35, 37, 53–4, 57, 87, 143, 163, 165–6, 187

mantles 1–2, 71, 84, 140, 146, 153, 246–50

morning gowns 46, 145–7, 153, 156, 159–60, 247, 248–50

mourning clothes 25, 41, 55, 154, 181, 201, 250

night rails 141, 248

nightgowns 23, 39, 41, 46, 50, 55, 57, 147, 153, 156, 159–60, 173, 181, 246–7, 248–50

petticoats 23–4, 29, 34–5, 38, 40, 43, 46, 50, 53–4, 77, 84, 86–7, 106, 108, 110, 113, 117, 139, 146–9, 153–4, 156–7, 159, 162, 163, 167–70, 173, 181, 201, 246–9, 250

shifts 137, 141, 143, 160, 248, 250

shirts 84, 85, 248

sleeves 23, 25, 29146, 153, 84, 138, 140, 143, 207, 246–50

smocks 138, 141, 143, 204, 250

stays 29, 46, 153, 166–7, 249–50
stiff–bodied gowns 36–7, 46, 53, 153, 167, 169, 173, 248–9
stomachers 29, 104, 247–8, 250
sultanes 47–8, 279
wadded gowns 156, 250
waistcoats 23, 29, 34, 41, 57, 74, 84, 139–40, 145–7, 153, 165–7, 169–70, 173, 201, 207, 246–8
weeds 154, 250
zimarra 30
see also mantua gowns, robes of state
Gelin, George, tailor 29, 79, 143, 152, 184, 223
Genty, Charles, embroiderer and cutter 29, 164, 223
gentry 5, 11, 32, 41, 54, 68, 73, 96, 98, 122–3, 129, 143, 163, 191, 203, 206, 268
George, Prince of Denmark and consort of Queen Anne 4, 51, 53
Georgians 6, 57
Glorious Revolution 18, 44, 46–8, 51, 53, 66, 122, 126, 131, 133, 215
Godolphin, Francis, Earl of Godolphin 128
Godolphin, Henrietta, Duchess of Marlborough 127–8
Gowing, Laura 8, 12, 99, 122, 161, 204
Graydon, Elizabeth, milliner 1, 8, 87, 95, 122–3, 125–9, 133, 157, 215, 217, 227, 231, 234, 240, 254
Great Wardrobe 15, 19, 23, 63, 97, 138, 181, 206
    Master of 71
Griffey, Erin 22, 28, 30, 73, 85, 97
Griffiths, Elizabeth 11
Groom of the Stole 17, 63, 65–6, 68, 71, 90–1, 190–1, 251
Guilds
    French 135, 167–8
    leadership of 98–9
    Livery Companies of London 12, 14, 96–9, 134, 136, 141, 151–3, 161–2
    membership of 12, 98–9, 100, 136,
    records of 12, 14–15, 138, 141, 151, 161, 175
    women 12, 14–15, 19, 97, 99, 121, 135–6, 138, 141, 153–4, 161
    see also apprenticeship

Habsburg dynasty 27, 64
Hailwood, Mark 13
hair
    combs 84, 103, 196
    cutting 193–5
    hair pieces 84, 193–4, 196–7, 199
    favourites 197–8, 199–200
    powders 196
    rolls and padding for 196, 198–9
    storage of 197, 199
    styling 34–5, 110, 185, 193–6, 198
    towers 195–7, 199
    wigs 196–7
    see also accessories and tirewomen
Hanoverians 57
Harris, Barbara J. 90
Harrison, Jane, Indian woman 123, 234
Hart, Avril 160
Hawker (later Young), Susannah, petticoat–maker 53, 149–52, 184, 240
Hayward, Maria 33, 41, 85
Heath, Francis, periwig-maker 9, 169, 171–3, 217
Heath, Jane, mantua-maker 9, 86, 147, 152–4, 157–9, 163, 165, 168–74, 217, 228
Henrietta Maria, Queen Consort 4, 27–32, 35, 178
    clothing of 28–31, 57, 73–4, 83, 166
    household and wardrobe administration 18, 64–5, 71, 75, 80, 84, 181–3, 185, 192, 202–3, 207–8
    influence on fashion 31–2, 71, 100, 190
    tradespeople to 6, 29, 32, 79, 85, 97–100, 103–4, 140–1, 143, 152, 163–4, 193
Henry VIII, King of England 179, 206
Henshawe, Anna, widow 99–100
Henshawe, Benjamin, silkman 97–9, 220
Herbert, Barbara, Countess of Pembroke 88
Hibbard, Caroline 22, 97
Hicks, Baptist, cloth merchant 97, 123, 206
HMS Gloucester 110, 112, 125, 148
Hollar, Wenceslaus 30, 98, 104
Holme, Randle 143
hosiers 83, 151, 156, 220, 222, 224, 228–9, 231, 235, 238
Houben, Birgit 11
household 16–17
    departments 15–17, 63
    finances 7, 10, 12, 15–18, 23, 51–2, 63, 73–5, 79, 80–2, 84, 91–2, 97, 122, 128
    furnishings 117, 132, 137, 141, 185–7
    management 2, 9–12, 18, 61–4, 70–1, 73–81, 84–5, 90–1, 161, 177–86, 191–2, 196, 201, 203, 206–9
    records 12, 15–19, 87, 143
    women's roles 8, 10–12, 61–2, 71, 90, 129–131, 171, 177–8, 190–2, 202–4, 206
    see also courts, Office of the Robes, servants
housekeepers 172, 181
Howard, Lady Anabella 87–8

Howard, Barbara, Countess of Suffolk, Mistress of the Robes 65, 67
Howard, Catherine, Countess of Suffolk 71–2
Howe, Anne, mantua-maker or seamstress 1, 154, 156, 240
Huguenots 39, 54, 75, 114, 116, 152, 188, 193
Hugueny, Stephen [Étienne], glover 55, 75, 234, 241
Hunt, John, linen draper 99, 223
Hunt, Margaret R. 8
Hunter, Mary, embroiderer 1, 241
Huysmans, Jacob 35
Hyde, Anne, Duchess of York 4, 41–2

Inder, Pam 136
India 39, 119
    Madras 117
    Surat 117
Indian
    gowns 14, 39–40, 55, 146–7, 157, 248–9
    gown-maker 146, 228
    houses 87, 119–21, 123, 130–33, 215
    silks 39, 55, 116–18, 129, 163
    women 3, 8, 20, 119–21, 123, 129–33, 158, 186, 215, 226, 233–4, 239
    see also East Indies, garments, textiles
industrious revolution 8, 217, 178
Interregnum 33, 35
Ireland, Dorothy, seamstress and starcher 192, 205, 209
Ireland, Jane, seamstress and starcher 209
Italy 23, 41, 55, 168
    fashions from 30–1
    textiles 121, 147, 166, 250
    tradespeople 35, 168
    Venice 85
    women from 27, 33, 41, 170, 172

Jacobites 126
James VI and I, King of Scotland and England 4, 18, 22–3, 64, 97–8, 100, 141, 178, 206
James II, King of England and Scotland 4, 18, 35, 41–2, 44–5, 122, 203
    Duke of York 70–1, 110
    Exile 35, 45, 66
Japan 39, 45, 119, 132, 186–7
Jones, Frances, Countess of Scarbrough 119–20, 157, 191
journeywomen (workwomen) 126, 173–4, 217

Keeper of the Jewels 71, 83
Keeper of the Privy Purse 17, 63, 65–6, 79, 91, 191, 216
Kérouaille, Louise de, Duchess of Portsmouth 35, 119, 186
Kesterton, Zara 122
Killigrew, Charlotte, Mistress of the Sweet Coffers 179, 181–2
Kneller, Godfrey 43, 69, 88, 123, 127, 171, 200
Korda, Natasha 193, 204

La Hay, tailor 78, 154, 234
lacemen 43, 106, 141, 204, 227, 229–32, 235–6, 239, 241–3
Langrish, Barrell, milliner 104, 121–2, 125, 228
Langrish, Judith, milliner 110, 121–2, 125, 228, 241
laundry 7, 10–11, 177–8, 202–5
    Laundress of the Body 17, 178, 181, 192, 203–5, 208–9, 213–4, 237–8
    laundry maids 133, 192, 203–4, 209
    laundry rooms 203–5, 234
    milliners 209–10
    products 202–3
    washerwoman 203
    washing clothes 193, 202–5, 207, 209
    women's work 177–8, 202–4, 206
Lee, Elizabeth, embroiderer 141, 154, 235
Lely, Peter 35, 37, 42, 50, 67, 130
life events
    birthdays 40–1, 87
    childbirth 44, 51, 84, 149–51, 208
    funerals 114, 150, 197, 207
    marriage 7, 14, 27, 33–4, 51, 121, 128, 129–31, 149, 151, 203
    mourning 41, 55, 114, 181, 201
    pregnancy 44, 51, 151, 208
Lim, Amy 45
Lindberg, Erik 9
Lindström, Jonas 9
livery 15, 63, 91, 182
Lombard, Peter, tailor 55, 80, 152–4, 156, 163, 166–7, 184, 228, 235
London 3, 5–7, 12–14, 32
    Charing Cross 113
    Cheapside 6, 97, 100
    City of 12, 14, 97–100, 119, 122, 152, 162, 178
    Covent Garden 7–8, 100, 113–14, 121, 125, 152, 172–3
    Customs House 84, 181
    Dorset Garden 122

Great Fire of 14, 100
Hyde Park 100
Middlesex 14, 100, 125, 133, 149, 151–2, 215
Mincing Lane 119
New Exchange 7, 100,
Pall Mall 100, 123, 129
Port of 123
Royal Exchange 85, 97–8, 100, 120–1, 125, 141
season 100, 143, 215
Spitalfields 55
St James's Park 100, 124
St Martin-in-the-Fields 100–1, 151–2, 174
St Paul's Cathedral 89
The Strand 100, 121, 152, 178
West End 6, 14, 100, 122, 134, 152, 215
Westminster 100–1, 124, 133, 149
Westminster Abbey 23, 150, 196–7, 207, 213
see also courts, guilds, palaces
Louis XIV, King of France 6, 32, 35, 39, 116, 152, 169

magnificence 1, 29, 51, 57, 61, 82–3, 89, 95, 174, 177
Maitland, Elizabeth, Duchess of Lauderdale 114, 120,
     161, 187
Mancini, Hortense, Duchess of Mazarin 33, 37–8, 126,
     157, 159, 170, 172, 254
Mandove, Mary, Indian gown-maker or couturière 14,
     143–7, 156, 159, 166–8, 228
Mansell, Charmian 178, 202
mantua gowns (mantos) 35–8, 41–2, 46–9, 53–4, 56–7,
     108, 135, 143–6, 154–5, 157–8, 162–5, 170, 173,
     248–50
     construction of 145–6, 153–6, 158–61, 163–5, 167,
          169, 173
     French 35, 37–8, 84, 170
     linings of 154, 164–6
     robings of 155, 163, 299
     tailors 153–4, 161
mantua-makers 6–7, 9, 12, 135, 151
     journeywoman 173–4, 217
     occupational identities 11, 143–7, 151–2
     partnerships 157–9, 162–3, 168–73
     payments to 80, 154, 156, 159–60
     relationships with clients 62, 86–7, 157–8, 170–1
     skills of 160–1, 163, 165–8, 170
     training of 135–6, 170, 173–4
     work of 39, 53, 57, 85, 87, 143, 151, 153–4, 165–6,
          170, 173
     see also couturières

marchandes de modes 96, 104–6, 122, 217
Markham, Bridgett, Privy Chamber Woman
     74–5, 83
Mary II, Queen of England and Scotland 4, 45–51, 54,
     58–9, 100, 114, 121–3, 127, 133
     clothing and furnishings of 45–51, 57, 106, 122, 148,
          154, 156, 187, 189, 190, 200, 210
     household and wardrobe administration 18–9, 65–8,
          71, 74–5, 79–80, 92, 126, 181–3, 185, 191–2, 196,
          203, 205, 209
     influence on fashion 45–6, 186
     Princess of Orange 45, 48, 51, 59, 189
     tradespeople to 45, 54–5, 80, 103, 106, 119, 121–3,
          131, 133, 140–1, 147–8, 154, 156, 161–2, 196–7,
          200, 209–10
Mary of Modena, Queen Consort 4, 41–5, 208
     clothing of 41–4
     Duchess of York 42, 70, 110
     household and wardrobe administration 18, 65–6,
          74, 80, 183, 191, 201, 203, 208
     tradespeople to 42–3, 126, 157
Masham, Abigail, Baroness Masham 89, 91, 190, 196
Massey, Anne, mantua-maker 87, 241
Master of the
     Great Wardrobe 63, 71
     Robes 71, 81, 90
material literacy 62, 73, 82–3, 89, 93, 202, 215
McKendrick, Neil 3
Medina, Solomon de, merchant 45, 123, 229, 235
mercers 43, 50, 55, 97–9, 125–6, 137, 151, 156, 172,
     220–7, 229–33, 238–43
merchants 5, 8, 13, 22, 79, 89, 97, 103, 122, 206
     Anglo-Dutch 45
     cloth 97, 120, 123
     Dutch 45, 54, 132
     East Indies 45, 117–8, 123, 186
     French 35, 38–9, 40, 105, 113
     women 119, 129
Mercure galant 35, 38, 114, 116, 144, 157, 164
Middle East 39, 117
     Armenia 40
     Persia 40, 55, 117
     Turkey 40
middling sorts 3, 5, 7, 12, 32, 54, 75, 79, 96, 117, 123, 185,
     190, 268
migrants
     French 9, 14, 87, 113, 116, 136, 152–3, 168–70, 173–4,
          197, 217

Dutch 45, 66, 79
  see also Huguenots
milliners 12, 81, 83, 149, 124–33
  gender of 97, 103, 105–6, 112, 121, 209
  goods sold by 1, 35, 75, 95–6, 104–7, 110, 112, 114,
    119–21, 126, 129, 169, 188, 197, 200, 209–10
  French 113–4
  journey women 126, 129
  occupational identities 8, 11, 96, 143, 149
  partnerships 121–2
  payments to 106, 122
  relationship with clients 12, 123, 127–31
  reputation of 96, 122–3, 128–9, 131, 133
  training of 110, 112, 141, 207
  shops 7, 85, 107, 119, 121, 123
Mistress of the Robes 9, 17, 55, 61–81, 83–93, 95–6, 126,
    129–31, 134, 170, 179, 181–2, 190, 214–16
Mistress of the Sweet Coffers 9, 17, 63, 178–82, 184–5,
    216
Montagu, Lady Mary Wortley 130
Mordaunt, Penelope, Countess of Peterborough,
    Mistress of the Robes 65–6, 73
Morgan, Anne, tailor or petticoat-maker 77, 147, 149,
    154, 156, 229
Morrison, Rebecca 160
Motteux, Peter, Indian goods retailer and playwright 87,
    116, 242
Mountjoy, Marie, tirewoman 193, 220
Muldrew, Craig 125
Mulys, Katherine, lacewoman 140, 235

necessary women 17, 63, 182, 191–2
needlework 74, 136, 138–41, 185, 206–7, 242, 246
Netherlands *see* Dutch Republic, Spanish Netherlands
North, Susan 138, 202
Nun, Elizabeth, Laundress of the Body 203, 205,
    208–9

Office of the Robes 2, 13, 15–19, 61–2
  management of 73–82, 91–3, 181–6
  offices within 63, 75, 79, 80, 91, 181–2, 202, 181, 202,
    214, 216–7
  of the Stuart kings 71, 73, 90
  tradespeople to 13, 52–3, 81–2, 103, 152–3,
    219–43
  see also Mistress of the Robes, Mistress of the Sweet
    Coffers
Onslow, Hester, haberdasher 99, 220

Pages
  of the Robes 17, 63, 181–2
  of the Backstairs 17, 190, 208
  of the bedchamber 208
palaces
  Greenwich 64, 181
  Hampton Court 34, 152, 181, 185, 203–4
  Kensington 51, 71, 85, 100, 149, 152, 181, 186,
    194
  Somerset House 18, 100, 152, 178–9, 181, 185–6,
    194, 202, 207
  St James's Palace 100, 124, 151–2, 178, 181, 194
  Westminster 100
  Whitehall 35, 66, 100, 151–2, 178–81, 201, 203–4,
    209, 234
  Windsor 85, 152, 181, 194
Palmer, Barbara, Duchess of Cleveland 33, 37, 119
Parliament 27, 32–3, 53, 55, 154, 196
  Houses of 6, 100
  member of 5, 68, 97–8
  politicians 45, 51, 126, 129, 133
  robes 154, 184, 240
patriarchy 9–10, 28
patronage 3, 5–8, 15, 22–3, 27, 31–2, 34, 38, 42, 54, 62,
    80–3, 87, 96–7, 103, 105, 121, 131, 133, 136, 147,
    152, 156, 171, 174, 201, 203, 206, 214–18
pattern cutters 29, 85, 164, 166, 204, 223
Paul, Tawny 151
Pearce, Michael 22–3
Pearse, Elizabeth, Laundress of the Body 203, 208
Pepys, Samuel 5, 34, 37, 39, 73, 113, 185, 190, 209
perfumers 185, 202, 219, 221–3, 239
periwig-maker 9, 170, 196
petticoat-makers 3, 53, 95, 148–9, 151–2, 154, 156, 174,
    184, 216, 238, 240
Portugal 18, 32–4, 209
  colonies 39
  dress 34, 41
  Lisbon 34, 202
  trade 39
  see also courts
Poska, Allyson 9
Potter, Jane, milliner and Indian woman 8, 123, 129–31,
    133–4, 186, 215–6
Privy Chamber 17, 63–4, 207
  women 63–4, 74, 192, 207
privy purse 18, 35, 37, 55, 75, 79, 113–14
  see also Keeper of the Privy Purse

Rawcliffe, Carole 202
ready-made goods 3, 119, 136, 137, 151, 156, 173
recreative practice 160, 165, 204
refugees 39, 114, 116
    see also Huguenots
Renault, Monsieur, Parisian tailor 84, 161
retailing
    new forms of 5–7, 13, 95–6, 103–6, 112, 116–19
    revolution 13
    shops 3, 7–8, 32, 85, 98, 100, 103, 107, 113–14,
        119–23, 129–33, 146, 156–8
    women 13, 32, 96, 106, 119–23, 126–33, 149
Ribeiro, Aileen 47
Robes of State 22, 150, 202
    Order of the Garter 1, 46
    St George insignia 1–2, 46, 250, 252
    see under coronation, parliament
Roche, Luis, tailor 152, 229
rubanières 104–6
Rutland, William, laceman 141, 204, 229

Sarti, Cathleen 61
sartorial politics 21–2, 25–7, 29–31, 33–5, 39, 41, 45–6,
    48–51, 53–5, 57–9
Sayers, Catherine, Laundress of the Body 209
Scotland 23, 33, 85, 110, 194
    Edinburgh 194, 220
    fashion 194
    tradespeople 163, 220
    see also courts
seamstress 81, 84–6, 90, 95, 99, 103, 110, 112, 114, 135–9,
    141–3, 148–9, 151–2, 160–1, 163, 167, 170, 174–5,
    178, 181, 184–5, 192, 204–5
servants 5, 10–12, 15, 19, 62, 73, 79–80, 92, 99, 131, 143,
    163, 172, 177, 181–2, 186, 190–2, 202–4, 206,
    208–10
Seymour, Elizabeth, Duchess of Somerset, Mistress of
    the Robes 70
    Countess of Ogle 87, 129–30, 169
    courtship and marriages 129–31
    estates 186
    household accounts 46, 79, 87, 129–30, 159, 195
    Mistress of the Robes 65, 71–3, 79, 90–1
    tradespeople to 87, 119, 121–2, 126, 156–7, 159–60,
        169, 173–4, 186, 195–6, 200
Shakespeare, William 193
Shepard, Alexandra 8

shopping 5–7, 83–5, 88–9, 114, 119, 123, 128, 131, 133,
    158
    gender 11, 82–3, 126
    locations 85, 98, 100–1, 113–4, 116, 119–21, 141, 178,
        193, 215
silkmen 83, 97–9, 137, 140–1, 156, 219–20, 222–3, 227,
    230
silkwomen 74, 90, 99, 110, 112, 136–41, 143, 152, 174,
    206–7, 209, 211, 215, 221
Simonton, Deborah 15
skills
    gendered 11, 15, 19, 73, 82, 136, 138, 151, 156, 160–3,
        175
    hierarchies of 15, 95, 136, 138, 149, 151, 160–1,
        167–8
    migration 14, 39, 152, 169
    tacit knowledge 170
    see also material literacy
skincare 112, 185, 189, 200–1
    perfume 85, 181, 182, 185
    sweet waters 200
    see also cosmetics, dressing room
Small, Gerard (Bert), tailor 154, 231, 236
Smuts, Malcolm 27, 61, 98
social
    climbing 5, 68–9, 157, 185, 123, 129, 131, 133, 185,
        206, 217
    networks 14–15, 64–8, 71, 86, 88–9, 96–7, 121,
        123–33
    see also credit, gentry, middling sorts
Spain
    diplomacy with 25, 27
    fashions 23, 25, 53, 84, 194, 246–7
    imports from 23, 55, 246, 249–50
    war with 33, 123
Spanish Netherlands 33
    Bruges 35
Speckard, Dorothy, silkwoman 112, 138, 206–7, 209, 211,
    215, 221
Stanley, Elizabeth, Countess of Derby, Mistress of the
    Robes 65, 68, 71, 75, 78, 91–2, 191, 251
starcher 79, 178, 192, 204–9, 211, 214–15, 238
stay-makers 14, 53, 154, 163, 197, 239, 240
Stuart, Frances, Duchess of Richmond and Lennox 90,
    119, 126, 149–50, 196–7, 254
Stuart, Henry Frederick, Prince of Wales 27
Stuart, James Francis Edward 208

Stuart, Princess Elizabeth 193–5
Styles, John 55, 82, 135, 163
sumptuary laws 5
Sutton, Anne 138
Swansted, Blanche, tirewoman 193–4, 210, 221

tailors 5, 135, 151, 166–7
    royal 23, 29, 55, 79–81, 83–5, 143, 146, 148, 152–4,
        156, 161, 163, 166–7, 184, 197, 216, 220, 222–4,
        228–9, 231–2, 234–6, 240
    skills 138, 148, 160–3, 165–6, 168, 170
    training 135–6, 138, 161–2
    women 13, 136–8, 143, 146–7, 151, 161–3, 168
Telier, Hester Le, silkwoman 74, 139, 207, 221
Temple, Jane Martha, Countess of Portland 88, 90
ter Borch, Gerard 187–8
textiles
    alamodes 55, 249
    atlas 55, 84, 119, 249, 250, 295
    bengals 55
    brocades 51, 55, 149, 155, 163, 179, 246, 249, 250, 278
    calicoes 39, 55, 117, 119–21, 153, 163, 186, 246, 248,
        250, 301
    chintz 39, 55, 117, 119–20, 132
    cloth 51, 119, 163, 184, 246–8, 250, 301
    crape 41, 55, 114, 126, 157, 170, 201, 247–50, 301
    cuttanees 119
    cypress 140, 246, 250
    damasks 25, 55, 117–18, 121, 147–8, 163–4, 185, 246,
        248–50
    ermine 126, 195, 246–50
    figured silk 55, 250
    flannel 84, 149, 154, 248
    flowered 29, 38, 40, 55, 114, 117, 119, 153, 163, 179,
        248–50
    gauze 107, 114, 126, 247–50
    linens 39, 45, 74, 84, 104, 110, 119, 121, 139, 181, 201,
        209–10, 246–50
    longuins 119
    lustrings 159, 164, 248–50, 278
    muslins 39, 116–17, 119–21, 126, 163, 210, 248–50
    Persians 39, 55, 119, 121, 156, 248, 250, 301
    plush 84, 246
    sarcenet 153, 183–4, 246–50, 278
    satins 23, 25, 29, 39, 43, 55, 84, 106, 110, 121, 126,
        147, 155, 159, 163, 165, 179, 184–5, 193, 196, 207,
        246–50, 301

serge 39, 163, 248, 250
striped 40, 47, 55, 117, 119, 157, 186, 246, 250, 295
stuffs 38, 55, 62, 74, 163, 246, 248, 295
tabbys 149, 247–50, 278
taffetas 23, 25, 55, 84, 117, 121, 139, 163–6, 184,
    246–50, 278
tissue 36, 159, 249–50, 278
Turkey silks 40, 119, 247–8
velvets 84, 110, 166, 185–6, 195–6, 207, 246–50
see also Indian silks
theatre 47, 114, 122, 130–1, 133, 193
Thomas, Rachel, Yeoman of the Robes 79, 181, 216
Thynne, Thomas 129–31, 133
tirewoman 3, 14, 178, 193–201, 210, 214–15, 220–3, 227,
    238–9
trade
    global 3, 6, 39, 57, 59, 82, 95–6, 119, 210, 214
    Dutch 45, 116–17, 132
    East Indies 3, 39, 45, 116–19
    French 40, 114
    women 8, 119
    see also retailing, shopping

van der Borcht, Pieter 204–5
van Goltstein, Anna, First Woman of the
    Bedchamber and Keeper of the Privy
    Purse 79, 191, 196
Vickery, Amanda 82
Villiers, George, Duke of Buckingham 64, 66, 71

Waggit, Alice, seamstress 141, 163
Walsingham, Lady Audrey, Mistress of the Robes 62,
    64–5, 74, 83–4, 90
wardrobe
    cleaning 10, 181
    inventories 23–4, 46, 64, 154, 179–81
    spaces 179–82, 185
    storage 71, 81, 179–85, 202, 207, 210
    see also dressing rooms, Great Wardrobe
weavers 55, 120, 221
White, Livia, seamstress or silkwoman 74, 139, 221
Whittle, Jane 11, 13
Wilkins, Mary, milliner 129, 210, 243
William III, King of England and Scotland 4, 45–7, 51,
    87, 100, 122, 140, 185, 204, 209
William, Duke of Gloucester 51, 213
Woolley, Hannah 6

work
careers 62, 89–91, 93, 194
identity 3, 8, 83, 89–91, 93, 106, 136, 138, 147–9,
151–2, 194, 206, 214–5
sinecures 9–10, 61, 209–10, 215
unpaid 7, 10, 12, 79, 177
verb-orientated approaches to 9–10
wages and payments 8, 10–11, 61, 74–5, 79–81, 122,
126, 154–9, 178, 191–2, 194, 204, 206, 209

widows 9, 13, 76, 97, 99–100, 136–7, 139,
163
see also business, servants
women 5, 7–15, 19, 62, 73, 89–90, 96, 106, 122,
136, 138, 141, 153, 156, 163, 178, 202–3,
205–6, 214
working couples 8–9, 97, 104, 110–11, 114, 121–2, 151,
162–3, 169–70, 193, 196, 206–7
Wunder, Heide 9